w/D

FIFTY MAJOR ECONOMISTS

Fully updated to include the most recent developments in economic thought, this new edition explores the work of fifty major economists, from seventeenth century philosophers such as John Locke to contemporary economists such as Gary Becker, Robert Lucas, Amartya Sen and Joseph Stiglitz. Other entries include:

- Adam Smith
- Karl Marx
- John Maynard Keynes
- Milton Friedman
- Daniel Kahneman

Fifty Major Economists contains brief biographical information on each featured economist and an explanation of their major contributions to economics, along with simple illustrations of their ideas, references to their major works, guides to further reading, and a glossary of terms. This book is an important and accessible resource for students of economics.

Steven Pressman is Professor of Economics and Finance at Monmouth University, New Jersey. He is the author of *Quesnay's Tableau Économique* and editor (with Richard Holt) of *A New Guide to Post Keynesian Economics*, which is also published by Routledge. He also serves as co-editor of the *Review of Political Economy* and Associate Editor and Book Review Editor of the *Eastern Economic Journal*.

YOU MAY ALSO BE INTERESTED IN THE
FOLLOWING ROUTLEDGE STUDENT
REFERENCE TITLES:

Economics: The Basics
Tony Cleaver
0–415–31412–7

Business: The Key Concepts
Mark Vernon
0–415–25324–1

Fifty Key Figures in Management
Morgen Witzel
0–415–36978–9

The Routledge Companion to Global Economics
Edited by Robert Benyon
0-415-24306-8

Management: The Basics
Morgen Witzel
0-415-32018-6

Internet: The Basics
Jason Whittaker
0-415-25746-8

FIFTY MAJOR ECONOMISTS

Second Edition

Steven Pressman

Routledge
Taylor & Francis Group

LONDON AND NEW YORK

First published 1999
by Routledge
This edition published 2006
by Routledge
2 Park Square, Milton Park, Abingdon, Oxon OX14 4RN

Simultaneously published in the USA and Canada
by Routledge
270 Madison Ave, New York, NY 10016

Routledge is an imprint of the Taylor & Francis Group, an informa business

© 1999, 2006 Steven Pressman

Typeset in Bembo by Taylor & Francis Books
Printed and bound in Great Britain by MPG Books Ltd, Bodmin, Cornwall

British Library Cataloguing in Publication Data
A catalogue record for this book is available from the British Library

Library of Congress Cataloging-in-Publication Data
Pressman, Steven.
Fifty major economists / Steven Pressman.– 2nd ed.

p. cm.
Includes bibliographical references.
ISBN 0-415-36648-8 (hardback) – ISBN 0-415-36649-6 (pbk.)   1.   Economists–
Biography. 2. Economics–History. I. Title.
HB76.P74 2006

330.092'2–dc22

2005025713

ISBN10 0–415–36648–8 ISBN13 978–0–415–36648–9 (hbk)
ISBN10 0–415–36649–6 ISBN13 978–0–415–36649–6 (pbk)
ISBN10 0–203–01920–2 ISBN13 978–0–203–01920–7 (ebk)

To the memory of my parents, Jeffrey and Phyllis Pressman

CHRONOLOGICAL LIST OF CONTENTS

ALPHABETICAL LIST OF CONTENTS

PREFACE

It was with much joy that I approached revising and updating *Fifty Major Economists*. I learned a great deal while writing the original edition, and was looking forward to another good learning experience. Also, much has changed within the economics profession since the mid-1990s when I first began work on this project. Doing a second edition of the book has allowed me to think about and write about these changes. Two of the most important changes, the rise of the new Keynesian school of economics and the rise of behavioral and experimental economics, are reflected in the two new economists included in the book – Joseph Stiglitz and Daniel Kahneman.

But to add new chapters, and to keep to the constraints of having only fifty economists in the volume, someone had to go. This was probably the hardest part of revising and updating the volume, since I looked at each of the chapters of the original work as if they were my children. I had devoted a great deal of effort and love bringing them into existence, and so it was hard to let any of them go. Alas, Robert Owen and Oscar Lange were jettisoned. I had originally included Owen, despite many objections from my colleagues, because of his concern with labor issues, something I felt was important and underrepresented even with the Owen chapter. Since labor and unemployment is also a key concern of Stiglitz, I look at this as a somewhat sensible trade-off. Lange did work on economic planning and socialist economies. Over the past decade, interest in this issue has waned among both economists and policy-makers. Conversely, there has been greater interest in understanding human decision-making and in doing experiments to try to understand how people actually behave. The importance of these lines of research was recognized in 2002 when Daniel Kahneman was awarded a Nobel Prize for Economics. So it seemed logical to replace Lange with Kahneman.

In addition to the two new entries, all of the previous chapters have been revised. These changes corrected errors and dealt with instances where I was not completely clear in the previous edition. I also updated each chapter to reflect both the recent work of living economists and the recent secondary literature seeking to understand the contributions of these key figures. I hope the result will be as well received as the first edition of this book.

In all writing endeavors one incurs many obligations. This is especially the case in a work covering so many ideas, so much history, and so many figures. Many colleagues and friends read earlier drafts of this work and provided substantial comments in an attempt to correct my mistakes. For their hard work I thank Jane Agar, Nahid Aslanbeigui, Peter Boettke, Charlie Clark, Robert Cord, Milton Friedman, John Henry, Sherry Kasper, Mary King, Michael Lewis, Roger Koppl, Franco Modigliani, Laurence Moss, Douglass North, Iara Onate, Susan Pashkoff, Alessandro Roncaglia, Ruth Sample, Mario Seccareccia, John Smithin, Gale Summerfield and Naomi Zack. Any remaining errors remain my responsibility.

Several of my students at Monmouth University and the University of New Hampshire read and commented on many individual chapters, thereby forcing me to make the ideas of all fifty economists clear to someone who is not cursed by having a PhD in Economics. Special thanks here are due to Adam Hutchinson, Tad Langlois, Ivan Pabon, Lynn Van Buren, Flavio Vilela Vierira and Sarah Youngclaus.

My editors at Routledge all provided encouragement, ideas and suggestions at all stages, from writing the original book through the making of the revised volume. For their assistance and support I am very grateful.

But perhaps my greatest debt and gratitude goes to those people who typed the numerous revisions to each chapter, as I tried to get the ideas of these fifty economists exactly right, and as I tried to make each economist intelligible to a broad audience. For their hard work, and for their patience in putting up with endless revisions, I thank Beth Boyington, Nancy Palmer, Diana Prout and Donna Reeder.

INTRODUCTION

To outsiders, economists frequently seem confused and inconsistent. US President Harry Truman sought out a one-armed economist because when he asked for economic advice he was frequently told "on the one hand ... on the other hand ... ." And President Ronald Reagan lamented that, whenever he questioned his three main economic advisors, he would get four different answers.

Like all good jokes, these quips contain a good deal of truth. But there are also good reasons for this situation. The economy itself is complex, and one force driving the economy is human behavior, which is notoriously difficult to predict. As Isaac Newton observed, "I can measure the motion of bodies, but I cannot measure human folly" (quoted in Galbraith 1993: 44). In addition, people employ different perspectives when they analyze the world, or, to use Thomas Kuhn's (1962) famous phrase, they have different paradigms of how the world works. Different views of how the economy works inevitably lead to different policy prescriptions and conflicting economic advice. A good economic advisor should provide all perspectives and set forth all possibilities to the president.

The rise of economics as a discipline, and how different economists have sought to understand capitalism, is the story of this book. It is about the major figures responsible for our incomplete (and sometimes inconsistent) analysis of real-world economic issues.

In its infancy, before economics emerged as a discipline, there were no professional economists. For this reason, the earliest contributions to economics were made by philosophers and practical men seeking to understand how a market economy works.

Thomas Mun, our first major economist, was a merchant who ran the British East India Company, a firm that engaged in trade with the Far East. Much of his work justified this commercial activity and advocated a national trade surplus. He argued that foreign trade was beneficial to a country when the country sold more goods abroad than it bought from foreign countries because this would result in precious metals coming into the country, thereby increasing national wealth.

William Petty, our second major economist, was a land surveyor interested in measuring things. He tried to measure national economic activity (now our GDP), but this was not easy to do in the seventeenth century. Petty chose an indirect method, counting the number of homes in cities, and reasoning that wealthier nations had more people living in cities.

Richard Cantillon and François Quesnay were, respectively, an entrepreneur and a physician. They saw economies as a set of interrelated parts that interacted in a rather fixed and reliable manner. Cantillon and Quesnay described these interrelations, explaining how money circulates throughout the economy, going from manufacturers in cities to agricultural workers and landowners in rural areas, and then back again to the manufacturers in cities.

John Locke provided a philosophical justification for private property, and against religious doctrines which held that, since God gave land to everyone, so the land was owned by everyone. Locke also argued that people were rational and self-interested in their daily behavior. This conflicted with the prevailing view that people followed the dictates of religion. It also opened the door to an economic explanation of individual behavior, since if people's actions were based on religion we would need to consult religious texts and religious leaders to understand economic behavior.

David Hume provided a philosophical justification for the business activities carried out by merchants. He also recognized a problem with Mun's call for trade surpluses. In running a trade surplus, a country would sell goods abroad and receive gold in return. This would increase the national money supply and also increase prices. But with higher domestic prices, countries would buy more from abroad, thereby eliminating the trade surplus. Thus, according to Hume, there were economic forces at work tending to keep trade balanced among nations.

Another philosopher who made important contributions to economics was Jeremy Bentham. Bentham introduced the notion of utility into economics, and helped make economics into a discipline that studied how to increase utility. He also provided a defense of charging interest on loans, an activity disapproved of by the church (because it took advantage of the poor) since medieval times. Such a defense was important because it led to increased lending and commercial activity in Britain.

Adam Smith, generally regarded as the father of economics, was a philosopher who had written a treatise on moral philosophy before turning his attention to economics. His main concern was to understand how and why economies grew. His answer was that capitalism frees the entrepreneurial spirit, and that given economic incentives entrepreneurs would figure out how to produce goods more efficiently. As a result of greater productive efficiency, economies would grow and prosper, raising the standard of living for most people in the nation.

Thomas Malthus was a pastor, and is responsible for economics being called "the dismal science." In contrast to Smith, Malthus saw economies heading towards starvation as population growth exceeded the growth of the food supply. Malthus also was pessimistic about the overall outcome of allowing free rein to the entrepreneurial spirit. He saw high unemployment or "gluts" as a likely consequence of capitalism, rather than prosperity.

David Ricardo, like Mun and Cantillon, was a businessman. He made a fortune in finance before turning his attention to economic issues. Ricardo is best known for his theory of comparative advantage. In contrast to Mun, who thought that only nations experiencing a trade surplus would benefit from trade, for Ricardo free international trade would benefit all nations. He thus gave economics an argument for free trade. Ricardo also set forth a view that the value of goods is determined by their cost of production – mainly their labor costs – and thus the price of a good is determined mainly by the amount of labor used to produce it.

John Stuart Mill, like Locke, Hume and other early economic thinkers, was a famous philosopher. Mill was interested in the question of what made a discipline scientific. He explained that economics was a deductive science, like geometry. It begins with definitions and axioms that are supposedly self-evident, and then derives theorems about how the economy works. Mill himself provided a few of these theorems, explaining how the gains from international trade (identified by Ricardo) would be divided up between two countries, and providing an economic analysis of the factors that determine whether a country would prosper or decline in the long term.

Karl Marx was also a trained philosopher, and later turned his attention to the workings of a capitalist economy. Like Smith, Marx saw the promise of economic growth and higher living standards due to capitalism. But he also saw that capitalism generated a large number of problems. Marx saw capitalism as leading to the impoverishment of workers, polluted cities, firms growing and becoming monopolies, and the tedium of most work. He thought that these problems would eventually lead workers to rise up against business owners and establish a socialist economy where everyone shares in the ownership of all firms.

These early years of economics led to key contributions by individuals, but few schools of economic thought. Schools thrive best in academia, where like-minded individuals can be in the same place and turn out student followers. It was Alfred Marshall who first established economics as a separate subject, with its own degree, at Cambridge University; so it was Marshall who made possible different schools of economic thought and the many jokes about economists who cannot agree.

Although not a school of thought, most early economic thinkers adopted a particular approach when analyzing the economy. This approach, "classical economics," has several distinguishing characteristics. First, it looks at classes or groups of people rather than at individuals. Classical economics focuses on what determines the wages received by workers (on average) rather than how much was made by each individual worker, and on what causes the rate of profit to rise and fall in the whole economy rather than the factors affecting the profits of an individual firm.

A second characteristic of classical economic thought is that it focuses on explaining the generation and distribution of an economic surplus. Beginning with Quesnay, economists recognized that the productive power of the land yielded more grain than the grain required (as seed and as food) during the growing season. This extra grain was a surplus. Smith's famous pin factory example (see p. 34) describes how the division of labor can generate more output without additional input requirements (such as more food to feed more workers), and thus generate a surplus in the manufacturing sector of an economy.

With one exception, classical economics pretty much died during the twentieth century. That exception is Piero Sraffa, who demonstrated that the contemporary approach to economics was defective because it was logically inconsistent. For Sraffa and his followers, the neo-Ricardian school, the classical approach of studying how economies could generate a surplus was the only consistent way to do economics.

Most historians of economic thought attribute the demise of classical economics to the greater use of mathematics, especially the calculus, and the rise of marginal analysis, which was aided and abetted by the mathematics of the calculus. This focused the attention of economists on the small or marginal decisions faced by individual firms and consumers, rather than the behavior of large groups.

Augustine Cournot, professionally a mathematician, used the calculus to understand consumer behavior and firm behavior. He noted the inverse relationship between the price of a good and the quantity that people would buy, and he drew the first demand curve. Also, Cournot defined the modern notions of marginal cost and marginal revenue in mathematical terms, and demonstrated how firms could maximize profits by producing at the point where the two were equal.

Vilfredo Pareto sought to define the conditions under which we could say that one economic outcome was better for everyone than another outcome. Using these conditions and the calculus, he showed that free trade always leads to the best possible outcome for two people. Building on Pareto's work, Francis Edgeworth demonstrated that, not only would free trade benefit individuals, it would also benefit countries that traded with each other. This gave mathematical rigor to the arguments for free trade first developed by Ricardo.

William Stanley Jevons and Carl Menger were the first economists to analyze consumer behavior based on marginal analysis. They argued that consumers would buy whatever they enjoyed the most (given their incomes), and that free consumer choice would lead to the best results for individuals and for the nation. Arthur Pigou dealt with the one major exception to this rule – externalities, or situations where business firms impose costs on society rather than on just the people who buy their goods. Pollution is probably the best example of an externality; everyone pays when firms pollute the environment. Pigou advocated government policies (such as taxes on polluting firms) to deal with this problem, thereby making the externality a cost to the firm.

John Bates Clark brought marginal analysis to the question of what determines wages and firm profits. His answer was that wages and profits are determined by the marginal productivity of workers and machines, respectively. Knut Wicksell showed that, in a competitive economic environment, all factors of production would receive incomes equal to their marginal productivity, and that the sum of these incomes would equal the value of the output produced by the firm. With this, marginalism could explain how the revenue received from selling something gets divided up among all the factors contributing to its production, and how everyone received income equal to their contribution to production. This analysis provided an economic justification for the incomes that everyone receives in a market economy and for the existing distribution of income.

Today's main economic approach, neoclassical economics, arose out of marginalism. Like marginalism, instead of studying classes of individuals, neoclassical economics studies the optimizing behavior of rational and well-informed individuals; and instead of studying the

generation of an economic surplus, it focuses on the efficient allocation of resources resulting from individual optimization. Alfred Marshall and Leon Walras were the main early developers of neoclassical
economics. Marshall focused on one market at a time, and studied
firm decisions and industry outcomes. He combined the marginalist
insight about utility determining demand with the classical insight
about the costs of production determining supply (but with firms
using marginal calculations), and then argued that the two factors of
supply and demand jointly determined prices and output in an
industry. Walras focused on the general equilibrium of all markets at
once. He saw the entire economy as a set of supply and demand
equations for every good; he then solved these equations for equilibrium prices and quantities, and explained how economies would
reach this state of general equilibrium.

Once a school of economic thought develops, it is only natural
that alternative schools should arise. Two early oppositional schools
were the Austrians and the Institutionalists.

Austrian economics (so-called because its two founding fathers,
Carl Menger and Eugen Böhm-Bawark, were Austrian) is the more
conservative alternative to the neoclassical school. Austrians stress the
importance of entrepreneurship for economic growth, and argue that
being an entrepreneur does not mean balancing marginal costs and
marginal revenues. Rather, entrepreneurs must have a vision and take
chances in an uncertain world. Menger emphasized the importance
of the entrepreneur. Böhm-Bawark developed the Austrian notion of
production as a roundabout process that takes time. During this process it was important that entrepreneurs be rewarded. If they were
not, then they would not innovate and everyone would suffer. Friedrich Hayek picked up on these themes and argued that greater
government intervention in the economy always creates economic
problems because it hinders the entrepreneur. It also creates social
problems because government policies always limit individual
freedom.

The more liberal of the early oppositional schools, institutionalism,
was founded by Thorstein Veblen. Unlike neoclassical economists,
but similar to the classical school, institutionalists hold that individual
decisions about how to spend one's money do not arise from people
looking inside themselves and seeking to maximize their utility.
Rather, Veblen noted that people looked outside themselves (to
advertising and to the behavior of other people) for clues about what
they should value and how they should behave in the economic
world.

Institutionalism was a strong force in the early twentieth century, but declined thereafter as economists focused more on mathematical analysis rather than on individual behavior. None the less, there are strong institutionalist elements in the works of many major economists who wrote in the last half of the twentieth century. For example, John Kenneth Galbraith analyzed how firms mold and manipulate consumer behavior, and studied the large business firm as an institution seeking power over prices and over consumers. Institutionalist influences also exist in the work of Gunnar Myrdal, who studied poverty in the world economy. For Myrdal, our beliefs about the poor come from our neighbors and our peers. We see the poor as different, which leads to discrimination against the poor and continued poverty. Similarly, Barbara Bergmann has argued that institutions and habits of thought are responsible for women's second class economic status. For Bergmann, societal beliefs about the capability of women lead to discrimination against women in the job market and lower incomes for women, which in turn reinforce beliefs about women's abilities. Finally, the work of Amartya Sen, in explaining how our choices depend on the expectations of others, returns us to Veblen's point about the social aspects of consumption. Likewise, Sen's call for developing the capabilities of those mired in poverty seeks an escape from the vicious cycle of poverty and discrimination that institutionalized beliefs perpetuate.

While institutionalism declined in the late twentieth century, an offshoot of institutionalism, the new institutionalist school, has received more interest. Like Veblen, new institutionalists study the role of institutions in the economy. But they seek to explain how and why institutions arise from individual maximizing behavior, rather than studying how institutions affect individual behavior. A good example of this is Gary Becker's analysis of the family. For Becker, the family as an institution arose as a means of specialization. Tasks get divided up by family members to improve the efficiency of the family, just as the division of labor in the factory leads to greater efficiency.

Seeing institutions as the result of rational behavior, rather than looking at how institutions affect individual behavior, makes the new institutionalists more neoclassical than institutionalist (see Hodgson 1989). One main exception to this is the work of Douglass North. North sees institutions as important because they provide the rules of the economic game. Good rules help economies grow, according to North; bad rules provide incentives for people to engage in unproductive activities and lead to slower growth.

But the main opposition to neoclassical economics arose during the Great Depression of the 1930s. The Keynesian Revolution, stemming from the work of John Maynard Keynes, sought to explain how a prolonged bout of high unemployment was possible and what could be done to remedy this problem. Keynes blamed high unemployment on too little spending. He then argued for using fiscal policy (tax cuts and greater government spending) as well as monetary policy (more money and lower interest rates) to generate the needed spending in the economy and reduce unemployment.

After Keynes, economists devoted a great deal of effort to predicting economic recessions and formulating economic policy in order to make things better. John Hicks made these tasks easier by means of mathematical modeling. He formalized Keynes by putting his arguments into a set of equations and then showing how fiscal and monetary policy could be used together to improve economic outcomes.

In addition, economists put a great deal of effort into measuring the entire economy. The work of Simon Kuznets in measuring GDP or national income was critical in this endeavor, because until we measure the economy we cannot test our theories about what causes economies to grow and we cannot predict what will happen to the economy. So too was the work of Joseph Schumpeter, who classified different types of business cycles and explained why economies went through business cycles in the short run and in the long run. Irving Fisher did pioneering work in the formation of index numbers, which were used to measure inflation and help distinguish between increases in national income due to higher prices and increases in national income due to producing more things.

With numerical data and the aid of computers economists could begin to plot the exact relationships between the different parts of the economy. The input–output analysis of Wassily Leontief formalized the insights of Cantillon and Quesnay, enabling economists to identify all the inputs that would be necessary for an economy to expand its output or increase production. The empirical macroeconomic models developed by Jan Tinbergen let economists forecast how the overall economy would be likely to perform in the near future. They also allowed a more precise quantitative estimate of the impact of economic policies on the whole economy. Working in reverse, they let policy-makers figure out how much they needed to cut taxes or cut interest rates in order to get unemployment down to some desired level.

Building these models required understanding key parts of the whole economy. Many economists worked on understanding the main determinants of spending and the important relationships between key parts of the whole economy. Milton Friedman and Franco Modigliani developed the modern theory of consumer spending, focusing on how things like expectations and wealth impact current consumption. Modigliani examined factors that affected business investment and developed the area of finance, which looks at how firms make decisions about obtaining the revenue to build new plants and equipment (i.e. whether to borrow or to issue new stock). Paul Samuelson developed the notion of the accelerator, which showed the economic effects when investment responds positively to a growing economy. The accelerator showed that national economies were less stable and more likely to need policy intervention, as Keynes had stressed. Samuelson also developed the notion of the Phillips Curve, a trade-off between inflation and unemployment that arises when economies grow, which helped clarify macroeconomic policy-making decisions.

The work of Keynes also led to the rise of a Post Keynesian school. Building on the work of Keynes, this school seeks to understand how and why problems arise in capitalist economics, and then seeks to develop economic policies to improve economic performance. Joan Robinson and John Kenneth Galbraith saw monopoly power or imperfect competition as an important source of macroeconomic problems such as inflation and unemployment. Galbraith and Nicholas Kaldor both added incomes policies as a tool to control inflation in the face of this market power. Robinson and Kaldor advocated economic policies that would encourage manufacturing sector development and export-led growth to deal with unemployment.

As might be expected, the Keynesian Revolution met with considerable opposition. There was the existing Austrian school, already committed to a belief in the efficacy of free markets. Hayek strongly denounced the Keynesian Revolution and argued that it was taking countries down the road to serfdom.

Monetarism, a school led by Milton Friedman, provided a second counter-attack to Keynes. Friedman argued against both fiscal policy to lower unemployment and short-run solutions to economic problems. Unemployment, he argued, would naturally gravitate to its natural rate in the long run. Moving more quickly, or attempts to drive unemployment below its natural rate, he argued, would either result in inflation or have no impact at all.

The public choice school, led by James Buchanan, took aim at the Keynesian Revolution by bringing microeconomic analysis to bear on policy-making decisions. Buchanan saw politicians as individual utility maximizers. As such, he arrived at the conclusion that macroeconomic policy would be employed to benefit politicians and bureaucrats, but would not improve economic performance. The result would be large budget deficits and a larger role for government in the economy.

But the big challenge to Keynes came with Robert Lucas and the new classical or rational expectations revolution. Lucas began with the standard microeconomic assumption stemming from Locke – people were rational and would act in their own self-interest. From this he demonstrated that unemployment would never exist for long. Unemployed people would offer to work for less money, and rational employers would hire them at lower wages. Moreover, for new classical economists, Keynesian economic policy would be completely ineffective. Rational individuals will know that tax cuts or more government spending will lead to budget deficits. These deficits will have to be repaid in the future, which means higher taxes in the future. So people will save now to be able to pay the higher taxes in the future, and tax cuts will fail to increase spending or reduce unemployment.

The new classical school dominated macroeconomics from the late 1970s to the early 1990s. Although it rendered macroeconomics and microeconomics consistent, since both now assumed that all individuals were rational, its inability to explain the high rates of unemployment that prevailed during the Great Depression made many macroeconomists uneasy. New Keynesian economics arose in response to this unease.

New Keynesians assume individual rationality, but seek to explain why unemployment can exist in a world of rational individuals. Joseph Stiglitz, one of the leaders of the new Keynesian school, sees information problems as the main culprit. Stiglitz realized that rational individuals must always make decisions about how much information they need before making a choice. Sometimes it is just not worth seeking out additional information because information can be hard to get and may not lead to significantly better decisions. Stiglitz then showed how informational problems can result in high wages, high interest rates and high unemployment rates. The door was again open for Keynesian macroeconomic policies to improve economic outcomes.

Finally, we come to the most recent trends within the discipline of economics. Late in the twentieth century, economics started to broaden its horizons by expanding its method of analysis and by studying important aspects of people's lives that are normally considered beyond the scope of the discipline.

The public choice school, which brings economic analysis to bear on the question of how government officials actually make economic and social policy, is one good example of the latter type of broadening. Another good example is Kenneth Arrow's use of economic analysis to study health care systems and their problems. But perhaps the best example of this phenomenon is Gary Becker's work on how individual decision-making leads to social problems like crime and addiction, and how economic incentives and trade-offs affect the decisions of people to marry and have children.

In expanding its method, economics has moved away from its long history of analyzing the logical consequences of individual rationality. Economists have begun to do experiments, take surveys and engage in computer simulations to find out how people really behave and to figure out the economic consequences of real human behavior. In the mid-twentieth century John von Neumann pioneered game theory, which looks at individual decision-making when outcomes depend not just on individual decisions but also on what others decide. At first, game theory was used to study firm behavior in oligopolistic markets; but soon it was being used to analyze individual behavior in various settings and even nuclear strategies in a world containing two superpowers. One important result from game theory, known as the prisoner's dilemma, shows that individual rationality need not yield the best results in certain situations. But perhaps most important of all, game theory has been used in controlled experiments involving real people, and thus has given rise to a great deal of interest and work in experimental and behavioral economics. Psychologist Daniel Kahneman has been most instrumental in this endeavor to understand how real economic agents actually behave. His experimental results cast doubt on the economic notion of rationality, and open the door for a broader modeling of human behavior and its consequences.

Where these new techniques and methods will take economics in the future is anybody's guess. On the one hand, there may be few changes in how economists go about understanding the world they live in. Yet, on the other hand, we may be on the brink of another revolution in understanding how our economic system works.

References

Galbraith, John Kenneth, *A Short History of Financial Euphoria*, New York, Viking Press, 1993

Hodgson, Geoffrey, "Institutional Economic Theory: The Old versus the New," *Review of Political Economy*, 1 (November 1989), pp. 249–69

Kuhn, Thomas, *The Structure of Scientific Revolutions*, Chicago, University of Chicago Press, 1962

FIFTY MAJOR ECONOMISTS

THOMAS MUN (1571–1641)

Thomas Mun is the best-known and most respected member of a group of seventeenth century British merchant-economists called "the mercantilists." This group proposed that England run trade surpluses in order to prosper economically. As set forth by Mun ([1664] 1954, p. 125),

> The ordinary means ... to increase our wealth and treasure is by *Forraign Trade*, wherein wee must Ever observe this rule; to sell more to strangers yearly than wee consume of theirs in value. ... [T]hat part of our stock which is not returned to us in wares must necessarily be brought home in treasure.

Little is known about the life of Mun. His grandfather worked for the Royal Mint; his father was a textile trader. Mun himself became a merchant early in life, lived in Italy for many years, and quickly accumulated a great deal of wealth. He later became involved with the East India Company, a large British joint-stock company that traded (primarily) in the Far East. In 1615 Mun was elected to be a Director of the East India Company, and he remained a Director of the firm for the remainder of his life. After Mun achieved wealth and social status he was appointed to several British committees and commissions. Most of these commissions issued reports containing Mun's name as part of a long list of committee members; but Mun himself wrote only two economic tracts.

His first work (Mun 1621) defended the East India Company against critics who claimed that the firm was exporting gold and silver to the Orient (in exchange for spices) and that this loss of precious metals was hurting the British economy. *A Discourse of Trade* was rather unmercantilist in its orientation. Rather than advocating a trade surplus and the accumulation of gold, Mun advanced any and all arguments he could think of to support the East India Company.

He claimed that nations become wealthy for the same reasons that families become wealthy – by frugality and by making more than they spend. Likewise, nations and families become poor by spending too much money. Thus, Mun reasoned, as long as the East India Company made money it could not make Britain poorer.

Mun also pointed out that food, clothing, and munitions were necessities, so importing these goods improved the welfare of Britain. On the other hand, importing luxury goods was harmful to the nation. Mun then went on to argue that the East India Company was importing only items necessary for consumption.

Taking yet another line of defense, Mun argued that trade with India provided a market for British exports. In addition, trade with India was good for Britain because it eliminated trade with Turkey; had the same goods been imported from Turkey, Mun pointed out, the cost to Britain would have been much greater.

Finally, Mun argued that not all luxury imports were harmful; some imports were improved by British firms and re-exported, thus leading to a net influx of precious metals into Britain. The goods imported by the East India Company, Mun claimed, were generally goods needed by British exporters.

While the *Discourse* made Mun an apologist for the East India Company, his second book, published posthumously (1664), established Mun as an important early economic thinker. What is most noteworthy about *England's Treasure by Forraign Trade* is its much broader perspective. No longer does Mun try to defend the East India Company; rather he adopts the viewpoint of the nation as a whole. He looks at trade in general, rather than trade by the East India Company, and he makes the case that foreign trade enriches a nation whenever it leads to a trade surplus. Mun also examines the factors that cause a country to run trade surpluses. Finally, Mun advances a set of proposals that British leaders could implement if they wished to improve the national trade position.

The trade balance is merely the difference between what a nation exports and what it imports. When a nation runs a trade surplus, its exports exceed its imports. Sales abroad, over and above what is bought from foreign countries, must be paid for by foreigners. In the seventeenth century these payments were made with precious metals – gold and silver. Trade surpluses thus enabled a nation to accumulate wealth, thereby enriching a country. In contrast, domestic trade could not make Britain wealthier because the gain in precious metals by one citizen would equal the loss by another citizen. To generate trade surpluses, Mun noted, Britain must become more self-sufficient and reduce its need for foreign-made goods. Britain must also become more frugal so that more goods were available for export. Mun especially looked down on and discouraged the consumption of luxury goods.

With the domestic money supply rising as a result of these trade surpluses, a danger lurks that people might try to purchase more goods. This would cause domestic prices to increase and would eventually lead to the loss of exports, since domestically produced goods would become too expensive to sell abroad. But these consequences, Mun noted, could easily be avoided. To make sure that the inflow of money from abroad actually goes to benefit a nation, all new money must be re-invested. Reinvestment would also create more goods to be exported in the future. Here Mun recognized the importance of capital investment, and he viewed a positive trade balance as a way to accumulate productive capital.

Besides explaining the benefits of trade surpluses, Mun also explained what could be done to encourage such surpluses. First, there was price policy. Mun wanted exports sold at the "best price"; that is, the price that brings in the most revenue and wealth. Where Britain had a monopoly in world trade, or something close to a monopoly, her goods should be sold at high prices. But when foreign competition was great, British goods should be priced as low as possible. This would result in more sales for Britain and help drive out foreign competitors. When foreign competitors disappeared, Mun recommended that prices be raised, but not to the point that competitors are enticed to come back into the market.

Second, Mun explained that higher-quality goods would be in greater demand throughout the world and would also lead to greater exports for Britain. He then explained how the British government could help improve product quality. Mun wanted the government to regulate manufacturers and to establish a trade council (similar to the functions now performed by the US Department of Commerce, and the Ministries of Trade in Canada, Europe and elsewhere) that would advise the government on how to regulate trade and industrial activity. The regulations on British manufacturers, Mun thought, should be quite strict in order to ensure that Britain produced high-quality goods.

Finally, Mun explained how national tax policy could help generate trade surpluses. He recognized that (in opposition to the national interest) some firms might want to import luxury goods. In such a case, government policies must bring private and national interests into harmony. Mun looked to taxation to achieve this end. Export duties were to be discouraged because they would cost Britain sales in foreign countries. Import duties should be low on goods that are subsequently exported and high on goods that tend to be consumed by British citizens. Excise or sales taxes, Mun argued, did little harm. Although they raised the price of food and clothing, Mun believed that these taxes would lead to higher wages and thus be shifted to employers. Although Mun did not offer any explanation for why this was likely to happen, one possibility is that he had in mind a *subsistence theory of wages* (see **Smith**), whereby wages would have to increase to make sure that workers would make enough to survive.

When higher prices for necessities lead to higher wages, the standard of living for British workers remains the same and the excise tax is paid by the wealthy. In order to avoid paying this tax the rich had only two options: they could work longer and harder, or they could reduce luxury consumption. In either case, Mun argued, the nation would benefit.

Mun, however, did not want the state to collect tax revenues and then engage in lavish or wasteful spending. Tax collections had to be saved so that they were available for national emergencies, such as wars. At the same time, the state should not accumulate so much tax revenue that the national supply of capital falls. As a compromise, Mun proposed that each year the state should accumulate a surplus of taxes over spending that was equal to the annual trade surplus.

Mun and mercantilism came in for sharp criticism from other economists during the eighteenth and nineteenth centuries. David Hume explained how trade imbalances would correct themselves automatically. François Quesnay and Adam Smith both sharply criticized the mercantilists, and argued that less government restrictions on businesses would spur domestic production. Finally, David Ricardo advanced a strong case for free trade. All these anti-mercantilist views were quickly taken to heart by most economists.

Mercantilist thinking, however, experienced a revival of sorts in the twentieth century. John Maynard Keynes praised the mercantilists for recognizing that the demand generated by trade surpluses would increase economic growth. Chapter 23 of *The General Theory* (Keynes 1936), entitled "Notes on Mercantilism," credits the mercantilists with understanding that countries could create jobs and incomes for their own citizens by generating a trade surplus, while the influx of money due to the trade surplus would be used to increase business investment.

But perhaps the strongest support for mercantilist doctrines can be found in Asia. The success of the Japanese economy in the second half of the twentieth century was achieved with the aid of economic policies that were mercantilist in spirit, even if not in intent. The Japanese government set high product quality standards, which helped Japan become a producer of high-quality consumer goods. Economic success was also achieved by using tariffs and protectionism to stem imports, while encouraging domestic firms to export goods (see Johnson 1982).

Although he is not highly regarded by economists today, and although he did not make any ground-breaking discoveries, Mun did leave his mark on the history of economics. The idea that government economic policy should be used to generate a trade surplus, and the idea that the way to achieve economic growth is through the growth of exports, constitute his two lasting contributions.

Works by Mun

A Discourse of Trade from England unto the East-Indies (1621) in Early English Tracts on Commerce, ed. John R. McCulloch, Cambridge, Cambridge University Press, 1954

England's Treasure by Forraign Trade (1664) in Early English Tracts on Commerce, ed. John R. McCulloch, Cambridge, Cambridge University Press, 1954

Works about Mun

Buck, Philip W., The Politics of Mercantilism, New York, Octagon Books, 1964

Johnson, E. A. J., Predecessors of Adam Smith: The Growth of British Economic Thought, New York, Augustus M. Kelley, 1965

Magnusson, Lars, Mercantilism: The Shaping of an Economic Language, New York and London, Routledge, 1994

Other references

Johnson, Chalmers, MITI and the Japanese Miracle: The Growth of Industrial Policy, Stanford, California, Stanford University Press, 1982

Keynes, John Maynard, The General Theory of Employment, Interest and Money (1936), New York, Harcourt Brace & World, 1964

WILLIAM PETTY (1623–87)

William Petty was one of the very first people to think and write systematically about economics, and one of the first individuals to apply economic principles to the real world. His work provides insight into the nature of rent and taxation. But Petty is best known for his attempt to make economics a quantitative and statistical science through what he called "political arithmetic."

Petty was born in 1623 to a poor clothworker in the quiet market town of Romsey, on the River Test in Hampshire, southern England. His schooling consisted primarily of rote memorization; it was a typical education for the children of the lower classes at that time. None the less, Petty rose above his formal schooling because he possessed great curiosity and read widely in the areas of literature and science.

At the age of thirteen or fourteen, Petty left school and found a job as a cabin boy on a ship that continually crossed the English Channel. During his first year at work, Petty broke his leg. Since he was no longer useful to his employer, he was left on the French side of the Channel. Petty decided to stay in France and to attend the Jesuit College in Caen. He left Caen in 1640, spent three more years at sea, and then went to Holland to study anatomy and medicine.

In 1646 Petty returned to England to study medicine at Oxford. After receiving his doctorate in medicine, he was appointed Professor of Anatomy at Oxford. Petty established a name and reputation for himself by supposedly raising from the dead a woman who had been hanged (Strauss 1954, ch. 3). But within weeks of giving his first lecture, he decided that the academic life was not right for him, and he left Oxford to become chief physician of the Irish army. At the same time, Petty became chief surveyor of Ireland, and he used the knowledge he acquired in this job to accumulate much land and great wealth. In the 1660s Petty helped establish the Royal Society of London for the Improving of Natural Knowledge. Its agenda was to follow the scientific method of Francis Bacon – to use observation and experimentation in order to study the natural world and society.

Petty developed the method of political arithmetic as a result of applying the Royal Society research program to economic phenomena. In the preface to his *Political Arithmetic*, Petty ([1671] in Hull 1899) announced that his goal was to refute popular beliefs and show that England was suffering from neither economic decline nor a decline in trade. On the contrary, Petty claimed that England was richer than ever. He then sought to prove this thesis. Unfortunately, in seventeenth century England there were no government agencies to report economic data on a regular basis. Nor did newspapers provide every economic and financial statistic that one might care to know. Thus Petty assumed responsibility for gathering the figures necessary to make his case.

Essentially, the method of political arithmetic was "to express myself in terms of number, weight or measure; to use only arguments of sense; and to consider only such causes as have visible foundations in nature; leaving those that depend upon the mutable minds, opinions, appetites, and passions of particular men, for the consideration of others" (Hull 1899, p. 244). Political arithmetic employed quantitative methods to analyze economic and social phenomena. One aspect of this new method was to use numbers and measures to describe reality. Another aspect was to use these numbers to draw inferences about the way the world worked. For example, by showing that A and B increased together, Petty would draw the conclusion that in order to increase A it was necessary to increase B, and in order to increase B it was necessary to increase A. The final thrust of political arithmetic was an attempt to separate economic analysis from the morals or beliefs held by individuals, thereby making any study of the economy more objective.

It is well known that the scientific or experimental method is difficult to employ in economics. A true controlled experiment would require that we start with two identical economies, or two identical groups of people, placed in exactly the same situation. We would then alter one condition for just one of these two groups. Then we would observe how this one change affected each group. Unfortunately, in the real world it is virtually impossible to create or find such an environment. Political arithmetic attempted to substitute statistical analysis for experimentation, believing this is the best we can do in economics. This statistical method continues to be used in economics (see **Tinbergen**), although there have been recent attempts to make economics more "scientific" by figuring out how to run controlled experiments (Smith 1987, 1990; Burtless 1995) (also see **Kahneman**).

To prove that London was wealthy and that it had been expanding economically, Petty set out to show that the city had more people and more homes than Paris. Petty first examined the median number of burials per year in London and in Paris (using data from 1683–5 for London and 1682 for Paris), and found a greater number of burials in London (22,337) than in Paris (19,887). Assuming that death rates were the same in both cities, Petty concluded that the population of London was greater than that of Paris and that London was wealthier than Paris.

One key assumption in this analysis was that national wealth depended on the population of a nation. While this assumption may seem bizarre in an era where poor countries tend to be the most populous and whose populations grow at the fastest rates, this was a reasonable assumption when Petty was writing. In seventeenth century England there was no direct way to measure wealth; some indirect measurement was necessary. And Petty did choose a reasonable indirect measure. Before modern birth control methods came into existence, population and population growth depended primarily on the ability of children to survive. This, in turn, required a greater standard of living or greater national wealth. Greater wealth did actually lead to more rapid population growth; thus Petty's analysis was probably the best possible at the time.

Although Petty has been taken to be a mercantilist (see **Mun**) because he frequently called for England to run trade surpluses, Petty differed from the mercantilists in many respects. Unlike the mercantilists, Petty advocated trade surpluses to increase employment rather than to accumulate wealth. This makes Petty, more than Mun, the true precursor to Keynes. In addition, unlike the mercantilist writers, Petty recognized a number of benefits to free international trade. Finally, unlike the mercantilists, Petty did not look towards international trade to promote the economic growth of England. Rather, Petty thought that public finance, or government spending and tax policy, was a more important determinant of economic well-being than trade policy or accumulating large trade surpluses.

In fact, Petty became a harsh critic of English public finance, arguing that the English tax system was a major force hindering national economic growth. In seventeenth century England the cost of collecting taxes was high, there was great uncertainty about the taxes that people owed, and the many injustices stemming from actual collection were legendary. This all reduced the incentives that people had to work hard and better themselves. And when people lack such incentives, economies stagnate.

But Petty was not opposed to all forms of taxation. Nor did he think that taxes were necessarily bad and hurt a nation. The problem was with the actual English tax policy. Petty (in Hull 1899, p. 64) condemned English *poll taxes* because they were *regressive* in nature. Petty also condemned state lotteries as a means of raising revenues; this he regarded as "a tax upon unfortunate self-conceited fools" (Hull 1899, p. 64). Instead, he favored a *progressive tax* where people pay according to the "interest in the Public Peace; that is, according to their Estates or Riches." At times he also supported a proportional tax on consumption (Hull 1899, p. 91).

More important than how taxes were collected, though, was how tax monies were spent. According to Petty, taxation hurt the economy only when tax revenues were removed from circulation. If tax revenues were spent, they had few harmful effects. Government spending would return money to circulation and put people back to work. This would compensate for the loss of money in circulation and the loss of jobs that arose from taxation.

Moreover, Petty recognized the possibility that taxes could have positive effects. Anticipating Nicholas Kaldor, Petty held that, if taxation and spending encouraged the consumption and production of high-productivity goods, this would increase national output. In addition, tax monies spent to assure that the economy functioned in an orderly manner would promote national wealth. Petty thus considered it the responsibility of government to spend money on things such as defense, justice, schools, poor relief and public works including highways, bridges, and harbors (Hull 1899, p. 20). Finally, Petty noted the importance of government expenditure, even on useless items, in order to create jobs and eliminate idleness. Foreshadowing Keynes, he wrote the following about government spending: "'tis no matter if it be employed to build a useless pyramid upon Salisbury Plain, bring the stones at Stonehenge to Tower Hill, or the like" (Hull 1899, p. 31). All that really mattered was that spending of some sort be undertaken.

Despite his strong empirical and practical bent, Petty did make key theoretical contributions to economics. He was the first economist to define the notion of a *surplus* and he was the first economist to explain land rents based upon this notion (Roncaglia 1985, ch. 7). Although the view that rent is a surplus has come to be known as the *Physiocratic theory of rent*, the theory was really due to Petty rather than to Quesnay.

To grasp the notion of a surplus, think of a primitive agricultural economy that grows only corn. During the year, corn will be both an input into the production process and an economic output. As an input, corn will be used as seed and to feed workers. At the end of the year, corn will be harvested, to be used next year as food and seed. Petty defined the economic surplus as the difference between the total output of corn (at the annual harvest) and the input of corn needed to produce that output. Landowners, he thought, would tend to receive rental payments equal to the surplus generated on their land. No one would pay to rent land for more than the surplus that can be obtained from that land, since the renter would thereby lose money. On the other hand, competition among renters would push rents up to the level of the surplus.

Despite his contributions to the study of public finance, and despite his work on defining and explaining the notion of a surplus, Petty was an important figure mainly for his emphasis on using numbers or data to understand and explain how real-world economies work. Although he urged the development of better and more regular economic statistics to aid in this endeavor (see Hull 1899, p. lxvi, note 4), it would take another 250 years before reliable data became readily available (see also **Kuznets**). Hutchison (1988, p. 37f.) is surely correct that Petty was overconfident that government could collect reliable statistics in the seventeenth century; but Petty was also right that without any statistics it is virtually impossible to understand how economies change over time. Petty attempted to make such measurements and he used these measurements to try to understand the British economy. This constitutes his most important economic contribution and makes him the most important economic figure of the seventeenth century.

Works by Petty

The Economic Writings of Sir William Petty, ed. C. H. Hull, Cambridge, Cambridge University Press, 1899

Works about Petty

Hutchison, Terence, *Before Adam Smith: The Emergence of Political Economy, 1662–1776*, Oxford, Basil Blackwell, 1988

Letwin, William, *The Origins of Scientific Economics: English Economic Thought 1660–1776*, London, Methuen & Co., 1963

Roncaglia, Alessandro, *Petty*, Armonk, New York, M. E. Sharpe, 1985

Strauss, Erich, *Sir William Petty: Portrait of a Genius*, London, Bodley Head, 1954

Other references

Burtless, Gary, "The Case for Randomized Field Trials in Economic and Policy Research," *Journal of Economic Perspectives*, 9, 2 (Spring 1995), pp. 63–84

Smith, Vernon L., "Experimental Methods in Economics," in *The New Palgrave: A Dictionary of Economics*, ed. John Eatwell, Murray Milgate and Peter K. Newman, New York, Stockton Press, 1987, Vol. 2, pp. 241–9

Smith, Vernon L. (ed.), *Experimental Economics*, Aldershot, Edward Elgar, 1990

JOHN LOCKE (1632–1704)

The contributions that John Locke made to economics were primarily the contributions of a philosopher. He provided the first justification for private property and for limited state involvement in economic activity. This helped provide a philosophical foundation for the capitalism developing in seventeenth century England, and helped win its acceptance in an era dominated by religious concerns. Locke also made several contributions to the theory of money and interest rates.

Locke was born in Somerset, England, in 1632 to a moderately well-off family. His father was a country lawyer with considerable land holdings; one of his best clients and closest friends was Alexander Popham. Popham became a Member of Parliament in 1647 and helped Locke gain admittance to Westminster School, one of the most influential and best English public schools.

Locke did so well at Westminster that he won a scholarship to Oxford University, and entered Christ Church College in 1652. He received a bachelor's degree in 1656 and a master's degree in 1659. He then went on to teach at Oxford – becoming a lecturer in Greek in 1660 and a lecturer in Rhetoric in 1662.

Like many of his contemporaries, Locke was fascinated by William Harvey's discovery that blood circulated throughout the body, and he began to study medicine in his spare time. He became personal physician to Lord Ashley, who was Chancellor of the Exchequer, and soon became his personal assistant. From his relationship with Lord Ashley, Locke learned about the important economic issues of the day, such as trade with the British colonies and interest rates.

Because of the knowledge and expertise he developed about colonial problems, in 1673 Locke was made Secretary to the Council for Trade and Plantations. Two years later he returned to private life and to another love – philosophy. Over the next few years Locke worked on *An Essay Concerning Human Understanding* (1690a) and *Two Treatises on Government* (1690b). These two works established his reputation as a great philosopher. None the less, Locke retained an interest in economic issues, particularly monetary matters, and continued to exert political influence in England until his death.

Locke made five contributions to economics, three of a philosophical nature and two that were more economic in nature. He set forth philosophical justifications for private property and for the state, and he developed a methodology that helped make economics "scientific." This latter contribution involved assuming that people act rationally and respond to financial incentives. Locke's contributions to economics concerned the theory of money and interest. He argued against government regulation of interest rates, and against a government plan to devalue the British currency, because such actions would have bad economic consequences.

Probably the most important philosophical contribution made by Locke was his justification for an individual's right to private property. In seventeenth century England, commercial activity was growing rapidly and came into conflict with the dominant feudal and religious institutions. It was generally accepted that God gave the earth to all men in common. To own the resources of the earth meant that those resources were not available for someone else. This made it hard to justify private ownership.

Yet Locke provided such a justification. He first set forth the rather uncontroversial proposition that men had a right to their own labor and the fruits of their labor. Men acquired land as their lawful property by combining their labor with the land. This was acceptable as long as there remained an ample supply of land for others, and as long as what someone took from the land did not spoil before it was consumed (Locke [1690b] 1953, pp. 130ff.).

Locke then went from this limited defense of property (based on what could be consumed) to a more extensive defense of private property. Money or capital, Locke recognized, was really the product of past labor. Thus, ownership of money could be justified because people had to work in order to acquire it. Money also allowed man to accumulate more and more property, since money did not spoil before it was consumed. The only constraint on unlimited accumulation was the right of the poor to enough income to be able to survive whenever no land or jobs were available, and whenever they were physically unable to support themselves (Locke 1690b). In addition, Locke argued that private property had practical value, because when men were allowed to accumulate property they were more productive.

Locke's second philosophical contribution was his justification for the state in economic society. In line with contemporary beliefs, Locke held that natural law dictated that the ultimate source of political rule was the individual. The state could come into existence only when a group of individuals agreed to turn over some of their rights to a common ruler. Locke saw the state as a company whose shareholders were men of property. Men put themselves under the rule of government to protect their life, liberty, and land. All citizens (or at least those owning land and wealth) therefore had an interest in joining civil society; and presumably all citizens gave their tacit consent to the rule of government. Rulers, in turn, had to protect the interests of their citizens; otherwise they would be removed from office and replaced with someone who would uphold the social contract (MacPherson 1962). Since the state arose as a result of individual decisions about laws and rules, the state could be justified by appeals to natural law.

A final philosophical contribution made by Locke involved the methodology of economics, or how economics should be done. Locke viewed people as rational self-interested individuals, who responded to economic incentives. This was quite different from the prevailing religious view that people were altruistic, or that they primarily followed religious dictates. Because people could be counted on to behave in certain ways, economic laws and principles could be developed. For example, Locke recognized that, when the price for some goods increased, people would substitute cheaper goods for the goods they usually consumed; similarly, sellers would respond to greater profit opportunities by producing and selling more (Locke 1968, pp. 2–3, 46–68). As a result, economic laws could be developed analogous to Boyle's Law in chemistry and Newton's laws of motion in physics. Just as gases behaved according to the mathematical expressions contained within the laws of chemistry and physics, so too humans would behave rationally and in their own self-interest when making economic decisions (Vaughn 1980).

In the area of economics proper, Locke made contributions to the theory of money and the theory of interest. In the mid-seventeenth century, Josiah Child held that the state should limit interest rates to 4 percent (see Letwin 1963, p. 157), arguing that lower interest rates would benefit merchants and others wanting to borrow money for useful purposes, and thus benefit the nation as a whole. The only people who would be hurt by this policy, according to Child, were lenders charging high interest rates.

Locke (1691) refuted this claim, and made a case against government regulation of interest rates. He argued that *usury laws* merely redistribute the gains from trade between the merchant and the lender; they do not benefit the nation as a whole because they do not increase borrowing and investing. For example, if a merchant could make 10 percent on borrowed money and current interest rates were 5 percent, the lender and the merchant split the gains from trade 50–50. But if the government prohibits loans at more than 4 percent, 60 percent of the gains from trade go to the merchant and 40 percent go to the lender. There would be no additional investment and no net gain for the nation here. In fact, there could be a net loss for the nation if some people were unwilling to lend money at a 4 percent rate. It would be better, Locke concluded, if interest rates were allowed to go to their natural level rather than be set by government decree.

The natural rate of interest for Locke was the free market interest rate, the rate determined by the laws of supply and demand. When money was in short supply, its price (or the rate of interest) would rise because lenders would know that they could charge more. Behaving rationally, lenders would charge higher interest rates and make more money. Conversely, when there was more money to lend than borrowers wanting this money, the natural rate of interest would fall. Rational borrowers would shop for good deals, and only those lenders reducing their rates would find someone who was willing to borrow their money (Locke [1691] 1968, pp. 9–11).

Locke was also a prominent figure in the recoinage question. In seventeenth century England, most coins were made of precious metals. Because these metals had value people began clipping or filing off the edges of coins. These scraps would then be melted down and sold as gold or silver. Clippers thus accumulated wealth, while clipped coins continued to circulate in exchange for goods and services. This behavior led Sir Thomas Gresham to formulate one of the first economic principles. *Gresham's Law* simply states that "bad money drives out good money." By this, Gresham meant that rational people held the best (least-clipped) coins, and spent those coins that were clipped the most and contained the least amount of precious metal.

As early as 1690 the English government proposed solving the problem of clipped or depreciated coins by reducing the weight of precious metals in all coins, or essentially devaluing the national currency. Locke opposed this solution, and he argued against devaluing and in favor of recoining with the accustomed amount of precious metals. Reducing the precious metal content in all coins, he thought, would not help matters because the value or purchasing power of money was determined by its silver or gold content. This natural value of money could not be set by public authorities or by government laws (Letwin 1963, p. 171). Debasing the currency would merely lead merchants to demand more coins (and thus the same precious metal content) in exchange for goods. Although he entered this debate at a rather late stage, Locke helped to convince government authorities not to devalue the British currency and to recoin using the accustomed precious metal content.

His argument that reducing the precious metal content of each coin (and producing more coins) would lead to higher prices makes Locke an important forerunner of the *quantity theory of money* (see **Fisher**). However, Locke has remained a key figure in economics primarily for the important philosophical contributions he made to the subject. His justifications for private property, and for letting economic activity take place without outside interference by government, have been accepted by most economists throughout history – even up to today.

Works by Locke

An Essay Concerning Human Understanding (1690a), Amherst, New York, Prometheus Books, 1994

Two Treatises of Government (1690b), 2nd edn, New York, Cambridge University Press, 1953

Some Considerations of the Consequences of the Lowering of Interest and Raising the Value of Money, 1691, in Locke 1696

Several Papers Relating to Money, Interest and Trade (1696), New York, Augustus M. Kelley, 1968

Works about Locke

Kramer, Matthew, *John Locke and the Origins of Private Property*, New York, Cambridge University Press, 1977

Letwin, W., *The Origins of Scientific Economics*, London, Methuen, 1963

MacPherson, C. B., *The Political Theory of Possessive Individualism: Hobbes to Locke*, Oxford, Clarendon Press, 1962

Vaughn, K. I., *John Locke: Economist and Social Scientist*, London, Athlone, 1980

RICHARD CANTILLON (1687?–1734?)

Richard Cantillon (pronounced KAN-till-LON) is a mysterious and fascinating figure. Few details of his birth and youth are known, and his financial activities as well as his death remain shrouded in controversy. Despite devoting most of his life to making money, Cantillon wrote the first real economic treatise, a study describing the interrelationships and workings of the economic system. He also contributed to monetary theory and was the first person to explain the important economic role played by the entrepreneur.

Cantillon was born into a Catholic family in Ballyronan, a small town in northwest Ireland, sometime between 1680 and 1690. The exact date of his birth remains uncertain because parishes did not keep birth records in Ireland during the seventeenth century. Brewer (1992, p. 2) makes a plausible case for a birth year of 1687 based on the fact that Cantillon took French nationality in 1708, and he would have had to be twenty-one to do this.

Little is known about Cantillon's upbringing or when he left Ireland. From 1711 to 1713 he was a clerk for the British Assistant Paymaster General in Spain, who had the responsibility for paying and outfitting British troops fighting in Spain. In 1716, he went to France to take over his cousin's bank.

Cantillon made a small fortune in 1720 on John Law's Mississippi scheme, which involved selling shares of stock that represented entitlement to all the gold and silver thought to be contained in the Mississippi River area. Having accumulated much wealth in this way, Cantillon lent money to others who were speculating on the value of Mississippi shares. In order to get around French *usury* laws, Cantillon disguised his loans as foreign exchange transactions – he lent money to others in one currency and demanded repayment in another currency. As a result of all his wheeling and dealing, Cantillon was constantly involved in legal battles. In an attempt to put an end to them, he decided to return to England and live a life of luxury with the vast wealth he had made from his investing and lending activities.

If some mystery surrounds his birth, the death of Cantillon is downright confusing. On the night of 14 May 1734, shortly after his return to England, a fire engulfed Cantillon's home in Albemarle Street in London. At the time it was thought the fire was an accident or that Cantillon had been murdered. But Murphy (1986) argues that Cantillon was not in the house at the time of the fire. He thinks Cantillon fabricated his own death to end all the litigation arising from the fortune he amassed. In support of this view, Murphy notes that Cantillon withdrew È10,000 the day before the fire, that a neighbor reported seeing what was supposed to be Cantillon's burnt corpse without a head, and that Cantillon's personal papers were found many years later in the Dutch colony of Surinam in South America. It is surely hard to believe that a thief would take valueless personal papers, and hard to understand how these papers turned up in Surinam – unless, of course, Cantillon himself took them there.

Cantillon wrote only one surviving work in economics, his *Essay on the Nature of Commerce* (Cantillon 1755). This book was published more than twenty years after the fire that engulfed his London home. A statistical supplement, which is referred to in the text, has never been found. There are reports of other writings by Cantillon, but these too have never been found.

Divided into three books or parts, the *Essay* sets forth a simple set of overarching principles that explain how economies work. The first book describes how the real economy operates, or the principles according to which goods are produced and people get hired to produce those goods. Book Two focuses on the monetary system, and explains how money and the real economy are related. Finally, international trade and foreign exchange are brought into the picture in Book Three.

Book One of the *Essay* depicts the economy as an interconnected system, or a circular flow of money and goods. It also explains how the different parts of this system interact with one another. Cantillon breaks into the circle of production and exchange by focusing on the money that gets spent by landowners. This spending supports manufacturers in cities and towns. It also supports agricultural workers in rural areas, by creating jobs and incomes for them. Manufacturing sector workers and agricultural sector workers will need to buy some manufactured goods, and they will need to purchase a lot of agricultural goods. This creates more jobs and more income for those working in both these economic sectors. Because the need for food and agricultural goods is greater than the need for manufactured goods, money tends to flow from the manufacturing sector to the agricultural sector in exchange for food. At some point agricultural workers will have to pay landowners for the use of their land, and so money will find its way back into the pockets of the landowners, ready to start a new cycle of spending and production.

Within this framework, Cantillon ([1755] 2001, p. 53) observed that production in different occupations is determined by the demand for different goods. If landowners want more manufactured goods and less food, people and resources will flow from the agricultural sector to the manufacturing sector; more manufactured goods and fewer agricultural goods will then be produced. In more modern terms, if consumers want more running sneakers and fewer regular shoes, makers of regular shoes will do less business. Some shoemakers will go bankrupt and new businesses will start up that produce running sneakers. The same principle also applies to different geographic regions within a nation. If more labor is wanted in cities and less labor is needed in rural areas, workers will move from rural areas to urban areas.

Cantillon also analyzed the economic role of the entrepreneur within this circular production process. The term "entrepreneur" goes back to ancient and medieval times, when it referred to people who got things done. Early eighteenth century entrepreneurs were contractors; in particular, they were people who had a contract with the government. This was a rather riskless occupation since governments generally paid their bills. Cantillon borrowed this popular term and redefined it. He made the entrepreneur a risk taker, rather than someone receiving a regular salary. Cantillon recognized that the future was uncertain and that all economic activity was inherently risky. However, someone must take risks now in the hope of making a profit later. If not, no production would take place. The risk-taking entrepreneur was thus essential for the circular production process to operate well and for economies to prosper.

Book Two of the *Essay* looked at how money affected this circular process. By analyzing the economic impact of money, Cantillon can legitimately be regarded as the founder of classical monetary theory (Bordo 1983). Money in the eighteenth century meant gold and silver coins; it could be created in either of two ways – by mining gold and silver, or by selling goods to other nations. When miners or traders had more money, their demand for goods and services increased, and so employment and output would expand in other industries or sectors. Greater demand would also raise prices, but not necessarily in proportion to the increased supply of money (Cantillon 1755, book II, chs 6, 7), since higher prices induce increases in output, and since sometimes there can be more money but not more spending of the additional money.

Economists now describe this uncertain impact of money as the *Cantillon Effect*. The economic effect of new money is uncertain because it depends on who gets the money and what they do with it. If the money goes primarily to merchants and exporters there will be more money saved and more investment. With more production, rather than more spending, prices will not tend to rise. But if the money goes to landlords who revel in luxury consumption, there will be a greater increase in prices and luxury goods will tend to go up in price the most.

At some point, Cantillon thought, the greater prosperity due to more money would likely come to an end. It is primarily through the effect of money on international trade that this occurs. Rising prices will make exports less competitive in international markets at the same time that imports become relatively cheap and attractive to domestic consumers. A trade deficit will result, meaning that gold will be shipped abroad in order to pay for all the imported goods flowing into the country. With gold going abroad, the domestic money supply is reduced and domestic production stagnates. Cantillon thus discovered the *specie flow mechanism* (see **Hume**).

Book Three of the *Essay* discusses trade policy, and pretty much follows the recommendations of the mercantilists (see **Mun**). Cantillon favored protectionism, and supported the running of trade surpluses in manufacturing. However, he advocated these policies more for military purposes than for economic reasons. Protectionist mercantilist policies, Cantillon thought, would increase the population of Britain. A trade surplus in manufacturing would allow Britain to import food, and this food could then support a larger population and make Britain a stronger nation.

Cantillon has been a much neglected figure in economics. He is known primarily for his influence on Quesnay and the Physiocrats, and for developing the notion that money flows connect the different sectors of the economy. Yet the place of Cantillon in history is more important than this. His *Essay* can legitimately be regarded as the first real economic treatise. It envisioned the economy as an interrelated system, and explained how that system worked. For this reason, Cantillon probably deserves to be regarded as the first real economist.

Works by Cantillon

Essay on the Nature of Commerce in General (1755), New Brunswick, New Jersey, Transaction Publishers, 2001

Works about Cantillon

Bordo, Michael, "Some Aspects of the Monetary Economics of Richard Cantillon," *Journal of Monetary Economics*, 12 (1983), pp. 235–58
Brewer, Anthony, *Richard Cantillon: Pioneer of Economic Theory*, London and New York, Routledge, 1992
Murphy, Antoin, *Richard Cantillon: Entrepreneur and Economist*, Oxford, Clarendon Press, 1986
Spengler, Joseph, "Richard Cantillon: First of the Moderns I," *Journal of Political Economy*, 62, 4 (August 1954), pp. 281–95
Spengler, Joseph, "Richard Cantillon: First of the Moderns II," *Journal of Political Economy*, 62, 5 (November 1954), pp. 406–24
Tarascio, Vincent, "Cantillon's Theory of Population Size and Distribution," *Atlantic Economic Journal*, 9, 2 (July 1981), pp. 12–18

FRANÇOIS QUESNAY (1694–1774)

François Quesnay (pronounced KEN-nay) is best known as the creator of the first economic model ever developed, the *Tableau Économique*, and as leader of the Physiocrats, the first school of economic thought. However, Quesnay has been admired for many other things – his *laissez-faire* policy proposals, his analysis of the generation and distribution of an economic surplus, and his vision of the economy as a closely integrated set of inter-dependent parts.

Quesnay was born in 1694 in the village of Méré, around 15 miles west of Versailles. His father was a peasant farmer and shopkeeper, and so Quesnay received little formal schooling. But Quesnay was enamored with books, and would often walk to Paris to purchase secondhand copies of Plato and Aristotle (Beer 1939, p. 101).

At age seventeen Quesnay decided to become a surgeon. Although dissatisfied with his medical training, which included bleeding patients, Quesnay continued with his studies. In 1717 he passed his medical examinations, obtained a license, and opened a practice in the village of Mantes, just south of Paris. After publishing several books on medical subjects, his reputation as a surgeon grew. In 1735 Quesnay was asked to serve as personal physician to the Duke of Villeroy. In 1744 he received a doctorate in medicine and became a member of the French Academy of Sciences. Five years later he settled in Versailles to become personal physician to Madame de Pompadour, the powerful mistress of Louis XV, as well as a medical consultant to the king.

At this point in his life (age fifty-five) Quesnay became interested in economics and mathematics. His broad interests, and his connections with those in high places, brought him an invitation to write several articles for Diderot's *Encyclopedia*. The articles he wrote earned him great fame and a large following. His disciples called themselves "Physiocrats," from the French term *Physiocrate*, meaning rule of nature.

The *Encyclopedia* articles all analyzed economic processes as a circular flow of money, goods, and people from one sector of the economy to another, akin to the flow of blood through the human body. "Corn" (in Meek 1963) was the most important *Encyclopedia* article because it first set forth the doctrine that only the agricultural sector of the French economy was productive. That is, only in agriculture could a *surplus* be generated, or only in agriculture does output exceed the inputs needed to produce that output. Quesnay thought that this surplus arose from the natural, generative properties of the land. This idea was important because it emphasized that wealth was generated in the process of production, rather than through exchange or trade as the mercantilists had claimed. Another consequence of this view, one that resulted in much criticism, was that manufacturing activities were not productive because they did not create a surplus.

Cantillon had already described the workings of an economy as a set of circular flows or economic interrelationships. Quesnay developed this idea further, and quantified the various relations between parts of the economy in greater detail in his *Tableau Économique*. The *Tableau* was thus the first attempt to mathematically model an entire economy, and to actually show the relationships between its various parts. Quesnay began with the assumption that the economy could be described in terms of three different classes or sectors. First, there is an agricultural sector that produces food, raw materials, and other agricultural goods. Second, a manufacturing sector produces manufactured goods like clothing and shelter as well as the tools needed by both agricultural and manufacturing workers. The manufacturing sector for Quesnay also includes what we today call the service sector, since it is responsible for facilitating domestic and international trade. Third, a class of landowners produces nothing of economic value; but these landowners have claims on the surplus output produced in agriculture. Rents represent the payment of this surplus to landowners, and this view has become known as the *Physiocratic theory of rent*.

Following his position in "Corn," Quesnay always assumed that only agricultural production was productive. Most *Tableaux* showed that inputs employed in agriculture yield twice the amount of output; however, Quesnay was aware that this assumption about the relationship between inputs and outputs depends upon the techniques of production employed in the agricultural sector. Some of his important policy proposals involve attempts to increase productivity in the agricultural sector.

Finally, Quesnay assumed that all income was spent, and that spending was divided equally between agricultural goods and manufactured goods. These assumptions led Quesnay to his famous zig-zag model of the economy, shown in Figure 1.

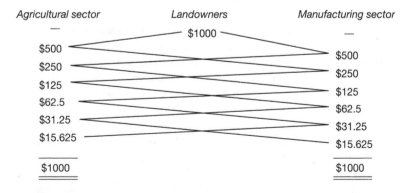

Figure 1 The *Tableau Économique*

According to this model, landowners take their $1,000 rental receipt and spend one half of it on manufactured goods and the other half on agricultural goods. These two sectors now each have $500 in money income. Those employed in these two sectors spend half their new income on goods produced by the other sector. This spending leads to incomes of $250 for each producing sector. Again, half of this additional income gets spent on the goods of the other producing class. This process continues until the amount of additional spending gets to be very, very small. We can then add up all the spending on agricultural goods and all the spending that takes place on manufactured goods. As Figure 1 shows, these both total $1,000.

What happens within each sector is probably more important than what happens across the different sectors, because it is within each sector that production takes place, and it is within sectors that an economic surplus gets generated. So let us look more closely at each sector (for more details see Pressman 1994).

Proprietors buy and consume $1,000 worth of goods – $500 worth of food and $500 worth of manufactured goods. During the year they produce nothing. They thus subsist on the output of the two producing classes or sectors. In particular, they receive rental payments from agricultural farmers equal to the agricultural surplus, and use these payments to buy and consume goods.

The other sectors take their initial $500 income and use it to buy necessary inputs so that more food and manufactured goods can be produced in the next year. The manufacturing sector buys (in total) $500 of agricultural goods through the zig-zags of Figure 1 and has $500 in cash. It uses this $500 in cash to buy more inputs from the agricultural sector and then takes its $1,000 of inputs to produce $1,000 worth of manufactured goods.

The agricultural sector has produced $2,000 worth of goods, but has sold only $1,000 to the proprietors and the manufacturing class. In addition, it has bought $500 worth of manufactured goods, as depicted in the zig-zag diagram of Figure 1, and it sold another $500 worth of goods to the manufacturing sector, as described in the previous paragraph. These two transactions balance each other out, and leave the agricultural sector with $1,000 worth of inputs. It also has the $1,000 in cash needed to pay the proprietors their rents and start a new production distribution cycle. Since inputs yield double the amount of output, the agricultural sector will produce another $2,000 worth of agricultural goods in the next production period. This process will continue from year to year, barring some outside factor disturbing the reproduction process.

Like the mercantilists, the Physiocrats viewed economic theory as a means to appropriate economic policy rather than as an end unto itself. The purpose of the *Tableau* was not just to explain the principles by which economies reproduce and grow, but to set forth policies to help stimulate economic growth. Moreover, Quesnay the physician tended to look upon the economy as if it were a sick patient in need of help.

Towards these policy ends, Quesnay usually presented two *Tableaux*, a sort of controlled experiment. One *Tableau* would be the control case, showing the present state of affairs in France. The other *Tableau* would show the effects of introducing various policy changes into the French economy. A good policy, Quesnay was able to show, would lead to economic growth; the French economy would prosper. This would be demonstrated by increased output of agricultural and manufactured goods. A poor policy, in contrast, would cause the French economy to decline and stagnate. In line with the name they adopted for themselves, the Physiocrats believed that all correct economic policies were consistent with the rules of nature.

One important policy conclusion of the *Tableau* was that taxes should be placed only on landlords. Taxes could not be placed on the manufacturing sector because they produced no surplus to tax. Any attempt to tax this sector would tax away the inputs used in producing manufactured goods. Since input exactly equals output in manufacturing, any reduction in inputs would lead to lower manufacturing output and therefore would result in the decline of the manufacturing sector. To the extent that the agricultural sector required goods produced by the manufacturing sector, it too would experience economic decline.

Similarly, any tax placed on the agricultural sector would reduce the inputs available in this sector and lead to its decline. Since agricultural advances double during production, each tax dollar imposed on agriculture would lower national output by two dollars. This outcome is even worse than taxing the manufacturing sector.

If neither manufacturing nor agriculture could be taxed without harming the economy, taxes had to fall on the landowners, the class that produced nothing. Since a tax on landowners does not reduce the inputs available in either manufacturing or agriculture, it would not lead to economic decline.

A second important policy conclusion of the *Tableau* was that the French agricultural system had to be restructured. Two important changes were especially needed. First, agriculture had to be modernized. Small plots of land, farmed with outdated technology, were terribly inefficient. By expanding the size of French land holdings, new cultivation methods could be employed that would only be feasible if done on a large scale. Investment in new technology, Quesnay recognized, would only be profitable and would only take place if its costs were spread out over many acres and many agricultural goods. Second, agriculture had to become more capitalist in nature, following the example of English agriculture. Quesnay argued that these reforms would improve agricultural productivity, or increase the surplus generated in agriculture, by providing greater economic incentives for successful farmers.

With such restructuring, agricultural inputs might lead to output that is triple the volume of the inputs; and thus, with more food produced, there would be more inputs available to the manufacturing sector and so more manufactured goods would be produced. All of France would therefore prosper.

A third policy prescription following from Quesnay's model was that saving, or hoarding money, was bad for the economy because it interrupted the circular flow of money and goods. Any lack of demand would lead to a reduction in national output and cause the French economy to stagnate. In this respect, Quesnay was an important forerunner of John Maynard Keynes.

Finally, in contrast to the mercantilists, Quesnay supported free trade of goods among nations. For the Physiocrats, wealth depended upon the total output of goods produced rather than the precious metals that a nation accumulated. More goods, in turn, required greater agricultural production. Quesnay thought that free international trade would increase the demand for French agricultural goods, and shift economic resources or inputs from the unproductive manufacturing sector to the productive agricultural sector. As a result of more inputs and greater production in the agricultural sector, the economic surplus generated within France would increase and the country would prosper (see Pressman 1993).

In one sense, history has not been kind to Quesnay. He has as much right as Adam Smith to be regarded as the father of economics. But while Smith has become a household name, Quesnay is virtually unknown outside the society of professional economists. Economists also parrot the criticism, first made by Smith, that Quesnay was wrong when he assumed that manufacturing is unproductive. Finally, the *Tableau* has been harshly criticized for being extremely difficult to follow and understand.

Yet, in another respect, history has been good to Quesnay. Virtually all economists, regardless of their orientation, think highly of him (no small feat!). Mathematically-minded economists look favorably upon Quesnay for his role as a pioneer in economic modeling. Leontief (1941, p. 2) claimed that the *Tableau* was an important precursor of his input–output analysis. Conservative economists value Quesnay's *laissez-faire* policy proposals and his opposition to placing taxes on the productive sectors of the economy. More liberal economists have been attracted by his Keynesian vision of spending as an important determinant of economic growth and decline. Even Marx (1954) lavished praise on Quesnay for recognizing the importance of an economic surplus arising in production, and for showing how this surplus enables capitalist economies to reproduce and grow. Quesnay is truly an economist for all seasons.

Works by Quesnay

L'Ami des Hommes, 5 vols, Avignon, 1762, with Victor de Riquetti, Marquis de Mirabeau
Philosophie Rurale, 5 vols, Amsterdam, Chez les Libraries Associés, 1764
The Economical Table, New York, Bergman Publishers, 1968
Quesnay's Tableau Économique, ed. Marguerita Kuczynski and Ronald L. Meek, New York, Augustus M. Kelley, 1972

Works about Quesnay

Beer, Max, *An Inquiry Into Physiocracy*, London, George Allen & Unwin, 1939
Higgs, Henry, *The Physiocrats*, London, Macmillan, 1897
Meek, Ronald, *The Economics of Physiocracy: Essays and Translations*, Cambridge, Massachusetts, Harvard University Press, 1963
Pressman, Steven, "Quesnay's Theory of Economic Growth and Decline," in *Economics as Worldly Philosophy*, ed. Ron Blackwell, Jaspal Chatha and Edward J. Nell, London, Macmillan, 1993, pp. 305–21
Pressman, Steven, *Quesnay's Tableau Économique: A Critique and Reassessment*, Fairfield, New Jersey, Augustus Kelley, 1994
Vaggi, Gianni, *The Economics of François Quesnay*, Durham, North Carolina, Duke University Press, 1987

Other references

Leontief, Wassily, *The Structure of the American Economy 1919–1929*, Cambridge, Massachusetts, Harvard University Press, 1941
Marx, Karl, *Theories of Surplus Value*, 3 vols, Moscow, Foreign Language Publishing House, 1954

DAVID HUME (1711–76)

David Hume was a world-famous philosopher who argued that knowledge could arise only from experience. But he also made several contributions to economics when the discipline was just developing. These involved analyzing the impact of money on an economy, and on the trade that takes place between nations.

Hume was born in Edinburgh, Scotland, in 1711. His father, a country gentleman, died when Hume was very young, so Hume was raised by his mother. However, his father left plenty of money to the family. This allowed Hume to receive an excellent education, primarily by private tutors at home. He then enrolled at the University of Edinburgh, intending to study the classics. But Hume quickly became dissatisfied with the education he was receiving and he decided to drop out of school, go to France, and become a great philosopher.

Despite having written several books that are now regarded as philosophical classics, Hume could not support himself as a philosopher. Unable to get a teaching job at any Scottish university, he agreed to tutor the Marquis of Annandale in 1745. Several years later he accepted a position as secretary to an army general. These jobs provided Hume with enough money that he soon achieved financial independence and could spend most of his time reading and writing.

In 1752 Hume was hired as a librarian at the Advocates Library in Edinburgh. This provided him with additional income as well as ready access to a large number of books. The result was a prodigious outpouring of philosophical works as well as a six-volume *History of England* (Hume 1757–62). In 1763 Hume became secretary of the British embassy in Paris, and in 1767 he became Undersecretary at the Foreign Office. Two years later he resettled in Edinburgh, where he died in 1776.

As an economist, Hume made several contributions to the theory of money and the theory of international trade. He analyzed the impact of money on interest rates, on economic activity, and on prices. He also explained how and why countries would not be able to experience trade imbalances for long periods of time. Finally, Hume addressed the important question: "What happens when rich countries trade with poor countries?" His answer was that international trade would benefit both rich countries and poor countries.

In mid-eighteenth century England, the mercantilists were proposing that government policies be enacted to support the meritorious merchant (see **Mun**). But they provided no justification for their program. Hume filled this void by explaining the economic function of the businessman. For Hume, the merchant was praiseworthy because he was frugal. Businessmen tend to save their income and accumulate capital. More capital lowers interest rates and tempts other businesses to borrow and expand their operations, thereby increasing competition and lowering profit rates. In contrast to the merchant, wealthy landowners typically borrow money in order to consume more goods. They therefore reduce the stock of productive capital and push up interest rates on loans.

This analysis not only explains the functions of the merchant or businessman; it also provides a theory of interest, now called the "*loanable funds theory*." According to Hume, interest rates are determined by the supply of savings and the demand for savings. Greater savings lowers interest rates and also allows more money to be borrowed. Lower savings has the reverse effect – it increases interest rates and discourages borrowing. Moreover, Hume's analysis of saving and investment provides a justification for savings. Savings are needed for new investment, and thus savings are needed for economic growth.

Hume also analyzed the economic effects of changes in the money supply. He explained the positive effects of more money on the economy and then explained how, in the long run, the entire effect of more money would be to raise prices, leaving output and employment unchanged. This analysis, as Mayer (1980) notes, makes Hume an important precursor of the modern doctrine of *monetarism* (see **Friedman**), Finally, Hume analyzed the economic effects of money leaving one country and going to another. This analysis of the international flow of money has been called the *specie flow mechanism*. Although historically this transmission mechanism was first identified by Cantillon, Hume is the first person to have published something on this process and is usually given credit for its discovery. With his discovery of the specie flow mechanism, Hume took one large step away from mercantilist thinking and one large step toward the classical macroeconomic theory that was to develop in England during the late eighteenth and early nineteenth centuries.

The short-run effects of money were a consequence of the fact that prices did not immediately change. In fact, Hume (1875, p. 314) thought that prices would be sticky over a rather long period, one lasting several years. When gold and silver is mined, according to Hume, it is put into circulation by being spent. Money thus gets concentrated in the hands of a few merchants. As these merchants spend the money for investment purposes, industry begins to expand and employment begins to rise. Even if prices rise a bit, this inflation is a good thing because it increases business profits, which further stimulates economic expansion.

At some point, however, the rise in employment will lead to higher wages. Also, at some point in the process of money being spent and dispersed throughout the economy, businesses will not be able to keep up with demand and their inventories will start to fall. These two effects alter the money transmission mechanism. Rather than leading to greater output and employment, the additional money now increases prices. As time goes on, the entire impact of minting more money will be felt on the price side, and there will be no more production or employment than we had originally.

Hume next analyzed the impact of additional money on foreign trade. This led him (1955, pp. 60–77) to develop the specie flow mechanism, which explained how economic forces automatically lead to a position of balanced trade for all countries. It also explained how economic forces would establish a natural distribution of money throughout the world economy.

Consider again what happens to a nation when gold is discovered and mined. We have seen that this increase in the domestic supply of money eventually causes a rise in prices. But this price increase has further economic consequences. Higher prices will make a country's goods more expensive abroad, and so it will export less. Conversely, with higher domestic prices, goods produced abroad will be relatively less expensive. As a result, more goods will be purchased that were made in other countries. Both declining exports and rising imports will worsen the national trade balance. More money will go abroad to buy foreign goods than comes back through selling goods to other countries. This will lead to a loss of money from the domestic economy. In the long run, with less money and less spending, the domestic price level will decline somewhat.

One important consequence of this analysis is that trade imbalances cannot be maintained for long periods of time. Countries running trade surpluses will see their money supply rise and will experience inflation; this will tend to reduce their trade surplus. Countries running trade deficits, in contrast, will see their money supply decline and their prices fall. This will tend to reduce their trade deficit. A further consequence of this analysis is that the amount of gold in a country will remain the same, or reach an equilibrium level, whenever its imports equal its exports.

Although many economists regard Hume as a mercantilist thinker, the specie flow mechanism raises considerable doubt about this interpretation. One fundamental tenet of mercantilism was that countries should strive for trade surpluses and that governments should assist national businessmen in this endeavor. But the logic of the specie flow mechanism makes this goal an impossible dream. Any trade surplus will lead to an influx of precious metals and higher domestic prices. This will tend to eliminate the surplus. What the mercantilists desired could not be achieved, according to the logic of the specie flow mechanism. And Hume, to his credit, did *not* push for mercantilist economic policies that would generate trade surpluses.

Finally, Hume went on to examine the question of what happens when poor countries and rich countries trade with one another. Many times since the eighteenth century this issue has been the subject of heated debate. It is an eternally important question because it is closely related to the issue of what causes economies to grow. At the end of the twentieth century and the beginning of the twenty-first century, the debate has focused on the economic consequences of German unification, of bringing countries like Greece and Spain into the European Union, and of a North and South American trading bloc. Also, the debate has focused on the outsourcing of jobs from developed nations to less developed countries and the economic consequences of this outsourcing.

According to Hume (1955: 60–77), trade helped poor nations, but it did no harm to wealthier nations. Trade enabled poor countries to grow and develop; their standard of living would converge with that of their wealthier neighbors and trading partners. In contrast, Gunnar Myrdal would later argue that *cumulative causation* leads to a divergence of world living standards, with the rich getting richer at the expense of poor countries.

One mechanism that Hume identified as leading to converging living standards is the transfer of technology from more advanced to less advanced economies. As the recent examples of South Korea, Malaysia, Taiwan, and Hong Kong show, advanced technology allows the living standard of less developed countries to rapidly approach that of more developed nations. Later, Hume (1955, pp. 78–82) made the case that trade between unequals also benefits wealthy countries because it provides them with export markets. He then used these arguments to support free trade and oppose mercantilist restrictions on exchange between nations (see Elmslie 1995).

Starting with the questions raised by the mercantilists and the economic issues of his time, Hume began to develop economic analysis by showing the impact of money and trade on each other and on economic growth. But his place in the history of economics comes from more than his attempts at economic analysis. Hume is an important transitional figure between the mercantilists and the British classical economists who would follow on his heels.

Works by Hume

History of England (1757–62), Indianapolis, Liberty Fund, 1985

Essays, Moral, Political, and Literary, ed. T. H. Green and T. H. Grose, 2 vols, London, Longmans, Green, 1875

Writings on Economics, ed. Eugene Rotwein, Madison, Wisconsin, University of Wisconsin Press, 1955

Selected Essays, New York, Oxford University Press, 1998

Works about Hume

Berdell, John, *International Trade and Economic Growth in Open Economies: The Classical Dynamics of Hume, Smith, Ricardo and Malthus*, Cheltenham, Edward Elgar, 2002

Elmslie, Bruce, "The Convergence Debate between David Hume and Josiah Tucker," *Journal of Economic Perspectives*, 9, 4 (Fall 1995), pp. 207–16

Johnson, E. A. J., "Hume, the Synthetist," in *Predecessors of Adam Smith: The Growth of British Economic Thought*, New York, Augustus Kelley, 1965, pp. 161–81

Mayer, Thomas, "David Hume and Monetarism," *Quarterly Journal of Economics*, 95, 1 (August 1980), pp. 89–101

Mossner, Ernest, *The Life of David Hume*, Oxford, Clarendon Press, 1970

ADAM SMITH (1723–90)

Although others wrote about economic issues and principles before him, Adam Smith is regarded by most people as the father of economics. This honor stems neither from the originality of his ideas nor from the techniques of economic analysis that he pioneered. Rather, Smith is regarded as the father of economics due to his vision of capitalism as an economic system that makes everyone better off. Smith was the first person to see the benefits stemming from greater competition and to argue for policies that promote greater competition. This required both reduced government involvement in the economy, and also government actions to counter monopolistic tendencies and practices.

Smith was born in 1723 in Kirkcaldy, a small town near Edinburgh, Scotland. His father, a lawyer and comptroller of customer duties, died shortly before he was born, so Smith was raised by his mother and by guardians appointed in his father's will (Ross 1995, p. 2).

Although he was a sickly child, Smith had a great passion for books and was an avid reader. At age fourteen, he was sent by his parents to the University of Glasgow, where he studied moral philosophy, mathematics, and political economy. In 1740, he won a scholarship to Oxford University and studied at Balliol College for the next six years.

Smith found Oxford to be intellectually stultifying. Little teaching took place, and even less learning occurred. Since so few of the faculty actually lectured, Smith was able to spend many hours in the library doing what he liked best – reading, especially in the areas of literature, philosophy, and history. Smith's ([1776] 1937, p. 717f.) suggestion that teachers be paid based on the number of students in their classes probably stems more from his bad experience at Oxford than from a desire to spur competition among faculty members.

In 1751 Smith was hired to fill the Chair of Logic at the University of Glasgow. A year later he took over the Chair of Moral Philosophy. His lectures on ethics were well attended and formed the basis of his first literary success – *The Theory of Moral Sentiments* (Smith 1759).

The Theory of Moral Sentiments tried to explain how people acquired the moral feelings that enabled them to distinguish right from wrong. It found the answer in the ability people had to put themselves in the position of an impartial spectator. This allowed people to judge actions not only from the viewpoint of their own selfish interests, but also from the perspective of an objective observer. Like the conscience, this ability led people to act in ways that were morally right.

When Charles Townshend read *The Theory of Moral Sentiments* he decided that he could do no better than to put his stepson, the Duke of Buccleuch, under the tutelage of Smith. So Townshend hired Smith, and Smith resigned from his professorship at Glasgow to accompany the young Duke to France. This new job gave Smith lots of free time to read and reflect, and by traveling to France, Smith was able to meet the leading Physiocrats, including François Quesnay. In early 1764, Smith began writing a book "to pass away the time" (Rae 1895, p. 178), as he noted in a letter to his friend David Hume.

After traveling around France for three years, Smith returned to Kirkcaldy and then spent the next decade finishing his book. *The Wealth of Nations* was published in 1776, and it brought Smith both fame and fortune. In contrast to *The Theory of Moral Sentiments*, *The Wealth of Nations* assumed that people act according to their own self-interest. Yet, *The Wealth of Nations* argues that individual acts of selfishness contribute to the public good. In a famous passage, Smith

([1776] 1937, p. 423) describes this process: when each individual works, "he ... intends only his own gain ... [but] is ... led by an invisible hand to promote an end which was no part of his intention." That unintended end was economic growth and improved living standards for the whole nation.

The Wealth of Nations set out to analyze what caused the national standard of living to rise, and to show how self-interest and competition contributed to economic growth. It also examined how governments affect economic performance. These studies of the principles of economics also led to an attack on the economic theories and policies of the mercantilists (see **Mun**).

According to Smith it was the process of mechanization and the *division of labor* that enabled economic growth to take place. Living at the onset of the Industrial Revolution in England, Smith saw first-hand the economic consequences of technological innovation. In the 1730s the flying shuttle was invented, which was more efficient than the handloom and thus made the weaving process go much faster. In 1769 the spinning jenny was invented, which allowed one person to spin several threads simultaneously. These, and many other new technological innovations, allowed individual workers to be many times more productive than they would have been without the aid of machinery.

The Wealth of Nations begins by pointing out how the division of labor enabled the productivity of workers to increase. Smith ([1776] 1937, p. 4) describes the production process in a pin factory:

> The way in which this business is now carried on ... it is divided into a number of branches, of which the greater part are likewise peculiar trades. One man draws out the wire, another straightens it, a third cuts it, a fourth points it, a fifth grinds it at the top for receiving the head; to make the head requires two or three distinct operations ... and the important business of making a pin is, in this manner, divided into about eighteen distinct operations.

Smith reports that he saw pin factories where ten people divided up all these tasks and produced more than 48,000 pins per day. Yet, if these people had to work separately and independently, Smith claimed, they would not be able to produce much more than twenty pins per day. The division of labor thus yielded a 2,000-fold increase in the number of pins produced.

By dividing up the tasks, workers become more productive for a number of reasons. First, by concentrating on only one task, the skill and dexterity of the individual worker improves, and workers can perform their task more quickly. Second, time is saved moving from one task to another. Third, when focusing all their attention on just one job, workers are more likely to come up with labor-saving devices that allow them to produce more with less effort.

Smith felt that the natural tendency of people to buy and sell goods, and the natural tendency of people to improve their material condition (i.e. self-interest), were the driving forces behind the division of labor and the resulting improvements in productivity. However, Smith did recognize one important limit to the division of labor. If firms could not sell the additional pins they manufactured, there would be no incentive for them to divide up the many production tasks, employ more machinery, and increase the number of pins produced. It was, therefore, critical to expand the market for British goods.

Towards this end, Smith supported free international trade among nations. Free trade would allow British firms to sell their goods in an international arena rather than only within Britain. Moreover, Smith argued that free trade would benefit Britain because it would allow firms to obtain goods more cheaply from abroad. This would lower the cost of producing goods for export.

The case for free trade naturally developed into a critique of *mercantilism*. Because the mercantilists wanted to limit trade in goods, their policies would limit the market for domestic producers and keep British living standards from rising. The mercantilists were also wrong about the gains accruing from English colonies in the New World, according to Smith. England did not gain because it could sell goods to America and obtain gold in exchange. Rather, England gained because it could sell more goods, further divide up the tasks done by workers, and produce more goods with the same work force.

Smith did not give his unqualified support to free trade, however. Because national defense was more important than national wealth, he ([1776] 1937, p. 429) opposed trade whenever it increased the military might of countries other than Britain or reduced that of Britain. Smith thus supported the English Navigation Acts. These laws forced American ships to stop in England and transfer their cargoes to British ships before the goods moved on to their final European destination. Smith reasoned that this policy would increase both the number of British ships and the number of trained British seamen; in times of war these two assets would be important for the defense of an island nation like Britain.

On the other hand, Smith opposed retaliatory tariffs on those countries placing restrictions on the sale of British goods; he claimed that one bad policy did not warrant another bad policy. Smith thought that any British worker who lost a job due to free trade would soon find another job at a better wage as long as guild restraints and apprenticeship rules did not keep labor from moving to new areas and more productive uses. Realizing that this would not occur quickly in the real world, Smith advocated a gradual lowering of protective tariffs, rather than their immediate elimination, so that the transition process could take place slowly and smoothly.

Smith also rejected the popular *infant industry argument* for protective tariffs. This was the claim that protectionism was necessary for a country just beginning to develop a particular industry. Since new domestic firms would be less experienced and knowledgeable in producing goods than already-established foreign firms, domestic firms would face a competitive disadvantage compared to their foreign rivals. For a nation to develop expertise in a new industry, so the argument runs, domestic firms must receive protection until they obtain the requisite experience. Smith ([1776] 1937, p. 425) opposed the infant industry argument because he thought it created inefficient monopolies and diverted scarce capital resources to these monopolies.

Monopoly was another enemy of free trade, of expanding the market for British goods, and of rapid economic growth. Smith identified four negative effects of monopolistic practices. First, monopolies led to higher prices for consumers, and thus made consumers worse off. Smith ([1776] 1937, p. 128) noted that businessmen had a penchant for getting together and devising schemes to raise the price of their goods and services. The fewer the number of firms and the larger their size, the easier it would be for firms to conspire against the public by raising prices.

Second, Smith ([1776] 1937, p. 147) held that monopolies were "a great enemy to good management." Competition, he believed, forced managers to operate as efficiently as possible and to seek out ways to improve the efficiency of their operations. With competition, if your firm did not become as efficient as possible, other firms surely would, or new firms would start up that operated more efficiently. Poorly run firms would then be driven out of business by their more competitive rivals.

Third, Smith held that monopolies were more likely than competitive firms to pressure government to support their monopoly position, and were more likely to be successful in this endeavor. This would result in bad and oppressive laws being passed. One example that Smith gives ([1776] 1937, p. 612f.) involves prohibitions on the export of sheep. Draconian laws against selling British sheep were passed by Parliament in order to maintain the monopoly power of woolen cloth manufacturers. Without British sheep exports, other countries would not be able to produce woolen goods and sell them in England.

Finally, Smith noted that monopolies led to a misallocation of resources. Because of the high prices they could charge, monopolists would make huge profits. This would stimulate production in these industries. Resources would thus go to making goods not because people want those goods most, and not because there were many possibilities for improving the division of labor and reducing costs, but only because a monopoly existed.

This critique of monopolies also turned into a critique of mercantilism. Because mercantilist policies kept out foreign competition, these policies helped to promote national monopolies ([1776] 1937, p. 595). They thus hurt consumers and severely hampered national economic growth.

While generally regarded as the patron saint of *laissez-faire* economics and an opponent of government, Smith did not really oppose all government intervention into economic affairs. In fact, he recognized four important functions for government. The first, as we have seen, is in preventing monopoly or guaranteeing a competitive environment.

Second, Smith recognized that only governments could provide for the defense of the entire nation against outside threats. It is for this reason that Smith supported the Navigation Acts and large government expenditures on defense. Third, government had to provide for internal order and defense; that is, it had to protect each member of society from every other member of society. Government was thus responsible for setting up a police force and a judicial system.

Finally, Smith opened a door that Milton Friedman (1977) and other conservative thinkers were later to bemoan, by approving government provision of public goods in cases with large *externalities*.

For most economic transactions, all the costs of production are paid for by the person who buys and consumes the good. Likewise, all the benefits of production go to the consumer of the good. However, in some situations, many outsiders gain or lose significantly from economic transactions. These gains and losses imposed on those outside the market transaction are referred to as "externalities." One good example of a negative externality is pollution. In this case, some production costs (a less clean environment) will fall on people living near the polluting plant who do not buy the good produced in the plant. Education is a good example of a positive externality. Everyone benefits from a better-educated labor force, since it leads to higher productivity and more goods. Here, those people who do not spend more time in school *gain* from the greater education of others. Under such circumstances, there is less incentive for me to spend time and money on my own education, since I receive the benefits of a high living standard due to other people's efforts. But when everyone reasons in this manner we get too little education and everyone loses. The moral in this case is that too little will be spent on education unless education is provided by the government.

In addition to explaining how economies grow, Smith also attempted to explain how incomes were divided from producing goods and services. As the first economist who attempted to explain the principles determining income distribution, Smith made several contributions. These centered around his analysis of what determined the price of goods and what determined the returns going to those who produce goods.

Smith began by distinguishing the market price of a good from the natural price of a good. The market price was the price that people paid in their everyday economic transactions. Market prices were determined by the fixed quantity of goods brought to market as well as by the demand for those goods. In contrast, the natural price of a good was an equilibrium price, or the price towards which market prices moved or gravitated (Smith [1776] 1937, p. 55).

Smith thought that an automatic mechanism would bring the natural price and the market price into equality. If market price exceeded natural price for some good, then landowners and employers would shift their land and capital to produce more of this good. This would tend to reduce market price and move the market price closer to the natural price. On the other hand, if market price were below the natural price, landowners and employers would seek some other good to produce, or some other use for their land or capital. This would reduce the supply of this good, increase its market price, and move the market price towards its natural price.

Smith next tried to explain what determines the natural price of each good. He adopted a cost-of-production theory of price, where natural price was the sum of the costs of paying land, labor, and capital for their role in production. Each of these factors was to be paid their natural rates, and so Smith needed to explain what determined these natural rates.

His remarks about natural rents were quite confusing. At times Smith ([1776] 1937, p. 145) regarded rent as a monopoly price that exists because land is scarce. At other times he ([1776] 1937, p. 146) provided a *Physiocratic theory of rent* (see **Quesnay**), noting that rent was a payment for the *surplus* output obtained from using land to grow things. And at yet other times, Smith ([1776] 1937, p. 147) hints at a *differential theory of rent* (see **Ricardo**), whereby rent is a payment to the owners of more productive land.

Smith's theory of natural profits is even less satisfactory than his theory of natural rent. Smith says that natural profits are a return to capital, which results from savings. But this is merely a definition of natural profits; it does not explain what determines the level of natural profits.

To explain natural wages, Smith developed the *subsistence theory of wages*, a doctrine that was to dominate economic analysis for the century following publication of *The Wealth of Nations*. On this view, the natural wage was the rate that just allowed workers to survive and reproduce. If wages fell below subsistence levels, workers would die; and with fewer workers offering their services, wage rates would have to go up. On the other hand, if wages rose above subsistence levels, higher living standards would mean that fewer workers died and more of their children would survive. Here the increased number of workers would eventually force wages down to subsistence levels.

Whether or not Smith was indeed the father of economics, he was no doubt father of the field within economics known as "public finance." As we have seen, *The Wealth of Nations* described the proper role for government in a thriving economy. It also discussed how governments could best raise revenues.

Given public expenditure decisions, funds had to be raised through taxation to pay for this spending. Smith laid down four rules or maxims for taxing the public. First, he held that taxes should be *proportional*, meaning that everyone should pay about the same percentage of their income in taxes. While today many taxes (like the individual income tax) are *progressive* in their incidence, taking larger fractions of income from the rich than the poor, when Smith was writing most taxes were *regressive*, taking larger bites from the income of poor families than from wealthy families. A proportional tax therefore would have reduced the tax burden on low-income families and increased the tax burden on those with large incomes and wealth.

Second, Smith held that taxpayers should not be kept in the dark about their taxes. They should know in advance haw much they owe and when their tax payments were due. Moreover, tax laws should not be changed radically from year to year, which would make tax payments each year arbitrary rather than certain.

A third principle of taxation was that taxes should be levied at a time, and in a manner, that is most convenient for people to pay. The current practice of taxing capital gains when they are realized, rather than when they accrue, provides a good example of this maxim in practice. If capital gains taxes were imposed every year on the appreciation of assets that each person owns, people might be forced to sell their assets just to pay the taxes they owe on their gains. Taxing gains only when assets are sold makes it easier for people to pay their taxes.

Fourth, Smith maintained that the best tax was the one that was least costly to collect. Taxation should not require great numbers of tax collectors; it should not damage economic incentives or create excessive efforts to evade taxes (for example, smuggling goods so that taxes don't have to be paid on imports); and it should not impose penalties that are so severe they will ruin tax evaders. All these principles were designed to generate the greatest growth, or to have taxes do the least amount of damage to economic growth.

With Marx and Keynes, Smith ranks as one of the three most important figures in all of economics. His vision was of self-interest and the national interest in perfect harmony, leading to continued economic growth and prosperity. The only potential problems were government intervention in the free market, monopolistic practices by businesses, and bad tax policies. Thus Smith argued against mercantilist restraints on trade, and wanted the British government to control monopolies and observe care in the manner by which it taxed its citizens.

Smith's vision was an optimistic one, involving competitive capitalism increasing living standards and making everyone better off. In the time since *The Wealth of Nations* was published, this vision has largely come to pass. But it was not a quick transformation. Nor was it an easy one. What Smith did not live long enough to see was the set of serious and deep problems that would accompany economic growth – unemployment, pollution, the poverty of British workers, and the deterioration of industrial cities in Britain. These were the problems that Smith's successors were forced to grapple with.

Works by Smith

The Theory of Moral Sentiments (1759), New York, Augustus M. Kelley, 1966
Lectures on Justice, Police, Revenue and Arms [notes taken by a student in 1763], New York, Augustus M. Kelley, 1964

An Inquiry into the Nature and Causes of the Wealth of Nations (1776), New York, Modern Library, 1937
The Early Writings of Adam Smith, ed. J. Ralph Lindgren, New York, Augustus M. Kelley, 1967
Lectures on Rhetoric and Belles Lettres, New York, Oxford University Press, 1985

Works about Smith

Friedman, Milton, "Adam Smith's Relevance for Today," *Challenge*, 20, 2 (March–April 1977), pp. 6–12
Hetzel, Robert, *The Relevance of Adam Smith*, Richmond, Virginia, Federal Reserve Bank of Richmond, 1977
Hollander, Samuel, *The Economics of Adam Smith*, Toronto, University of Toronto Press, 1973
Rae, John, (1895) *The Life of Adam Smith*, Seattle, University Press of the Pacific, 2002
Ross, Ian Simpson, *The Life of Adam Smith*, Oxford, Clarendon Press, 1995

JEREMY BENTHAM (1748–1832)

Jeremy Bentham is known primarily as a philosopher and social reformer, and it is as a philosopher that Bentham made his main contribution to economics. This involved introducing the notion of utility into economic analysis.

Bentham was born in London in 1748. His father was a prosperous attorney who was able to provide an excellent education for his children. Like many of the major figures in economics, Bentham was something of a child prodigy. It is reported that he knew the alphabet even before he could speak (Everett 1931, p. 5).

Bentham was educated at Westminster School in London. He enrolled in Queen's College, Oxford, at the age of twelve. He received a bachelor's degree in 1767 and then went on to study law, first at Lincoln's Inn in London and then at Oxford. Admitted to the Bar in 1769, Bentham never practiced law. In part this was because he disliked the law. But a more important consideration was that Bentham wanted to change the world, or at least to improve things in England. So instead of following in his father's footsteps, Bentham began to read widely in philosophy and political theory. He also assumed the role of social reformer, attempting to persuade political leaders and the public to adopt his many schemes to improve life in England.

Some of the more noteworthy reform proposals advanced by Bentham were birth control, adult suffrage (including women), the legalization of unions, and the development of a civil service. But his pet project was always prison and penal code reform. In the 1790s Bentham launched a campaign to construct a model prison, the Panopticon Penitentiary, which he envisioned as "a mill for grinding rogues honest, and idle men industrious" (quoted in Mitchell 1950, p. 194). While this plan was never implemented in England, a Panopticon was built in St Petersburg in the early nineteenth century (Halévy 1949, p. 296).

These many reform proposals gained Bentham considerable fame and numerous followers, and he soon became the leader of a group of British reformers known as "the philosophical radicals." They earned this title because their proposals were radical by the standards of late eighteenth century England and were justified by the philosophical doctrine of *utilitarianism*, or the view that all actions should promote the greatest happiness for the greatest number of people.

The only significant contribution Bentham made to economics proper was his badly titled *Defence of Usury*, which was published in 1787 (in Bentham 1952–4, vol. 1, pp. 124–207). Since the Middle Ages, heated disputes have raged over whether limits should be placed on interest rates. In centuries past, the issue was primarily whether it was moral to charge any interest at all on loans. In the late twentieth century, the issue became whether interest rate ceilings should be placed on credit cards and consumer loans. But while the focus of the debate has shifted somewhat, the main positions have not. On one side of the debate is the argument that borrowers are poor people who desperately need money; thus charging interest or charging high rates of interest takes advantage of the weak and destitute. On the other side, it is argued that lending money involves some risk. Compensation is thus required for the many times that one lends money but does not get repaid.

Adam Smith ([1776] 1937, p. 339) supported public regulation of interest rates through the establishment of interest rate ceilings. Bentham thought this was inconsistent with Smith's *laissez-faire* principles, and he pointed out that there was "no more reason for fixing the price of the use of money than the price of goods" (Bentham 1952–4, vol. 1, p. 125). Bentham also argued that, since one party had agreed to pay high interest rates, it was hard to consider usury an offense that should be prohibited by legislation.

But the main case against laws regulating interest rates was the negative economic consequences that would follow. First, people would not lend money if they could not earn interest on their loan. Anti-usury laws, designed to help people in need, would actually hurt the poor by making it more difficult for them to borrow the money they needed. Second, usury laws kept innovative business-men, as well as the poor, from borrowing money. This hurt every-one's standard of living, the poor as well as the affluent. Third, Bentham argued that if the poor could not borrow the money they needed to survive they would find other, less socially desirable ways to secure the funds. Fourth, Bentham held that making usury illegal led to the rise of a black market for loans at even higher rates of interest. Again, anti-usury laws would only hurt those people the laws were supposed to help. Finally, anticipating new institutional economics (see **North**) to some degree, Bentham held that any law as bad as usury prohibition would cause people to disrespect all laws and thereby harm social relationships as well as economic relation-ships. After reading Bentham's book, Adam Smith was persuaded that his support of usury laws was in error, and that there should be no government regulations on interest.

Bentham's main contribution to economics was not his case against government regulation of interest rates, but his work developing the notion of utility and bringing considerations of utility maximization into economic analysis. Contemporaries of Bentham had been employing the term "utility" in legal, political, moral, and economic discussions. But their use of this notion was vague and imprecise. It was not clear what this term actually meant, how utility could be measured, or how different utilities could be compared. Attempting to put the social or human sciences on a par with the natural sci-ences, Bentham wrestled with these issues. His hope was that through these efforts he would become the Isaac Newton of the moral world (Mitchell 1950, p. 180).

Bentham began his *Introduction to the Principles of Morals and Legis-lation* (1948, p. 1) with the following bold and often-quoted state-ment regarding human behavior: "Nature has placed mankind under the governance of two sovereign masters, *pain* and *pleasure*." He then went on to define the principle of utility as a moral principle – considerations about pleasure and pain determine "what we ought to do," and the right thing to do will always be whatever maximizes net pleasure, or total pleasure minus total pain.

This implies that individuals could measure their pleasures and pains. Bentham held that such measurements were made by each individual and involved considering seven dimensions of pleasure: (1) its intensity, (2) its duration, (3) its certainty, (4) its propinquity, (5) its fecundity, (6) its purity, and (7) the number of individuals to whom it extends. Bentham enumerated fourteen simple pleasures, including wealth, skill, power, a good name, memory, imagination, bene-volence, and malevolence; and he identified twelve simple pains including disappointment, regret, and desire. He also set forth various factors that influenced pleasure and pain, such as health, gender, age, education, and firmness of mind. Thus, while his contemporaries talked in general terms, Bentham spoke concretely and tried to be precise and specific about measuring utility.

Bentham argued that all pleasures were equal, regardless of their source. For example, the pleasures from watching television count as much as the pleasures received from reading a book on economics or philosophy; and the pleasures received by the poor count as much as the pleasures enjoyed by the very rich. Since the pleasure of one person counts no more than anyone else's pleasure, economic and social policies should not favor the rich, as most policies did at the time Bentham was writing.

A further implication of utilitarianism was that education and leg-islation were needed to promote the maximum amount of happiness within the nation. Education was important because it enables people to do a better job of adding up and comparing the pleasures and pains that result from different actions. Legislation was necessary to penalize acts that did not maximize happiness, and also to provide incentives for people to act morally or in ways that contribute to the maximum happiness of the population. Government, for Bentham, became a mechanism for helping to increase the net happiness of its citizens.

The doctrine of utilitarianism also provides a means for evaluating government policies and legislation. Government acts were good that increased net utility in the nation, while government action that decreased net utility in the nation was bad. As such, the utilitarian calculation is an important forerunner of contemporary *cost–benefit analysis*. In fact, Bentham's *Manual of Political Economy* contains the first use of cost–benefit considerations to justify public expenditure. Bentham proposes that public spending should be evaluated by comparing the benefits from that expenditure with the costs pro-duced by the "most vexatious and burthensome tax" (Bentham 1952–4, vol. 2, p. 202). He argued that, if the benefits from govern-ment spending exceed the costs produced from having to tax citizens, the spending should take place. On the other hand, if the costs aris-ing from additional taxation were greater than the benefits of the public expenditure, the spending should not take place and taxes should not be imposed for this purpose.

Despite its usefulness as a moral guide and a policy tool, utilitar-ianism also gave rise to numerous problems that would greatly perplex later economists. First, although Bentham struggled to make the notion of utility concrete, it is not clear how someone could, in practice, measure this elusive notion. It is also not clear how we could go about comparing, let alone adding up, the pleasures and pains experienced by different people. Second, many people have criticized utilitarianism for being an immoral doctrine, since it ignored the notion of justice or fairness as a means of judging government and individual actions. For example, under utilitarianism, discrimination would be justified if it led to maximum happiness in the nation. Finally, there is a curious conflict between Bentham's view of human nature and his view of morality. If people by nature are always under the domination of pleasure and pain, and if they always act to maximize their net pleasure, then people cannot behave any differently than they actually behave. Under such circumstances, it is hard to talk about right and wrong actions, or to hold people responsible for their actions.

To be fair, Bentham was aware of these problems with his theory. His response was that, despite such problems, his system was the best one available for organizing society and for running a government. The only alternative would be to have everyone pick their own standard for how government and society should be run; and this alternative, according to Bentham, could only lead to chaos and anarchy.

By providing a detailed explanation of the principle of utility, as well as a concerted argument for using this notion in economic analysis, Bentham earned the title "father of utilitarianism." He also became a philosophical guiding spirit for the many generations of economists that were to follow him.

Works by Bentham

Economic Writings, ed. W. Stark, 3 vols, London, Allen & Unwin, 1952–4

Manual of Political Economy, in Bentham 1952–4, vol. 2

Introduction to the Principles of Morals and Legislation, Riverside, New Jersey, Hafner, 1948

Works about Bentham

Everett, C. W., The Education of Jeremy Bentham, New York, Columbia University Press, 1931

Halévy, Elie, The Growth of Philosophical Radicalism, New York, Augustus Kelley, 1949

Mitchell, Wesley C., "Bentham's Felicific Calculus," *Political Science Quarterly,* 33 (June 1918), pp. 161–83. Reprinted in *The Backward Art of Spending Money and Other Essays*, New York, Augustus M. Kelley, 1950, pp. 177–202

Other references

Smith, Adam, *The Wealth of Nations* (1776), New York, Modern Library, 1937

THOMAS ROBERT MALTHUS (1766–1834)

Thomas Robert Malthus (pronounced MAL-thuss) is one of the most controversial figures in the history of economics. He achieved fame chiefly from the population doctrine that is now closely linked with his name. Contrary to views that it was possible to improve people's living standards, Malthus held that any such improvements would cause the population to grow and thereby reverse these gains. Malthus also sparked controversy with his contemporaries on issues of methodology (by arguing that economics should be an empirical rather than a deductive science), over questions of theory (by holding that economies can experience prolonged bouts of high unemployment), and on policy issues (by arguing against free trade and against government assistance to the poor).

Malthus was born in 1766 in the town of Wotton, in Surrey. His father was a well-to-do country squire, who made sure that Malthus received a good education. At first, Malthus was instructed by his father and private tutors in his home. Then he was sent off to excellent private schools. At the age of eighteen he enrolled at Jesus College, Cambridge, where he studied mathematics and natural philosophy.

Although his father wanted him to become a surveyor, Malthus decided to enter the church. He was ordained in 1788, thus becoming Reverend Malthus. In 1793 he became a fellow of Jesus College and curate of Okewood, a little chapel in Wotton.

While he was working at Wotton, Malthus got into a heated argument with his father about the ability to improve the economic well-being of the average person. His father thought this was possible; Malthus remained skeptical. The dispute prompted Malthus to do some reading, and then some writing, on the topic. The outcome was his *Essay on Population*, which was first published in 1798.

The population essay brought Malthus instant fame, and then (in 1805) a job as Professor of History, Politics, Commerce, and Finance at the New East India College near London. The college was primarily a training school for employees of the East India Company who were about to take administrative posts in India. The teaching position made Malthus one of the first academic economists. And, as is true of many teaching jobs, it required little time and effort. This left Malthus much free time to socialize, to correspond with his many friends (especially David Ricardo), and to stir up controversies regarding economic principles and policies. In addition to the controversies surrounding his principle of population, Malthus became embroiled in important debates with Ricardo over the British Poor Laws and Corn Laws, the benefits of free trade, and the possibility of gluts or insufficient demand for goods.

In mid-eighteenth century England the Industrial Revolution was in full swing. However, workers lived near the level of physical subsistence, and their condition worsened in the latter half of the century. Monotony and repetition characterized factory work; the tyranny of the factory clock and the pace of the assembly line were beyond the control of all workers. The division of labor, praised by Adam Smith in *The Wealth of Nations* as the means to productivity growth and rising living standards, made work so routine that women and children could perform jobs just as easily as men. Business owners logically preferred such workers because they could be hired for less.

These circumstances gave rise to numerous champions of the working class. Among the best known were the Marquis de Condorcet, Robert Owen, and William Godwin. Condorcet (1795) argued that greater economic equality and more security for workers would improve their material well-being. Towards this end he advocated two reforms – a welfare system to provide security for the working poor, and government regulation of credit to keep down interest rates so that needy families could borrow money at lower cost. Owen (1857–8) attempted to develop utopian communities in industrial towns that would improve both the economic and the social conditions of working class families. Godwin (1793) was even more radical in his analysis and his policy proposals. He blamed the capitalist system for the poverty of workers. He then demanded that property be taken from its owners and given to those whom it would benefit the most. This, Godwin claimed, would end all poverty, injustice, and human suffering in the world.

The *Essay on Population* (Malthus 1798) was inspired by these men; yet it was written to refute their arguments about the possibility of improving economic conditions. Malthus thought that human betterment was impossible because poverty and misery were the inevitable lot of the majority of people in every society. Moreover, he argued that all attempts to alleviate poverty and suffering, no matter how well-intentioned and no matter how well thought out, would only worsen things. It is this position that led Thomas Carlyle to call economics "the dismal science," an appellation that has stuck for more than two centuries.

Malthus held that the human condition could not be improved, for two reasons. First, he believed that people were driven by an insatiable desire for sexual pleasure. This led to population increases which, if left unchecked, would grow geometrically – 1, 2, 4, 8, 16, etc. Second, Malthus believed that *diminishing returns* operated in agriculture; that is, as more and more land was brought into cultivation, each new plot of land would be able to grow less food than the previous plot. For this reason, food production could at best increase in arithmetical proportions – 1, 2, 3, 4, 5, etc. Since population was growing more rapidly than the food supply, at some point the population would exceed the food that could be grown to feed everyone. Starvation would ensue if there were no other checks on population growth.

In the first edition of the *Essay on Population* Malthus allowed only "positive checks" on a growing population. These were factors that raised death rates – famine, natural catastrophe, plague, and war. But in the second and subsequent editions of the *Essay* Malthus added a set of "preventive checks" – sexual abstinence, birth control, and delayed marriage. These had the effect of lowering birth rates and population growth. Allowing preventive checks on population growth also toned down the pessimistic nature of the economic forecast. But Malthus still held that, because of the strong human desire for sexual pleasure, population growth could not be reduced very much by preventive checks; the conclusion still followed that it was impossible to improve overall economic well-being.

The case against Condorcet, Owen, and Godwin followed simply from this analysis. If wealth and income were distributed more equally, as Godwin advocated, or if the poor were made better off through various social reforms, as Condorcet and Owen suggested, working families would respond by having so many children that they would shortly find themselves impoverished again. It is for this reason that Malthus opposed every attempt to legislate relief for the poor, and was opposed to granting charity to the poor. This, he thought, would only lead to more poor people.

Present-day Malthusians (for example, Murray 1984) make similar arguments, maintaining that government aid merely causes welfare recipients to have more children, thus worsening their economic plight.

Several years later, in a pamphlet entitled *An Investigation of the Cause of the Present High Price of Provisions* (in Malthus 1970), Malthus went even further in arguing against relief for the poor. This work argued that poor relief would also lead to increases in the price of corn in England. Thus, not only would poor relief hurt the poor, but, by raising the price of necessities, poor relief would also hurt all British citizens.

Although he was best known for his population doctrine, Malthus also made several theoretical and policy contributions to economics.

At the theoretical level, Malthus provided a justification for profits (see the *Essay on Rents* in Malthus 1970). As we have seen, Adam Smith really had no theory of profits and could not explain what determined the level of profits. Malthus filled in this gap left by Smith. For Malthus, profits were a return to the capitalist for his part in producing goods. Workers who had tools and machinery were more productive than workers lacking this capital equipment. By allowing such capital to be employed in the production process, capitalists contributed to production and deserved to be remunerated based on this contribution.

The *Essay on Rents* also developed the *differential theory of rent* (see **Ricardo**). According to this doctrine, rents existed because of differences in soil fertility and because landlords made improvements on their land. If the best plot of land could grow 1000 bushels of corn, and the second-best plot could produce only 800 bushels, the owner of the best plot would be able to charge rent equal to the value of the extra 200 bushels. Rent was thus a payment to land-owners, made for the privilege of using better parcels of land. According to Malthus, economic progress meant that the demand for agricultural goods would increase and less fertile lands would have to be used to feed people. Differences in land fertility would therefore rise, and so would rents. In contrast to Ricardo, for Malthus high rents were the result of economic prosperity and a measure of prosperity.

At the policy level, Malthus (1820) attempted to explain why economies were subject to periodic depressions or gluts – times when businesses could not sell goods and when unemployment remained very high. The answer Malthus gave was that gluts were due to insufficient demand or too little spending. Conversely, Malthus held that rising prices (i.e. inflation) stemmed from too much spending taking place in the economy. It is for this reason that Keynes (1964, pp. 362ff.) cited Malthus as an important precursor of his theory of business cycles.

Just as Malthus was writing his *Principles of Political Economy* (1820), Great Britain suffered a major depression. The cause of this problem, according to Malthus, was that as economies grew there was a tendency for capitalists to receive too much income. In fact, he argued, capitalists got more income than they could profitably invest. There were two reasons for this. First, new machinery requires new workers. While it is easy to build new machinery in a short period of time, to get more workers requires fifteen years or more. During this time there will be a shortage of labor; wages will rise, profits will fall, and capitalists will prefer to hold their income as cash rather than investing. Second, Malthus held that new machinery increases the productivity of labor and reduces the need for workers. Because capitalists received more income than they could profitably invest, they ended up saving too much. Private virtue thus became public vice – too little spending leads to a surplus of goods and reduces the need for workers.

The solution that Malthus proposed for the problem of gluts followed directly from his analysis of its causes. He wanted the state to alter the distribution of income so that capitalists received less income and landowners received more income. Malthus believed that landowners spent almost all their income; if they received more income they would consume it by hiring more servants and engaging in luxury consumption. For this reason Malthus supported the British Corn Laws (which were passed in 1815 and then repealed in 1846). This legislation prohibited the import of grain into Britain until certain price levels were reached. With fewer grain imports, Malthus reasoned, more land would be used in Britain for growing food. This would increase (differential) rents due to *diminishing returns* in agriculture, and provide more money to landowners. In addition, Malthus believed that wages would rise in proportion to the increased price of corn due to trade restrictions. The losers would be the capitalists, whose savings would fall as their income declined.

Despite his many theoretical contributions, and despite being a forerunner of Keynesian economics, Malthus remains an important figure in economics primarily because of his population doctrine. The term "Malthusian" will always connote pessimism about the ability of mankind to improve its economic condition.

Works by Malthus

An Essay on the Principle of Population as it Affects the Future Improvement of Society, with Remarks on the Speculations of Mr. Godwin, M. Condorcet, and other Writers (first edition, 1798), New York, Oxford University Press, 1999

The Principles of Political Economy Considered with a View to their Practical Application, London, Murray, 1820

The Pamphlets of Thomas Robert Malthus, New York, Augustus M. Kelley, 1970

Works about Malthus

Bonar, J. R., *Malthus and His Work*, New York, Augustus M. Kelley, 1966

Grampp, William D., "Malthus and His Contemporaries," *History of Political Economy*, 6, 3 (1974), pp. 278–304

Hollander, Samuel, *The Economics of Thomas Robert Malthus*, Toronto, University of Toronto Press, 1977

James, Patricia, *Population Malthus: His Life and Times*, London, Routledge & Kegan Paul, 1979

Keynes, John Maynard, "Malthus," in *Essays in Biography*, New York, Norton, 1951, pp. 81–124

Other references

de Cariat, Jean-Antoine-Nicholas, Marquis de Condorcet, *Outlines of an Historical View of the Progress of the Human Mind*, London, J. Johnson, 1795

Godwin, William, *An Enquiry Concerning Political Justice* (1793), New York, Woodstock Books, 1992

Keynes, John Maynard, *The General Theory of Employment, Interest and Money* (1936), New York, Harcourt Brace and World, 1964

Murray, Charles, *Losing Ground: American Social Policy, 1950–80*, New York, Basic Books, 1984

Owen, Robert, *The Life of Robert Owen*, 2 vols, New York, Gordon Press, 1973

DAVID RICARDO (1772–1823)

First and foremost David Ricardo was interested in issues concerning income distribution and economic growth. He sought to understand how the economic pie was divided up among rent, wages, and profits; and he sought to understand the principles causing economies to grow and decline. Ricardo saw free international trade as one important force leading to greater economic growth. But he saw diminishing returns in agriculture as a counterforce, one which tended to squeeze profits and slow economic growth.

Ricardo was born in London in 1772, to a prosperous Jewish family. His education prepared him to follow his father into the world of trade and finance. True to plan, at age fourteen Ricardo entered his father's brokerage firm. He took to the business rather quickly. He was regarded as an extremely able negotiator, and rather adept at difficult and arcane operations such as currency *arbitrage* (see **Cournot**).

Ricardo became estranged from his father when he married a Quaker and converted to Christianity. Penniless, and having to support a family, Ricardo borrowed all the money he could and began his own brokerage firm. While the first years were difficult, he quickly made a great fortune and became independently wealthy by the age of twenty-six. This allowed him the leisure time to pursue his intellectual and scientific interests. These included starting up a laboratory, beginning a mineral collection, and joining the Geological Society of Britain.

Ricardo came across a copy of Adam Smith's *The Wealth of Nations* in 1799 while on vacation with his wife. According to legend, after reading Smith he decided to spend his spare time studying economics. Ricardo also joined a group of distinguished economists who met regularly to discuss economic issues. This group included James Mill (the father of John Stuart Mill), Bentham, and Malthus.

In 1819, Ricardo bought a seat in the House of Commons. The seat was in the Irish borough of Portarlington, an area that Ricardo never visited. To be somewhat fair, at the time it was not uncommon for wealthy people to buy seats in Parliament. Ricardo quickly became a recognized expert in Parliament on financial matters, and he spoke up frequently on critical economic issues such as currency and banking, tariffs, taxation, and the agricultural depression.

Economists remember Ricardo primarily for his theory of comparative advantage. This theory provides the justification virtually every economist uses to support free trade. But Ricardo made several other lasting contributions to economics. He explained how national income got distributed among wages, profits, and rents; how income distribution changed over time; and what the consequences of changing income distribution were for Britain. He is also responsible for developing the labor theory of value.

In *The Wealth of Nations*, Adam Smith held that a country would export goods to other countries if it were more efficient at producing these goods. Smith called this "*absolute advantage.*" According to this view, if Japan produced cars, computers, food, and clothing more efficiently than the US, Japan would export all these goods to the US. The US would run a large trade deficit with Japan, giving it money in exchange for these Japanese goods. The US would likely be hurt by this trade deficit, since American jobs would be lost to Japan.

Bur for Ricardo there was no problem if one country was less efficient at producing everything. Trade, he contended, depended on *comparative advantage*, or relative efficiency, rather than on absolute efficiencies. Ricardo then demonstrated that countries would tend to sell those goods it was relatively more efficient at producing, or that it was relatively less inefficient at producing. Through specialization *each country* would gain from foreign trade.

A simple numerical example can help make this point clear. Suppose both Japan and the US each produce two goods – automobiles and rice. In the US, one worker can produce either one car or one ton of rice in any given year. In Japan, one agricultural worker can produce two tons of rice in a year, and one manufacturing worker can produce three cars in one year. For both rice production and automobile manufacturing Japanese workers are absolutely more productive than American workers. However, Japanese workers are relatively more efficient at producing cars and US workers are relatively less inefficient at producing rice. Japanese workers are three times more efficient in manufacturing cars, and US workers are only half as efficient as the Japanese when it comes to growing rice.

What Ricardo demonstrated is that both the US and Japan would gain from specializing in what each does better at making, and then trading with each other. The argument runs as follows. Suppose the US has 200 workers and Japan has 100 workers, and that workers are divided equally between car production and rice production in each country. The US then produces 100 cars and 100 tons of rice, while Japan produces 150 cars and 100 tons of rice for the year. Combined output for both countries is 250 cars and 200 tons of rice.

Now consider what happens when Japan specializes in car production and the US specializes in rice production. In Japan, 100 workers make 300 cars; in the US, 200 workers produce 200 tons of rice. World output has gone up by 50 automobile due to specialization. Many people will be better off because more cars get produced.

The next important question that must be answered is who gets this extra output. Ricardo noted that this depends on the rate of exchange between the two goods. If Japan trades 100 cars to the US for 100 tons of rice, Japan winds up with 200 cars (the initial 300 produced less the 100 traded to the US) and 100 tons of rice, while the US winds up with 100 cars and 100 tons of rice (the 200 produced domestically less the 100 traded for cars). Here all the gains from specialization and trade go to Japan. On the other hand, if Japan trades 150 cars to the US for 100 tons of rice, all the gains from specialization (the 50 cars) go to the US.

Within these boundaries (1 ton of rice trading for 1 car and 1 ton of rice trading for 1.5 cars) both countries will benefit from trade. Since people in both countries can benefit from economic specialization and trade only if the rate of exchange falls within these boundaries, strong forces will operate to push the rate of exchange between cars and rice within this range (or push the exchange rate between the US dollar and the Japanese yen into this range, so that specialization and trade are possible). Ricardo, unfortunately, did not explain where actual exchange rates would fall within this range, or how gains from trade would actually get divided up between two countries. That job was left to John Stuart Mill.

A second theoretical contribution of Ricardo was the first concerted theory of income distribution. Ricardo also drew out the important practical consequences of his theory.

Ricardo's theory of distribution had three elements – a theory of rent, a theory to explain wages, and a theory of profits. His theory showed how national income was divided up into these three categories, and what happened to rents, wages, and profits over time as economies grew. In analyzing rent, Ricardo followed Malthus (1970) in advancing a *differential theory of rent*. According to the differential theory, rents stem from the different fertility of various plots of land. Whenever there is an ample supply of rich and fertile land, people will not pay for the use of this land and there will be no rent on the land.

But usually there is a limited supply of good land. When the most fertile land is used up, the next most fertile plot of land has to be cultivated. Gains immediately accrue to those who own the most fertile land. If the most fertile land yields ten bushels of corn per acre and the second-best land yields eight bushels per acre, some farmers should be willing to pay close to two bushels of corn for using the best land rather than the second-best land.

As worse and worse quality land gets brought into use, differential rents will rise. "When land of the third quality is taken into cultivation, rent immediately rises on the second, and is regulated . . . by the difference in their productive powers. At the same time, the rent of the first quality will rise" (Ricardo 1951–5, vol. 1, p. 70). If the third-best land yields seven bushels per acre, rent on the best land will rise to around three bushels per acre, while the second-best plot of land now commands a rent of one bushel per acre.

Worker wages, Ricardo held, depend upon subsistence requirements – the minimum that workers would need to survive. Unlike Smith, Ricardo interpreted this minimum in conventional terms rather than in physical terms; it "essentially depends on the habits and customs of the people" (Ricardo 1951–5, vol. 1, p. 97). As the general standard of living improves, so too does the minimum wage that can be paid to workers. The minimum income needed to survive in twentieth-first century England is not the same as the minimum income needed in nineteenth century-England. Indoor plumbing and private baths, while uncommon in the nineteenth century, were essential at the start of the twenty-first century. Wage levels in the twenty-first century must therefore take account of the higher living standards to which people have grown accustomed.

Finally, Ricardo held that profits were a residual, or what was left over for the capitalist after paying workers their wages and land-owners their rents. Ricardo also held that profit rates would be the same in every industry, since, if one industry received higher profits, more capital would enter that industry and push down prices and profits. Similarly, capital would leave industries earning low profits. This would tend to raise prices and profits.

These theories of rent, wages, and profit led Ricardo to a rather unhappy conclusion. Over time, as a country grows, its population will likewise grow. More people mean more mouths to feed and more food that has to be produced. Consequently, less–fertile land must be brought into use. This will raise the rent on all land and increase the rents that must be paid to landowners. As the cost of producing food rises (due to higher rent payments), so too must the price of food. The subsistence theory of wages maintains that higher food prices must lead to an increase in wages. Only with such a pay increase can workers buy higher-priced food and maintain their standard of living.

With both wages and rents rising, the profits of the capitalist must get squeezed. Landowners receive higher rents, wages rise to keep up with rising food costs, and so profits must fall. Moreover, as profits fall, the motivation for accumulating capital disappears. At this point, economic progress comes to an end and the economy stagnates.

Ricardo made several suggestions for dealing with this looming crisis. First, he argued for a repeal of the British Corn Laws. First passed in 1660, the initial goal of the Corn Laws was to stabilize the price of grain in England. High duties on imports and low export duties were imposed when the domestic supply was great. When the harvest was bad, import fees were removed, thereby allowing more grain to come into England, and export duties were imposed. This initially helped exert a downward pressure on grain prices in times of shortages. But over time, problems developed and the legislation did not seem to work as intended. By the early 1800s, the Corn Laws were not stabilizing prices; rather, they were keeping up grain prices and protecting the incomes of landowners who gained from the high prices of corn grown on their land.

Ricardo saw that a repeal of the Corn Laws would increase imports of foreign grain into Britain. This would have two beneficial effects on profits. By keeping down the price of food, grain imports would keep down wages and stop the squeeze of wages on profits. Greater grain imports would also mean that Britain itself would need to produce less grain. This would reduce the amount of land used domestically to grow food. Since the least-fertile land would be taken out of cultivation, and since rents were a differential, rents in Britain would fall and reduce the squeeze on profits.

A second policy reform advocated by Ricardo was greater capital accumulation. More capital equipment would improve the productivity of land. If all land were improved equally, there would be no change in differential rents. And with wages determined by habitual subsistence requirements, wages would not be affected by greater productivity. Thus the gains from capital accumulation would go primarily to profits. Moreover, this increase in profits would generate greater investment in the future, the hiring of more workers, and even greater productivity growth.

Ricardo eventually came to entertain considerable doubt that capital accumulation could improve British living standards. The third edition of his *Principles of Political Economy* (Ricardo 1951–5, vol. I) added a chapter entitled "On Machinery." This chapter discusses the possibility that new machinery would harm workers by displacing labor. Before Ricardo, virtually all economists agreed with Adam Smith that machinery assisted the division of labor and thus contributed to economic growth. In addition, following Smith, most economists thought that the introduction of machinery would not lead businesses to lay off workers. Early editions of the *Principles* concurred in this view and claimed that greater use of machinery would lower the price of goods rather than displacing labor. Thus all society would benefit.

But after reading a pamphlet by John Barton (1817) entitled *Observations on the Condition of the Labouring Classes*, Ricardo changed his mind. With the aid of numerical examples, Barton showed how capitalists might make more money by hiring fewer workers and employing more machines. Based on these examples, Ricardo concluded that workers were right to fear and oppose the introduction of new machinery on the grounds that it would likely lead to what we now call "technological unemployment."

One consequence of the new machinery chapter was that Ricardo came to agree with Malthus that continued high unemployment was possible. Another consequence was that it made Ricardian economics even more pessimistic. With technological unemployment looming on the horizon, not even capital accumulation could be counted on to improve the welfare of society (see Hicks 1969).

Finally, no summary of the contributions made by Ricardo would be complete without mentioning his theory of value. Ricardo's theory of value began with observation that "commodities derive their exchange value from two sources: from their scarcity and from the quantity of labor required to obtain them" (Ricardo 1951–5, vol. 1, p. 12). Scarcity was only important in determining the value of those goods that cannot be reproduced – things like rare paintings, books, coins, and wine. These goods were not important in Ricardo's opinion. The vast majority of goods were reproducible, and what was important in determining their value was the amount of labor needed to produce them. Two sorts of labor were necessary – direct labor and indirect labor. Direct labor is the amount of work-time or the number of workers needed. Indirect labor is the machinery used in the production process. Since machinery is a reproducible good, its value gets determined by the direct and indirect labor needed to produce it. By going back in time, the value of every good could reduce to the amount of labor needed to produce it directly and the amount of labor needed to produce the machinery required in the production process.

Ricardo held that reproducible goods would exchange at rates that mainly depended on the amount of labor (direct plus indirect) needed to produce them. If it took twice as much labor to produce a boat as it took to produce a car, the boat would be twice as expensive as the car. But if it took three times as much labor to produce a boat, the boat would cost three times as much as a car. One important implication of this theory of value is that (relative) prices depend exclusively on production and technology. The demand for cars and boats is irrelevant. All that matters is the way that cars and boats each get produced – in particular, how much labor is required to make each good.

Ricardo did not hold a total labor theory of value. He recognized that different capital structures might be required to produce different goods. If two goods both require 1,000 hours of labor, but one good employs only direct labor while the other uses a lot of machinery, the two goods may not cost the same amount to produce. The reason for this is the interest cost on the labor used to produce machinery. Interest does not have to be paid when producing some good with only direct or current labor. But interest must be taken into account when using past labor or machinery, since money will have to be borrowed to pay the workers making the machinery. Ricardo (1951–5, vol. 1, p. 36) thought that the proportion of capital and labor used in producing every good was roughly the same. Hence, the quantity of labor needed to produce a good was a reasonably good approximation of the value of every good; however, it was not a perfect measure of relative prices (see Stigler 1958).

With Smith and Marx, Ricardo was one of three giant figures in classical economics, the period stretching from the late eighteenth century to the late nineteenth century. He made several lasting and important contributions to economics – the labor theory of value and the theory of comparative advantage being the most prominent. Ricardo also developed the first rigorous economic theory of distribution, and drew out its consequences. Finally, he had a vision of an economic system where relative prices were determined mainly by the costs of production, and where demand and utility played little or no role. This vision was subsequently adopted and formalized by Piero Sraffa, and became the basis of the neo-Ricardian or Sraffian school of economic thought.

Works by Ricardo

Works of David Ricardo, ed. Piero Sraffa, 10 vols, Cambridge, Cambridge University Press for the Royal Economic Society, 1951–5

Works about Ricardo

Blaug, Mark, *Ricardian Economics*, New Haven, Connecticut, Yale University Press, 1958

Hicks, John, "Ricardo on Machinery," in *A Theory of Economic History*, New York, Oxford University Press, 1969, pp. 168–71

Hollander, Samuel, *The Economics of David Ricardo*, Toronto, University of Toronto Press, 1979

Stigler, George J., "The Ricardian Theory of Value and Distribution," *Journal of Political Economy*, vol. 60 (June 1952). Reprinted in *Essays in the History of Economics*, Chicago, University of Chicago Press, 1965, pp. 156–97

Stigler, George J., "Ricardo and the 93 Per Cent Labor Theory of Value," *American Economic Review*, 48 (June 1958). Reprinted in *Essays in the History of Economics*, Chicago, University of Chicago Press, 1965, pp. 326–42

Other references

Barton, John, *Observations on the Circumstances which Influence the Condition of the Labouring Classes of Society*, London, John & Arthur Arch, 1817

Malthus, Thomas Robert, *The Pamphlets of Thomas Robert Malthus*, New York, Augustus M. Kelley, 1970

ANTOINE AUGUSTIN COURNOT (1801–77)

Antoine Augustin Cournot (pronounced CORE-KNOW) developed much of contemporary microeconomics. He was the first economist to draw a demand curve, he explained how market structure affected prices, and he provided the first analysis of how markets reach equilibrium. But Cournot is best known for his analysis of the process of arbitrage and for his analysis of pricing behavior in industries with only two firms (duopolies).

Cournot was born in Gray, a small French town east of Dijon, in 1801. He attended the local high school until he was fifteen and then spent four years studying on his own. During this time he primarily read treatises in law and mathematics. In 1821 Cournot was admitted to the École Normale Supérieure in Paris, but when the school was closed for political reasons he transferred to the Sorbonne.

After graduating in 1823, Cournot spent ten years helping a French marshal write his memoirs. This job provided ample free time, and Cournot used his time well. He wrote a thesis in astronomy, a doctoral dissertation in mechanics, and he obtained a law degree. Cournot also began writing articles on mathematics. These articles earned him substantial notoriety among distinguished French mathematicians, and eventually a position as professor of analysis and mechanics at the University of Lyons.

Cournot turned out to be an excellent administrator as well as an excellent mathematician. He soon became Rector of the Academy of Grenoble, and over the next several decades he held many other administrative posts. Cournot was Inspector General of Education in

Paris, served as Commander of the Legion of Honor, and was Rector of the University of Dijon.

In 1862 Cournot retired from administration and returned to Paris in order to devote the last years of his life to scholarly research and publishing. Unfortunately, with his eyesight deteriorating, Cournot was able to produce little during his retirement.

Early in his professional career, Cournot published mainly in the field of mathematics. He then developed an interest in philosophy, and wrote about the philosophy of history and the theory of knowledge. Only later in life did Cournot become interested in economics. His major economic treatise, *Researches into the Mathematical Principles of the Theory of Wealth* (Cournot 1838), was the first work in economics to bring the differential calculus into economic analysis, and the first application of calculus to the pricing behavior of the firm.

Surprisingly, Cournot's contemporaries showed no interest in this pioneering and revolutionary approach to microeconomic analysis. Many historians of economic thought have speculated that Cournot was ignored because other French economists failed to understand the mathematics of the calculus or what light the calculus could throw on economic principles. However, Ekelund and Hébert (1990) put some of the blame directly on Cournot. They contend that Cournot was ignored because he failed to apply his mathematical economics to the main issues of the day.

A quarter century after publication of his *Researches*, Cournot took another stab at economics. Hoping to reach a larger audience, he removed all the mathematics from his treatise. But this book (Cournot 1863) also made no impression on his contemporaries. Cournot then made a third and final attempt to simplify his theories (1877). This work also was ignored.

Although his contemporaries may have failed to appreciate him, subsequent economists have recognized the many analytical advances due to Cournot. These advances involve developing microeconomic concepts and modes of analysis. The most important microeconomic ideas due to Cournot are his analysis of demand, his analysis of firm costs and production decisions, and his explanation of how arbitrage guaranteed that prices of goods would be roughly equal throughout the world.

Cournot (1960, ch. 4) was the first economist to describe and define the downward-sloping demand curve, noting that the quantity demanded for any good, such as a bottle of French wine, depended on the price of that good. He noted that rising prices would reduce the quantity of wine that people would buy, while falling prices would increase the quantity of wine demanded. Cournot then drew the first demand curve relating prices and the amount of wine consumers would purchase. Unlike the demand diagrams of today, where price is put on the vertical axis and quantity on the horizontal axis (see **Marshall**), Cournot recognized that the quantity of goods demanded by consumers was the dependent variable in the relationship and that price was the independent variable; so Cournot correctly put quantities on the vertical axis and prices on the horizontal axis.

Cournot (1960, p. 81) next showed that an equilibrium price existed at the point where demand and supply were equal. If demand exceeded supply for some good, the price of that good would rise. With demand greater than supply, businesses would see their inventories decline; this would be a signal to the firm that it could charge higher prices for each bottle of wine. At this higher price, demand would be lower; thus demand would come to equal supply more closely. Conversely, if supply exceeded demand, sales would be sluggish and business inventories would not be bought up. In this case, firms would know that if they wanted to sell their stock of wine they would have to lower prices. This would increase demand, thereby bringing it closer to supply.

Cournot also introduced several economic concepts concerning business costs. He was the first to distinguish variable costs from fixed costs. Fixed or overhead costs, such as insurance and the rent payments on a wine bottling plant, stay constant as the firm produces more and more wine. Variable costs include expenses on raw materials, parts, and labor. Expenditures on these items must rise as output increases. To produce more wine, firms require more grapes, more bottles and corks, and more workers.

Cournot recognized the practical importance to the firm of knowing whether costs and revenues will rise or fall as production changes. He defined *marginal cost* as the cost of producing one more unit of output (one more case of wine) and noted that the marginal cost of producing one more unit could be increasing, decreasing, or constant as more goods were produced. Similarly, he defined *marginal revenue* as the additional revenue going to the firm as a result of producing and selling one more unit of output or case of wine.

Using these two notions, Cournot explained how a monopolist should behave in order to maximize its profits. He proved that profits are at their maximum when the firm produces at the level where marginal cost equals marginal revenue, and then sets a price based upon the demand for that quantity of goods. If the last case of wine a monopolist is considering producing has a marginal cost greater than its marginal revenue, the firm should not produce that case for it loses money by doing so. On the other hand, if the marginal revenue from producing one more case of wine exceeds the cost of producing that wine, profits will rise and the firm should produce that case of wine.

Once the firm compares marginal cost and marginal revenue to determine how much to produce, it must decide how much to charge for what it produces. Here the demand curve plays an important role. Wanting to receive as much money as possible, the firm looks to demand, which shows the price that people are willing to pay for that level of output, and it charges the price indicated by that curve.

At the opposite end of the spectrum from monopoly lies the market structure called "perfect competition." Cournot defined the characteristics of this type of industry. Perfect competition requires a large number of small firms. It also requires no restrictions on new firms entering the industry. Such restrictions could be in the form of government regulations or they could be the high start-up costs for any new firm. Cournot (1960, p. 90) noted that only with perfect competition are sellers unable to alter market price by varying the amount that they supply.

Cournot also analyzed the pricing principles for a duopoly, a market which has two sellers and two sellers only. For his analysis, Cournot assumed that neither seller could set prices. He also assumed that each seller knew the demand for the good it produced, and that costs were similar for both firms.

From these assumptions Cournot was able to show how the decisions of each firm affected the price in the market and thus the output decisions of the other firm. If one firm increased production in an attempt to raise profits, that firm would have to lower its price to sell the additional output. This would require the second firm also to lower its price if it is to remain competitive. Moreover, the second firm faces similar decisions regarding how much to produce. It too can attempt to increase production and profits. Any decision made by the second firm will affect the price that the first firm could charge and the profit it could make. When the second firm changes production and prices, the first firm has new information, and might need to make a new decision about how much to produce and what to charge. This decision, in turn, will affect the situation facing the second firm. It too will have new information and will have to make a new decision about production. One might think that the process of each firm altering its price and output decisions in response to the decisions of its rival might go on forever. But Cournot showed that this would not be the case. Eventually a situation would result where neither firm could improve their position (make more profit) by increasing or decreasing the amount of the good that they produced. This was a duopoly equilibrium (see Machlup 1962).

Finally, Cournot (1960, ch. 3) turned his attention to international prices or the price of foreign currencies. Here he explained how *arbitrage* guarantees an equilibrium set of exchange rates among a number of different currencies that will be totally consistent.

Arbitrage is merely the process of buying and selling in different places and making money on any price differences. For example, if a bushel of corn goes for $1 in Mexico and $1.10 in Canada, one can earn profits by buying corn in Mexico and then reselling the corn in Canada. Moreover, this activity will increase the demand for corn in Mexico and thus push up its price. In Canada, the greater supply of corn will tend to lower prices. Thus, arbitrage pushes prices to the same level all over the world. Prices may not be exactly the same in Mexico and Canada because of the costs of transporting goods from country to country, but arbitrage should make the price of goods converge all over the world.

What is true of buying and selling corn is likewise true of trading foreign exchange – arbitrage will equalize the price of foreign currency throughout the world. In 2005, 100 yen cost around $1, and the British pound cost around $2. For exchange rates between the yen, the dollar and the pound to be consistent, one British pound had to equal 200 Japanese yen. Arbitrage assures that this will be the case.

Consider what would happen if this were not so – for example, if È1 traded for 400 yen. From an American perspective 100 yen costs $1, but in England 100 yen costs only 50 cents, since 50 cents will buy a quarter of a British pound and a quarter pound buys 200 yen. Arbitrage works here just like it did in the corn example. Americans would make money buying yen in England and selling yen in Japan for US dollars. These trades would push up the price of yen in England (due to greater demand) and reduce the price of yen in Japan (due to the greater supply). This process of arbitrage would continue until the price of all three currencies became consistent throughout the world.

Cournot is surely one of the more underrated figures in the history of economics. Given the many important conceptual and analytical advances he made, and given the mathematical nature of these advances, it is surprising that his reputation has not been much greater. In part, this is probably due to the fact that Cournot focused too much on technique. Another likely reason is that he had few disciples to promulgate his ideas and his approach to economics. None the less, his many contributions to microeconomic theory have held up over time and they remain the heart of contemporary microeconomic analysis.

Works by Cournot

Researches into the Mathematical Principles of the Theory of Wealth (1838), trans. Nathaniel T. Bacon, New York, Augustus M. Kelley, 1960
Principes de la théorie des richesses, Paris, Hachette, 1863
Revue sommaire des doctrines économiques, Paris, Hachette, 1877

Works about Cournot

Ekelund, Robert B. and Hébert, Robert E., "Cournot and His Contemporaries: Is an Obituary the Only Bad Review?," *Southern Economic Journal*, 57, 1 (July 1990), pp. 139–49
Machlup, Fritz, *The Economics of Sellers' Competition*, Baltimore, Maryland, Johns Hopkins University Press, 1962
Moore, Henry Ludwell, "The Personality of Antoine Augustin Cournot," *Quarterly Journal of Economics*, 19, 3 (1905), pp. 370–99
Plantz, Don V., "Cournot's *Researches:* Some Insights on Its Influence Upon the Development of Economic Thought," *Western Economic Journal*, 2 (1964), pp. 195–208

JOHN STUART MILL (1806–73)

John Stuart Mill was an important transitional figure in economics. In some ways he was part of the classical school that included Smith, Malthus, and Ricardo; but in other respects Mill was an important forerunner of the marginalist school that began to develop in the late nineteenth century.

Mill was born in London in 1806. His father, James Mill, was a prominent historian. James Mill devoted considerable time each day to teaching his children, and he attempted to give them the best possible education. The story of these efforts is quite remarkable. Mill ([1873] 1957, p. 5) reports: "I have no remembrance of the time when I began to learn Greek. I have been told that it was when I was three years old." At seven years of age, Mill was reading the philosophical dialogues of Plato. At eight he began to learn Latin. Over the next four years mathematics was added to his studies. Mill learned elementary geometry and algebra thoroughly, as well as the differential calculus and higher mathematics. On reaching age twelve, the advanced stage of his education began with the study of logic and philosophy. One year later Mill ([1873] 1957, p. 19) went through "a complete course in political economy," which included attending many discussions between his father and David Ricardo.

But it was the constant presence of Bentham in the Mill household that had the greatest impact on the young Mill. Conversations with Bentham, and reading his works, convinced Mill to follow in Bentham's footsteps and become a social reformer. On reaching adulthood, Mill sought to spread the gospel of Bentham throughout the world. From 1834 to 1840 he edited the *Westminster Review*, a major intellectual periodical in Britain and the vehicle of communication for the Philosophical Radicals (see **Bentham**). He then began publishing books on economics, philosophy, politics, and social theory. These works made Mill one of the best-known and most respected figures in nineteenth century England.

In his many books and articles Mill made several important contributions to economics. Some of these extended and completed classical economic analysis; others broke new ground by analyzing economic phenomena as relationships and trade-offs. Mill also made several contributions to the broad area where economics and philosophy overlap. These explained the philosophical foundations of economics, and set forth justifications for individual freedom and limits on government intervention in economic and social affairs.

The *Principles of Political Economy* (Mill 1848) was essentially a textbook summarizing the economic wisdom of the time. The book went through numerous editions, and dominated economic teaching in England for half a century (until the publication of Marshall's *Principles*).

One important contribution of Mill's *Principles* was its analysis of future economic growth. Here Mill attempted to find a middle path between Smith and Malthus. As we have seen, Smith saw societies becoming wealthier as a result of greater freedom to trade, technological innovation, the division of labor, and capital investment. Malthus, on the other hand, saw economic progress limited by the press of people against fixed resources. Mill saw both sets of forces operating at once. Rather than predicting the ultimate outcome of these conflicting forces, he (Mill 1848, book 4) set forth several possibilities or scenarios for the future. As a result, Mill deserves credit for being the first economist to recognize that long-run trends or outcomes cannot be forecast with certainty, but depend on how various opposing forces work themselves out over an extended time period.

A first scenario followed pretty much along Malthusian lines – population grew more quickly than could capital and technology increase output. In this case, as in Malthus, the result would be lower wages and higher profits. The living standard of the ordinary worker had to decline.

A second scenario closely followed the analysis of Smith – capital accumulation increased faster than the population grew. Here real wages rose, thus making the average worker better off.

In a third scenario, the supply of capital and the population increased at the same rate, but technology was relatively stable. Because the supply of labor and the demand for labor increased at the same rate, there would be no change in real wages. But since technology did not improve, inferior land had to be used to feed the growing population because the most fertile land would be used first (see **Ricardo**). This increased the cost of producing food. With food prices and rents increasing, profits had to fall. This is essentially the Ricardian outcome.

Fourth, Mill noted that technological advances might improve more rapidly than capital and population grew. This would make it easier to grow food, and would lower both wages and rents. As a result profits would rise, and the economy would prosper.

Mill thought that the third scenario was the most likely of all the possible future outcomes. Living in the middle of the Industrial Revolution, and having no experience with long-term technological advance, it was somewhat natural for Mill to believe technological progress must come to an end. When this happened, Mill argued, capital accumulation and economic growth also would come to an end, as Ricardo predicted.

Most classical economists feared the end of economic growth. Mill, in contrast, thought that the stationary state would have many benefits. The most important benefit of all was that the end of growth would end the perpetual rat race of industrial life.

> I am not charmed with the ideal of life held out by those who think that the normal state of human beings is that of struggling to get on; that the trampling, crushing, elbowing, and treading on each other's heels ... are the most desirable lot of human kind ... (Mill 1848, p. 334)

Mill helped bring classical theory to completion in other ways as well. One problem left unanswered by the theory of comparative advantage was how the gains from international trade get divided up between countries. Mill explained that most of the gains from trade would go to that country with the lower demand and the greater *elasticity of demand*. If demand is elastic, a change in price will yield a large change in quantities bought by consumers. On the other hand, if demand is inelastic, consumers will not be swayed much by price changes (see **Marshall**).

Demand is inelastic when you are hooked on a good and just have to have it – maybe because there are no available substitutes, or maybe because psychologically the good is something you just must have. So, if the US has less need for Japanese automobiles and can easily do without Japanese automobiles (i.e. if US demand for Japanese automobiles is relatively elastic), while Japan cannot do without American food and has a great appetite for American food, most of the gains from specialization and trade would go to the US. The US would sell food to Japan at a high price and get their automobiles cheaply. On the other hand, if Americans are hooked on Japanese automobiles and cannot get these goods elsewhere, while Japan finds alternate sources of food, most of the gains from trade will go to Japan. In this case, the high and inelastic demand for cars in the US means that Americans pay high prices for Japanese cars, while the low and inelastic demand in Japan means that the Japanese get American food cheaply.

Mill made his most lasting contributions to economics, not when he extended classical economic analysis, but when he began to think in new ways. He was one of the first economists to speak of supply and demand as schedules or relationships (Stigler 1965). In the work of Smith, Ricardo, and other classical economists, supply and demand were treated as quantities of goods brought to market and as quantities of goods bought by consumers. Mill recognized that quantities responded to changes in price. As prices increased, businesses would bring forth greater quantities of goods to the market; and as prices fell, consumers would purchase greater quantities of the goods provided by businesses.

Mill was also the first to formulate the notion of *opportunity cost*. Any human action involves giving up the opportunity or ability to do something else. The opportunity cost of any action includes financial costs as well as non-financial costs. Deciding to pursue a college education requires spending money on tuition, books, and other things. There are opportunity costs involved, since other goods cannot be purchased because a college education was bought. These other goods are given up, or are lost consumption opportunities. But there are further opportunity costs of a college degree. When going to school one is not earning money. Thus one gives up the income that could have been earned by not going to school. The total opportunity cost of a college education includes both the money spent for schooling and the lost wages from attending school.

Mill's most important contribution to economics may be his rejection of the classical *wage fund doctrine*. This doctrine holds that worker wages were a form of capital and were paid out of a fund that businesses accumulated before producing goods. On this view, the only way to increase both wages and employment would be for the entrepreneur to accumulate more profits. Mill (1869b) argued that there was no fixed amount that businesses had to pay labor. The amount of money that firms could pay as wages was flexible, and it was determined by the willingness of employers to pay workers more. Mill also noted that business owners could always reduce their own consumption of goods, for example by buying $5 million homes rather than $20 million homes. This would make more money available for workers. Consequently there was no fixed wage fund. More money was always available to increase wages or to hire more workers; and business owners and workers can always negotiate over wages.

Mill achieved fame not only for his economics, but also for his philosophical and political writings, both of which dovetailed with his economic work. Mill (1863) defended the utilitarian philosophy developed by his father and Bentham, and that has come to form the foundation for much of economics.

More important, his "On the Definition of Political Economy" (in Mill 1844) was the first attempt by an economist to examine the issue of economic method. Mill wanted to know if the social, behavioral, and moral sciences (such as economics) were like the natural sciences. His answer was "no," because controlled experiments were not possible outside the natural sciences. It is impossible to set up two economies, identical in all respects except for the one factor we wish to alter in order to study its overall impact. Since economic knowledge could not come from experience, Mill reasoned that it must come from introspection. We know from examining ourselves that people behave in ways that attempt to maximize the pleasure they received. And we know that all attempts to maximize pleasure are constrained by nature – we can only work so hard and so long, and we can only produce so much in any given year. Economics, for Mill, is thus the science that deduces the consequences of these assumptions, just like geometry is a science that proves theorems about triangles and circles after starting with some basic definitions and assumptions about points, lines, and angles.

Finally, *On Liberty* (Mill 1859) discussed the limits of government and societal restrictions on individual freedom. Mill argued that the state and society had a right to restrict individual freedom only to keep one individual from harming another individual. *On Liberty* was thus a ringing endorsement of *laissez-faire*. In contrast to Smith, who argued for *laissez-faire* because it maximized material well-being, for Mill *laissez-faire* was desirable primarily because it resulted in the greatest individual development. Similarly, *The Subjection of Women* (Mill 1869a) also advocated equality for women on the grounds of self-development. Mill argued that the greatest obstacle to the liberation of women was received opinion and custom that relegated women to a subordinate position in society. This limited the development of half the population. It also limited the ability of society to progress. By allowing women to compete with men for jobs and for all other positions, society would gain by having the best and most qualified person in every position.

During his lifetime, Mill was regarded as one of the two or three most prominent economists. However, today Mill is not counted among the very best and most important economists. Part of the reason for this is that, while he added bits and pieces to economic analysis, Mill made no major advances. Moreover, as a transitional figure, Mill left no school of followers to further and continue his work. Yet another factor is that there was no single area of economics in which Mill specialized and made major contributions. Rather, the work of Mill encompassed numerous and disparate areas – methodology, theory, policy, labor economics, international trade, and political theory.

Works by Mill

Essays on Some Unsettled Questions of Political Economy (1844), New York, Kelley, 1968
Principles of Political Economy, 2 vols (1848), New York, Oxford University Press, 1994
On Liberty (1859), Indianapolis, Indiana, Hackett, 1978
Utilitarianism (1863), Indianapolis, Indiana, Bobbs Merrill, 1957
The Subjection of Women (1869a), Cambridge, Massachusetts, MIT Press, 1970

"Thornton on Labour and Its Claims," *Fortnightly Review*, 5, May 1869b, pp. 505–18. Reprinted in *Collected Works of John Stuart Mill, Vol. 5, Essays on Economic and Society*, London, Routledge & Kegan Paul, 1967, pp. 631–68
Autobiography (1873), Indianapolis, Indiana, Bobbs-Merrill, 1957

Works about Mill

Capaldi, Nicholas, *John Stuart Mill: A Biography*, New York, Cambridge University Press, 2004
Hollander, Samuel, *The Economics of John Stuart Mill*, Toronto, University of Toronto Press, 1985
Schwartz, Pedro, *The New Political Economy of J. S. Mill*, Durham, North Carolina, Duke University Press, 1972
Stigler, George J., "The Nature and Role of Originality in Scientific Progress," in *Essays in the History of Economics*, Chicago, Illinois, University of Chicago Press, 1965, pp. 1–15

KARL MARX (1818–83)

Although Karl Marx is most closely associated with socialist economic systems, Marx actually wrote very little about socialism. Rather, he studied the operation of capitalist economies and analyzed the problems that arise under capitalism. He then argued that these problems could not be remedied by economic policies, or by other actions to make the system work better, because they were essential characteristics of capitalism. These problems, Marx thought, would continue to fester and eventually destroy capitalist economies.

Marx was born into a middle class Jewish family in Trier, Germany, in 1818. He was first educated at home by his parents and Baron von Westphalen, a close friend and neighbor of his father. Marx then went on to attend high school in Trier. Upon graduating, he decided to go to the University of Bonn to study law, but shortly after beginning his studies he became bored with legal issues and developed an interest in philosophy. In order to pursue this interest Marx transferred to the University of Berlin, which at the time was the hub of Hegelian philosophy.

According to Hegel, human life was constantly in flux; every idea and every force generated an opposite force and the tension generated by these two opposing forces would inevitably lead to change. Marx embraced the Hegelian notion of change; his idea that all economic systems generate opposing forces and then undergo radical transformation derives from the philosophy of Hegel. It should go without saying that this vision threatened political leaders, who preferred the status quo, and business leaders, who saw Marx and his followers as attempting to ruin their good thing.

In 1841 Marx received a PhD in Philosophy, and in 1843 he married the daughter of Baron von Westphalen. Unable to get an academic job teaching philosophy, and without many marketable skills, he worked as editor of the liberal-left newspaper *Rheinische Zeitung*. Within a year the paper was banned by Prussian censors. Seeing no future in Germany, Marx moved to Paris, where he began to associate with numerous socialists and communists. In Paris, Marx also met Friedrich Engels. Engels was the son of a wealthy textile manufacturer and a well-known economist in his own right. His classic, *The Condition of the Working Class in England* (Engels 1844), described the sad state of working class families in the industrial towns of northern England. Engels and Marx quickly became friends and collaborators. Perhaps as important, Engels provided financial support to Marx during the rest of his life.

Because of his radicalism, Marx was expelled from Paris after a short period of time. He tried living in Brussels, but was soon expelled from there as well. Finally, he moved to London, where he was accepted by political authorities, although not necessarily with open arms. Marx lived the last 33 years of his life in London, spending most of his time at the British Museum, reading and writing economics.

The economic writings of Marx attempt to understand how capitalist economies work, and where capitalism fits into the economic history of mankind. Marx saw capitalism as just one phase of an historic process that all economies move through. Human economic activity, Marx noted, began in hunter–gatherer societies. Then people settled down and formed agricultural communities, which shortly developed into feudal economies. Under feudalism, landowners provided protection for peasant farmers, and peasants provided part of their output to the landowner. Feudalism, in turn, was transformed into capitalism due to the rise of businessmen who engaged in small-scale manufacturing and who traded goods both domestically and internationally. As was true of each economic epoch, Marx recognized that capitalism possessed both positive and negative aspects. Among its positive attributes was the ability to increase average living standards through the use of more advanced technology and machinery (see **Smith**), and the ability to attract workers to towns and cities and away from "the idiocy of rural life."

But the negative attributes of capitalism dominated the positive ones, according to Marx. Moreover, Marx saw these problems as being integral parts of the capitalist system. Reform efforts, which attempted to mitigate the negative aspects of capitalism, could not really solve the deep-seated problems or save capitalism from its ultimate fate. Indeed, in *The Communist Manifesto*, Marx and Engels (1948, ch. 2) advocated a number of such reform measures, including free public libraries, free education, the abolition of child factory labor, a graduated income tax, the end to all inheritances, government control of communications and transportation networks, and the establishment of a national bank. But Marx saw these policies as "band-aids" to make life more tolerable under capitalism; he did not think they could fundamentally change the way capitalism operated or keep it from self-destructing. No matter what policies were put into effect, the capitalist system was destined to collapse at some point under the weight of the many problems that it created. Most of the economic writings of Marx attempted to identify and explain these problems.

One crucial characteristic of capitalism, according to Marx, is that it exploits individual workers. To understand the notion of *exploitation*, it is necessary to understand Marx's analysis of the value of any good. Following Ricardo, Marx adopted a *labor theory of value*. This theory held that the value of any good depended upon the amount of labor spent producing it. This labor could either be direct labor, which is current work effort, or indirect labor, which is the amount of labor that went into making the machinery that was used in producing the good.

Marx then divided the value of all goods into three categories – constant capital, variable capital, and surplus value. Constant capital refers to the machinery, plants, and equipment used up in the production of a good; this notion is similar to the notion of depreciation that is familiar to all accounting students. Variable capital refers to the current wage bill, or what workers are paid to help produce goods. Marx defined *surplus value* as the value of a product over and above wage and depreciation costs. It is similar to the more familiar notion of profit. Marx provided a second, and similar, perspective on surplus value. He noted that the essence of capitalism was to take money (M), use this money to buy things (labor and machines) that could produce some commodity, and then sell that commodity for a greater amount of money (M'). Surplus value could thus also be defined as the difference between M' and M. Marx held that the appropriation of surplus value by the owners of capital constitutes exploitation.

Exploitation was made possible by the fact that workers had to offer their services or work effort because they owned no capital and could not support themselves in any other way. Through their daily efforts, workers created something of value. They produced goods, and they produced machinery that could help produce even more goods in the future. But workers did not receive the full value of everything they produced. Some of the value they created was taken by their employer in the form of surplus value. At the beginning of the working day, workers produced enough goods so that the sale of these items would pay for their wages plus wear and tear on the machinery used in production. For the rest of the day, however, laborers worked to enrich their employer.

Marx noted that capitalists had three means at their disposal to increase surplus value and thus the exploitation of workers. First, they could increase the length of the working day, so that during each day more surplus value was created. Second, they could increase the intensity of work effort, so that workers produced more goods in a given time period. One means of increasing work intensity was to increase the speed of the assembly line. Another was to increase the monitoring and control of workers, so that workers were less able to slack off. In these cases, workers produced more during the day; and, with variable and constant capital fixed, more output would translate into greater surplus value.

Finally, capitalists could increase surplus value by reducing the wage bill. One obvious way to do this would be to lower the wages of current employees. Alternatively, women and children could be hired to replace men at lower pay. In the early twenty-first century we can look at firms moving their production facilities to less developed countries (where labor costs are much lower), or outsourcing services to these countries, as other examples of how firms can reduce their wage bill. These three strategies all have the same effect – they lower wages and increase exploitation or surplus value.

Marx did recognize that there were limits to the exploitation of workers by these methods – workers could physically endure working just a certain number of hours each day, technology and physical capabilities limited the extent to which an employer might speed up the assembly line, and families had to be paid enough to buy the necessities that would enable them to survive and work in the future. Competition, however, forced firms to maximize their exploitation of workers. In a competitive environment, not every firm will be profitable and thrive. Firms unable to do as well as their competitors will invariably go out of business. Competition among firms thus forces each firm to exploit its workers more in order to lower costs, increase profits, and remain in business. Only those firms exploiting their workers to the fullest extent possible will survive; other firms will cease to exist because their costs of producing goods will be too high. Competitive capitalism thus guarantees that workers live on the edge of subsistence and that they get exploited to the maximum extent possible.

A second major problem with capitalism that Marx noted is that it creates alienated workers. Alienation has four aspects. First, under capitalism workers become alienated from how they produce. Marx thought that human beings were naturally creative and wanted to control and shape their environment. But, *contra* Adam Smith, the division of labor did not promote dexterity and skills; rather it transformed the production process into simple, monotonous tasks. Work became boring and had no meaning except as a source of income; it destroyed the creative, emotional, esthetic, and intellectual potential of the worker (see Braverman 1974). Thus, rather than work being an integral part of human life, this aspect of alienation leads to the familiar aphorism "life begins when work ends."

A second reason for alienation under capitalism is that workers lose control over the goods that they produce. The individual craftsman, Marx noted, could take pride in what he produced. For the assembly-line worker, however, this is not the case. These workers are not responsible for producing the final product and can take little pride for the small part they play in producing it. In addition, the capitalist system leads inexorably to the production of cheap and shoddy merchandise. Capitalists always seek to produce at the lowest possible costs. Again, survival is at stake. One way to cut costs is to cut corners. Thus quality tends to suffer, and workers tend to turn out cheap junk that they can take no pride in having made. By losing control over the means of production workers become alienated from what they produce.

A third reason for alienation is that under capitalism the surplus value created by workers goes to enrich their employer. People work hard all day long. But these efforts only improve the absolute position of the capitalist; they do not improve the absolute standard of living of the individual worker who puts in all the effort. Workers always and only receive subsistence wages. This means that the relative position of the worker worsens as a result of working hard. The standard of living for workers remains at the bare minimum necessary for survival, while capitalists increasingly become richer and richer. Marx believed that this characteristic of capitalism stemmed from the fact that capitalists monopolized the means of production. Workers had to work in order to earn enough money to eat and survive. Capitalists, in contrast, owned enough property so that they could live well without working or producing. Thus workers were at a great disadvantage relative to capitalists and were forced to accept subsistence wages.

Finally, Marx contended that under capitalism the labor power of the worker becomes the property of the capitalist employer. The worker is thus alienated from herself. There is a loss of individual freedom and self-respect; employment becomes a form of slavery for the worker.

Alienation and exploitation of workers lead inevitably to a class struggle between capitalists, who own the means of production, and workers, who do not. This struggle, Marx thought, would lead to the destruction of the capitalist system when the pressures on workers became too great. And competition among capitalists guaranteed that such pressures would continue to rise and build.

Marx always placed his analysis of the class struggle in an historical context, noting over and over that capitalism arose out of a predominantly agricultural and feudal society. Capitalism destroyed feudal ties. It would therefore not be surprising if capitalism were replaced with another socio-economic system, socialism, where workers owned the means of production and made decisions regarding working conditions, quality of output, prices, wages, etc. Moreover, the forces that would eventually cause capitalism to self-destruct were all integral parts of the capitalist system.

First, capitalism was about taking fortunes and using them to create larger fortunes. Large fortunes are needed because they bring power and prestige. Also, each capitalist was always under pressure from other capitalists. Anyone trying to stand still would quickly be forced out of business by competitors, lose prestige and power, and have to seek employment as a worker (i.e. become exploited and alienated).

Second, capitalism was characterized by an unending drive towards monopoly and economic concentration. Monopolists made huge profits. In contrast, the firms in a competitive environment tend to compete away their profits. All firms, therefore, desire to become large and all desire to be monopolies. The process of competition crushes the weak and the small, or they become absorbed by the big and the strong. Furthermore, to remain competitive a firm had constantly to improve worker productivity; but technological improvements required increasing amounts of capital. Thus larger and larger firms were needed to supply this rising capital requirement. These tendencies towards monopoly meant that small businesses would be bankrupted by large firms, small businessmen and women would soon become workers for these large monopolies, and more and more people would come to resent monopolies.

A final force leading to the demise of capitalism was the tendency for profit rates to fall. Capitalism is all about trying to accumulate more and more wealth. To win at the game, more and more efficient machinery must be bought and used. As such, the production process comes to rely on relatively more capital and relatively less labor. The profit rate equals total profits divided by the initial monies put out to produce goods. In Marx's terminology, the rate of profit equals the ratio of surplus value to constant plus variable capital. Since surplus value comes from exploiting workers, using more machinery and fewer workers can only reduce surplus value and the rate of profit.

The tendency to replace labor with machinery also increases unemployment. This "reserve army" of the unemployed helps to keep wages down and counters the tendency of the rate of profit to fall. But at the same time, higher unemployment and lower wages lead to greater social unrest. And it is this, more than anything else, that will help bring about the end of capitalism.

These many pressures on the capitalist system, Marx thought, would continue to build until the system is finally destroyed. As Marx (1957–62, vol. 1, p. 929) writes:

> [T]he mass of misery, oppression, slavery, degradation and exploitation grows; but with this there also grows the revolt of the working class, a class constantly increasing in numbers, and trained, united and organized by the very mechanism of the capitalist process of production. ... The centralization of the means of production and the socialization of labor reach a point at which they become incompatible with their capitalist integument. The integument is burst asunder. The knell of capitalist property sounds; the expropriators are expropriated.

Marx had little to say about economic life after capitalism. He was clear that workers rather than capitalists would own the plants and factories used to produce goods and services. This is the traditional definition of a socialist economic system. It is also clear that Marx envisioned a more equal distribution of income and wealth under socialism than existed under capitalism. But beyond this, there is nothing in the work of Marx. Yet, even without a clear vision of the future, Marx continued to inspire nineteenth century workers to organize and to rebel against capital oppression.

Along with Adam Smith and John Maynard Keynes, Marx must be regarded as one of the three great figures in the history of economics. Unlike Smith, who primarily saw the benefits that would accrue from a free-market capitalist economy, Marx mainly saw the dark side of capitalism and saw this as leading to its ultimate demise. And unlike Keynes, who looked towards rational government policy to save capitalism, Marx thought capitalists would buy out government officials. Politicians, therefore, would not put into place any policies such as unemployment insurance, welfare systems, maximum hours or minimum wages, which might improve the condition of workers and keep class conflicts from becoming violent and revolutionary. Likewise, Marx did not think government policy would be used to keep unemployment down, provide legal recognition for labor, or help labor unions gain bargaining power. Yet many social policies were put into effect throughout the world in the twentieth century, governments did assist labor unions, and labor–management conflicts were reduced to manageable proportions.

In the end it seems that Marx underestimated the flexibility of the capitalist system and its ability to change in order to save itself. He also seems to have underestimated the ability of democratic governments to rise above the capital–labor conflict, and to implement policies that soften the harsh, and sometimes brutal, aspects of capitalism. But despite these flaws in his predictions, probably no one has understood the dynamics of the capitalist system, and the tensions it creates among its various participants, better than Marx.

Works by Marx

The Communist Manifesto, New York, International Publishers, 1948, with Frederick Engels
Capital, 3 vols, Moscow, Foreign Languages Publishing House, 1957–62
Theories of Surplus Value, 3 vols, Moscow, Foreign Language Press, 1963
Value, Price and Profits, New York, International Publishers, 1976
Wage-Labor and Capital, New York, International Publishers, 1976

Works about Marx

Heilbroner, Robert, *Marxism: For and Against*, New York, Norton, 1980
McLellan, David, *Karl Marx: His Life and Thought*, New York, Harper & Row, 1973
Robinson, Joan, *An Essay on Marxian Economics*, London, Macmillan, 1960

Sweezy, Paul, *The Theory of Capitalist Development: Principles of Marxian Political Economy*, New York, Monthly Review Press, 1970

Wheen, Francis, *Karl Marx: A Life*, New York, Norton, 2000

Wolff, Robert Paul, *Understanding Marx: A Reconstruction and Critique of Capital*, Princeton, New Jersey, Princeton University Press, 1984

Other references

Braverman, Harry, *Labor and Monopoly Capital*, New York, Monthly Review Press, 1974

Engels, Friedrich, *The Condition of the Working Class in England* (1844), Moscow, Progress Publishers, 1973

LÉON WALRAS (1834–1910)

Léon Walras (pronounced VOL-ras, with a German W and the S enunciated) is known primarily for developing general equilibrium analysis. He took a very abstract and theoretical problem about how all markets in an economy are related, applied sophisticated mathematics to the problem, and arrived at a solution. His solution showed that all the markets in the economy could simultaneously achieve equilibrium.

Walras was born in Evreux, France (around 90 kilometers west of Paris) in 1834. His father, a teacher and an economist, stressed that mathematics would come to be used increasingly in the social sciences. Walras revered his father and wanted to live up to the high expectations that his father set for him. So, after graduating from high school, Walras applied to the prestigious *École Polytechnique*. Ironically, he was turned down because he lacked the necessary background in mathematics and twice failed the entrance examination. As a result, Walras wound up at the *École des Mines* studying engineering rather than social science. Not really interested in engineering, he spent his time reading literature, philosophy, art, history, and the social sciences. Eventually he dropped out of school. Walras then started writing novels, but he was not successful at this endeavor either.

In 1858, during an evening walk, his father suggested that making the social sciences akin to the natural sciences was one of the major jobs remaining to be accomplished in the nineteenth century. Walras promised his father he would give up writing novels and devote his life to developing a scientific economics. Inspired by his reading of Cournot, as well as by his father, he decided to make this scientific economics a mathematical economics.

Progress towards this end, however, was slow and hard. Walras wrote articles for economics journals, but all he had to show for his efforts was a pile of rejection letters. None the less, Walras learned more mathematics and he continued to praise the virtues of making economics more quantitative. During the 1860s, while working on his mathematical economics, Walras supported himself as a newspaper columnist and as an administrator for a railway company. Finally, his efforts began to pay off. In 1870 he received a teaching position with the law faculty of the Lausanne Academy.

Walras was not happy teaching at Lausanne. Neither his few students nor his law faculty colleagues were especially interested in mathematical economics. However, Walras persevered and continued to write. He sent his articles, free of charge, to others, financing this work with the inheritance he received following the death of his mother. These articles helped Walras achieve international recognition and numerous awards for his contribution to economic science. Towards the end of his life he was made an honorary member of the American Economic Association.

Walras made several important contributions to economics. Along with Jevons and Menger, he was one of several independent discoverers of the notion of *marginal utility*. He was one of the first and strongest advocates of *methodological individualism*, the belief that all explanations of economic phenomena should be based upon individual acts of choice (Hicks 1934, pp. 347f.). But Walras is best known for constructing a general equilibrium economic model, which views the economic system as a set of interrelated mathematical equations. Walras then explained how to solve this set of equations for all prices and quantities.

The notion that different sectors of an economy are related to each other has a long history in economics; the idea goes back at least as far as Cantillon and Quesnay. Walras added two important things to this vision – a mathematical representation of how all markets were interrelated, and an argument that economies would move towards equilibrium in all markets.

Walras recognized that whenever one market moved towards equilibrium, or whenever one market was affected by outside forces, these changes would upset the markets for other goods. For example, in the 1970s when OPEC raised oil prices, consumers wound up paying more for gasoline and heating oil. With more consumer dollars going to energy-related products, less could be spent on other goods. As a result, the producers of these other goods had to cut back production and lay off workers. These layoffs, in turn, would further reduce consumer spending, leading to further production cutbacks and layoffs.

In addition, the energy shock affected the costs of producing goods. Even those goods using little energy in production still require energy when transported from where they are produced to where consumers buy them. Similarly, the parts required for production have to be transported from elsewhere. On the other hand, the layoffs due to reduced spending will push down wages. Consequently, the rising cost of energy should increase the price of some goods (those using little labor and much energy) and reduce the price of other goods (those using little energy and much labor). Consumers will tend to cut back their spending on those goods whose prices rise, and will buy more of those goods whose prices fall or remain stable. But these changes in consumer spending will change the quantities of inputs (such as workers and energy) that businesses want to hire. This changed demand for inputs will, in turn, change input prices. Again, when input prices change, the cost of production will change and so too will the final price of each good.

The question raised by the notion of general equilibrium is whether all these changes tend to slow down and stabilize at some point, so that all markets reach a point where there are no more forces of change affecting any good or input. Walras answered this question with an unqualified "yes." To support this answer he set up a series of mathematical equations representing the market for every good and for every input in the economy.

There were four sets of equations in his economic model. The first set showed the quantity of each good that consumers demanded. Consumer demand was based upon individual preferences and the price of every good that consumers could purchase. Each good sold to consumers could be represented by a mathematical equation that related the amount of the good consumers wanted to their income and to the price of every good.

A second set of equations described what determines the price of every good bought by households. Walras assumed that all markets were competitive and that firms could not charge high prices based upon their monopoly power. This enabled him to set the price of each good equal to its cost of production (the price of inputs times the quantity of each input used).

These first two sets of equations dealt only with product markets, or goods sold to consumers. But another set of markets operates in all economies. These are factor or input markets. They are where remuneration is determined for the factors of production – the wages received by workers, the rental payments received by landlords, and the profits received by owners of capital.

Factor markets contribute two more sets of equations. One set shows the quantity of inputs or factors (land, labor, and capital) offered to help produce goods. Owners of factor inputs (workers, landowners, and capitalists) determine the quantity of factors they wish to supply. This decision will be based upon how disagreeable it is to work or supply their input into the production process, and also on how much can be bought with the income received from helping to produce goods. The reward for working, in turn, depends on the price of goods and the income received from working.

A final set of equations shows the quantity of inputs or factors that businesses want to buy. This depends on the final demand for goods (how much consumers want to buy at different prices), on production technology, and on the cost of all inputs (enabling businesses to figure out the least costly way to produce things). For example, if consumers decide to spend more money on clothing, clothing manufacturers will need to hire more workers and buy more machinery. Alternatively, higher wage costs or new labor-saving technology will reduce the demand for labor and increase the demand for machines.

So far we have four sets of equations – one showing the quantity of goods demanded, one relating price to cost of production, one showing the quantity of inputs supplied, and one showing the quantity of inputs demanded. We also have four sets of unknowns that we need to solve, for: (1) the price of each good; (2) the quantity of each final good bought and sold; (3) the price of each factor of production; and (4) the quantity of each factor supplied and bought by business firms.

But Walras adds one more equation to his mathematical system. This equation stipulates that all the money received by various factors of production must be used to buy something. This can be done either directly, by each household spending all their income, or indirectly, by some households saving money and then lending this money to other households.

This extra equation created a difficult problem for Walras. As all students of algebra learn, to solve a set of mathematical equations it is necessary that the number of equations equals the number of unknowns. Walras now had one more equation than the number of unknowns. To deal with this problem Walras selected one good, G1, arbitrarily; the prices of all other goods would be determined relative to G1. The price of G1 thus would be a standard of comparison, or *numéraire*. Mathematically, the number of unknowns would now equal the number of equations in the general equilibrium representation of the economy. The system could thus be solved for the price of all goods relative to G1. The solution could not explain the absolute level of prices, or why a gallon of milk cost $2 rather than $1 or $4. But it could explain why a gallon of milk costs twice as much as a dozen eggs and three times as much as the daily newspaper.

This vision of the economic system as a set of equations is quite abstract. One question that naturally arises after working through a mathematical proof for the existence of general equilibrium is "what, if anything, does this have to do with the real world?" After all, in the real world things change all the time; and in the real world there is no master economist who solves a large set of equations in order to determine the price of each good and the wage received by each worker. Walras believed that his mathematical solution to the system of equations would be the same solution reached by markets in the real world. But how could the real world achieve equilibrium without a master economist to solve the many mathematical equations?

Walras devised an answer which he felt showed that his abstract model and his mathematical equations were good depictions of actual reality. His answer was twofold. First, Walras held that all traders wanted to maximize utility, and that utility maximization and competition moved the whole economy to the set of equilibrium prices ground out by his equations. Second, Walras introduced the notions of the auctioneer and the *tâtonnement* (which means groping) process.

Imagine a big auction, where producers bring their goods to sell and where consumers come to buy goods. Producers set prices for their goods and these prices are called out by the auctioneer. Of course, at some prices, some goods will have too many buyers and other goods will have too few buyers. The auctioneer then notes these cases of too many buyers and too few buyers, and raises prices in the former case while lowering prices in the latter case. Buyers and sellers would then revise their offers to buy and sell goods. Again, there may be shortages of some goods while other goods will find too few buyers. The auctioneer would take this new information into account and again revise prices accordingly. Through successive iterations of this process, Walras argued, the auctioneer would grope towards the set of equilibrium prices for the whole auction. Only then would exchange take place and, at this set of equilibrium prices, all markets would clear. Walras thought that market prices naturally behaved the way that the mythical auctioneer did. Market prices do rise when there are more buyers than sellers, and they do fall whenever there are more sellers than buyers. In this way, the market system gropes its way to a position of general equilibrium.

Unfortunately, the auctioneer and the *tâtonnement* process do not fully solve the problem of real-world applicability. The groping process seems as divorced from reality as a set of mathematical equations proving general equilibrium. In the real world, trades take place *before* the final set of general equilibrium prices is reached through the groping process. Also, the final equilibrium will likely be affected by any exchanges that take place before the whole system balances (Hicks 1934).

Another problem with the *tâtonnement* process is that in the real world it is suppliers who change prices rather than omniscient auctioneers; and, being human, they may make mistakes and raise rather than lower prices (or vice versa). Moreover, many firms set prices based upon *expected* demand in the near future rather than on current conditions.

Finally, as von Neumann was quick to recognize, the mathematical solution to a Walrasian set of equations could conceivably contain negative prices. It could also contain prices whose value is zero. Yet in the real world this is impossible. Businesses will not give away goods for free. Nor will they produce goods and then pay people to purchase them, which is what would occur when we get negative prices after we solve a set of Walrasian equations.

All these problems, however, do not detract from the great achievement of Walras. Walras forced economists to focus on the interrelationships among different markets. He formalized the notion of general equilibrium, and showed economists how it was possible to study an interrelated economy as a set of mathematical equations. He raised the important issues of convergence to equilibrium and the stability of economic equilibrium, and he attempted to explain how economies could reach general equilibrium. For these achievements, Walras must certainly be regarded among the half dozen most important figures in the history of economics.

Works by Walras

Elements of Pure Economics (1874 and 1877), Homewood, Illinois, Irwin, 1954
Correspondence of Léon Walras and Related Papers, 3 vols, ed. W. Jaffé, Amerstam, North-Holland, 1965

Studies in Applied Economics:Theory of the Production of Social Wealth, London, Routledge, 2004

Works about Walras

Hicks, John R., "Léon Walras," *Econometrica*, 2, 4 (October 1934), pp. 338–48

Jaffé, William, *Essays on Walras*, ed. Donald A. Walker, Cambridge, Cambridge University Press, 1983

Jaffé, William, "The Antecedents and Early Life of Léon Walras," *History of Political Economy*, 16, 1 (1984), pp. 1–57

Schumpeter, Joseph, "Marie Esprit Léon Walras," in *Ten Great Economists*, New York, Oxford University Press, 1951, pp. 74–9

WILLIAM STANLEY JEVONS (1835–82)

William Stanley Jevons (pronounced Jev-uns, with a short e) is best known for developing a theory of relative prices, or exchange values, based upon the notion of marginal utility. In contrast to early nineteenth century classical economists, who held that the costs of production determined relative prices, Jevons argued that relative prices depend upon subjective assessments by people of the satisfaction to be gained from purchasing different goods. Jevons also made contributions to growth theory and business cycle theory.

Jevons was born into an upper middle class family in Liverpool, England, in 1835. His father was an iron merchant and his mother came from a prosperous family of bankers and lawyers. The family wealth enabled Jevons to receive an excellent education. At first he was tutored at home; then he attended private schools and University College, London, where he studied metallurgy and mathematics (with the world-famous Augustus DeMorgan).

When the British railway boom ended, the family iron business went bankrupt. To help his family deal with their financial problems, Jevons abandoned his studies in 1854. He then trained as an assayer and took a job at the Sydney Mint in Australia (Könekamp 1962, pp. 255f.).

A dispute over the funding of a railway line for New South Wales initially sparked his interest in economics, and Jevons was soon reading the great classical economists, especially Smith, Malthus, and Mill. A powerful desire to make the world better, especially a wish to help nations grow and prosper, prompted Jevons to continue his education. Returning to England in 1859, and to University College in 1860, Jevons studied mathematics, political economy, philosophy, and history. Although he was disappointed with his political economy courses and felt that he got more from reading on his own than from attending lectures, he continued with his studies and received both an undergraduate and a master's degree in political economy from University College.

Jevons then accepted a position at Owens College in Manchester, where he taught for the next thirteen years. In 1876, he left Owens College to become Professor of Political Economy at University College, London. This appointment had light teaching and few administrative duties, thus allowing Jevons the time to pursue his own writing. But by 1880 Jevons again found it difficult to juggle both his teaching duties and his writing ambitions, so he resigned from University College in order to focus more on writing. Unfortunately, by that time his health had deteriorated due to overwork, and two years later he collapsed while swimming and drowned.

The first book that Jevons published, *The Coal Question* (1865), was alarmist and Malthusian. It forecast a severe energy shortage for England. Jevons began by estimating the existing supply of coal in England. He then estimated the rate at which coal consumption was increasing. Putting these two estimates together, Jevons found a continually increasing demand for a depleting supply of coal reserves. The consequences could only be sharply rising coal prices. Even worse, at some point the dwindling supply of coal would stop economic growth in England.

Jevons was not optimistic that energy substitutes for coal could be found. Nor did he think conservation efforts could do anything but push back slightly the date at which economic growth would come to an end. More surprisingly, Jevons ignored two obvious policy solutions – a tax on coal and a prohibition on British coal exports. Instead, he advocated repaying the national debt so that, when the day of reckoning came, and the existing supply of resources was exhausted, there would be no other burdens on future generations.

The Coal Question brought instant fame to Jevons. Stories of the impending coal shortage filled British newspapers. John Stuart Mill praised Jevons in Parliament, and a Royal Commission on Coal was established to investigate the problem. However, panic about an energy crisis was premature. Jevons estimated that coal consumption in Britain would be 2,607 million tons by 1961 (based on 1861 levels of coal use and then current annual growth rates of 3.5 percent). Yet in 1962, actual coal usage in England was around 10 percent of his estimate – only 192 million tons (Black 1981, p. 16).

The primary reason Jevons was so far off the mark is that he did not foresee the development of coal substitutes such as petroleum, natural gas, and hydroelectric power. A personal disposition to fear what the future had in store apparently also came into play. Concerned about a shortage of writing paper, Jevons purchased such large stocks of paper that more than 50 years after his death his children had still not used it all up (Keynes 1951).

Jevons's lasting claim to fame, however, stems not from his fears about energy shortages, but from his efforts to bring utility analysis into economics. Jevons, J. B. Clark, and Menger, each independently, discovered the notion of subjective utility and the principle of diminishing marginal utility. These were both important discoveries, as they brought consumers and consumer behavior into economic analysis for the first time. But Jevons went even further than Menger by drawing out the implications and possible applications of utility analysis.

The discovery of the principle of diminishing marginal utility appears to have taken place in the late 1850s while Jevons was working in Australia. This idea is simply and concisely encapsulated in a letter of 1860 that he wrote to his brother: "One of the most important axioms is, that as the quantity of any commodity, for instance, plain food, which a man has to consume, increases, so the utility or benefit derived from the last portion used decreases in degree" (quoted in Keynes 1951, p. 280).

Several years later Jevons (1871) set forth the important distinction between total utility and marginal utility. This distinction led to the development of the modern theory of consumer behavior. Jevons noted that, as people consume more and more of any good, the total utility they get from consuming that good generally increases. But, as people consume more and more, the utility they get from each additional quantity, or the good's marginal utility, declines. Thus, the first glass of water to a thirsty man provides more satisfaction than the second or third glass. By the fifth or sixth glass, the man derives little additional utility from consuming more water. As we consume more and more water, our total utility goes up, but the extra utility that we get from the last glass falls.

According to Jevons, consumers will buy those goods that provide them with the greatest satisfaction. Whenever the consumer can freely switch purchases, buying more things that give him a lot of utility and reducing his spending on goods that provide little utility, the consumer will be better off. Going even further, Jevons argued that each consumer would alter his purchases so that they reach a state where no further spending could increase total utility.

This doctrine forms the foundation of *laissez-faire* policies that keep the government from regulating or taxing the goods and services that consumers buy. For example, if cigarettes or alcohol or drugs are freely available, consumers will buy only the amount of these goods that maximize their utility. If governments prevent the sales of these goods, or make their purchase difficult by imposing onerous regulations on producers or taxes on their sale, consumer satisfaction will fall because consumers will buy other goods, goods that they desire less. What is true of cigarettes and alcohol and drugs is true of all goods. The unrestricted availability of goods, without taxes and without any government regulations, raises the utility of each consumer and increases national well-being.

Jevons next applied the notion of utility to labor. By so doing, he helped show how wages are determined and how labor markets work. Jevons assumed that labor was disagreeable and therefore involved negative utility or disutility for the worker. On the other hand, labor also yields positive utility, since workers are paid for their efforts and can use this income to buy goods. Individuals have to balance the disutility of work against the utility of the goods that could be bought with the fruits of one's labor. As long as the utility of consumption exceeded the disutility of work, people would continue to work (Jevons 1957, ch. 5). At the point where the disutility of work exceeded the utility of consumption, people would stop working and enjoy leisure time instead.

This application of utility analysis to the labor market had several important consequences. First, the distinction between productive and unproductive labor, as originally set forth by Quesnay, was shown to be mistaken. All labor was productive in the sense that it yielded utility to individual workers, who could take their pay packet and buy goods with it. Second, employing utility theory to study labor casts doubt on the classical theory of wages (see **Malthus**). Humans were not at the mercy of a *subsistence wage*; rather, the labor supply depended upon the going wage. If wages got too low, workers would withdraw from the market and enjoy leisure. Third, in contrast to Ricardo and Marx, for Jevons there is no opposition between labor and capital. Labor makes its own decisions about whether or not to work, carefully balancing the gains and the losses from employment. Capitalists also make similar decisions when deciding whether or not to invest and hire more workers.

Finally, no accounting of the economic thought of Jevons would be complete without mentioning his theory of the business cycle. While doing extensive research on economic growth, Jevons (1884) noted a close relationship between sunspot activity and economic activity. Between 1721 and 1878 business cycles had an average duration of 10.46 years, while sunspot activity showed a periodicity of 10.45 years. Jevons felt that this relationship was too close to be accidental. He even set forth a few creative explanations for this similarity. If sunspot activity affected the weather, and the weather affected British harvests, then sunspot activity should be correlated with grain prices. A good harvest would increase the supply of grain and lower its price, while bad harvests would lead to higher grain prices. Jevons also looked to foreign trade to explain the similar solar and economic cycles. A more active sun, according to Jevons, influenced the rice harvest in India. A good harvest in India led to high demand for British manufactured goods. This, in turn, caused the British economy to expand. In contrast, less sunspot activity meant poor Indian harvests, little demand by India for British goods, and a slumping British economy.

Few contemporaries of Jevons, and few subsequent economists, have taken the sunspot theory of business cycles seriously. In addition, more recent data cast doubt on the figures Jevons used; astronomers have increased the solar sunspot cycle to 11.1 years, while economists have reduced the length of the business cycle to 7 or 8 years (Keynes 1951, p. 279). And, in contrast to Jevons, most contemporary economists look towards the economy itself, rather than outside forces, as the cause of periodic turns in prosperity and depression. Nevertheless, Jevons deserves recognition as one of the originators of business cycle theory.

Despite his linkages to the future through worries about the depletion of energy resources, and despite his linkages to the past as a business cycle historian, the major contribution of Jevons to economics remains his development of marginal utility theory and his use of this theory to explain consumption and work decisions. In all his work, Jevons was a pioneer, and the many advances due to Jevons make him one of the three or four most important nineteenth century economists.

Works by Jevons

The Coal Question: An Inquiry Concerning the Progress of the Nation, and the Probable Exhaustion of Our Coal-Mines, London, Macmillan, 1865
"Notice of a General Mathematical Theory of Political Economy," Statistical Journal, 29 (June 1866). Reprinted as an Appendix in Jevons (1957), pp. 303–14
The Theory of Political Economy (1871), New York, Kelley & Millman, 1957

The Principles of Science: A Treatise on Logic and Scientific Method, London, Macmillan, 1874

The State in Relation to Labour (1882), New Brunswick, New Jersey, Transaction Publishers, 2001

Investigations in Currency and Finance (1884), North Highlands, California, Best Books, 1984

Works about Jevons

Collison Black, R. D., "W. S. Jevons, 1835–82," in *Pioneers of Modern Economics in Britain*, ed. D. E. O'Brien and John R. Presley, London, Macmillan, 1981, pp. 1–35

Keynes, John Maynard, "William Stanley Jevons 1835–82," in *Essays in Biography*, New York, Norton, 1951, pp. 255–309

Könekamp, Rosamond, "William Stanley Jevons (1835–82): Some Biographical Notes," *Manchester School of Economic and Social Studies*, 30, 3 (1962), pp. 251–73

Maas, Harro, *William Stanley Jevons and the Making of Modern Economics*, New York, Cambridge University Press, 2005

Pert, Sandra, *The Economics of William Stanley Jevons*, London, Routledge, 1996

Schabas, Margaret, *A World Ruled by Number: William Stanley Jevons and the Rise of Mathematical Economics*, Princeton, New Jersey, Princeton University Press, 1990

CARL MENGER (1840–1921)

Carl Menger (pronounced MEN-GERR) is regarded as the founding father of the Austrian School of Economics. This is because he is responsible for developing two pillars of Austrian economics. First, Menger helped to establish a subjective theory of value. Second, he argued that economic knowledge can come only from deducing the consequences of assumptions that are known to be true.

Menger was born in 1840 in Neu-Sandec, Galicia (then part of Austria but now part of Poland). Very little is known about his upbringing or his education. His father was a lawyer, and Menger followed in his father's footsteps by studying law and political science, first at the University of Vienna and then at the University of Prague. In 1867 he received a doctorate in law from Kracow University.

After graduating, Menger worked first as a financial journalist for the leading Viennese newspaper and then in the press office of the Austrian Prime Minister. It was during this time that he worked on the *Principles of Economics* (Menger 1985).

With his reputation growing due to the *Principles*, Menger was appointed to a lectureship in the Law Faculty at the University of Vienna in 1873. Three years later he was promoted to the position of Professor Extraordinarius; but he soon resigned this position in order to tutor Crown Prince Rudolph and travel with him throughout Europe. In 1879, Menger accepted a teaching position in Vienna, and thereafter led the life of an academic economist – devoting all his energy and efforts to teaching and writing. Although he was made a member of the upper chamber of the Austrian Parliament in 1900, Menger preferred his work in economics to taking part in any political deliberations or debates (Hayek 1934, p. 417).

Menger made two important contributions to economics. One involved value theory and the other concerned economic methodology. Menger was one of the first economists to discover the marginal utility theory of value and the principle of diminishing marginal utility, and he was one of the earliest advocates of a subjective theory of value. Menger was also involved in a heated debate over the nature of economics and the proper way to do economic analysis.

During the late nineteenth century, classical economics was held in low esteem on the European continent. Especially dissatisfying was the highly abstract and theoretical nature of British economics. Menger sought to bring economics back to the real world. His starting point in this endeavor was a recognition that goods have value because they meet human needs.

In contrast to the classical British economists, Menger argued that value was determined by subjective factors (utility or the beliefs of people about what gives them pleasure) rather than by objective factors (the costs of production). For Menger, value did not exist objectively within goods themselves. Rather, value arises because people make judgments about the worth of particular goods. Diamonds and gold are not valuable in and of themselves. They have value only because human beings desire them and find them useful.

Value, for Menger, thus comes from the satisfaction of human needs. Human needs create a demand for goods; they also become the driving force for the development of institutions such as private property and money that help them to meet their needs. Finally, human needs result in economic exchange and help determine prices. Furthermore, Menger argued that, since human needs were greater than the goods available to satisfy these needs, people would choose rationally among all alternative goods made available to them.

Menger (1985, p. 127) illustrated these principles with a table, which is reproduced here as Table 1. Each column in the table represents a different type of good. The numbers under the Roman numerals represent how important a particular good is to some individual, or the degree of satisfaction obtained by consuming that good. Goods must satisfy the subjective needs of consumers, according to Menger, and consumers must recognize this fact if goods are to have any value.

Table 1 Menger's principles of value

I	II	III	IV	V	VI	. . . X
10	9	8	7	6	5	1
9	8	7	6	5	4	0
8	7	6	5	4	3	0
7	6	5	4	3	2	0
6	5	4	3	2	1	0
5	4	3	2	1	0	0

Menger also recognized that, as one purchases greater and greater quantities of a good, each succeeding quantity purchased will yield less satisfaction to the consumer. That is, people experience *diminishing marginal utility* when they consume more of any good (see **Jevons**). Thus, Table 1 shows that the first units consumed of any kind of good yield the greatest utility, and each succeeding unit yields less and less utility.

Unfortunately, Menger gave few examples of the goods that belong in each category. He stated that Category I goods are those that preserve life; Category II goods preserve health; Category III goods provide for individual welfare (that is, future life and health); and Category IV goods are various types of diversions. Category I might thus represent food; Category II medical care; and Category IV entertainment.

Menger was also not clear about what the numbers in his table actually measure. It is clear, however, that the numbers are supposed to measure relative wants or the satisfaction received from consuming different goods (Menger 1985, pp. 163–76). Menger was also clear about how individuals make decisions regarding what to consume or how to spend their money. Since consumers have limited income at their disposal, individuals will first buy those goods that satisfy greater needs. Goods with a subjective value of 10 will be consumed before goods with a value of 9, which in turn will be consumed before goods valued with 8 or less.

One important consequence of this theory of value is that all activities yielding subjective satisfaction are productive activities. In contrast to the British classical economists, trade was productive according to Menger because people would not trade unless they felt the goods that they received would give them more utility than the goods they gave up. And in contrast to Quesnay, agriculture and manufacturing could both be productive activities because the goods produced by each of these economic sectors yield satisfaction to consumers.

Another implication of the subjective theory of value is that the classical *labor theory of value* (see **Ricardo**) had to be wrong. As Menger (1985, p. 145) noted:

> The determining factor in the value of a good, then, is neither the quantity of labor or other goods necessary for its production nor the quantity necessary for its reproduction, but rather the magnitude of importance of these satisfactions with respect to which we are conscious.

Since value comes from the individual, according to Menger, economic analysis must begin with studying the individual. This position has come to be known as *methodological individualism*.

Menger also recognized that factors of production (land, labor, and capital) have value because they satisfy wants indirectly; these factors are needed to produce the goods that people directly desire. To find the actual value of a factor of production, Menger thought that we should withdraw one unit of the factor (say one worker) and observe the loss in output. The value of this output is the value added by that worker. It represents the consumer satisfaction produced by that worker. The value created by each factor of production thus depended upon its *marginal productivity*; and the return or payment to each factor used in producing goods should depend on the anticipated value created by that factor (Menger 1985, p. 124).

From 1875 to 1884 Menger was absorbed in a heated methodological dispute with Gustav Schmoller, a leader of the German Historical School. Dispute might be too euphemistic a description of what was more an exchange of insults than a true scholarly debate. Moreover, the exchange itself was quite strange considering that Menger dedicated his *Principles* to Roscher, another leader of the Historical School.

According to the Historical School, economic laws have to be found in historical facts accumulated over long periods of time. Until the facts were set forth, it would be premature to develop any economic theories. The right way to understand an economy was to look at historical data, find regularities, and then make inferences about how the economy worked. The Historical School rejected the abstract-deductive method of doing economics, where economic principles were derived from assumed characteristics of people and markets. Instead, they accepted a relativism regarding economic relations and economic policy. For the Historical School the world worked differently at different times and in different places.

In contrast, theory development took precedence over data accumulation for Menger. Menger thought that proper scientific method involved the search for essential characteristics of economic phenomena, or necessary connections between economic variables (such as the fact that lower prices for some good causes people to buy more of that good). Historical or empirical economics could not do this, since sometimes prices fall and people expect further price declines, so they buy less now. Consequently, historical economics could not yield definitive results. Only introspection yields absolute and necessary truths, according to Menger. Trying to refute laws of economics by pointing to contrary real-world evidence was like trying to refute the laws of geometry by measuring the angles of a triangle to see if they equaled 180 – even the attempt to do this shows a fundamental misunderstanding of geometry.

Menger's *Investigations into the Method of Social Sciences* (1883) sought to put economics on firm theoretical and methodological foundations. In so doing, Menger defended his method of doing economics and argued against the method of the Historical School. Menger strongly emphasized the individualistic method of analysis and the fact that economic knowledge is derived *a priori*, or before the experience of real-world economies. Studying economics for Menger involved studying individual preferences (or demand) and explaining how these lead to observable phenomena like different prices for different goods.

The *Investigation* provoked hostile attacks from members of the Historical School, including Schmoller. These attacks were responded to in kind by Menger's students and followers. Schmoller refused to have any more books written by Menger reviewed in his journal, and he announced publicly that followers of Menger were not fit to fill any teaching positions (Hayek 1934, p. 407).

Eventually the debate ended, more as a result of boredom than through a final resolution of the issues. Menger's method became the accepted method of doing economics, although there have been many prominent critics of this methodology (see **Leontief** and **Bergmann**). The major effect of the debate has probably been to give economic *methodology*, a study of the methods used to obtain economic knowledge, a bad reputation. As Schumpeter (1951) notes, most economists have felt this debate to be a total waste of time; and from it they have generalized the lesson that all methodological discussion in economics is a waste of time. But this outcome has probably hurt the economics profession, for, as Hutchinson (1973, p. 36) points out, "critical examination of the assumptions, concepts and theories of economists . . . is seldom, if ever, a waste of time."

Major economists usually leave a legacy of ideas and theories that come to be accepted by other economists and that form part of the economic wisdom taught to future generations. A few make their mark because they dared to step outside the mainstream and were able to inspire a group of students or followers. Menger is the rare figure who fits into both categories. His emphasis on the individual, and his argument that we must explain the economic world as responses to subjective individual assessments, make Menger a founder of the Austrian School of Economics (Alter 1990; Vaughn 1994). But with his discovery of utility as a source of value and his discovery of the principle of diminishing marginal utility, Menger also fits into the former category.

Works by Menger

Principles of Economics, trans. J. Dingwall and B. F. Hoselitz (1871), New York and London, New York University Press, 1985

Investigations into the Method of the Social Sciences (1883), Grove City, Pennsylvania, Libertarian Press, 1990

The Collected Works of Carl Menger, 4 vols, ed. Friedrich Hayek, London, London School of Economics and Political Science, 1934–6

Works about Menger

Alter, Max, *Carl Menger and the Origins of Austrian Economics*, Boulder, Colorado, Westview Press, 1990

Bloch, Henri-Simon, "Carl Menger: The Founder of the Austrian School," *Journal of Political Economy*, 48, 3 (1940), pp. 428–33

Caldwell, Bruce J. (ed.), *Carl Menger and His Legacy in Economics*, Durham, North Carolina, and London, Duke University Press, 1990

Hayek, Friedrich, "Carl Menger," *Economica*, 1 (November 1934), pp. 393–420

Hutchinson, T. W., "Some Themes from *Investigations into Method*," in *Carl Menger and the Austrian School of Economics*, ed. J. R. Hicks and W. Weber, Oxford, Clarendon Press, 1973, pp. 15–37

Schumpeter, Joseph, "Carl Menger, 1840–1921," in Joseph Schumpeter, *Ten Great Economists From Marx to Keynes*, New York, Oxford University Press, 1951, pp. 80–90

Stigler, George, "The Economics of Carl Menger," *Journal of Political Economy*, 45 (April 1973), pp. 229–50

Vaughn, Karen L., *Austrian Economics in America*, New York, Cambridge University Press, 1994

ALFRED MARSHALL (1842–1924)

Alfred Marshall is responsible for what Keynes (1951, p. 157) called "diagrammatic economics," or the translation of economic concepts into simple graphs. He is also responsible for introducing many of these concepts into economic analysis. Finally, more than anyone else, Marshall helped make economics a field of study in its own right.

Marshall was born in Bermondsey, a working class district of London, in 1842. His father was a clerk at the Bank of England; his mother was a butcher's daughter. Although the family were not well-to-do, they placed a high value on education and sent Marshall to good schools. Like John Stuart Mill, Marshall was pushed hard by his father and forced to study late into the night. Despite the fact that his father stressed the classics and languages (and perhaps even because of this), Marshall was drawn to mathematics rather than the humanities.

With financial help from his uncle, Marshall attended Cambridge University, where he studied mathematics, philosophy, and political economy. His interests in philosophy were particularly strong. During frequent mountain-climbing excursions in the Alps, Marshall would find a good spot for reading and contemplation, and there he would study the classic works in philosophy.

However, Marshall decided to specialize in economics. One important factor in this decision was his walks through "the poorest quarters of several cities . . . looking at the faces of the poorest people" (Keynes 1951, p. 137; also see Rima 1990). After receiving a degree in the moral sciences (there was no economics degree at Cambridge at the time), Marshall taught for nine years at St. John's College, Cambridge. He then taught briefly at Bristol and at Balliol College, Oxford. In 1885 he returned to Cambridge, where he taught until his retirement in 1908.

Many of the notions and modes of analysis introduced by Marshall still provide the basis for undergraduate education in microeconomics, particularly in introductory microeconomics courses. Marshall studied individual markets in isolation, pretty much ignoring the impact that one market has on other markets and that these other markets, in turn, have on every market. This made Marshall the founder of *partial equilibrium analysis*. In contrast, Léon Walras studied the many interrelationships among all markets in the economy, or *general equilibrium analysis*. While neither as complete nor as comprehensive as general equilibrium analysis, partial equilibrium analysis has the advantage of focusing on the practical problems facing a particular firm and industry.

In order to study individual markets, Marshall developed the tools of supply and demand analysis. The upward-sloping supply curve demonstrated the *law of supply* – as prices rise, firms will produce more and bring to market greater quantities of any good. The downward-sloping demand curve showed the *law of demand* – as prices fall, consumers buy greater quantities of a good. The "two scissors" of supply and demand determined the price for each good and the amount of each good that would be produced. In contrast to the demand-driven approach of Jevons, and in contrast to the supply-driven approach of Ricardo, Marshall emphasized that supply and demand jointly determined prices and production.

Marshall argued that competition would force actual prices towards the equilibrium price. If prices were set above the equilibrium level, firms would not be able to sell what they produced and would see their inventories pile up. This would signal to the firm that it must lower prices and cut production. On the other hand, if prices were set below equilibrium, shortages would result. People would line up to buy a limited stock of goods and many consumers would have to be told that some good was "sold out." Businesses would take this as a sign to increase prices and production. As Figure 2 shows, only at the equilibrium point would firms sell all they produced and tend to keep their prices the same (barring any change in either supply or demand).

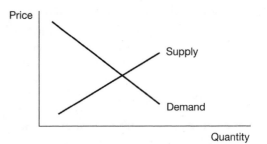

Figure 2 Supply, demand, and equilibrium

Marshall recognized that his "two blades" were complex constructions. He then went on to analyze supply and demand in greater detail. Following Jevons and others, demand was governed by the utility or satisfaction that people received from consuming a particular good. Consumers were forever attempting to get the greatest utility from what they purchase and consume. They would compare the additional satisfaction from buying one good with the additional satisfaction that would result from alternative purchases. When a good was priced highly, consumers could buy very little of that good because they could get more utility from using their money to purchase many other goods.

Marshall (1920, p. 97) defined a change in demand as the purchase of more (or less) of a good by people *at the same price*. Changes in the demand relationship, or shifts in the demand curve, could result from several causes – changes in wealth, population changes, changes in tastes, a change in the price of other goods, or changed expectations about future prices (Marshall 1920, book 3, ch. 4). Greater wealth and a larger population would increase demand, as shown in Figure 3. This would push up prices. Advertising could change consumer tastes and cause demand to increase. Likewise, expectations of greater prices in the future would push up demand and prices since people would want to buy now, before prices go up.

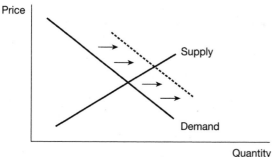

Figure 3 Shifts in demand

The impact of a change in the price of other goods is a bit more complicated to analyze. Normally, when the price of some good, such as gasoline, increases, people buy less gasoline and spend their money on other items. Thus demand for goods other than gasoline should rise. However, there are some cases when the reverse is true. *Complementary goods* are sets of goods usually consumed together. Any good consumed with gasoline, like automobiles (especially "gas guzzlers"), would experience reduced demand when the price of gasoline rose.

Supply, in contrast to demand, was governed by the costs of production. Producers, like consumers, were always trying to maximize; but the producer wanted to maximize profits from production. Due to *diminishing returns* and the rising cost of parts and labor, greater output could be produced only at rising costs. Businesses would therefore only produce more goods if they received a higher price. Hence the Marshallian supply curve was positively sloped.

Like demand, the supply relationship could shift. And like shifts in demand, a shift in supply means more (or less) of the good gets produced and sold *at each price*. The main factor causing supply to shift is a change in the costs of production. Higher wages, for example, would raise the costs of production – no matter how much was produced. Business could make the same amount of profit only if they pass these higher costs on to consumers in the form of higher prices. An increase in wages would therefore shift supply to the left. This shift would lead to higher prices. In contrast, improved technology, by reducing the amount of labor necessary to produce goods, would lower unit costs, shift supply down (or to the right). This leads to lower prices, as shown in Figure 4 (Marshall 1920, book 5, ch. 3).

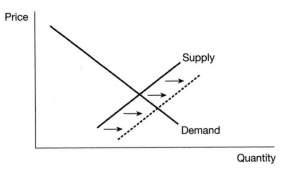

Figure 4 Shifts in supply

One of Marshall's most important contributions to economics was his formulation of the notion of elasticity. Virtually all economic relationships are cause-and-effect relationships. The notion of elasticity attempts to ascertain *how much* of an effect a given cause has. If some cause has a large effect, the relationship is said to be elastic; if the cause has a small effect, the relationship is inelastic. Marshall also developed a mathematical formula to measure exactly how elastic or inelastic any economic relationship was.

The price *elasticity of demand* concerns how much a given change in price alters the amount of a good consumers would purchase (Marshall 1920, book 3, ch. 3). Marshall identified several factors that determined whether the demand for a particular good was likely to be elastic or inelastic. One important factor was the ease of substitution. If goods were necessities and there were few alternatives, then demand for the good was likely to be price inelastic; consumers would have to keep buying the good when its price increased because they had no alternatives. During the energy crisis of the 1970s, for example, despite a quadrupling of gasoline prices, people still needed to drive. And they were stuck with their expensive cars that consumed a great deal of gasoline. So consumers paid the higher prices and cut back very little on their consumption of gasoline.

Marshall also explained why price itself was an important determinant of demand elasticity. For a container of salt, whose price is very low, a large percentage change in price would have little effect on consumption because the extra money spent on salt due to a large price increase would be rather trivial. In contrast, when expensive items (such as automobiles or a college education) increase in price by a large percentage, consumers must spend a good deal more of their income to buy these goods. Thus they are less likely to purchase them. Consequently, demand for expensive goods tends to be elastic and demand for inexpensive goods tends to be inelastic.

Finally, Marshall stressed that time was an important factor in determining the elasticity of demand, with demand becoming more elastic over time. As we have seen, after the large increases in gasoline prices in the 1970s people found it difficult to cut back on their gasoline purchases. But over time, they started buying more fuel-efficient cars, automobile manufacturers produced cars that gave better gas mileage, mass-transit systems were improved and expanded, and people learned to use car pools. All of these changes eventually helped to reduce the amount of gasoline bought.

Marshall also applied the notion of price elasticity to the supply relationship. The price elasticity of supply measured how much more businesses would produce and seek to sell in response to a given change in price. Here, too, time was an important factor.

The shortest time period of all Marshall called "the market period." It is best to think of the market period as the time after the farmer harvests his crops and sets out a stand displaying his fruits and vegetables. Everything that is brought to market must be sold or it will spoil. In this case, production cannot respond to price changes. The supply curve will be vertical, or nearly vertical, and demand will determine price.

In the short run, higher prices can affect production to some extent. Firms can work their current employees and equipment for more hours. But equipment cannot be expanded in the short run, and new firms cannot enter an industry in the short run. So there are limits to how many more goods can be supplied. Any increase in demand will lead to some increase in production and some increase in price.

The long run is the period of time that allows firms to expand their plants and equipment. In addition, in the long run firms can enter and exit the industry. Output can therefore be readily expanded at more or less constant cost, making the long-run supply curve fairly flat or horizontal. From this Marshall concluded that, over short time periods, demand was the more important determinant of price; but given enough time, it was supply or the costs of production that determined prices.

Since Marshall was drawn to economics by moral considerations and a desire to help the poor, it is not surprising that he was especially concerned with the problems of income distribution and poverty. Marshall traced the problem of poverty to the labor market (Rima 1990). The labor market operated just like the market for any good. The only difference was that in the labor market businesses were doing the demanding and households were doing the supplying. For Marshall, the supply of unskilled labor was determined by a Malthusian *population principle* – in response to higher wages, the population would increase and so would the labor supply. The demand for unskilled labor, however, was constantly decreasing due to mechanization. These two forces keep wages down for the unskilled, and kept them earning poverty-level incomes.

Marshall argued that individuals lacking broad and extensive skills, and individuals lacking any bargaining position in the labor market, could only receive low wages. This led to poor health and poor education, which in turn led to low productivity and low wages for their children. Poverty persisted from generation to generation because nothing was done to break the cycle of poverty (Marshall 1920, book 6, chs 4–6). Unfortunately, Marshall said little about how to raise wages for those with few skills, and even less about how to reduce poverty. He refused to advocate either minimum wages or legislation to help develop trade unions. His only suggestions were that the unskilled limit their family size and that progressive taxation be used to help the poor (Marshall 1920, p. 719; 1917, pp. 317–29). Ultimately, Marshall looked to education as a solution to the problem of poverty (Marshall 1920, pp. 717–18).

Although most famous for his contributions to microeconomics, Marshall did make some macroeconomic contributions as well. He employed the notion of *purchasing power parity* to explain what determines exchange rates between the currencies of two different countries (Marshall 1923). The idea behind this notion is rather simple and straightforward. Some goods are sold virtually everywhere throughout the world. By comparing the cost of these goods from country to country we can obtain a good measure of the relative value of two different currencies. If a McDonald's hamburger sells for $1 in the United States and for 100 yen in Japan, then $1 and 100 yen should represent equivalent incomes. According to the purchasing power parity theory, regardless of the actual exchange rate between the dollar and the yen, $1=100 yen should be used when comparing incomes in the US and Japan, since $1 and 100 yen have the same purchasing power or can buy the same things.

In addition, according to the purchasing power parity theory, exchange rates between the yen and the dollar will tend towards this level. Several forces operating in the world economy ensure this outcome. If goods are cheaper in Japan, those holding US dollars will seek to buy Japanese yen so that they can buy goods more cheaply in Japan and import them into the US. This will push up the price of the yen until purchasing power parity is reached. Conversely, if goods are cheaper in the US, the Japanese will seek to buy US dollars in order to buy cheaper US goods, thereby pushing up the price of the dollar for Japanese citizens and moving us towards purchasing power parity.

Despite the many new concepts advanced by Marshall, his main contribution to economics may have been institutional rather than substantive. Marshall, more than anyone else, is responsible for establishing economics as a separate subject and discipline. When Marshall returned to Cambridge University in 1885, economics was still part of the curriculum in the moral sciences and history. It was merely one subject that historians and philosophers were required to take in order to get their degree. Marshall set out to make economics an independent field of study in its own right, one with standards as high as the physical and biological sciences. Yet Marshall also wanted economics to be a practical science, assisting government officials and business leaders in making important decisions.

In 1903 Marshall succeeded in this endeavor; a separate school and degree in Economics was started at Cambridge University Other academic institutions soon followed the lead of Cambridge, and economics became a recognized discipline throughout the world. As a result, students throughout the world were able to major in economics, and to study the many notions introduced by Marshall. For all these reasons Marshall was the most eminent economist of his day, and remains among the half dozen or so most important figures in the history of economics.

Works by Marshall

Elements of Economics of Industry, London, Macmillan, 1879
Principles of Economics (1890), London, Macmillan, 8th edn, 1920
"National Taxation after the War," *After-War Problems*, ed. W. H. Dawson, London, Allen & Unwin, 1917, pp. 313–45
Industry and Trade, London, Macmillan, 1919
Money, Credit and Commerce, London, Macmillan, 1923
The Pure Theory of Foreign Trade, London, London School of Economics and Political Science, 1930
The Early Writings of Alfred Marshall, 1867–1890, 2 vols, ed. John K. Whitaker, New York, Free Press, 1975

Works about Marshall

Groenewegen, Peter, *A Soaring Eagle: Alfred Marshall 1842–1924*, Brookfield, Vermont, Edward Elgar, 1995
Keynes, John Maynard, "Alfred Marshall, 1842–1924," *Economic Journal*, 34 (September 1924), pp. 311–72. Reprinted in *Essays in Biography*, New York, Norton, 1951, pp. 125–217
Pigou, A. C. (ed.), *Memorials of Alfred Marshall*, London, Macmillan, 1925
Reisman, David, *The Economics of Alfred Marshall*, New York, St. Martin's Press, 1986
Reisman, David, *Alfred Marshall's Mission*, New York, St. Martin's Press, 1990
Rima, Ingrid, "Marshall's Concern about Poverty: A Hundredth Anniversary Retrospective," *Review of Social Economy*, 48 (Winter 1990), pp. 415–35

FRANCIS YSIDRO EDGEWORTH (1845–1926)

Francis Edgeworth studied how economies could achieve the best or optimal distribution of resources. His main contribution was to apply advanced mathematical techniques in an attempt to answer this question. In this endeavor, Edgeworth developed many modern tools of microeconomic analysis – utility functions, indifference curves, contract curves, and the Edgeworth box.

Edgeworth was born in Edgeworthstown, Ireland, in 1845 into a famous and wealthy family. His grandfather was the educationist, Richard Lovell Edgeworth, and his aunt was the novelist Maria

Edgeworth. Edgeworth received an excellent classical and humanistic education at the hands of private tutors. At the age of seventeen, he entered Trinity College, Dublin, to study languages. Then, in 1867, Edgeworth went to Oxford University to study the humanities. He obtained an MA degree in 1877 and also published his first book, a work on ethics (Edgeworth 1877) that attempted to bring other moral theories under the rubric of utilitarianism. Edgeworth then began to study commercial law and mathematics.

In the late 1870s Edgeworth lectured at Bedford College in London. His neighbor, William Stanley Jevons, interested Edgeworth in mathematics and statistics, and how they could be applied to economics. Edgeworth quickly saw that mathematics could aid economic reasoning and could check the arguments made in ordinary English (Creedy 1986, p. 15). He then began publishing articles and books that employed mathematical techniques to demonstrate economic principles. These publications eventually earned him a teaching position at King's College, London, and then a highly prized chair – Drummond Professor of Political Economy at All Souls College, Oxford.

In 1891, Edgeworth became the first editor of the *Economic Journal*. Over the next thirty-five years, he molded and developed the journal, making it into one of the most distinguished and important economic journals in the world. During this time period he served either as editor or joint editor (with Keynes).

In all his work, Edgeworth looked to the differential calculus as a "master key" that would unlock all the wisdom of economics. Starting with clear definitions and mathematically precise axioms, and proceeding with rigorous demonstrations of his conclusions, Edgeworth hoped to put economics on the same footing as mathematics and the hard sciences. Only then, he felt, could questions of economic policy be adequately addressed and solved. Edgeworth also felt mathematics was esthetically more elegant than mere prose, was more precise than prose, and was therefore philosophically superior to the verbal arguments of Adam Smith and the other classical economists. Ironically, his poor prose and his convoluted mathematics make Edgeworth difficult to read, even for those economists who have specialized trained in mathematical economics.

Edgeworth was primarily interested in the issues of exchange and distribution; in particular, he studied how the benefits of trade or exchange are distributed between individuals and between countries.

One important contribution due to Edgeworth (and Pareto) concerned the notion of utility, a concept that had become popular among British economists due to the influence of Bentham and Mill. Early utilitarians relied upon the notion of *cardinal utility*, which required that consumers know *how much* more utility they received from good A than they received from good B. Edgeworth moved economists from focusing on cardinal utility to focusing on *ordinal utility*, which involved a rank ordering of consumer preferences based upon the utility derived from each good. Ordinal utility was less stringent than cardinal utility because it required consumers to know only that they preferred good A to good B (or vice versa), or that they were indifferent between the two goods (see **Pareto**).

Edgeworth used this ordinal view of utility to develop the notion of an *indifference curve*. This curve is a set of points representing combinations of two goods that provide the same amount of utility to a particular individual. This notion is easiest to understand if we consider a simple case with just two goods – pretzels and beer. To start, let us take some combination of these goods, say three beers and three bags of pretzels. If I have either more beer or more pretzels, my utility should increase since I have more things. For my utility to remain at the same level, whenever I have more beer then I must have fewer pretzels (and vice versa). We can consider continually increasing the quantity of one good and decreasing the quantity of the other to make sure that utility stays the same for the consumer. The set of all such points would be an indifference curve for numerous possible combinations of beer and pretzels. Such a curve is shown in Figure 5.

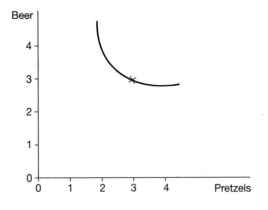

Figure 5 The indifference curve

Starting with more beer or more pretzels, we could trace out another indifference curve, one yielding greater utility than our original curve. This new curve would be to the northeast of the indifference curve sketched in Figure 5, and would include combinations like four beers and four bags of pretzels. Since more goods yield greater utility, this indifference curve would represent more utility, or a better situation for our consumer. Similarly, starting with fewer beers or fewer pretzels would let us trace out a new indifference curve yielding less utility than our original indifference curve. This would lie to the southwest of the curve sketched in Figure 5.

Edgeworth assumed that indifference curves would be convex to the origin, as shown in Figure 5, rather than a straight line. This is because of *diminishing marginal utility*. As I consume more and more beer, the extra utility I receive from another beer declines. The first beer quenches my thirst and helps me relax after a hard day at work; the second beer also helps me to relax. But the ninth beer provides few additional benefits over and above the eighth beer, and as cases of extreme drunkenness and alcohol poisoning show, may even provide negative utility. What is true of beer is also true of pretzels. A first bag satisfies my hunger, a second and subsequent bags provide less utility, while a tenth bag of pretzels is likely to make me sick.

Edgeworth next applied the tool of indifference curves to analyze exchange. Exchange can occur between two people (barter), which is how Edgeworth thought of it, or as trade between two countries, which is how many contemporary economists employ the Edgeworth analysis. This theory of exchange constitutes the main contribution to economics made by Edgeworth. It shows diagrammatically how exchange benefits both parties, and also shows how the final result of any exchange was likely to be indeterminate.

Consider two countries (Germany and Belgium), each of which produces two goods (again, pretzels and beer). In each country people have their own set of indifference curves, and firms in each country will want to satisfy consumer demand as best they can, for this is how they make money. So production within each country will tend to maximize the utility of its citizens, or reach their highest indifference curve (the best possible combination of the two goods). With their own national resources, Belgium finds its highest indifference curve, and produces 40 million cases of beer and 10 million tons of pretzels. Likewise, Germany seeks its highest indifference curve, producing 40 million cases of beer and 60 million tons of pretzels. The *Edgeworth Box* is constructed by flipping one country's indifference curve upside down and linking it with the indifference curve for the other country. In Figure 6, Germany is flipped around, so that higher indifference curves for Germany are further down or to the southwest. Point A in Figure 6 shows the optimal situation for the two countries before they engage in any international trade. It should be thought of as the best each country could do on its own.

Edgeworth noted that both Belgium and Germany could improve their well-being by moving from point A to any point within the ellipse or eyepiece formed by the intersection of their two indifference curves. Points like B and C lie on higher indifference curves for each country, and make each country better off. These points could be reached only if Germany and Belgium traded with one another. Belgium moves to a higher indifference curve by trading beer with Germany for more pretzels; and Germany moves to a higher indifference curve by giving up pretzels in exchange for beer.

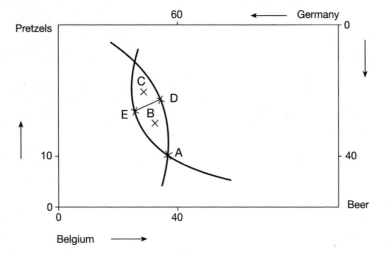

Figure 6 The Edgeworth Box

In contrast to this situation, consider what happens as we move along the line segment drawn between D and E. Belgium can become better off only if Germany becomes worse off, and Germany can become better off only if Belgium becomes worse off. If Germany goes to a higher indifference curve, then Belgium must be on a lower indifference curve, and vice versa.

Edgeworth called the set of points at which the indifference curves of Germany and Belgium can be tangent to each other (points between D and E in Figure 6) the *"contract curve."* These points represent the best possible situations for the two countries (starting at point A). In reality, however, the curve is as much a conflict curve as a contract curve. Both countries are better off when on the contract curve than when they reject trade (and remain at point A); yet once on the contract curve the two countries are in conflict – one country gets more if the other country gets less. At point E, Germany goes to a much higher indifference curve and receives all the gains from trade, while Belgium is neither better off nor worse off. Conversely, at point D, all the gains from trade go to Belgium. Edgeworth next sought to find out whether there would be one unique solution in a situation like this, or how the gains from trade would actually get divided up between the two parties. He discovered that there is not likely to be just one trading equilibrium point. The point on the contract curve that the two countries eventually settle on will involve bargaining between Belgium and Germany over the gains from trade. The country that gains more will be the one that is better at bargaining, or the country that can more easily do without the good produced by the other country (see **Mill**).

Edgeworth next went on to show that the degree of indeterminacy in the final outcome was a function of the number of traders on each side. If many countries produced pretzels for export and only a few produced beer, Germany would not be able to extract such a good bargain against Belgium. All the pretzel-producing countries would compete against each other by offering lots of pretzels for each beer received from Belgium. Similarly, with many beer producers and no other pretzel producers, the trading advantage would favor Germany. Everyone wants Germany's pretzels, but Germany can go to many different places to get beer.

In addition to his work in economic theory, Edgeworth (1996) made several contributions to statistical analysis, including work on drawing statistical inferences and developing the *correlation coefficient* (see Stigler 1978). This number, which can vary from zero to one, shows the association between two economic variables; in particular, it shows how closely two variables are related to one another. A correlation coefficient of zero shows that the two variables are not related at all and do not move together. A value of one shows the two variables move in unison; whenever one variable changes we can predict with 100 percent certainty how the other variable will change.

Rather uncharacteristically, his work in mathematical statistics had a very practical side to it, which Edgeworth drew out and explained.

In two papers Edgeworth (1886, 1888) showed how the past history of demand for withdrawals would let a bank estimate the probability that a certain amount of cash in the bank would be adequate to meet daily customer withdrawals. This computation allowed a bank to determine how much money it could lend out and how much money it had to keep on hand as a contingency fund against depositors coming to the bank to withdraw their money.

Notwithstanding this practical application of his work, Edgeworth wanted above all to establish theorems about economic principles. This approach to the study of economics has greatly influenced other economists. Edgeworth also developed several important tools of economic analysis. For these reasons, Edgeworth was one of the five or six most important economists of the early twentieth century.

Works by Edgeworth

New and Old Methods of Ethics: Or "Physical Ethics" and "Methods of Ethics", Oxford, Parker, 1877

Mathematical Psychics: An Essay on the Application of Mathematics to the Moral Sciences, London, Kegan Paul, 1881

"Problems in Probabilities," *Philosophical Magazine*, 22 (1886), pp. 371–84

Metretike, or the Method of Measuring Probability and Utility, London, Temple, 1887

"The Mathematical Theory of Banking," *Journal of the Royal Statistical Society*, 51 (1888), pp. 113–27

Papers Relating to Political Economy, 3 vols, London, Macmillan, 1925

Writings in Probability, Statistics and Economics, 3 vols, ed. Charles R. McCann, Hampshire, Edward Elgar, 1996

Works about Edgeworth

Creedy, John, *Edgeworth and the Development of Neoclassical Economics*, Oxford, Blackwell, 1986

Creedy, John, "F. Y. Edgeworth, 1845–1926," in *Pioneers of Modern Economics in Britain*, ed. D. P. O'Brien and John R. Presley, Totowa, New Jersey, Barnes & Noble, 1981, pp. 72–104

Hicks, John, "Francis Ysidro Edgeworth," in *Economists and the Irish Economy from the Eighteenth Century to the Present Day*, ed. Antoin E. Murphy, Dublin, Irish Academic Press, 1984, pp. 157–74

Keynes, John Maynard, "Francis Ysidro Edgeworth: 1845–1926," in *Essays in Biography by John Maynard Keynes*, New York, Norton, 1951, pp. 218–38

Stigler, Stephen M., "Francis Ysidro Edgeworth, Statistician," *Journal of the Royal Statistical Society*, 141, 3 (1978), pp. 287–322

JOHN BATES CLARK (1847–1938)

John Bates Clark was one of several people who independently discovered the ideas of marginal utility and marginal productivity in the late nineteenth century. Clark also used the notion of marginal productivity to develop a theory of income distribution. He then used this theory to justify the existing income distribution as fair and equitable. In addition, Clark studied the impact of large monopolistic firms and powerful labor unions on the American economy, and he argued that, when such economic power existed, it should be restrained.

Clark was born in Providence, Rhode Island, in 1847. His father owned a dry-goods store there; but poor health caused him to move to Minnesota, where he started a small plow manufacturing business. Clark attended Brown University and Amherst College, where he acquired interests in both philosophy and ethics. After graduating, he spent three years studying in Switzerland and Germany at the Universities of Zurich and Heidelberg. At this time there were few graduate programs in the United States, and travel to Europe was necessary to pursue advanced studies. When Clark returned to the United States he accepted a teaching job at Carleton College, where among his students was Thorstein Veblen. Other teaching positions followed at Smith College, Amherst College, and Johns Hopkins University. Clark finally settled down at Columbia University, where he taught economics from 1895 to 1923 (with the exception of the 1898–9 academic year when he replaced Irving Fisher, who was recovering from tuberculosis, at Yale). In 1880 Clark helped to found the American Economic Association, now the largest and most prestigious organization of economists in the world. Three years later he became its President.

While teaching at Columbia University, Clark became active in the Peace Movement. Convinced that the threat of war was a great obstacle to improving the economic condition of man, he joined the League to Enforce Peace, actively supported the League of Nations, and became director of the Economic and History Division of the Carnegie Endowment for International Peace, which studied international war and militarism.

Clark's most important contribution to economics was undoubtedly his development of the *marginal productivity theory of distribution*. The theory was designed to explain the principles that determine how much income different people receive, and thus the principles affecting the distribution of income in an economy.

The precise inspiration for the marginal productivity theory of distribution remains somewhat obscure. Clark (1899, pp. viii, 84–5) himself stated that the theory was developed in response to Henry George, and was intended to prove George wrong about income distribution. George (1929, pp. 167–9) had held that rents stemmed from the monopoly power of landowners, and that rents existed only because there was a fixed stock of land and someone was willing to pay to use that land. Rents, therefore, were not morally justified and were not the result of human exertion. As a result, he proposed (like Quesnay) abolishing all existing taxes and instituting a single tax on land values.

Yet Clark's son (J. M. Clark 1952) and John Henry (1983) both contend that Clark developed the marginal productivity theory as a response to Marx, who claimed that workers were exploited because employers kept some of the value (the *surplus value*) that workers created. Numerous passages in the writings of Clark (1899, p. 7; 1890a, p. 43; 1904, pp. 34–6) appear to support this interpretation.

More than likely, Clark had both George and Marx in mind when working on his marginal productivity theory of distribution. *Contra* George, the theory shows that rental income is earned income; and *contra* Marx, it shows that workers are not exploited because the income they receive is equal to what they produce and contribute to society. A third motivation for the marginal productivity theory may have been a more pragmatic one. Late-nineteenth century America was the age of the robber baron (Josephson 1934). Labor organizations, such as the Knights of Labor and the American Federation of Labor, arose in response to growing business power, and union attacks on capitalism grew. Quite possibly, the marginal productivity theory also stemmed from a desire by Clark to justify business profits and thus defend capitalism from these attacks.

Whatever its inspiration, Clark used marginal productivity theory to argue that the existing distribution of income was fair – so long as the incomes received were part of a competitive process. Clark (1899, p. v) set forth the essence of his theory in the introduction to his book *The Distribution of Wealth*:

It is the purpose of this work to show that the distribution of the income of society is controlled by a natural law, and this law, if it worked without friction, would give to every agent of production the amount of wealth which that agent creates. However wages may be adjusted by bargains freely made between individual men, the rates of pay that result from such transactions tend ... to equal that part of the product of industry which is traceable to the labor itself. ... So far as it is not obstructed, [the economic system] assigns to everyone what he has specifically produced.

To understand marginal productivity theory it helps to consider a particular firm, say an educational institution. Whenever the school hires an additional teacher it can offer more classes and more courses of study, so it should experience increased enrollments. From each new student the school will receive additional revenue. If the new faculty member has a national or international reputation, the gain will be even greater; students from all over the country or around the world will come to learn from the new faculty member. The marginal productivity of the new faculty member is the increased revenue coming to the school hiring that person.

Clark took the position that if everyone was paid the value of their marginal productivity, no one could legitimately complain about how much income they received. Everyone would get exactly what they contributed to the production of goods and services. The resulting income distribution would be fair and everyone would be justly compensated. On the other hand, if someone received less than the value of their marginal product they were being robbed or exploited. Such a condition, Clark felt, would lead to potential social problems, as Marx recognized.

Under the marginal productivity theory of distribution, land is treated just like labor. It contributes to the value of output because things could not be produced without a place to put buildings and factories. Similarly, the land contains important raw materials that are needed in producing goods and services. For land's contribution to the value of output, landowners must be paid some rent. Thus, Henry George was wrong to claim that such incomes were not earned. Land contributes to production, and the owners of this land deserve some reward for this contribution.

Similarly, according to the marginal productivity theory, profits are justified by the contribution that capital equipment or machinery makes towards producing goods. Thus profits are not robbery; they are a return to capital. Moreover, as long as workers receive their marginal product, they receive a fair return for their efforts, even though they do not receive the surplus value that they create while working.

One question immediately raised by this theory has come to be called the product exhaustion or *adding-up problem*. There are two ways to look at this problem. First, is there enough money from the sale of a good to pay all factors of production their marginal product?

Does my school, Monmouth University, receive enough revenue to pay all members of faculty their marginal product? If not, someone will be exploited, because they receive less than their actual contribution to the revenue of the school. Second, if everyone gets paid their marginal product, and you add up all such payments, is there anything left over? This is a potential problem because if anything is left over after Monmouth pays all its faculty members and all other factors of production, we need some way to determine who gets this income and we need some way of deciding whether the division of this extra revenue will be fair.

Clark (1890a, 1891) asserted that the sum of all marginal productivities equals the total value of goods and services produced by a firm, and even developed a set of diagrams attempting to show this result (1899, ch. 13). He argued that any other result would tend to be eliminated through competition. Clark's argument, however, was not mathematically rigorous, and he failed to identify the restrictive circumstances under which this result held. It was left to Knut Wicksell to demonstrate the correct solution to the adding-up problem. Wicksell showed that only in the case of *constant returns to scale* would all factor payments equal the value of the good produced. Wicksell then argued that competition would lead to constant returns. None the less, Clark got the gist of the solution right; only when the forces of competition are strong will product exhaustion or adding-up not pose a problem for the marginal productivity theory of distribution.

Clark also made important contributions to economics through his study of competition and monopolies. Beginning with Adam Smith, economists have worried about the concentration of economic power in the hands of a few firms. Monopolies, through their market power, could restrict output and raise prices, thus giving consumers fewer and more expensive goods.

As we saw above, Clark held that competition was a positive force in the economy because it tended to make sure that everyone got their fair share, or the value of their marginal contribution to production. Whenever there is competition among firms, if an employer tried to pay a worker less than her marginal product, she would offer her services to another employer. And she should be able to find ready employment because other firms would benefit from hiring her. The firm would gain additional profits plus the worker's marginal product. This would exceed the wage rate that the employer would pay to the worker. But in the absence of competition among firms, this worker has limited options and must accept the wage offered by her employer.

This analysis had several important policy implications. Anything disturbing competition was anathema and to be opposed. This included unions that threatened to strike, and used this threat to extract wages higher than worker marginal products. Clark (1894, p. 494) thus led the fight for right-to-work (open shop) laws in the late nineteenth century. Restraints on competition, however, could also come from businesses; so Clark began to study monopolies, other forms of imperfect competition, and business practices that restrained competition.

In several articles, Clark (1890b, 1901, 1904) defended large firms, holding that monopolies and oligopolies were natural phenomena. Large firms with monopoly power, Clark held, were never really a problem because of potential competition. If a firm earned excessive or monopolistic profits, other firms would soon enter the industry, seeking a share of these high profits. In addition, Clark argued that, if a large firm abused its monopoly power, consumers and labor unions would attempt to use the legislature and the courts to reduce prices and break up the monopoly.

However, Clark (1900) did recognize that in the competitive process some producers might set their prices below their costs. Such actions attempt to drive competitors out of business, leading to monopoly power and greater profits in the future. When done domestically, this practice is called "*predatory pricing*"; when done by a foreign firm it is called "*dumping*." To deal with this potential problem, Clark emphasized the need to prevent any unfair methods of competition.

The Sherman Act of 1890, and the Standard Oil case of 1911, made predatory pricing illegal in the US. Unfortunately, it is always difficult in practice to prove whether firms are engaging in predatory pricing, and Clark provided no clear test to help us determine whether firms are engaging in this practice. If a firm is pricing below cost, this may be due to lack of demand for their product or because competitors can produce and sell goods at this low price. In the latter case, to remain competitive, the firm will have to cut its price to the same low level and hope it can survive by cutting costs.

Arguments over this issue have recently been raised by American businesses, which have accused Japanese firms of dumping goods in the US in order to develop a large market share and drive US firms into bankruptcy. Like predatory pricing, dumping is regarded as an illegitimate form of business competition because its goal is to develop monopoly power. The General Agreement on Tariffs and Trade (GATT) has an anti-dumping code that all nations are supposed to adhere to. But like predatory pricing, dumping has been difficult to prove in practice.

The one dominant theme running through the economics of J. B. Clark is the importance of competition among business firms. Competition is necessary to make sure that everyone gets paid what they contribute to the production process, and that we have a fair distribution of income. Competition is also necessary to keep large firms from abusing their economic power.

Although Clark's achievements do not rank him with the major British economists or the Continental marginalists, they do make him the most distinguished American economist in the late nineteenth and early twentieth centuries. Europe was the center of economic thought when Clark was alive and writing. But Clark led a parade of major American economists that would soon grow very large.

Works by Clark

The Philosophy of Wealth (1886), Seattle, University Press of the Pacific, 2004

Capital and Its Earnings (1888), Seattle, University Press of the Pacific, 2003

"The Law of Wages and Interest," *Annals of the American Academy of Political and Social Science*, 1 (July 1890a), pp. 43–65

"The 'Trust': A New Agent for Doing an Old Work: Or Freedom Doing the Work of Monopoly," *The New Englander and Yale Review*, 16, 3 (March 1890b), pp. 223–30

"Distribution as Determined by a Law of Rent," *Quarterly Journal of Economics*, 5 (1891), pp. 289–318

"The Modern Appeal to Legal Forces in Economic Life," *Publications of the American Economic Association*, (December 1894), pp. 481–502

The Distribution of Wealth (1899), Seattle, University Press of the Pacific, 2002

"Trusts," *Political Science Quarterly*, 15, 2 (January 1900), pp. 181–95

The Control of Trusts, New York, Macmillan, 1901

The Problem of Monopoly, New York, Columbia University Press, 1904

Works about Clark

Clark, J. M., "J. M. Clark on J. B. Clark," in *The Development of Economic Thought*, ed. H. W. Spiegel, New York, Wiley, 1952, pp. 592–612

Henry, John, "John Bates Clark and the Marginal Product: An Historical Inquiry into the Origins of Value-Free Economic Theory," *History of Political Economy*, 15, 3 (1983), pp. 375–89

Henry, John, *John Bates Clark: The Making of a Neoclassical Economist*, New York, St. Martin's Press, 1995

Other references

George, Henry, *Progress and Poverty* (1879), New York, Robert Schalenback Foundation, 1929

Josephson, Matthew, *The Robber Barons: The Great American Capitalists, 1861–1901*, New York, Harcourt Brace, 1934

VILFREDO PARETO (1848–1923)

Vilfredo Pareto (pronounced pa-RAY-tow) is remembered by economists primarily as one of the fathers of mathematical economics. Yet, late in life, Pareto rejected the trend to formalize economics. He came to believe that this approach was too narrow and could not yield a comprehensive understanding of how real economies worked. He then tried to broaden economics by incorporating political and sociological variables into his analysis of the economic system.

Pareto was born in Paris in 1848 while his father, a civil engineer, was in exile for opposing the policies of the Italian government. His family was middle class, and provided Pareto with a good education. They also imparted to him the values of hard work and moderate living. In 1858 the family returned to Italy, so Pareto was educated mainly in Italian public schools. He then went on to attend the Polytechnic Institute of Turin, receiving an engineering degree in 1869 and finishing first in his graduating class.

After receiving his degree, Pareto worked as a civil engineer for a government-owned railroad. Other engineering positions followed. These jobs required that Pareto travel to England and Scotland, and so enabled him to observe the British economy. The success of the British government in promoting a free market, and the beneficial effects of this *laissez-faire* policy, were especially striking. As a result, Pareto joined the Adam Smith Society and became an active member of the society in the 1870s and 1880s. He contributed frequently to the society newsletter, supporting democracy, free trade, competition, and reduced government regulation of business and individual activities.

In his spare time, and during nights of insomnia, Pareto read extensively in political economy and sociology. In 1882 he retired from his government job to become an engineering consultant, and he began to write political and economic commentaries that attracted a great deal of attention. Pareto also put his training in mathematics and engineering to good use by translating economic theories from verbal, declarative sentences into mathematical equations. This work led to a faculty appointment at the University of Lausanne in 1893, where he succeeded Léon Walras.

At Lausanne, Pareto developed a worldwide reputation as a pioneer in making economics more mathematical. Despite his success, Pareto became troubled by the increasing narrowness of mathematical economics and did an about-face. He argued that, to understand real economies, one needed to understand the cultural and political context in which economic events took place. Pareto also attempted to incorporate sociological, political, and psychological factors into his analysis of how economies change.

In 1898, when his uncle died, Pareto inherited a substantial fortune. He used this money to purchase a country villa on Lake Geneva. There he was able to work in peace on his project to broaden economic analysis. He also became an eccentric hermit, living in a large house with more than a dozen cats.

In addition to making economics more mathematical, Pareto made three substantive contributions to economics – he developed a law of income distribution that still bears his name, he was responsible for switching the focus of economists from cardinal to ordinal utility, and he developed a test of whether economic outcomes could be improved.

While teaching at Lausanne, Pareto became interested in income distribution, and he began to study income inequality in various nations. These studies led to the discovery of a simple pattern governing income distribution. Pareto found that if you were to rank order families in one country by their income level, and then recorded family income levels, you would find that income does not increase proportionately or arithmetically Rather, Pareto found that income increases geometrically as we move along our rank ordering from the poorest to the wealthiest family. When income increases proportionately, if a family at the thirtieth percentile makes 20 percent more than a family at the twentieth percentile, a family at the fortieth percentile would make 20 percent more than a family at the thirtieth percentile and a family at the hundredth percentile would make 20 percent more than a family at the ninetieth percentile (see Figure 7). When income increases geometrically, income disparities grow as one moves along the ordered list of incomes. For example, if a family at the thirtieth percentile makes 10 percent more than a family at the twentieth percentile, a family at the fiftieth percentile may make 40 percent more than a family at the fortieth percentile and a family at the hundredth percentile may make twice as much as (100 percent more than) a family at the ninetieth percentile (see Figure 8).

Examining income statistics from the US and numerous European countries, Pareto found the pattern of income distribution to be pretty much the same everywhere. As a result, he called this pattern a "law" of income distribution. Because he found income

Despite the great controversy it generated, Pareto's work on income distribution marked a major advance in economics. Pareto was the first economist to seriously study income distribution data from around the world. He was thus a pioneer in this area. Pareto also made a major contribution by suggesting how income inequality could be measured. In this way, his work was path-breaking. Finally, the suggestion that income distribution might display some law-like order raises intriguing economic, social, and political questions which have been ignored by most subsequent economists.

Pareto made another important contribution to economics when he argued that *ordinal utility* rather than *cardinal utility* should form the basis of economic analysis. Measured in ordinal terms, the individual consumer is assumed to know that good A is preferred to good B. Measured in cardinal terms, the consumer is assumed to know not only that good A is preferred to good B, but also *by how much* good A is preferred to good B.

Shifting the focus from cardinal to ordinal utility reduces the demands that economists made of each consumer. Consumers need to know only that they prefer peaches to plums. This is something most consumers do actually know. It is also something that most consumers reveal through their everyday expenditures. Consumers, however, are not likely to know that they want peaches twice as much as plums or three times as much as plums. The shift to ordinal utility thus made economics more realistic in the way it described human behavior.

Also, by moving from cardinal to ordinal utility, it was no longer necessary to worry about how utility could be measured or how it was possible to compare the utility of different people. Since the times of Bentham and Mill, *utilitarianism* had been plagued by these problems. With ordinal utility, rather than cardinal utility, a measuring rod was no longer needed. The fact that two people traded with each other demonstrated that they preferred the goods they received to the goods they traded away. Likewise, interpersonal utility comparisons no longer had to be made. Ordinal utility could guarantee that total utility would rise as a result of any trade because utility for each party to the exchange had to be greater; if one person was not made better off by the trade, they would not have made such a trade.

A third contribution made by Pareto was the introduction of the notion of an optimal state of economic affairs, now called "Pareto Optimality." Pareto himself called such a state "ophelimite," from the Greek "*ophelimos.*" His goal was to argue that certain economic outcomes could not be improved upon. *Pareto Optimal* outcomes are situations where making one person better off requires that someone else be made worse off. Thus, no clear overall improvement is possible; the Pareto Optimal condition is the best that we can do.

Pareto began by noting that two individuals in a market will trade only if each of them gains something from the exchange. If one party gains and the other loses there will be no trading. If the two parties are unwilling to trade on their own, any attempt to redistribute goods between these people will make one person better off but the other worse off. Whenever a country allows free exchange in the market, the outcome for the nation will have to be Pareto Optimal.

The notion of Pareto Optimality can also be used to evaluate proposed policy changes. Tax cuts for the wealthy may increase investment and spur economic growth. If those with low incomes gain as a result of greater growth, this tax policy would lead to a Pareto Superior result. But if the tax cuts do not generate sufficient income growth, those with low incomes wind up worse off (because these tax cuts will have to be paid for by someone). In this case, the current tax system would be Pareto Optimal.

In the 1930s, many economists thought that the notion of Pareto Optimality could help evaluate economic performance without resorting to value judgments. This, they thought, would give economics a more scientific grounding. As a result, economists spent a great deal of effort trying to prove theorems about the existence of Pareto Optimality under certain conditions, and to determine whether Pareto Optimal situations were stable or likely to change. The main finding of this work is that competitive capitalism leads to an outcome that is both Pareto Optimal and stable.

However, this work has more recently received a good deal of criticism. First, all Pareto Optimal situations are based upon an initial distribution of income or resources. If we were to begin with other initial distributions, we would reach very different results. These outcomes would be Pareto Optimal also, and there is no way to decide among the various possible Pareto Optimal outcomes. Second, as Sen (1982) has pointed out, Pareto Optimality does not really yield a value-free or scientific welfare economics. It assumes that, if a change makes every individual in society better off, the society as a whole is better off. While this may very well be true, Sen points out it is still an individual opinion rather than a scientific truth. Finally, Sen (1987) has also argued that there is really nothing great about Pareto Optimal situations, since famines could be Pareto Optimal, while government redistribution to prevent mass starvation would not (see **Sen**).

Despite his many important substantive contributions, Pareto is best known for introducing mathematical forms of reasoning and analysis into economics. However, later in his life, Pareto grew dissatisfied with mathematical formalization and with abstract economic theory. Important questions about economic growth and overall economic performance, he thought, could only be understood within an historical and sociopolitical context. Pareto then sought to incorporate these factors into a theory of the business cycle. He noted that social factors influenced decisions to save, work, and consume, and thus the overall state of the economy. Pareto then began to develop a sociological theory of economic growth and stagnation. Economic growth, according to Pareto, required hard work and a willingness to delay gratification. Social norms of hard work, frugality, and professional commitment contribute to these behaviors; economic growth tends to soften and relax them. When their incomes rise, people become more hedonistic – they borrow and spend, and they engage in speculative activities to make money quickly. At some point, Pareto thought, excessive consumer debt would reduce consumer confidence and spending. This would slow down economic growth; but it would also lay the foundation for future growth by reinvigorating social norms and by providing more saving for future investment.

It is somewhat ironic that Pareto is remembered for contributing to the mathematical economics that he came to criticize and reject. But it is hardly surprising that a discipline which has become increasingly mathematical would praise the mathematical Pareto and ignore the sociological Pareto. None the less, for his many contributions to so many different areas within economics, and for his pioneering efforts to make economics more mathematical and scientific, as well as more historical and sociological, Pareto must be regarded among the dozen or so most important figures in the history of economics.

Works by Pareto

Manual of Political Economy (1906), New York, Augustus M. Kelley, 1971
The Mind and Society, New York, Harcourt, Brace, 1935
Sociological Writings, ed. S. E. Finer, New York, Praeger, 1966

Works about Pareto

Bruni, Luigino, *Vilfredo Pareto and the Birth of Modern Microeconomics*, Cheltenham, UK, Edward Elgar, 2002

Cirillo, Renato, *The Economics of Vilfredo Pareto*, London, Frank Cass, 1979

Powers, Charles H., *Vilfredo Pareto*, Newbury Park, California, Sage Publications, 1987

Schumpeter, Joseph, "Vilfredo Pareto: 1848–1923," *Quarterly Journal of Economics*, 63, 2 (May 1949), pp. 147–73. Reprinted in *Ten Great Economists: From Marx to Walras*, New York, Oxford University Press, 1965, pp. 110–42

Other references

Sen, Amartya, *Social Choice and Welfare*, Oxford, Basil Blackwell, 1982

Sen, Amartya, *On Ethics and Economics*, Oxford, Basil Blackwell, 1987

EUGEN VON BÖHM-BAWERK (1851–1914)

Eugen von Böhm-Bawerk (pronounced BAUM-BOW-work) made several related contributions to economics. He helped to develop the economic theories of capital and interest, and he explained why real interest rates had to be positive. Böhm-Bawerk was also among the first economists to incorporate time into economic analysis and to develop an economic theory in which time plays a crucial role.

Böhm-Bawerk was born in 1851 in the town of Brunn (now Brno) in Moravia (then part of the Austro-Hungarian Empire and now part of the Czech Republic). His father was a high government official. As a student, Böhm-Bawerk studied law, administration, and political science, and planned for a career in the civil service. Because his family was facing financial difficulties, he decided to study law at the University of Vienna and follow a more financially rewarding career path. The law curriculum required students to take several courses in economics. These courses likely sparked Böhm-Bawerk's interest in economics and led to another change in career plans (Hennings 1997, p. 9).

After obtaining a doctorate in law from the University of Vienna in 1875, Böhm-Bawerk received a government grant to study abroad and prepare for a teaching career in economics. Over the next five years, he studied in Germany at Universities in Heidelberg, Leipzig, and Jena, and he wrote a doctoral thesis. Being certified to teach in 1880, he accepted a job in Innsbruck, Austria.

Four years later he was promoted to full professor. In 1889, Böhm-Bawerk left academia to become a government economist in the Ministry of Finance. There he studied how to return Austria to the gold standard and worked on reforming the Austrian income tax so it would be a better source of revenue for the government (at the time, Austria relied heavily on sales taxes). In 1893 he became the Austrian Finance Minister, and over the next decade he held this position several times.

Böhm-Bawerk left the government in 1904 and returned to the University of Vienna, where he was given a chair in political economy. For the next ten years, until his death in 1914, Böhm-Bawerk spent most of his time defending himself from his many political and economic critics.

Today Böhm-Bawerk is remembered primarily for his theory of capital and interest. He made three important and interrelated contributions in this area – an analysis of production as a roundabout process, an explanation for why real interest rates had to be positive, and an equilibrium theory of interest rates that included time as an important variable affecting interest rates.

Economists usually view economies as moving towards equilibrium and ignore the fact that this process takes place over time. Since it may take considerable time before an economy can reach a state of rest or equilibrium, many other changes can occur to upset the initial equilibrium and move the economy down another path. Böhm-Bawerk refused to ignore time, and he stressed that time was an important factor in understanding how economies actually behaved.

Most important of all, time was a key factor in the decisions made by business firms about how to produce goods and services. Firms might use production techniques that yield goods relatively quickly; unfortunately, these methods usually yield few goods. Alternatively, the firm could use more roundabout techniques of production, wait longer for the goods to be produced, and in the end get more goods. To take one of Böhm-Bawerk's (1889, vol. 2, ch. 2) favorite examples, we can extract drinking water from a spring either by hand, by bucket, or by pipes. Each successive method of production is more roundabout; and each method is also more efficient and yields more water.

Roundabout production means using more tools or capital to produce final goods for the consumer, producing more intermediate goods, and having production take place in many different stages. Large assembly plants were just beginning to appear when Böhm-Bawerk was writing. With larger and more technologically advanced plants it was necessary to wait longer for the final output (for example, automobiles), since a plant must be built before any goods can be made and sold. Using robots will get us even more goods than an automated assembly line; but in this case we first have to build the robots and the automated plant and then stock the plant with robots. This is an even more roundabout production process. It requires more time and a longer waiting period for the final output than the assembly line. But this more roundabout production method also yields more goods over a long time period.

One problem with this theory is the difficulty of measuring roundaboutness in production, or determining which of two production processes was more roundabout. While this task is easy when comparing an automated assembly line with someone building a car in his garage, it is more complicated when two different assembly line techniques have to be compared or when two different systems of piping water into homes must be compared. And it is these latter decisions that most firms must make. Böhm-Bawerk did attempt to deal with the problem of measuring roundaboutness, but his efforts met with little success.

However, the notion of roundabout production contains a key insight – production involves a trade-off between having things soon, but having few things, and having more things, but having them in the distant future. One could have more goods in the future by giving up consumption for a long period of time; or one could consume goods now, but have fewer goods over the long haul.

Böhm-Bawerk analyzed this choice in terms of the subjective time preferences of economic agents. People decided whether they wanted goods now or whether they preferred to give up something now in order to get more in the future; and business owners determined whether more or less roundabout techniques are employed in producing goods based on whether they wanted to make some money now or more money in the future.

This idea of subjective time preference also provides the basis for Böhm-Bawerk's theory of interest. Böhm-Bawerk first laid the groundwork for his theory of interest by presenting and critiquing all previous theories. This was done in Volume 1 of his (1884) *Capital and Interest*, which showed that prior attempts to explain interest based on the productivity of capital, the abstinence from consumption, or the exploitation of workers, lacked any merit and made little sense. Volume 2 (1889) then went on to present a theory of interest based on time. It also tried to show that a positive rate of interest was inevitable and therefore justified.

For centuries economists had been trying, without success, to explain why real interest rates had to be positive. One can think of the *nominal interest rate* as the rate of interest two parties agree upon. In simple terms, if I borrow money from a bank for one year at a rate of 10 percent, I am paying back a stack of dollar bills that is

10 percent taller than the stack of bills that I borrowed. The *real interest rate* measures how much more the bank can buy with the stack of bills I repay it compared to the purchasing power of the stack of bills I borrowed. If over the past year the price of goods rises by 10 percent, the money I repay is worth less because it can buy less. In this case, a 10 percent bigger stack of bills and 10 percent inflation means the money I repay can buy no more (real) things than the money I borrowed, and the real interest rate is zero. By definition, the real rate of interest equals the nominal rate minus the rate of inflation. Alternatively, one can think of the real rate of interest as Böhm-Bawerk did – the real rate of interest paid by a consumer represents how many future goods he has to give up to consume goods now.

Böhm-Bawerk provided three explanations for positive real interest rates. First, there was an argument based on economic growth. Incomes usually grow over time. If people are going be richer in the future, they should be willing to give up more than one dollar in the future in order to get one dollar now.

Second, Böhm-Bawerk argued that people had a positive time preference; that is, they preferred consuming goods now because the future was uncertain. In the future one might not have the desire to consume goods, or the ability to do so (because no one knows how long they are going to live). Since we want things now, we have to be bribed to give up goods now in exchange for goods in the future. This bribe can only be more future goods.

Finally, Böhm-Bawerk argued that, since roundabout production processes were also more productive processes, borrowers could easily afford to pay positive real interest rates and should be willing to pay positive real interest rates.

After explaining why real interest rates had to be positive, Böhm-Bawerk went on to explain how interest rates actually get set. His analysis rested on standard supply and demand analysis – the supply of and demand for borrowed money determined its price, or the rate of interest.

Böhm-Bawerk's contribution here was to explain how roundabout production and consumer time preferences influenced the demand for money and the supply of money, respectively. As we have seen, for Böhm-Bawerk production was a process for transforming goods. It was a roundabout process that required other goods produced in the past. These goods must be paid for somehow. Also, to produce intermediate goods will require labor and raw materials; but workers must be paid and material must be purchased before final goods are sold to consumers. Roundabout production thus leads to a demand for money on the part of business firms. How many intermediate goods had to be stockpiled and how long the production process takes determines the demand for money.

The supply of money for Böhm-Bawerk was determined by preferences on the part of lenders for more goods in the future relative to having goods now. If people take a long-term perspective, and are willing to sacrifice now in order to have more later, they will be more willing to supply or lend money. On the other hand, if people crave immediate gratification, a high real rate of interest (or many future goods) will be needed to obtain the money necessary for more roundabout production to take place.

After setting forth this theory, Böhm-Bawerk (1896) used the theory to explain why, *contra* Marx, workers were not exploited. He assumed that all workers were paid the going wage rate. The difference between the output they produced and their wages was the profit of the entrepreneur. Workers could not receive the full future value of what they produced because employers had to pay interest during the time production was taking place. Profits were thus justified as a reward to capitalists for employing more roundabout production methods and for producing more goods. Profits also covered the interest cost that firms had to pay to borrow money and use more roundabout production techniques.

Schumpeter (1965, p. 147) hailed Böhm-Bawerk as one of the five or six greatest economists of all time. But since Schumpeter was a student of Böhm-Bawerk, this must be regarded as a rather biased assessment. For most economists, Böhm-Bawerk lacks the stature of the very best and most important figures in the history of the discipline. However, he did make several key contributions to economic theory. He recognized that time was important in understanding the economic role of capital and interest. And he also recognized that time played an important role in the production process.

Works by Böhm-Bawerk

Capital and Interest, 3 vols (1884 and 1889), trans. G. D. Huncke and H. E. Sennhole, South Holland, Illinois, Libertarian Press, 1959

Kard Marx and the Close of His System (1896), New York, Augustus M. Kelley, 1949

Further Essays on Capital and Interest, South Holland, Illinois, Libertarian Press, 1959

Shorter Classics of Böhm-Bawerk, South Holland, Illinois, Libertarian Press, 1962

Works about Böhm-Bawerk

Buechner, M. Northrup, "Roundaboutness and Productivity in Böhm-Bawerk," *Southern Economic Journal*, 62, 2 (October 1989), pp. 499–510

Hennings, Klaus H., *The Austrian Theory of Value and Capital: Studies in the Life and Works of Eugen von Böhm-Bawerk*, Cheltenham, UK, Edward Elgar, 1997

Hirshleifer, Jack, "A Note on the Böhm-Bawerk/Wicksell Theory of Interest," *Review of Economic Studies*, 34 (1967), pp. 191–9

Kuenne, Robert E., *Eugen von Böhm-Bawerk*, New York, Columbia University Press, 1971

Schumpeter, Joseph, "Eugen von Böhm-Bawerk, 1851–1914," in *Ten Great Economists: From Marx to Walras*, New York, Oxford University Press, 1965, pp. 143–90

KNUT WICKSELL (1851–1926)

Throughout his life Knut Wicksell was a highly controversial figure. On principle he refused to marry the woman with whom he chose to live and raise a family. In 1909 he served two months in jail for a speech that mocked the story of the Immaculate Conception. And he championed the rights of women, birth control, and universal voting long before these ideas gained acceptance in Sweden.

The economics of Wicksell was likewise controversial. An early advocate of the *marginal productivity theory of distribution*, Wicksell, in contradistinction to other proponents of this theory, drew policy conclusions from the theory that required greater government intervention in economic life. And in contrast to virtually all his contemporaries, Wicksell held that inflation or unemployment would continue indefinitely unless appropriate economic policies were employed.

Wicksell was born in Stockholm, Sweden, in 1851 to middle class parents. Because his mother died when he was very young Wicksell was raised by an uncle and aunt. He received a good high school education, showing talent in mathematics and natural sciences. In 1869, Wicksell enrolled at Uppsala University with the goal of becoming a Doctor of Philosophy and Professor of Mathematics. But his academic career turned out to be long and varied. He developed interests in poetry, feminism, and politics, and he published a collection of twenty-five poems in 1878. Then in the 1880s he became an ardent neo-Malthusian, and traveled throughout Sweden lecturing about the dangers of overpopulation and the need to control population growth through celibacy and birth control. As a result of these diversions, it was not until 1885 (fifteen years after he first enrolled at Uppsala) that Wicksell received a graduate degree in mathematics.

However, his interests continued their metamorphosis, moving from mathematics to economics and social reform. With an inheritance he received after the death of his father, Wicksell went to London in order to read the classics of economics at the British Museum. He returned to Sweden with a desire to teach and write about economics. But, at the time, economics was taught by the law faculty in Swedish universities. So Wicksell had to study law and obtain a law degree before he could receive an appointment teaching economics. In 1899, at the age of 48, Wicksell passed his law examinations and became a lecturer in political economy and law at Uppsala University. His academic career, understandably, was very short; Wicksell retired in 1916 at the age of 65.

Wicksell made substantive contributions in three distinct areas of economics – marginal productivity theory, monetary theory, and public finance.

Wicksell and British economist Philip Wicksteed each (independently) solved the adding-up or product exhaustion problem (see **Clark**). This involved describing when the marginal productivity theory could explain the distribution of *all* the output produced by one firm. Wicksell was an early proponent of the marginal productivity theory of distribution, which held that an individual's income depends upon their (marginal) contribution to firm revenues. One question left unanswered about this theory was whether the sum of all marginal productivities, and hence all incomes, was equal to the value of the output produced by the firm.

Wicksell demonstrated that whether this was true or not depended upon returns to scale. This economic notion concerns how output increases given a certain increase in inputs. To take a very simple example, consider a farm devoted exclusively to growing corn. If we double the number of acres used for growing corn and get exactly twice as much corn we have *constant returns to scale*. If we double the number of acres used, but output increases by less than 100 percent, we have decreasing returns to scale. Finally, if we double our acreage and our output of corn more than doubles we have *increasing returns to scale*.

Wicksell showed that if, and only if, there are constant returns to scale would the sum of all marginal products equal the value of output produced. In contrast, with increasing returns to scale the sum of marginal payments would exceed the value of the product produced; while with decreasing returns to scale the sum of marginal payments would be less than the total value of output. In the latter case, some value created in the production process could not be explained by marginal productivity. In the former case, the theory explained too much; the sum of all marginal productivities would be greater than the value of the output produced, so it would be impossible to pay everyone their marginal productivity.

Wicksell next explained how competition forced firms to operate at an optimal size, and argued that this optimal size would require constant returns to scale. He began by noting that firms face U-shaped cost curves. For the typical firm, costs fall as output rises, then remain constant for a while, and finally they begin to rise. It is not hard to understand why this should be so. As the size of a farm starts to grow the farmer can take advantage of *economies of scale*. A second tractor will not have to be purchased to grow more corn; one tractor can till more land. Likewise, a second barn will not be required. The output of corn can be doubled without doubling the inputs needed to grow that corn. At some point, though, economies of scale will be exhausted and the firm will reach its optimal or most efficient size. The farm now faces constant returns to scale and constant costs for producing additional corn. Beyond this level, additional capital equipment will be required, worse-quality land will have to be employed to grow corn, and the farm will become too large to run efficiently. Decreasing returns to scale thus set in.

Due to competition, firms are forced to operate at the most efficient level of production. This will be the point of minimum average costs, or the level of production where constant returns hold. Firms that do not produce at this level will be forced out of business by their competitors, those which do produce at minimum cost. Thus, competition forces firms to produce at minimum average cost and with constant returns to scale. As a result, Wicksell argued, the marginal products paid to all factors of production will tend to equal the value of the products they produce, and the marginal productivity theory will be able to explain how all income gets distributed.

A second major contribution made by Wicksell concerned monetary theory. During the time of Wicksell, monetary theory primarily studied the impact of money on prices. Ignored were any effects that money or interest rates had on the real economy – either on production or on employment. Wicksell changed monetary theory by arguing that changes in the rate of interest could affect the real economy.

Wicksell (1936, pp. 139–54) assumed that there was a natural rate of interest, or a natural rate of return on capital. He took this natural rate to be the rate of return (or the yield) on newly created plant and equipment. Innovations, or improvements in production technology, would increase the natural rate of interest, making investment yield a bigger return. In contrast, the market rate of interest is the rate charged by banks to those who want to borrow money. This rate was determined by the banking system.

Whenever the natural rate of interest exceeds the market rate of interest, businesses will want to invest and produce, since their gains from investment (the natural rate) will exceed their cost of borrowed funds (the market rate). Investment is able to exceed savings, Wicksell argued, because investment is financed *not* with savings, but with credit, or through the creation of new bank deposits when banks make new loans.

The economic expansion that begins under these circumstances will be cumulative and self-perpetuating. Rising investment demand will shift workers out of industries producing goods for consumption, and into industries that produce investment goods. With fewer consumption goods, the prices of consumption goods rise. As such, producers of consumer goods make greater profits and will want to expand production, or invest more. This process of greater investment and rising prices for consumer goods will continue unabated. Nothing will cause a slowdown in the process of growth and investment, according to Wicksell.

In contrast, if the natural rate falls below the market rate, the demand for investment falls. Businesses will not want to borrow money for expansion since the cost of borrowed funds (the market rate of interest) exceeds the gains from investment (the natural rate of interest). As a result, business production falls and employment drops. Deficient demand will lower prices and spending. But with sales down and prices low, business profits will suffer. Moreover, firms with excess capacity will not want to invest. The economic contraction will continue until investment rises. But this will not happen unless either the natural rate of interest rises or the market rate of interest falls.

The policy implication that follows this analysis is simple and straightforward – monetary authorities must prevent any divergence between the market and natural rates. Only by setting the market rate of interest equal to the natural rate of interest can monetary authorities prevent either continued growth and rising inflation or continued stagnation and rising unemployment. Another implication of this analysis concerns the causal relationship between money and interest rates. For Wicksell, in contrast to much twentieth century monetary theory (see **Fisher**), it is the rate of interest that determines bank lending and the supply of money (rather than the money supply determining the rate of interest).

The third main contribution of Wicksell concerns *public finance.* Wicksell supported a mixed economy containing a large role for government. Using *cost–benefit analysis* as his justification, he advocated a substantial increase in public ownership of firms. Wicksell pressed for public ownership of natural monopolies, such as utilities, as well as any other enterprises that showed a tendency towards monopoly or that began forming cartels for the purpose of restricting output and raising prices. It was better, Wicksell believed, that these firms be owned and operated by the government. Government ownership would give consumers more goods and services plus the benefits of lower prices.

Since price would most likely fall below the average cost of production, government-owned firms would be incurring losses on a continual basis. Wicksell suggested that these losses be financed from revenues raised through general taxation. He therefore did not think it was necessary for state-owned firms to make profits. Rather, the state was to assume ownership of firms in order to improve the allocation of national economic resources relative to a situation of monopoly. A second aspect of Wicksell's theory of public finance involved reducing the heavy reliance on *regressive taxation* in Sweden during the 1890s. Towards this end he advocated lowering excise taxes and tariffs, which fell heavily on low-income groups, and developing *progressive taxes* on individual and corporate incomes as well as on estates or inheritances. Wicksell also advocated modifying the Swedish property tax system so that it better taxed the rising share of "unearned" increases in land values. He stressed that earned income should be taxed at lower rates than unearned income (Uhr 1951, pp. 835–6).

As to the other side of the fiscal equation, Wicksell advocated more government spending for social services, especially education, in order to compensate for income inequalities that arise when income gets distributed based on marginal productivities. However, Wicksell also stressed the importance of broadly distributing government expenditures so that every member of society felt that they benefited from their tax payments.

These many proposals concerning public expenditure and taxation make Wicksell the founder of the Swedish mixed economy – with high taxes, progressive tax rates, large government benefits to workers, and substantial government ownership of production facilities.

Of our fifty major economists, Wicksell is one of the most underrated. One likely reason for this is that Wicksell made contributions in so many different and diverse areas. Another reason is that Wicksell did not develop any key economic notions, nor did he contribute to the mathematization of economic analysis. Finally, Wicksell himself must share some of the blame. He was too controversial, and too readily expressed great contempt for other economists and their theories. This was true of those with whom Wicksell agreed and those with whom he disagreed.

Works by Wicksell

Value, Capital and Rent (1893), London, Allen & Unwin, 1954
Interest and Prices (1898), London, Macmillan, 1936
Lectures on Political Economy (1901, 1906), 2 vols, London, Routledge & Kegan Paul, 1934–5
Kurt Wicksell: Selected Essays in Economics, London, Routledge, 1997

Works about Wicksell

Firsch, Ragnar, "Frisch on Wicksell," in *The Development of Economic Thought: Great Economists in Perspective*, ed. H. W. Spiegel, New York, Wiley, 1952, pp. 652–99
Garlund, Torsten, *The Life of Knut Wicksell*, Cheltenham, UK, Edward Elgar, 1996
"Symposium on the Theoretical Contributions of Knut Wicksell," *Scandinavian Journal of Economics*, 80, 2 (1978), pp. 127–249
Uhr, Carl G., "Knut Wicksell – A Centennial Evaluation," *American Economic Review*, 41, 5 (1951), pp. 829–60
Uhr, Carl G., *The Economic Doctrines of Knut Wicksell*, Berkeley, University of California Press, 1960
Uhr, Carl G., "Knut Wicksell, Neoclassicist and Iconoclast," in *The History of Swedish Economic Thought*, ed. Bo Sandelin, London and New York, Routledge, 1991, pp. 76–120

THORSTEIN VEBLEN (1857–1929)

Thorstein Veblen (pronounced VEB-LIN, the first syllable rhyming with WEB) was one of the sharpest and wittiest critics of orthodox economic theory. His criticism of traditional theory, and his own positive contribution to economics, stressed the impact that societal institutions have on individual behavior. Veblen saw behavior as driven by customs, by habit, by envy, and by other psychological dispositions, rather than seeing individuals as motivated by rational self-interest. Veblen then used these behavioral dispositions to explain the changes economies regularly undergo.

Veblen was born to Norwegian immigrants in 1857, on a small farm in Wisconsin. He was raised in rural Wisconsin and rural Minnesota. His parents stressed the importance of education, and pushed their children to excel and to pursue higher education. Veblen studied economics at Carleton College under John Bates Clark, who first formulated the *marginal productivity theory of income distribution* (see **Clark**). He then studied philosophy at Johns Hopkins University under Charles Peirce, a world-famous philosopher and founder of American pragmatism. At Johns Hopkins he also studied political economy under Richard Ely, an eminent economist who founded the American Economic Association. Despite having such distinguished teachers, Veblen was rather dissatisfied with Johns Hopkins and so he transferred to Yale. There he studied philosophy under *Social Darwinist* William Graham Summer, earning a PhD in philosophy in 1884.

Because of the bad job market for philosophers, Veblen was unable to find a position teaching philosophy. He spent the next seven years reading on his own, and then finally decided it was time to switch fields; so he entered Cornell University to study economics. One year later, Veblen moved to the University of Chicago with his Cornell mentor, J. Laurence Laughlin. He taught at Chicago for fourteen years but never rose beyond the rank of Assistant Professor, even though he wrote two highly successful and critically acclaimed books (Veblen 1908, 1978), published numerous essays, and edited the prestigious *Journal of Political Economy*.

After leaving Chicago, Veblen moved constantly from school to school, usually encouraged by college administrators to seek employment elsewhere. Part of the problem was the affairs he had with young co-eds and faculty wives. Another problem was that his caustic criticism of academia (Veblen 1918), and other economists, did not endear him to his colleagues. A further difficulty was that Veblen had no regard for academic rituals like department meetings, taking attendance in class, holding office hours, and grading. He usually gave all his students a "C" regardless of the quality of their work. Finally, there was the problem with Veblen the teacher. According to Dorfman (1972, pp. 248–9), Veblen "mumbled, he rambled, he digressed. His classes dwindled; one ended up with but one student."

Veblen was also renowned for his quirky lifestyle. Dorfman (1972, pp. 248–9) reports that Veblen furnished his living quarters with boxes that served as tables and chairs. Mundane household chores such as making up a bed were deplored as a waste of time. Dirty dishes were stacked in a tub until no clean dishes remained; then Veblen hosed them down. According to Diggins (1978, pp. 33–8), while teaching at the University of Missouri in the 1910s, Veblen lived in the basement of a friend's house, entering and leaving through the basement window.

Veblen's economics was nearly as quirky as his lifestyle. While other economists studied human behavior from their ivory towers, Veblen studied human behavior within the context of anthropology and other social sciences. For Veblen many forces influenced human behavior, and he brought these other forces into his economic analysis. As such, he sought to broaden and enrich economics with the insights from other disciplines.

Using the insights from other social sciences, Veblen rejected the economic assumption (stemming from Locke) that much behavior was rational and that people sought only their own pleasures. Instead, he saw people as behaving irrationally and following customs and habits rather than maximizing utility. In fact, Veblen turned traditional economic analysis upside down, arguing that human institutions and experience help determine what people believe to be pleasurable and painful.

Veblen is best known for his first book, a work that instantly made him famous. *The Theory of the Leisure Class* (Veblen 1908) rejects the traditional view of consumption as a means to human happiness, and rejects the view that individuals look inside themselves to determine the happiness that they would receive from consuming different goods. In its place Veblen develops a cultural theory of consumption. Habit, convention, and superstitious irrationality all determine human consumption.

Another important purpose of consumption, according to Veblen, is to impress others. Veblen called this "*conspicuous consumption.*" He then went on to provide an historical account of this phenomenon. He demonstrated that in early, predatory cultures unproductive consumption was a mark of human prowess and dignity. In more modern cultures, conspicuous consumption involves various sorts of ostentation – giving valuable gifts to others, driving expensive sports cars, and arranging expensive and extravagant feasts. These acts provide evidence of one's wealth and importance. Even in lower economic classes, conspicuous consumption can be demonstrated through a spouse who stays at home and does no work for remuneration in the marketplace.

The doctrine of conspicuous consumption undermines the traditional view of economic man. Money is *not* spent because it yields utility to the individual consumer. Rather, the doctrine of conspicuous consumption holds that consumers spend money in order to make their friends and neighbors jealous, and to keep up with the spending of their friends and neighbors.

This analysis has several important consequences. If I buy an expensive car because it makes my neighbor envious, and if my neighbor buys a similar car to keep up with me, neither one of us is better off. We both have more expensive cars, but we have failed to show up each other.

Things can be even worse than this. Suppose my neighbor buys a more expensive car than I bought in order to make me jealous. Not to be undone, I trade up to an even more expensive model. This process can continue indefinitely, with me and my neighbor continually buying more and more expensive cars. As a result of this process both of us seem to be far worse off – we have incurred a great deal of debt buying things we do not really want, and we have engaged in a competition that neither one of us can win and that is destructive to both of us. Because of human desires to emulate and "one-up" others, human decisions may actually reduce individual well-being.

Conspicuous consumption also undermines the doctrines of consumer rationality and consumer sovereignty. Once it is recognized that consumption patterns stem from habits and customs, consumption is no longer the outcome of rational calculation. And once it is recognized that consumption patterns depend upon the consumption of others and that culture can affect consumption decisions, then consumers are no longer autonomous beings who know what they want and then buy these things. Rather, people are human beings with human flaws, who usually do not know what they really want. They listen to advertising and ascertain what others are doing when they make consumption decisions. People are not, according to Veblen, passive agents who merely add up the pleasure they might receive from doing different things or consuming different goods.

Besides studying consumer spending habits, Veblen (1978) also studied the dominant characteristics of American capitalism at the beginning of the twentieth century. These included the rise of an industrial economy dominated by machines and robber barons, the inability of moral systems to control the power of modern business, severe business cycles, and the rise of powerful monopolies like US

Steel and Standard Oil. Unlike most of his contemporaries, who focused on how the economy would move towards a stable equilibrium, Veblen attempted to understand and explain the changes he saw taking place in the real world.

Towards this end, Veblen distinguished business activities from the machine process, and analogously the capitalist from the engineer. The business enterprise for Veblen was run by capitalists who were only interested in making profits. The capitalist was a predator, interested in making money rather than goods. Goods could be useless and of poor quality, but as long as money was being made nothing else was important.

In contrast, machine processes were the technical procedures used in producing goods. These processes were designed and run by engineers. Unlike the capitalist–businessman, engineers were concerned with productivity, serviceability, and efficiency. And unlike business activities, the machine process valued workmanship. Its output was functional or useful goods that satisfied man's needs to eat, to work constructively, and to satisfy his curiosity.

Business activities were the root causes of the business cycle (Veblen 1978, p. 237). Businessmen borrowed money based on their expectations of future profits. This borrowing increased economic activity and prices, leading to higher profits. With their expectations confirmed, businessmen would form even more optimistic views of future profits. And with things going so well, businesses could borrow more and make even more money. At some point, however, unease about continued profits would arise and some businessmen would see the possibility of making money in a contraction. Loans would be called in, small businesses would start to go under, and a recession would follow. Stagnation would then continue until businessmen saw enough opportunities for greater profit and were willing to borrow and expand their operations.

In sharp contrast to other economists writing on business cycles in the early twentieth century, Veblen saw no tendency for the economic system to equilibrate. Rather, he saw unending instability and oscillation. Any analysis of how economies reached an equilibrium was therefore unscientific, according to Veblen. For economic analysis to be scientific, it had to focus on the evolutionary changes of institutions over time rather than on the way an economy moves to a static equilibrium point.

Where did Veblen think this process was heading? Somewhat naively, Veblen thought the machine process and the engineer would help solve the many economic problems facing America.

The machine process would allow greater planning of production and distribution. It would allow us to do away with the price system. It would also end the waste of unemployment on the one hand and the waste of conspicuous consumption on the other hand.

Veblen was one of two or three best-known American economists in the early twentieth century. He attempted to give economics greater breadth by bringing to it the insights from other social sciences. More specifically, he showed how habits, culture, and institutions mold human behavior, and how changing human behavior affects the economy. As a result of this work, Veblen has become the intellectual father of the institutionalist school of economics.

Works by Veblen

The Theory of the Leisure Class (1899), New York, Macmillan, 1908

The Theory of Business Enterprise (1904), New Brunswick, Transaction Publishers, 1978

The Instinct of Workmanship and the State of the Industrial Arts, New York, Macmillan, 1914

The Higher Learning in America: A Memorandum on the Conduct of Universities by Business Men, New York, B. W. Huebsch, 1918

The Place of Science in Modern Civilization (1919), New Brunswick, Transaction Publishers, 1990

The Vested Interests and the State of the Industrial Arts, New York, B. W. Huebsch, 1919

The Engineers and the Price System (1921), New Brunswick, Transaction Publishers, 1983

Absentee Ownership and Business Enterprise in Recent Times, New York, B. W. Huebsch, 1923

A Veblen Treasury: From Leisure Class to War, Peace and Capitalism, ed. Rick Tilman, Armonk, New York, M. E. Sharpe, 1993

Works about Veblen

Diggins, John, *The Bard of Savagery*, New York, Seaburg Press, 1978

Dorfman, Joseph, *Thorstein Veblen and His America* (1934), New York, Augustus M. Kelley, 1972

Jorgensen, Elizabeth and Jorgensen, Henry, *Thorstein Veblen: Victorian Firebrand*, Armonk, New York, M. E. Sharpe, 1999

Mitchell, Wesley C., "Thorstein Veblen," in *The Backward Art of Spending Money and Other Essays*, New York, Augustus Kelley, 1950, pp. 279–312

Riesman, David, *Thorstein Veblen: A Critical Interpretation*, New York, Charles Scribner's Sons, 1953

Tilman, Rick, *Thorstein Veblen and His Critics, 1891–1963*, Princeton, New Jersey, Princeton University Press, 1992

IRVING FISHER (1867–1947)

Irving Fisher spent his career studying questions about money and the economy – how money affects interest rates, how money affects inflation, and the impact of money on overall economic activity. For this work, he is regarded as the father of monetary economics.

Fisher was born in 1867 in Saugerties, New York. His father was a clergyman, and so Fisher grew up in a highly religious environment. More than likely, this contributed to the sense of mission that characterized his personal life as well as his professional life.

Fisher received a good public school education and excelled in mathematics. When he decided to attend college at Yale, his family moved with him to New Haven. Graduating first in his class, Fisher remained at Yale to do graduate work in both mathematics and economics. He began studying economics with William Graham Sumner, an advocate of Social Darwinism, the philosophy holding that in social life the best competitors would always win out and that human improvement requires a competitive struggle (see Hofstadter 1944). Under the influence of Summer, Fisher took every economics and social science course offered at Yale (Allen 1993). However, it appears that the philosophy of Summer had little influence on Fisher. Most of his work in economics at Yale, as well as his doctoral dissertation, involved making economics more quantative rather than bringing philosophy or social issues into the realm of economics.

When Fisher graduated from Yale in 1892 he was already regarded as one of the leading mathematical economists of his day, and Yale immediately hired him as an economics professor. Many accolades and awards soon followed. In 1918 Fisher was elected President of the American Economic Association. In 1930 he helped to found the Econometrics Society and became its first President.

During the 1920s Fisher applied his knowledge of economics and financial markets to Wall Street. Speculating heavily in stocks, he soon became a multimillionaire. But Fisher lost half his net worth in the crash of 1929. Believing that stocks were a good bargain following the crash, Fisher borrowed heavily to buy more stock. When the market continued to fall, Fisher lost his entire fortune and then some. He remained heavily in debt for the rest of his life and lived the simple lifestyle that comes with such indebtedness.

Fisher devoted his life to many causes and wrote many popular books advocating those causes. He was a crusader for healthy living and a wholesome lifestyle. He advocated eating well and getting sufficient exercise, and he started the Life Extension Institute in 1913. He opposed smoking, eating meat, and drinking alcohol. And he devoted much time and effort to causes such as Prohibition and US entry into the League of Nations.

Fisher was also an economic policy crusader. His success in this arena, however, was no better than his success on Wall Street or his success in getting the US to join the League of Nations. Neither his (Fisher 1935) proposal to require that banks keep all their deposits on hand instead of lending out these funds, nor his (Fisher 1942) plan for taxing individual expenditures rather than income (see **Kaldor**), nor his (Fisher 1920) plan to control inflation by backing the dollar with a diverse set of goods (see Patinkin 1993) was ever taken seriously.

In contrast to his policy proposals, Fisher's theoretical work earned him the reputation of being a first-rate economist. His main interests were monetary theory – money, interest rates, prices, and how they were all related. His main contributions were to explain monetary concepts and how money affected the economy.

It was Fisher who first defined precisely the notions of income, capital, and wealth. To understand these terms requires knowledge of the differences between stocks and flows. Fisher claimed this distinction clicked into his mind during a mountain-climbing trip in the Swiss Alps when he saw water cascading down a mountain into pools of water (Allen 1993, pp. 66–7). The pools of water at the bottom of the mountain constituted a stock; the water flowing down the mountain was an addition to the stock and increased the size of the stock.

Fisher (1906) used this distinction to clarify several economic notions. He defined capital as a stock of wealth at one point in time, analogous to a stock of water in a pool at the bottom of a mountain. Out of current income would come a flow of savings which, like the water cascading down the Swiss mountain, adds to our stock of wealth. Too much spending (or spending more than your income) would cause a flow out of current wealth, thus reducing the stock of wealth.

Fisher (1907, ch. 5) also distinguished *real interest rates* from *nominal interest rates* (see **Böhm–Bawerk**), and he (Fisher 1920, pp. 35–9; 1928) coined the term "*money illusion*" to refer to an inability to distinguish a dollar from the purchasing power of the dollar (or what the dollar could buy after inflation). Interest rates on bank deposits provide one good example of money illusion. When the rates on cert-ificates of deposit fall, people generally complain about the low returns they are getting. Yet these people may have been doing worse with higher nominal interest rates and higher inflation. Money illusion also frequently occurs when workers get pay increases. Since wages are a major component of business costs, higher wages usually lead to higher prices.

Workers suffering from money illusion will be happy with a bigger pay check even though their bigger check can buy fewer things.

For Fisher (1923, 1925), money illusion was a prevalent phenomenon. He also thought it was responsible for the business cycle. Businesses, believing that real interest rates are high during times of inflation and high nominal interest rates, stop borrowing and investing. This slows down economic activity. Then, when a slowing economy reduces nominal rates, businesses mistake this for a cut in real rates and increase their borrowing and investment. As the economy expands, money illusion eventually brings the expansion to a halt. As the expanding economy generates inflationary pressures, banks must raise nominal rates to maintain the real rate of interest they make on their loans. Again, businesses mistake this for higher real rates and invest-ment falls. According to Fisher, economic expansion and contraction follow one another continually as a result of this process.

Fisher also tackled the difficult problem of how to measure inflation for the entire economy. Inflation is simply the change in prices faced by a typical family. Since each family purchases a diverse set of goods, and since the goods it buys change regularly, developing a single number to represent the average change in prices becomes a complex problem.

The simple solution to this problem of measuring inflation is to measure the price change for a set of goods that the typical family buys at one point in time. One problem with this method is that, when prices change for some good, people buy less of that good. This problem became particularly acute in the 1970s, when oil prices rose dramatically and energy consumption fell. Do we use the origi-nal quantities here or do we use the quantities bought after the price change? Today all nations use the set of goods bought by people before prices change when calculating inflation. Nations have adop-ted this method for practical reasons more than anything else. It is both expensive and time-consuming to take regular surveys of con-sumer purchases. Surveys therefore are only taken every few years. But this decision has important consequences for our measurement of inflation; it implicitly assumes that consumers will not change their spending patterns when prices change.

Fisher (1922) recognized that using original purchases would overstate the actual inflation rate because it assumes that people are buying large quantities of the good (gasoline, in our example) that increases most in price. He also recognized that taking the opposite approach, and using quantities bought by families *after* the price change, would underestimate the loss in purchasing power to the family when some good rises in price by a large amount. Fisher suggested that an ideal index number, or inflation measure, should employ the average of quantities bought before the price change and quantities bought after the price change.

While Fisher devoted a great deal of effort and energy to clarifying economic notions, he did more than just help define concepts. His main contributions to economics involved analyzing what factors determined interest rates and what factors caused inflation.

Fisher's theory of the rate of interest is still taught to most economics students today, and is regarded by most economists as a correct analysis of what determines interest rates for a particular economy. Fisher (1930) proposed that interest should be viewed as an income flow that comes from using anything in production. In particular, interest is the income flowing to someone who allows their stock of wealth to be used in producing goods. When wealth gets used in the production process, someone lends money to a business firm and does not spend it. Interest was thus a reward for not consuming things today, and so Fisher's theory is usually referred to as a time-preference theory of interest. Because most people desire to consume things now, they have to be paid to wait until next year or the year after to consume goods. Interest is thus a bribe to keep people from spending everything now.

Two forces determine interest rates, according to Fisher. On the supply side, the key is the preferences of individuals for present consumption versus future consumption. If people look toward the future, and are worried about how they will support themselves in old age, they will accept low interest rates to save rather than spend. On the other hand, if people only think about enjoying life now, they will not save unless they are paid grandly to do so.

On the demand side, interest rates depend upon available investment opportunities and the productivity of capital (including *human capital*). Greater productivity will lead to greater demand for borrowed money. With greater productivity, profits increase and business owners will want to expand more. To do this they will need to borrow or will demand more money.

The equilibrium rate of interest is the rate of interest at which the quantity of funds that borrowers want to lend equals the quantity of funds that lenders are willing to give up. Fisher made it clear that the forces affecting both supply and demand were unstable. Moreover, in addition to economic factors, supply and demand were also affected by social and psychological factors such as the habits, intelligence, self-control, and foresight of both borrowers and lenders.

Finally, Fisher (1911) set forth the now-famous *equation of exchange*, and he used it to identify the causes of price inflation. The equation, MV=PQ, says that the money supply (M) times its velocity (V, the number of times a unit of money is used during a year to purchase goods and services) must equal the output of goods and services (P times Q). This equality must be true as a result of the definitions of the various terms. If the British economy has a money supply of 1 trillion pounds, and if each pound is used seven times during the year to purchase things, then 7 trillion pounds worth of goods and services will be purchased during the year. This is the national output or gross domestic product of the British economy. This output, in turn, can be further divided into price (P) and quantity (Q) components. The quantity represents real things that are produced, while the price component measures how much each thing costs on average (Fisher's price index).

Using this equation Fisher was able to explain the three potential causes of inflation. First, if V and Q are both constant, prices will vary with changes in the money supply; that is, inflation will be due to too much money in the economy. Second, if M and Q are constant, prices will vary with changes in velocity. In this case, inflation stems from people trying to spend their money too quickly, or trying to buy more goods than the economic system can produce. Finally, if M and V are constant, prices go up if quantities go down. Here, a shortage of goods leads to inflation.

Taking his analysis one step further, Fisher (1910) analyzed the factors that affect M, V, and Q. Most important was his explanation of how the spending habits of individuals, and the means by which people get paid, affect the velocity of money. To keep things simple, suppose all workers get paid at the beginning of every month. During the month they will normally use just about all their pay to buy goods and services. By the end of the month, then, all money is again held by employers and can be used to pay next month's wages. In this case, each British pound will be used 12 times during the year to purchase goods (once each month), and the velocity of money will be 12. On the other hand, if British workers were paid two times a month, the same process of wage payments followed by spending would occur 24 times a year, and the velocity of money would be 24 instead of 12. Because the frequency with which people are paid is relatively constant, the velocity of money should also be relatively constant. This leaves changes in the money supply (M) as the main cause of economic fluctuations. For Fisher, changes in M could affect either prices or real output. Contemporary monetary economists tend to follow Friedman, rather than Fisher, and contend that changes in the money supply affect only prices in the long run.

Although probably not as well-known by the general public as Thorstein Veblen, Fisher ranks as the most important American economist in the first half of the twentieth century. Lacking Veblen's breadth and vision, Fisher made up for this with the large number of contributions he made to monetary theory – defining important notions, showing how money affects the economy, and explaining what determines interest rates.

Works by Fisher

Appreciation of Interest, New York, Macmillan, 1892
The Nature of Capital and Income, New York, Macmillan, 1906
The Rate of Interest, New York, Macmillan, 1907
The Purchasing Power of Money, New York, Macmillan, 1910 (Revised 1922)
Stabilizing the Dollar, New York, Macmillan, 1920
The Making of Index Numbers, New York, Houghton Mifflin, 1922
"The Business Cycle Largely a 'Dance of the Dollar'," *Journal of the American Statistical Association*, 18 (December 1923), pp. 1024–8
"Our Unstable Dollar and the So-Called Business Cycle," *Journal of the American Statistical Association*, 20 (June 1925), pp. 179–202
The Money Illusion, New York, Adelphi, 1928
The Theory of Interest, New York, Macmillan, 1930
100% Money: Designed to Keep Checking Banks 100% Liquid, to Prevent Inflation and Deflation; Largely to Cure or Prevent Depressions; and to Wipe Out Much of the National Debt, New York, Adelphi, 1935
Constructive Income Taxation, New York, Harper, 1942

Works about Fisher

Allen, Robert Loring, *Irving Fisher: A Biography*, Oxford, UK, and Cambridge, Massachusetts, Blackwell, 1993
Fisher, Irving Norton, *My Father, Irving Fisher*, New York, Comet Press, 1956
Patinkin, Don, "Irving Fisher and His Compensated Dollar Plan," *Economic Quarterly* (Federal Reserve Bank of Richmond), 79, 3 (Summer 1993), pp. 1–33
Schumpeter, Joseph, "Irving Fisher's Econometrics," *Econometrica*, Vol. 16, 3 (July 1948). Reprinted in *Ten Great Economists*, New York, Oxford University Press, 1965, pp. 222–38

Other references

Hofstadter, Richard, *Social Darwinism in American Thought*, Philadelphia, University of Pennsylvania Press, 1944

ARTHUR CECIL PIGOU (1877–1959)

A. C. Pigou (pronounced PEE-GOO) is known as the father of modern *welfare economics*, which studies how to make economies operate more efficiently as well as the trade-offs between efficiency and equity. Pigou is also one of the founders of modern *public finance*. This work developed the means to analyze how taxes impact the economy and the justification for government intervention in economic affairs.

Pigou was born in 1877 at Ryde, on the UK's Isle of Wight. His father was an officer in the British army; his mother came from a long line of Irish government officials. Pigou studied first at Harrow, an elite English private school, and then at King's College, Cambridge. He began studying history at Cambridge; but in his third year he came under the influence of Alfred Marshall and Henry Sidgwick, who convinced him to study political economy. Like Marshall, Pigou was attracted to economics for its practical value. He sought to teach his students that "the main purpose of learning economics was to be able to see through the bogus economic arguments of the politicians" (Champernowne 1959, p. 264).

When Marshall retired from Cambridge in 1908, Pigou succeeded him in the Chair of Political Economy. From then until his retirement in 1943, Pigou was the main expositor of Marshallian economics at Cambridge.

World War I became a life-altering experience for Pigou. He continued teaching at Cambridge, but also served in the Ambulance Corps close to the front line during vacations. Johnson (1960, p. 153) reports that "this experience was responsible for transforming the gay, joke-loving, sociable, hospitable young bachelor of the Edwardian period into [an] eccentric recluse." Besides being a recluse, Pigou was also known as an extremely frugal human being, especially when it came to clothing. He frequently wore tatty, stained clothing, and showed up "at the Marshall Library one day in the fifties proudly wearing a suit bought before the First World War" (Johnson 1960, p. 150).

The main economic contributions of Pigou fall into two broad categories. First, his analysis of externalities provides the foundation for modern public finance, environmental economics and welfare economics. Second, Pigou was the first major opponent of the macroeconomic revolution started by Keynes.

Pigou's (1906, 1912) first works in economics were on industrial relations and import duties. These studies led to an interest in how government policy could increase national well-being. Pigou (1912) raised this general question, and then spent most of his life trying to answer it. In so doing, he invented a good deal of modern public finance, especially the arguments and rationale for government intervention in the economy.

For some goods, all production costs are borne by the firm and passed on to the consumer via the price of the good. Pigou (1920) showed that the (private) production costs to a firm may not reflect all the social costs of production. When producers manufacture a good they take into account only their private costs – the labor, the raw materials, and the capital that they have to purchase. But production inevitably pollutes the environment, and these costs are paid for by third parties who neither produce nor consume the good. Here the social costs of production exceed the private costs; the firm and the consumer get others to pay part of the cost of producing that good. Market outcomes are not the best possible outcomes in this situation. We get too many goods that pollute the environment; and firms tend to use technology that creates excessive pollution since the costs of pollution are imposed on third parties but are free to the firm. As a result, the market system produces too much polluted air and water, as well as excessive noise and congestion in urban areas.

On the other hand, production can yield benefits to society greater than the benefits received by those consumers who purchase it. The lighthouse, an example developed by British economist and philosopher Henry Sidgwick in 1883, is typically used to make this point. A lighthouse benefits all ships that cross its path, not only those ships that frequent the waters and would want to pay for its construction. Other examples of this sort include police and fire protection, national defense, and spending on health care and education. The individual who purchases a cold remedy benefits because he feels better as a result of taking this medication. But if this medication also makes it less likely that others will be infected, there are greater social benefits than private benefits.

These divergences between private costs and social costs are called "*externalities*," "spillover effects," and "third-party effects." Pigou stressed that in the presence of externalities the market system is inefficient, and that this might justify government intervention into the market place.

Whenever there are large positive externalities, people gain whether or not they pay anything. This ability to obtain the benefits of some good or service without having to pay for it gives rise to what is called "*the free rider problem*." Each person, looking at things from their own individual point of view, will recognize that if they do not contribute money towards the national defense, a defense system will be built anyway; and they will still reap the benefits of greater defense spending. If the US is attacked from abroad, my house will be protected whether or not I helped to pay for the national defense. Moreover, if I do not contribute to the national defense, a defense system will still be constructed. And my failure to contribute anything will make little difference to the type of defense system that gets built or the quality of that defense system. By not contributing to the national defense I save my hard-earned money, but I lose nothing.

The problem here is that, when everyone reasons in this manner, no money gets spent on defense and everyone is worse off. The solution to this problem is for the government to improve upon market-based outcomes. The government must develop a defense system and must tax all beneficiaries (its citizens) for the cost of its construction.

In many cases the government can remedy problems that stem from externalities through taxes and subsidies. But sometimes legal remedies are sufficient to solve the problem. For example, in the *Economics of Welfare*, Pigou (1920, pp. 129–30) argued that railroads should compensate farmers and other property owners who suffered losses from the damage of sparks and smoke emitted from trains. In this case, the main policy change needed was in British liability laws. If the railroads had to compensate others for the damage done by their trains, Pigou thought they would be more careful and would run fewer trains. Private and social benefits would thus no longer diverge, and externalities would be internalized, or become part of the cost of transporting goods via rail.

Finally, in some cases no government intervention is justified to remedy the problems stemming from externalities. When the costs imposed on third parties are small and the costs of any remedy are large, *cost–benefit analysis* leads to the conclusion that externalities should be allowed to persist. Consider the noise coming from trains. If this imposes only minor inconveniences on local residents, then the cost of forcing the railroads to move their lines or develop quieter trains may far exceed the cost to people of hearing trains go by their home every few hours.

Pigou (1920, ch. 1) asserted that one job of the economist was to identify externalities, and to help eliminate them by showing how and when government action would improve upon market outcomes. He even thought that economists had a moral responsibility to identify externalities. But Pigou was not only interested in eliminating externalities. His main concern was how to increase the economic well-being of a nation. This, he noted, depended on both the size of the economic pie and its distribution.

More output would increase general welfare, since people desire to have things, and the more things they have (in general) the better off they are. Redistributive economic policies would likewise increase general welfare. This conclusion followed from Pigou's belief that the satisfaction derived from money declines as one has more and more money. Another few hundred dollars means little to Bill Gates, who is fabulously wealthy, but to someone who is unemployed this extra money may make the difference between life and death. Consequently, the loss of welfare from taxing the rich must be less than the gain in economic welfare from giving that money to the poor. *Progressive taxation* and transfer programs to aid the poor could thus be justified as improving the overall well-being of the nation.

Pigou did recognize that progressive taxes and transfers might reduce the size of the economic pie, and that there could be a trade-off between growth and equity. When there was no trade-off the implications were clear. Anything that increased national output, but did not make the poor worse off, increased national welfare. And anything that increased the share of national output going to the poor, but did not reduce the total size of the output, also increased well-being.

However, when these two criteria clashed (when transfers to the poor reduced output) the situation was quite different. Judgments would be required about how much output to give up in order to improve the position of the poor. Arthur Okun (1975, ch. 4) has vividly described this trade-off in terms of a leaky bucket. Transfers from the rich to the poor are always made with a leaky bucket, which will lose some of its contents as it redistributes income. The leaking water represents the inefficiencies or the reduced national output due to these transfers. Okun (1975, p. 94), a strong supporter of equality, thought transfers should be stopped when the leakage hit 60 percent. Pigou (1920), was not quite as precise, but he did state that sacrificing a little output was worth the gains that come from greater equity.

Despite his many contributions to welfare economics and to public finance, Pigou has probably attained greatest notoriety as an opponent of the Keynesian Revolution that began at Cambridge during the 1930s. Keynes (1936) made Pigou his whipping boy in the *General Theory*. For many reasons, Pigou was an easy target. He was a recluse with few followers who would come to his defense; he dressed badly and was a comic figure at Cambridge; and he was part of the older establishment against whom Keynes was rebelling.

Keynes lumped Pigou with the classical school of economics and attributed to this school the belief that supply would always create its own demand (a doctrine known as "Say's Law" after the French economist J. B. Say, who is usually credited with being the first person to make this claim). According to Keynes, the classical economists held that this was true for both goods and labor; they believed that unemployment was impossible because when people offered their services to some employer there would have to be some demand for their labor services. If not, wages would fall until someone was willing to hire these workers.

There is a certain degree of validity to this picture of Pigou. He published a popular work entitled *Unemployment* (1914), which argued that in the long run unemployment was due to inflexible and high wages. Many years later (1927), he argued that reduced demand by businesses for workers would lead to higher unemployment, but that this problem could be remedied if workers let their real wages fall. And *The Theory of Unemployment* (Pigou 1933) argued that, if wage levels were greater than the *marginal productivity* of workers, businesses would not hire anyone since the cost of doing so would exceed the benefits of hiring that worker. Although Pigou never actively advocated wage cuts, in all these cases the solution to the unemployment problem seemed to be a reduction in wages. And it was for this reason that Keynes criticized Pigou.

Pigou was deeply offended by the *General Theory*, both for its attacks on himself and its attacks on the Marshallian tradition at Cambridge. Reviewing the *General Theory*, Pigou (1936) accused Keynes of misrepresenting his views, and claimed there was nothing at all of merit in the book. He argued that in his previous work he recognized that expansionary policies could increase prices, thereby reducing real wages and increasing employment in the short run. Pigou (1943, pp. 349f.) later developed his own criticisms of Keynesian economics. He formulated the *real balance* or *Pigou Effect*, which described one way that the problem of high unemployment would tend to be self-correcting and not require Keynesian economic policies. Pigou pointed out that prices generally fall during periods of high unemployment because firms cannot sell goods otherwise. As a result, real wealth, or the purchasing power of prior savings, increases during a recession. Being wealthier, people tend to spend more. This additional spending will then spur production, and businesses will

JOHN MAYNARD KEYNES (1883–1946)[1]

With Adam Smith and Karl Marx, John Maynard Keynes (pronounced CANES) stands as one of three giant figures in the history of economics. As Smith can be viewed as the optimist of this trio, seeing economic improvement as the main consequence of capitalism; and as Marx can be viewed as the pessimist, believing that its many serious problems would cause capitalism to self-destruct; Keynes can be viewed as the pragmatic savior of capitalism. Recognizing both the benefits and the flaws of capitalism, Keynes looked to economic policy as a means of mitigating the problems that arise in a capitalist economy. Intelligent government policy could save capitalism, he thought, allowing us to reap its benefits without experiencing its dark side.

Keynes was born in Cambridge, England in 1883 with the proverbial silver spoon in his mouth. His father, John Neville Keynes, was the registrar at Cambridge University and a distinguished economist and philosopher at the University. His mother was, for a time, the mayor of Cambridge.

Keynes was educated at the best schools in England – Eton and King's College, Cambridge. At Cambridge, he studied the classics, philosophy with G. E. Moore, mathematics with Alfred North Whitehead, and economics with Alfred Marshall. Keynes also became part of an exclusive club of intellectuals at Cambridge, which later became the Bloomsbury group. The group included major literary and artistic figures such as Virginia Woolf, E. M. Forster, and Lytton Strachey.

After graduation, Keynes sat for the British Civil Service exam and received the second-highest score of all those taking the test. This gave Keynes the second choice among all open civil service positions. Although he craved a job at the Treasury, this position was taken by Otto Niemeyer, who had first choice by virtue of scoring highest in the exam. Ironically, Keynes received the highest scores in Logic, Psychology, Political Science, and Essays; but he scored second overall because of a relatively low score in Economics. Later in life, Keynes would quip that he "knew more about Economics than my examiners" (Harrod 1951, p. 121).

Settling for a post in the India Office, Keynes helped to organize and coordinate British interests involving India. "His first major job, lasting for several months, was ordering and arranging for the shipment to Bombay of ten young Ayrshire bulls" (Moggridge 1992, p. 168). Things did not get any more interesting after this and Keynes, understandably, became bored with his job. Two years later, in 1908, he returned to Cambridge to teach economics. Three years after that he assumed editorship of the *Economic Journal*, which at the time was the most prestigious economics journal in the world.

Public acclaim first came to Keynes following publication of *The Economic Consequences of the Peace*, a book about the Versailles Peace Treaty ending World War I. During World War I Keynes served in the British Treasury and was primarily responsible for obtaining external finance to support the British war effort. As the end of the war drew near, Keynes was made a member of the British delegation at Versailles that was negotiating German war reparations. Besides containing biting portraits of the major participants at the peace conference (US President Wilson, French Chancellor Clemenceau, and British Prime Minister Lloyd George), Keynes (1971–89, vol. 2) also provided an angry critique of the peace treaty itself. According to his calculations, Germany could not possibly make good on the British and French demands for reparations. The economic consequence would be the impoverishment of Germany, and rising German hostility towards France and England. The political consequence, which Keynes equally feared, would be the rise of an angry and militant Germany in the future.

Now a figure of national prominence, Keynes turned his attention to questions of economic theory and policy. His *Tract on Monetary Reform* (Keynes 1971–89, vol. 4) warned of the dangers of inflation. It looked to central bank control of the money supply as a means of stabilizing the price level and keeping inflation under control. This work also contained Keynes's famous and misunderstood dictum "in the long run we are all dead." Many have taken this phrase to mean that Keynes was willing to sacrifice long-term economic performance for short-term economic benefits. Yet this is not at all what Keynes was driving at. Keynes meant to criticize others who believed that the problem of inflation would eventually remedy itself, without any active government involvement. To the contrary, Keynes felt that, rather than waiting for inflationary problems to correct themselves in the distant future, it would be better to employ economic policy and improve things now. His point was that there was no reason to wait for elusive future gains, when more rapid progress could be made solving economic problems by intelligently employing economic policies.

In the 1920s, inflation receded and Britain found itself increasingly subject to economic fluctuations and prolonged periods of high unemployment. Keynes thus turned his attention to these new problems. *A Treatise on Money* (Keynes 1971–89, vols 5 and 6) examined in detail the relationships between money, prices, and unemployment. Keynes singled out the saving–investment relationship as the main cause of economic fluctuations. According to Keynes, when people attempted to save more than businesses wanted to invest, businesses would soon find themselves with excess capacity to produce goods and too few buyers for the goods they produced. On the other hand, when investment exceeded saving, there would be too much spending taking place in the economy. Consumers would be spending rather than saving, and businesses would demand more workers to produce goods and more workers to build plants and equipment. All this spending would bid up wages as well as other costs of production, and also increase the price of all consumer goods. Inflation would be the natural outcome.

The problem, Keynes stressed, was that savings decisions and investment decisions were made by different groups of individuals. As a result, there was no guarantee that the two would be equal. Keynes then argued that it was the responsibility of the central bank to keep these two variables equal to one another, and thus the responsibility of the central bank to prevent inflation and recessions. If savings exceeded investment, the central bank would need to lower interest rates, thus both reducing savings and stimulating borrowing. On the other hand, if investment exceeded savings, the central bank would need to raise interest rates, thus increasing savings and reducing borrowing for investment purposes.

Keynes, though, is best known for his 1936 classic, *The General Theory of Employment, Interest and Money* (Keynes 1971–89, vol. 7). This work has been responsible for the development of a whole branch of economics (*macroeconomics*), and was the most referenced and debated work in economics during the twentieth century. The work itself is both an attack on the predecessors of Keynes, and a theory of what determines the amount of production and employment in a country. Although the book says very little about economic policy, it provided the theoretical foundation for government policy action to end the Depression that was plaguing virtually every country in the 1930s.

Keynes begins *The General Theory* by attacking Say's Law, the view that "supply creates its own demand." According to this dictum, unemployment was not possible because whatever the existing supply of workers (or whatever the existing supply of goods in the economy), there will be a demand for these workers (or a demand for these goods). Keynes then proceeded to turn Say's Law on its head, arguing that aggregate or total demand determined the supply of output and level of employment. Whenever demand was high, economies would prosper, businesses would expand and hire more workers, and unemployment would cease to be a problem. But when demand was low, firms would be unable to sell their goods and they would be forced to cut back on production and hiring. If things got very bad, there would be massive layoffs, high unemployment, and a depression.

For obvious reasons, Keynes turned next to study aggregate demand and the causes of changes in aggregate demand. Analyzing the two most important components of demand, Keynes developed the modern theories of consumer spending and business investment (which means firms expanding their operations by purchasing more plants and equipment).

Keynes identified two broad determinants of consumer spending – subjective factors and objective factors. The subjective or psychological factors affecting consumption were uncertainty regarding the future, the desire to bequeath a fortune, and a desire to enjoy independence and power. Greater fears about one's economic future, a greater desire to leave money to one's children, or a greater desire for independence, would lead to more saving and less spending. Conversely, a secure economic future, no heirs, and indifference to one's economic independence would reduce savings and increase spending.

The objective factors affecting consumption were economic variables like interest rates, taxes, the distribution of income and wealth, expected future income and – most important of all – current income. When interest rates rose, consumers would become reluctant to borrow money in order to buy homes, new cars, and other goods on credit. Conversely, with low interest rates, consumers would freely incur debt and spend money. Likewise, when wealth, current income, or expected future income went up, people would spend more and save less; and with less wealth, less current income, and lower expected income in the future, people would spend less and save more.

In contrast to the many factors affecting consumption, business investment depends on just two factors according to Keynes – the expected return on investment, and the rate of interest. The former constitutes the benefits from investing in new plant and equipment; the latter constitutes the cost of obtaining funds to purchase the plant and equipment. If the expected rate of return on investment exceeded the interest rate, business firms will expand, building new plants and filling them with machinery to produce goods. However, if interest rates exceeded the expected rate of return on investment, that investment will not take place.

Changes in expectations and changes in interest rates lead to changes in business investment. When business owners are optimistic about the economy (believing that they will be able to sell many goods in the future and get a good price from consumers for these goods), they will expect high rates of return on money used to build new plants and equipment. However, when pessimism sets in, business decision-makers expect fewer sales to consumers and think that only if they offer goods at low prices will consumers purchase these goods. In this case, expectations are for meager rates of return on new investment, and little new plant is built.

Keynes next had to explain what determined interest rates. The interest rate was determined, according to Keynes, in money markets where people and businesses demand money and where central banks control the money supply. The demand for money came from portfolio decisions made by people and businesses – they could hold money or they could hold their wealth in the form of stocks, bonds and other assets.

By necessity, the supply of money existing in the economy must be held by someone. When central banks increase the money supply they buy government bonds. A bond is merely a promise to pay the person who owns the bond a fixed sum of money at some point in the future. To keep things simple, consider a bond that promises to pay its owner $1,000 one year from today. If I were to purchase this bond for $800, my interest rate, or the rate of return on the money I lent to whoever printed the bond, will be 25 percent (a $200 gain on the $800 I paid for the bond). If the price for the bond were $909 rather than $800, I would be getting back around 10 percent on my money (a $91 gain on the $909 I paid for the bond). And had I bought the bond for $990, I would be making only around 1 percent on my money ($10 additional on the $990 I lay out now). Consequently, bond prices and interest rates are inversely related – as one goes up, the other goes down, and vice versa.

When central banks buy bonds, this drives up the price of bonds and lowers the rate of return on these assets. On the other hand, when central banks want to reduce the money supply, they must sell bonds. To get people to hold these bonds the central bank must offer them at a low price. Those buying the bonds will thus be receiving a good rate of return on their money, or interest rates will rise.

After his critique of classical economic theory, and his presentation of the determinants of total demand for goods and services, Keynes, surprisingly, had little to say about how to reduce unemployment and end depressions. This is especially surprising since Keynes was interested first and foremost in economic policy.

He supported both money creation (*monetary policy*) and tax cuts as well as greater government spending (*fiscal policy*). In a much-quoted passage, Keynes writes about the need for more houses, hospitals, schools, and roads. But he notes that many people are likely to object to such "wasteful" government spending. Another approach (money creation) was therefore necessary.

> If the Treasury were to fill old bottles with banknotes, bury them at suitable depths in disused coal mines which are then filled up to the surface with town rubbish … private enterprise [would] dig the notes up and there need be no more unemployment (Keynes 1971–89, vol. 7, p. 129).

And in a much maligned passage, Keynes (1971–89, vol. 7, p. 378) calls for "a somewhat comprehensive socialization of investment." While many have taken him to be advocating government control of all business investment decisions, what Keynes really advanced was government spending policies to stabilize the aggregate level of investment in the national economy (Pressman 1987). Keynes believed that consumer spending was relatively stable, and changed little from year to year. Business investment, however, was driven by fickle "animal spirits." Changes in business confidence or expectations about the future of the economy would change the level of investment and would have a major impact on the economy. Moreover, self-fulfilling prophesies were likely to be at work. When businesses were confident about the economy, they would invest more and the economy would expand. This boom would reinforce expectations about profits, and lead to even greater optimism and investment. On the other hand, expectations about a poorly performing economy would lower investment, slow economic activity, and reinforce and strengthen business pessimism about future profits. As a result of all this, when optimism took hold the economy would boom, but when pessimism set in there would be dramatic declines in investment and massive unemployment.

Keynes's solution was to have government stabilize the level of investment. When private investment was low, the government should borrow money (i.e. run a budget deficit) and engage in public investments such as building new roads and bridges as well as spending more money on schools and better education. This would expand the economy as well as improve expectations. In contrast, when business investment was high due to great optimism, government should stop borrowing, repay its past loans and cut back on its public investment.

The 1940s found Keynes again working for the British government. He also returned to policy issues surrounding the war effort. He helped negotiate British loans from the US to help fight World War II, and he developed a proposal to help Britain finance its war effort. Rather than raising taxes (which would reduce British incomes), and rather than doing nothing to finance war spending (which would generate inflation due to shortages of goods and high demand), Keynes proposed a plan of compulsory savings or deferred pay. His idea was that all British citizens with incomes greater than some minimal level would have money taken out of their regular pay checks and put into special bank accounts to help finance the war. These accounts would earn interest during the war, but the money in them could not be withdrawn except under emergency circumstances. These savings could then be lent to the government and used to finance the war effort. After the war, the money in these accounts could be freely withdrawn and used for consumption needs. As an added benefit, this additional spending would help prevent another depression after the war.

When World War II ended, Keynes worked on the new international monetary arrangements being developed by the victorious governments. He believed that one major cause of the world depression of the 1930s was that every country tried to export unemployment to its trading partners. By running a trade surplus, each country could produce more and create more domestic employment; its trading partners would import goods instead of producing them within their borders. As a result, fewer workers would be needed abroad and unemployment would rise abroad.

Most countries attempted to generate trade surpluses through devaluing their currencies. By making foreign money and foreign goods more expensive, national governments knew that their citizens would buy fewer foreign goods and buy more goods made by domestic firms. Similarly, by making domestic money and domestic goods cheaper for people in other countries, devaluation would increase exports. The problem was that, whenever one country devalued its currency in an attempt to create exports and employment for its citizens, other countries would follow suit. The result was a series of currency devaluations that did not benefit any country.

In order to prevent competitive currency devaluations, Keynes proposed a system of relatively fixed exchange rates. This system was agreed to by the Allied victors at Bretton Woods, New Hampshire, in 1944, and came to be known as the Bretton Woods system. Bretton Woods required that each country peg its currency to an ounce of gold and keep it there. Because every currency was tied to gold, the value of every currency was tied to every other currency. If the US government said each dollar was worth 0.1 ounces of gold, and if the British government decreed that each pound would be worth 0.2 ounces of gold, then $2 had to equal È1, since both were equal to 0.2 of an ounce of gold.

The Bretton Woods agreement operated for about twenty-five years. During this time the world economy grew at unprecedented rates and unemployment rates in developed countries reached their lowest levels of the twentieth century.

But difficult problems simmered below the surface. At the agreed fixed exchange rates, gold was rapidly leaving the US, and the US feared it would soon run out of gold. Something had to be done to stop this. Bretton Woods died in August 1971, when President Nixon ended the convertibility of dollars into gold, and then announced that he would let the dollar float relative to an ounce of gold. The current system of flexible and variable exchange rates was born.

A second way to stem the deflationary impact of each country attempting to run a trade surplus was to set up some mechanism to discourage or prevent this from happening. Keynes wanted to establish an international system that would lend money to countries running trade deficits and penalize countries that persistently ran trade surpluses. Like the fiscal and money policies contained in *The General Theory*, this would encourage countries to spend money on foreign goods and so would counter any tendencies towards another depression. The clearing mechanism and the lending facility Keynes wanted were also established at Bretton Woods; these are the International Monetary Fund and the World Bank. Unfortunately, these institutions did not fill the role that Keynes hoped they would. The US expected it would run trade surpluses because its manufacturing capacity was not destroyed in the war; and so it refused to support any system that would penalize countries with persistent surpluses. Keynes pushed hard for a policy of penalizing surplus countries, but the US had all the bargaining chips because of all the money it had lent to Britain during World War II (see Block 1977). Ironically, such a policy would have been a great benefit to the US in the late twentieth and early twenty-first centuries because of its enormous trade deficits (exceeding $700 billion in 2005).

Keynes suffered a series of heart attacks while negotiating details of the final compromise on the nature of international financial institutions and arrangements. He died at his country home in Tilton, East Sussex, in 1946.

Without doubt, no twentieth century economist has had a greater impact than Keynes. At the theoretical level Keynes developed macroeconomic analysis, and macroeconomics as it is taught in colleges and universities today still relies on the concepts and modes of analysis developed by Keynes. Even contemporary macroeconomists opposed to the ideas of Keynes (see **Friedman** and **Lucas**) find it necessary to start with Keynes, and then explain the limitations and problems with his theory. At the policy level, the many tools employed by central banks and central governments to help control the business cycle, and the international mechanisms that exist to deal with trade imbalances and financial problems, are primarily due to Keynes.

Note

1 An earlier version of this piece appeared in the *Encyclopedia of Political Economy*, ed. Phil O'Hara *et al.*, New York and London, Routledge, 1998.

Works by Keynes

The Collected Writings of John Maynard Keynes, ed. D. Moggridge, 30 vols, London, Macmillan, 1971–89. Paperback editions of *Essays in Biography* and *Essays in Persuasion* are published by Norton. Harcourt, Brace & World publishes a paperback edition of *The General Theory of Employment, Interest and Money*.

Works about Keynes

Dillard, Dudley, *The Economics of J. M. Keynes*, New York, Prentice Hall, 1948

Hansen, Alvin, *A Guide to Keynes*, New York, McGraw Hill, 1953

Harrod, Roy, *The Life of John Maynard Keynes*, New York, Norton, 1951

Lekachman, Robert, *The Age of Keynes*, New York, Random House, 1966

Moggeridge, Donald, *Maynard Keynes: An Economist's Biography*, London and New York, Routledge, 1992

Pressman, Steven, "The Policy Relevance of *The General Theory*," *Journal of Economic Studies*, 14 (1987), pp. 13–23

Skidelsky, Robert, *John Maynard Keynes*, 3 vols, New York, Viking, 1983, 1992, and 2001

Other references

Block, Fred L., *Origins of the International Economic Order*, Berkeley, California, University of California Press, 1977

JOSEPH SCHUMPETER (1883–1950)

For Joseph Schumpeter (pronounced SHUM-PAY-ter) economics was all about change. He studied both short-run economic fluctuations and the long-run tendencies of capitalism. In these studies he identified the phases and causes of business cycles. He also examined the factors contributing to the rise and decline of capitalism.

Schumpeter was born to middle class parents in Triesch, Moravia (then part of the Austro-Hungarian Empire and now part of the Czech Republic) in 1883. His father, who owned a textile factory, died when he was very young. His mother soon remarried and moved to Vienna, where Schumpeter attended high school with the aristocratic elite. He received an excellent education in the humanities, but inadequate grounding in mathematics and science. As a law student at the University of Vienna, Schumpeter took several courses in economics. A seminar taught by Böhm-Bawerk sparked his interest in the long-term future of capitalism.

After receiving a doctorate of law in 1906, Schumpeter went to Cairo to practice law and to manage the finances of an Egyptian princess. In 1909 he accepted a teaching job at the University of Czernowitz (then in the Austrian Empire, but now in Ukraine), and two years later was appointed to a chair in political economy at the University of Graz.

Schumpeter then became interested in politics. In 1918 he became a member of the German Socialization Commission, which argued for socializing German industry in order to make it more efficient. In 1919, he became Finance Minister of Austria. His political career, however, was both short and unsuccessful. He proposed an unpopular tax on capital to control inflation. A flippant remark about the Austrian dollar ("a crown remains a crown") in the face of rampant inflation was viewed as insensitive to the plight of most Austrians. And there was much criticism of his plans to nationalize Austrian firms.

Unable to handle the pressures of political life, Schumpeter resigned after just seven months in office (Shionoya 1955, p. 18). He then became President of the Biedermann Bank in Vienna. Shortly thereafter, the bank became insolvent. At the same time Schumpeter invested in highly speculative activities and lost his shirt while incurring massive debts, which it took him many years to repay.

Unable to succeed in the real world, Schumpeter decided to return to academic life. In 1925, he accepted an appointment as Professor of Economics at the University of Bonn. Seven years later he accepted a position at Harvard, where he remained until his death in 1950. In 1949, Schumpeter served as President of the American Economic Association, thus becoming the first non-American to be so honored.

For Schumpeter, all capitalist economies had two prominent characteristics – they were unstable, and they experienced rapid growth. Schumpeter sought to analyze and understand these features of capitalism.

Schumpeter (1939) was one of the first economists to study business cycles, the regular fluctuations that economies experience. He identified three different cycles occurring simultaneously. First, there were short-run fluctuations of three to four years, which Schumpeter called "Kitchin Cycles," after economist Joseph Kitchin who first discovered them. These cycles were due to changes in business inventories. For one to two years, businesses would expand their inventories in order to keep ahead of rising sales. But when the growth of sales slowed, inventories would begin to pile up in warehouses. As a result, businesses would cut back production for a year or so in order to reduce their inventory backlog. When inventories finally returned to more desirable levels, and sales picked up, businesses would again seek to expand their inventories.

A second cycle was associated with changes in business investment in new plant and equipment. These cycles lasted eight to eleven years, and Schumpeter called them "Juglar Cycles," after Clement Juglar who first discovered them. Usually when people speak of "*the* business cycle," they refer to these economic fluctuations. Expansions lasting four to five years, Schumpeter thought, were due to the desire of businesses to expand and modernize their capital equipment. But after most businesses have expanded and modernized, they have little need for new investment. Consequently, spending on plant and equipment is cut back during the next four or five years. Over this period, capital equipment becomes worn out and outdated, thus setting the stage for another investment boom of four to five years.

Finally, there are long-run cycles, or *Kondratieff waves*, lasting 45 to 60 years. Schumpeter named these cycles after Russian economist Nikolai Kondratieff, who first noticed them but could not explain what caused them (see **Kuznets**). Schumpeter saw invention and innovation as the driving force behind long-run cycles. In times of slow economic growth, businesses would not likely introduce new innovations. As a result, new discoveries and innovations would pile up for several decades. When rapid economic growth finally begins, the stockpile of innovations gets employed in the production process and economies grow rapidly. Schumpeter regarded the Industrial Revolution, which introduced the steam engine, the spinning jenny, and other discoveries, as the beginning of one long-term economic expansion. Railroad construction in the mid-nineteenth century began a second Kondratieff wave. In the early twentieth century, electricity, automobiles, and chemicals sparked a third Kondratieff wave.

In his early work, Schumpeter (1911) held that invention was determined by non-economic forces and could not be understood through studying economics. In later work, Schumpeter (1942) held that innovation was shaped by economic forces inside the large firm. But throughout his life, Schumpeter refused to believe that innovation was a rational activity; instead he thought it was a creative activity that could neither be explained nor understood as the result of rational thinking processes. The agent of innovation and invention was the entrepreneur.

Unlike many of his contemporaries, Schumpeter did not believe that entrepreneurs merely hired resources in order to produce goods and meet consumer demand at minimum cost. Rather, like Cantillon, he thought that entrepreneurs were individuals willing to take risks. As such, they were the key force causing capitalist economies to grow. When there were many entrepreneurs, capitalism would thrive; on the other hand, if the entrepreneurial spirit was destroyed or severely hindered, capitalism would quietly transform itself into socialism.

For entrepreneurs to succeed, Schumpeter held that they had to mold and shape consumer tastes. In contrast to other economists, who saw firms responding to consumer tastes, Schumpeter held that "the great majority of changes in commodities consumed has been forced by producers on consumers who, more often than not, have resisted the change and have had to be educated up by elaborate psychotechnics of advertising" (Schumpeter 1939, vol. 1, p. 73). Consumer preferences do not lead to production and innovation; rather, innovation leads to new goods and services that consumers either reject or develop tastes for.

Invention and innovation by the entrepreneur was the driving force behind long-run economic cycles, according to Schumpeter (1911). Invention, backed by bank credit, leads to innovation and growing prosperity. This soon attracts imitators, and the original innovation leads to economic prosperity. But imitators are always less effective than innovators, and many arrive too late in the expansion cycle. Miscalculation and tighter credit will push some firms into bankruptcy, and lead to recession or depression. But these bankruptcies also weed out inefficient firms, thus correcting the errors of the past expansion. Inventions accumulate during the contraction, when entrepreneurs cannot find the funds to convert them into new products and processes. They remain dormant, but are available to start a new cycle of growth when the time is right and the economy begins to rebound.

In *Capitalism, Socialism and Democracy*, Schumpeter (1942) adopted an even broader perspective on economic change. Rather than examining the cyclical changes that a capitalist economy goes through, he examined the very future of capitalism. The big question he asked was "Can capitalism survive?" The answer he gave was "No. I do not think it can" (Schumpeter 1942, p. 61). In essence, he thought that Marx was right in believing that socialism would replace capitalism. However, rather than being destroyed by its failures, as Marx predicted, Schumpeter believed that capitalism would be destroyed by its many successes.

Schumpeter (1942, p. 83) thought that *creative destruction* was one main reason for the success of capitalism. Capitalism is not only about successful innovation; it is also about destroying old and inefficient processes and products. This replacement process makes capitalism dynamic and causes incomes to grow rapidly. Problems arise, however, because smaller firms are constantly being replaced by larger firms. Through this process, managerial bureaucrats, rather than innovative entrepreneurs, come to run the firm. These managers are employees rather than owners. They prefer a steady income and job security to innovation and risk-taking. As a result, capitalism loses its dynamic tendency towards innovation and its spirit of continual improvement and change.

Schumpeter (1942, pp. 121–5) also saw potential problems stemming from the fact that capitalism requires rational calculation and logical decision-making from all participants. This leads people to develop a skeptical and critical frame of mind. In addition, because capitalism is so successful at increasing incomes, it can support a large number of middle class intellectuals. With much free time on their hands, these individuals will criticize the capitalist system and push for measures that enhance the economic role of government bureaucrats. Resentment against the income inequalities that make capitalism possible will also be strong among intellectuals, and they will push for measures that try to keep incomes equal. These actions also will reduce the incentive to take risks and innovate.

Finally, Schumpeter (1942, pp. 160–1) thought that capitalism undermines the family. Capitalism is all about satisfying individual wants, while the family requires sublimating one's desires and compromising. If everyone just focuses on satisfying their own wants, it is hard to see how long-term relationships can last. One such relationship, the family, is important for capitalism because it is a main reason for saving. Families save so that, if anything happens to the main breadwinner, other family members will be provided for. By undermining the motivation to save, capitalism destroys its own foundation – the capital needed for future growth.

Long-term economic growth has always been a central economic-concern. Adam Smith and most classical economists saw capitalism as the best way to achieve rapid growth. By the late nineteenth century, however, economists came to focus more on the question of economic efficiency, and they lost interest in the issue of growth. The main contribution of Schumpeter has been to redirect the attention of economists to the issue of long-term economic growth. In so doing, he stressed the importance of non-economic factors like innovation and the entrepreneur for a healthy, thriving, and growing capitalism.

Works by Schumpeter

Theory of Economic Development (1911), Cambridge, Massachusetts, Harvard University Press, 1954

Economic Doctrine and Method: An Historical Sketch (1914), London, George Allen & Unwin, 1954

Business Cycles. A Theoretical, Historical and Statistical Analysis of the Capitalist Process, 2 vols, New York, McGraw Hill, 1939

Capitalism, Socialism and Democracy, New York, Harper, 1942

Ten Great Economists, New York, Oxford University Press, 1951

History of Economic Analysis, New York, Oxford University Press, 1954

Works about Schumpeter

Allen, Robert Loring, *Opening Doors: The Life and Work of Joseph Schumpeter*, 2 vols, New Brunswick, Transaction Publishers, 1994

Heertje, Arnold (ed.), *Schumpeter's Vision: Capitalism, Socialism and Democracy After 40 Years*, New York, Praeger, 1981

Heilbroner, Robert, "Was Schumpeter Right?," *Social Research*, 48, 3 (Autumn 1981), pp. 456–71

Oakley, Allen, *Schumpeter's Theory of Capitalist Motion: A Critical Exposition and Reassessment*, Hampshire, Edward Elgar, 1990

Rosenberg, Nathan, "Joseph Schumpeter: Radical Economist," in *Exploring the Black Box: Technology, Economics, and History*, Cambridge, Cambridge University Press, 1994, pp. 47–61

Shionoya, Yuichi, *Schumpeter and the Idea of Social Science*, New York, Cambridge University Press, 1995

Stolper, Wolfgang E., *Joseph Alois Schumpeter: The Public Life of a Private Man*, Princeton, New Jersey, Princeton University Press, 1994

PIERO SRAFFA (1898–1983)

Piero Sraffa (pronounced SRAH-fah) made two contributions to economics. First, Sraffa pointed out that the marginalist theory of value is logically inconsistent. Second, he attempted to construct an adequate theory of value based upon the work of Ricardo and the classical notion of a *surplus* that is generated during the production process.

Sraffa was born in Turin, Italy, in 1898 into a wealthy and distinguished Jewish family. His father was a well-known lawyer, who both practiced law and taught law at various Italian universities. As his father moved from one university to another, Sraffa moved from city to city and from school to school. After graduating from secondary school, Sraffa enrolled in the law faculty at the University of Turin, where he studied political economy under Luigi Einaudi, a well-known specialist in *public finance* and later President of the Italian Republic. Following a brief stint in the Italian army, Sraffa completed his degree in 1920, writing his doctoral thesis under Einaudi on monetary inflation during the period 1914–20 in Italy.

After graduation, Sraffa worked at an Italian bank, but he left this job in the spring of 1921 in order to spend time in England studying British monetary problems. Through a friend of his father, Sraffa made the acquaintance of John Maynard Keynes.

In 1922, at the invitation of Keynes, Sraffa wrote two articles on Italian banking. One was published in the *Economic Journal*, a scholarly journal edited by Keynes (Sraffa 1922a), and concerned the bankruptcy of an Italian bank. The second article appeared in the *Manchester Guardian* (Sraffa 1922b), and criticized the reporting procedures of Italian banks as well as government supervision of bank reporting procedures. This article was soon translated into four languages, including Italian. As a result, it came to the attention of Mussolini, who became enraged and called it "an act of true and real sabotage of Italian finance" (Kaldor 1985, p. 618). Mussolini contacted Sraffa's father, insisting on a full and complete retraction. Sraffa refused; but he had to flee Italy until Mussolini calmed down.

Despite his precarious relationship with Mussolini, Sraffa held numerous jobs in Italy during the 1920s. He set up a government department in Milan to collect labor statistics, but resigned as soon as the Fascist regime took power. Then he lectured in Public Finance and Political Economy at the University of Perugia, and he held the position of Professor of Economics at Cagliari University in Sardinia.

As the Fascist government became increasingly repressive, Sraffa sought employment outside Italy, and Keynes helped to arrange a lectureship for Sraffa at Cambridge University. Sraffa, however, found lecturing difficult. He disliked talking about his ideas in public and felt uncomfortable having to lecture in English. Again Keynes came to the rescue, getting Sraffa a job as head of the Marshall Library of Economics at Cambridge. Keynes also arranged for Sraffa to edit the works of David Ricardo for the Royal Economic Society. This project helped shift Sraffa's interests from money and economic policy to the abstract and theoretical issues of value theory. Sraffa spent a good deal of time in the 1930s, 1940s, and early 1950s compiling the ten-volume edition of Ricardo's *Works and Correspondence* (Sraffa 1951–5). While he received many awards for this scholarly endeavor (including the Soderstrom Gold Medal of the Swedish Royal Academy of Sciences, a precursor to the Nobel Prize in Economics), it is mainly through his work on the theory of value that Sraffa made his mark.

By the 1920s, supply and demand analysis had come to dominate economic thinking in Europe. But Sraffa was dissatisfied with this mode of thinking. His contributions to value theory were two-fold – one destructive and one constructive. First, he pointed out the logical flaws in the Marshallian analysis of supply. Second, he developed a more adequate theory of supply that relied on the classical notion of a *surplus*.

In 1925 Sraffa published an article in the *Annali di Economia* of Bocconi University attacking the foundations of orthodox Marshallian economics. Edgeworth read this paper in Italian and told Keynes about it. He also asked Keynes to have Sraffa write a shorter version of the paper for the *Economic Journal* (Sraffa 1926). Both articles pointed out logical problems with the supply curve of Marshall.

According to Marshall, the supply curve of any firm was independent of the supply curves of all other firms in the industry. An industry supply curve was derived by simply adding up the supply curves of every firm in the industry. If there were 200 firms in the industry, and 100 would produce 1,000 coffee mugs at $1, while the other 100 firms wanted to produce 2,000 coffee mugs if the price was $1, total output in the industry would be 300,000 coffee mugs if the price was set at $1. Similar calculations could be made for other possible prices. Adding up the quantity of coffee mugs produced at each different price, we get the industry supply of coffee mugs.

Sraffa argued that the conditions of production, and thus the supply curve, for any one firm had to affect the conditions of production for all its competitors. For example, when one firm expands its production of coffee mugs it will increase its demand for the materials (e.g. clay) that are needed to produce coffee mugs, and so the price of these materials will increase. But if the cost of making coffee mugs rises because of higher material costs, *all firms* make less profit by producing coffee mugs. As a result, other firms will want to produce fewer coffee mugs at each price. Because of such interdependence, Sraffa contended, it was illegitimate to draw Marshallian supply curves for any industry (see Mongiovi 1996).

Sraffa's second criticism was an attack on the assumption of *diminishing returns* in production. He argued that most production, especially manufactured consumer goods, occurs under conditions of *increasing returns*. Harking back to his other criticism of Marshall, he also showed that diminishing returns cannot apply to a particular industry or good in isolation, since changes in the cost of production in a particular industry will affect the cost of production in all other industries that require this good in the production process. For this reason, Sraffa held that the economic model of perfect competition had to be abandoned. Moreover, it had to be replaced with a model acknowledging firm interdependence and the existence of monopoly and oligopoly. This critique led to the development of models of monopolistic competition by Joan Robinson and others (see Harcourt 1986).

Sraffa was responsible for other criticisms of orthodox microeconomics. The *Cambridge Controversy* (see **Robinson**), suggested by Sraffa to Robinson, involved the argument (being made in Cambridge, England) that the orthodox theory of value was circular. Another approach to value theory was thus needed. Sraffa went back to the economics of Ricardo and the classical notion of a surplus, and began to develop this approach.

According to Sraffa, a logically consistent theory of value and distribution had to return to the classical conception of the circular nature of production – goods used to produce goods, and a *surplus* being created if you wind up producing more goods than you start with. Sraffa (1960) then went on to show the consistency of this model. He showed how such a model can be used to explain value or relative prices, as well as the principles that determined the distribution of income between wages and profits.

Beginning with a given technology that details what is necessary to produce goods, and given either a real wage (determined by the subsistence needs of workers) or the rate of profit, Sraffa demonstrated that relative prices would be determined. One key implication of the Sraffian model is that the distribution of income between wages and profits is determined outside the model; it arises from the subsistence wage paid to workers and/or the rate of profit in the economy. Another key implication of this analysis is that current technology, or the cost of production, determines relative prices.

Let us take a simple case, one with no surplus, to demonstrate this point. Suppose that the economy produces only two types of goods – manufactured goods (M) and agricultural goods (A). The technological requirements for producing these goods are as follows:

$$2A+2M=6A$$
$$4A+1M=3M$$

Two bushels of seed corn and two plows are required to produce six bushels of corn, while four bushels of corn and one plow are needed to produce three plows. Starting with six bushels of corn and three plows, and producing these goods during the year, we wind up with six bushels of corn and three plows. Our economy reproduces itself, but creates no surplus or fails to grow during the year.

If we think about prices in terms of this model or set of equations, we should recognize that the cost of inputs must equal the value of the output produced in each sector. Thus we can think of A as the price of a bushel of corn and M as the price of a plow. To find the prices of these two commodities we need to solve the above two algebraic equations for A and for M. Unfortunately, there is no unique mathematical solution here; but we do know that the mathematics of production technology will require A to equal 2M, or the price of a bushel of corn must be twice the price of a plow. The technology of production thus determines values or relative prices, although it does not tell us what the price of each good will be.

Sraffa was able to extend this model to a world of many goods and again show that the technology of production still determines relative prices. He was also able to extend the model to cases where a surplus is produced. Here things become even more complicated, and Sraffa had to make a few simplifying assumptions. First, he assumed that capital mobility would lead to a uniform rate of profit for all industries. This is a fairly reasonable assumption, since capital should flow to those industries or sectors yielding greater returns and should leave those industries or sectors with lower returns. This should reduce profit rates in the former set of industries and increase profit rates in the latter set of industries. Next, Sraffa assumed that the rate of profit depended on the rate of interest (Roncaglia 1993). With these two assumptions, Sraffa was able again to demonstrate that it was technology or the cost of production that determined relative prices.

This analysis has several key theoretical implications. Values or relative prices could be explained without resorting to the circularity of marginalist analysis. In addition, economics does not have to employ the suspect notion (as shown in the *Cambridge Controversy*) of aggregate capital. According to Sraffa's classical model, the distribution of income between wages and profits is determined by monetary policy, by competition, and by other forces that affect interest rates and worker wages.

This return to a more classical theory of distribution also has a number of important real world implications (see Sen 2003, pp. 1246–7). Profits and the high wages received by some people are no longer the result of the productivity of capital or the high productivity of some workers. Rather, profits and high wages are the result of technology, political decisions regarding interest rates, and the economic power held by different economic actors.

Sraffa's place in the history of economics is rather difficult to pinpoint. He made several telling criticisms of standard economic theory, and he began to develop a new and different theory of value. Yet few economists, even the majority of economists who are critical of traditional economic theory, have followed the path pioneered by Sraffa.

Works by Sraffa

"The Bank Crisis in Italy," *Economic Journal*, 32 (June 1922a), pp. 178–97

"The Current Situation of the Italian Banks," *Manchester Guardian Commercial: The Reconstruction in Europe*, Supplement No. XI, (7 December 1922b), pp. 675–6

"The Laws of Return under Competitive Conditions," *Economic Journal*, 36, (December 1926), pp. 535–50

"General Preface" and "Introduction," in *On the Principles of Political Economy and Taxation*, Vol. 1 of *The Works and Correspondence of David Ricardo*, 10 vols, ed. Piero Sraffa, Cambridge University Press, 1951–5

Production of Commodities by Means of Commodities: Prelude to a Critique of Economic Theory, Cambridge, Cambridge University Press, 1960

Works about Sraffa

Kaldor, Nicholas, "Piero Sraffa 1898–1983," *Proceedings of the British Academy*, 71 (1985), pp. 615–40

Mongiovi, Gary, "Sraffa's Critique of Marshall: A Reassessment," *Cambridge Journal of Economics*, 20 (1996), pp. 207–24

Potier, Jean-Pierre, *Piero Sraffa: Unorthodox Economist (1898–1983)*, London and New York, Routledge, 1991

Roncaglia, Alessandro, "Piero Sraffa's Contribution to Political Economy," in *Twelve Contemporary Economists*, ed. J. R. Shakleton and G. Locksley, New York, Wiley, 1981, pp. 240–56

Roncaglia, Alessandro, "Towards a Post-Sraffian Theory of Income Distribution," *Journal of Income Distribution*, 3, 1 (Summer 1993), pp. 3–27

Roncaglia, Alessandro, *Piero Sraffa: His Life, Thought, and Cultural Heritage*, London, Routledge, 2000

Sen, Amartya, "Sraffa, Wittgenstein, and Gramsci," *Journal of Economic Literature*, 41 (December 2003), pp. 1240–55

Other references

Harcourt, G. C., "On the Influence of Piero Sraffa on the Contributions of Joan Robinson to Economic Theory," *Economic Journal*, 95 (1986), pp. 96–108

GUNNAR MYRDAL (1898–1987)

The economics of Gunnar Myrdal (pronounced mirr-DALL) has two distinguishing characteristics – a focus on real-world economic issues and an effort to bring the insights from other disciplines into economic analysis. Myrdal spent much of his life studying the problems of race relations, unemployment, and poverty. He also sought to understand how economies change over time, and he looked towards psychological, historical, sociological, and cultural factors as the cause of these changes.

Myrdal was born in 1898 in the village of Solvarbo, in a rural, farming area of central Sweden. His father was a wealthy landowner who was able to provide Myrdal with an excellent education. Myrdal studied mathematics at the Royal Gymnasium and then enrolled at Stockholm University to study law. He chose this course of study because he wanted to understand how society worked. Although Myrdal received a law degree in 1923, the grueling course of study killed his interest in the law. His wife Alva then convinced him to study economics, a discipline that combined science and mathematics with an attempt to understand the workings of society (Angresano

1997, pp. 146–7). After studying under Knut Wicksell, Myrdal received a PhD in Economics from Stockholm University in 1927 and then began teaching there.

In 1932 Myrdal was appointed by Sweden's social democratic government to a new housing and population commission, and was thus able to influence Swedish housing policy. From 1934 to 1936, and again from 1942 to 1946, he served in the Swedish Parliament, and in the late 1930s he served on the Board of the National Bank of Sweden. In the mid-1940s, Myrdal became chairman of the Swedish Post-War Planning Commission and Minister for Trade and Commerce.

Because of his economic ideas and his many positions of political influence, Myrdal became one of the main architects of the Swedish welfare state. Furthermore, he was a strong advocate of using Keynesian *fiscal policy* in Sweden. Kindleberger (1987, pp. 394–5) credits Myrdal with convincing Finance Minister Ernst Wigters to spend money for public works and run budget deficits in order to reduce unemployment during the depression of the 1930s. In 1974, Myrdal shared the Nobel Prize for Economics with Friedrich Hayek.

Myrdal had wide and diverse interests, and he made important contributions to both economic theory and policy analysis. At the theoretical level, he introduced the *ex ante–ex post* distinction to help clarify some confusing aspects of macroeconomic analysis, and he developed the notion of *cumulative causation* as an alternative to equilibrium analysis. At the policy level, Myrdal explained the persistence of poverty throughout the developing world and among blacks in the US, and he suggested numerous policies to deal with the problem of poverty.

The lack of a distinction between expectations and actual outcomes created much confusion in economics during the 1920s. Businesses, for example, invest to make a profit; yet they sometimes lose money. Businesses even invest at times when there is no additional savings; but all economists know that savings must equal investment. Myrdal (1939) helped clarify these matters with his distinction between expected outcomes and final outcomes, or between *ex ante* and *ex post* economic variables. Expected or *ex ante* economic variables are measured at the beginning of some process; final or *ex post* variables are measured at the end of the process.

With this distinction Myrdal was able to explain how an increase in investment over *ex ante* saving would lead to additional savings (through increases in profits and other incomes), so that *ex post* savings will equal investment. By the same token, greater savings, *ex ante*, would cause a recession and lead to layoffs and lower profits for businesses. Unable to sell what they already produced, businesses would scale back investment. Again, when measured *ex post*, savings will equal investment.

Although the *ex ante–ex post* distinction helps to explain how economies will move towards an equilibrium where savings equal investment, for the most part Myrdal was opposed to equilibrium analysis and proposed an alternative way to understand how economies work. *Cumulative causation* involves a positive or negative feedback mechanism involving two or more variables. Since changes in any one variable lead to similar changes in other variables, the entire system moves along in one direction. The principle of cumulative causation was first applied in economic analysis by Wicksell, when he examined what happens when real and natural interest rates diverge. It was Myrdal, however, who first described this principle and recognized its importance.

A cumulative economic process can be contrasted with a unidirectional causal schema, where A causes changes in B, but B has no further effects on A. With unidirectional causation, changes in A lead to changes in B and things end there; the system reaches a new stable equilibrium with higher (or lower) values for the variables A and B.

With cumulative causation, the variables A and B impact each other. Changes in A will affect B, which will further affect A, again impact B, etc. There is no equilibrium or point of rest for the system. When A and B both increase, we have a virtuous cycle or positive feedback loop; and when A and B both decline, we have a vicious cycle or negative feedback loop. Myrdal used the idea of cumulative causation to explain economic problems like poverty and race relations.

In 1938, while lecturing at Harvard, Myrdal was approached by the Carnegie Corporation to study racial problems in the US. He accepted the invitation and spent the next five years working on the pathbreaking *An American Dilemma* (Myrdal 1944). This book argued that there was a moral conflict in America. On the one hand, Americans believed in the ideals of justice and equal opportunity, and did not think blacks were less able than whites. On the other hand, in practice blacks and whites were not treated equally and America did not live up to its high ideals. Much of *An American Dilemma* attempted to trace the discrimination existing in America against blacks. It documented the political and socioeconomic condition of blacks and whites, and it marshaled considerable empirical evidence to show that blacks were treated differently from whites.

In his typical fashion, Myrdal brought sociological, historical, psychological, and political insights into his analysis. He also showed the damage stemming from racial segregation and discrimination. He argued that the entire American society suffered by denying blacks a decent education, by not providing them with job training, and by discriminating against them in employment and housing. Myrdal also made the case that America's treatment of blacks was inconsistent with the needs of a technologically advanced society, and so the US economy performed poorly as a result of discriminating against blacks.

Myrdal also used the notion of cumulative causation to help explain the socioeconomic condition of black Americans. Prejudice against blacks led to lower living standards for blacks. Seeing that blacks do indeed have lower living standards, white prejudices were reinforced. This led to further declines in black living standards relative to whites. As Myrdal (1944, p. 381) succinctly put it, "*Discrimination breeds discrimination.*"

Myrdal went on to document the many ways black Americans were kept down due to a cumulative process of discrimination. Discrimination in education, for example, meant that blacks were less likely than whites to become doctors. Discrimination in education also meant that blacks would be less knowledgeable about health and sanitation. In addition, blacks had less money than whites for medical care. For all these reasons, blacks receive less adequate medical treatment and are in poorer health than whites. Consequently, blacks find it harder than whites to obtain and keep a job; and with lower incomes, black education will suffer (Myrdal 1944, p. 172).

Myrdal (1944, p. 956) also noted that segregation leads to white stereotypes of blacks and causes whites to focus on the differences between blacks and themselves. This, in turn, affects how whites regard blacks. When whites have less regard for blacks, they are less likely to associate or interact with blacks, and blacks will be less likely to work or live with whites who have little regard for them. Segregation and racial stereotypes are thus further reinforced.

The view that the condition of black America results from a negative feedback process has one important policy implication – this situation can be remedied in any one of a number of ways. Improvement in any one area will lead to gains in other areas through a cumulative process of improvement. But where to start?

Myrdal looked to American institutions to break into the vicious cycle of discrimination against black Americans. Organizations such as churches, schools, trade unions, and the government were repositories of the American creed of justice and equality. Moreover, many of these institutions could immediately improve the socioeconomic condition of blacks, thus reducing prejudice against blacks and beginning a positive or virtuous cycle. For this reason Myrdal proposed expanding the role of the federal government in the areas of education, housing, and income security. Laws making it easier for blacks to vote would also help to break the cycle of discrimination and prejudice. In addition, Myrdal (1944, pp. 198ff.) advocated migration from the rural South to the industrial North and West, where discrimination was not so prevalent and where high-paying jobs were more plentiful. Incorporating blacks into the labor movement would help both American labor and black Americans. Finally, Myrdal advocated using fiscal policy to achieve full employment, so that blacks migrating to Northern and Western cities could get jobs and become integrated into the post-war industrial economy.

Myrdal (1957) later applied the principle of cumulative causation to the study of economic development and used it to explain persistent poverty in South Asia (Myrdal 1968). He contrasted "spread effects," which create a positive cumulative cycle, with "backwash effects," which create a negative cumulative cycle. Once a region begins to develop economically, it will attract capital and labor from other regions. These new resources will assist in the development process. On the other hand, persistent poverty normally leads to high fertility rates, poor nutrition, and low labor productivity, all of which contribute to even greater poverty.

Following along the lines of his policy recommendations for reducing black poverty in the US, Myrdal (1970) stressed the need to end the vicious cycle of poverty and begin a virtuous cycle of growth and development. First and foremost, developing nations must spend more money on education. Second, efforts had to be concentrated on improving sanitation, providing clean water, and developing other public amenities. Third, income support programs had to address the problem of income inequality and the lack of adequate income received by most citizens in these countries.

While most economists have claimed that a trade-off exists between equality and growth (see **Kuznets** and **Pigou**), Myrdal held that there is no such trade-off, and that greater equality would lead to more rapid growth. Myrdal (1970, p. 51) argued that inequality leads to slower growth because of the physical and psychological consequences of poverty, and because the poor are unable to utilize their talents. Because it raises productivity growth, greater consumption is really greater investment in developing countries. Also, a welfare state that redistributes income will have higher levels of demand and more rapid growth.

Throughout his entire life Myrdal was highly critical of the methods employed in orthodox economic analysis. We have seen how he rejected equilibrium analysis in favor of cumulative causation. Myrdal (1969) also criticized social scientists in general, and economists in particular, because they could not write and speak to ordinary people. Instead, professionals generally write and speak only to each another. This reduces the importance of social science scholarship. Myrdal (1965) also criticized the attempt by economists to hide their normative or value assumptions behind the façade of scientific objectivity. He was not against economists making value judgments; he was only opposed to their refusal to acknowledge them. Even after winning the Nobel Prize, Myrdal claimed that the prize was inappropriate for an unscientific field like economics. He often quipped that the only reason he accepted the prize was that the award committee called him very early in the morning, before he was fully awake.

Myrdal is the rare economist who has made significant contributions to both economic theory and economic policy. His principle of cumulative causation provides a theoretic alternative to traditional equilibrium analysis. And the proposals to help reduce poverty and unemployment that follow from this theory provide an alternative to traditional *laissez-faire* policy prescriptions.

Works by Myrdal

The Political Element in the Development of Economic Theory (1929), Cambridge, Massachusetts, Harvard University Press, 1965

Monetary Equilibrium, London, Hodge, 1939

An American Dilemma, New York, Harper & Brothers, 1944

Rich Lands and Poor: The Road to World Prosperity, New York, Harper & Brothers, 1957

Asian Drama: An Inquiry into the Poverty of Nations, New York, Pantheon Books, 1968

Objectivity in Social Research, New York, Random House, 1969

The Challenge of World Poverty, New York, Pantheon Books, 1970

Against the Stream: Critical Essays on Economics, New York, Pantheon Books, 1972

Works about Myrdal

Angresano, James, *The Political Economy of Gunnar Myrdal*, Cheltenham, UK, Edward Elgar, 1997

Dostaler, Gilles, Ethier, Diane and Lepage, Laurent (eds), *Gunnar Myrdal and his Work*, Montreal, Harvest House, 1992

Jackson, Walter A., *Gunnar Myrdal and America's Conscience: Social Engineering and Radical Liberalism*, Chapel Hill, North Carolina, University of North Carolina Press, 1990

Kindleberger, C. E., "Gunnar Myrdal 1898–1987," *Scandinavian Journal of Economics*, 89 (1987), pp. 393–403

Lundberg, E., "Gunnar Myrdal's Contributions to Economic Theory," *Swedish Journal of Economics*, 76 (1974), pp. 472–8

Pressman, Steven, "*An American Dilemma*: Fifty Years Later," *Journal of Economic Issues*, 28, 2 (June 1994), pp. 577–85

Reynolds, Lloyd G., "Gunnar Myrdal's Contributions to Economic Theory, 1940–70," *Swedish Journal of Economics*, 76 (1974), pp. 479–97

Streeten, Paul, "Gunnar Myrdal," *World Development*, 18, 7 (1990), pp. 1031–7

FRIEDRICH HAYEK (1899–1992)

Friedrich Hayek (pronounced HI-YACK) achieved worldwide recognition as a champion of the free market and an opponent of government interference with the right of individuals to engage in free exchange through the market. His work makes a strong case that individual choice, rather than government decision-making, yields both economic benefits (greater efficiency) and non-economic benefits (greater liberty and freedom).

Hayek was born in Vienna in 1899. His grandfather, a mountain-climbing companion of Austrian economist Böhm-Bawerk,o was trained as a physician and then taught botany at the University of Vienna, but never became a professor. Hayek grew up hoping to become a university professor, in part because of his father's unfulfilled dreams (Caldwell 2004, p. 135).

During World War I, Hayek served in the Austrian army on the Italian front. Returning from the war he enrolled at the University of Vienna and earned two doctorates – one in law (1921) and one in *Statswissenschaft*, a field encompassing both political science and economics (1923). While working on the latter degree, Hayek encountered Menger's *Principles of Economics*, which hooked him on economics for life (Caldwell 2004, p. 139).

After the war, Hayek got to experience at first hand the hyperinflation that destroyed the economies of Germany and Austria. With prices rising several-fold every day, workers would demand half their daily pay at lunchtime so they could go out and buy necessities before the price of these goods would double or triple during the afternoon. This experience probably contributed to Hayek's vehement opposition to inflation and to Keynesian policies that sought to stimulate the macroeconomy.

Ludwig von Mises, head of the Austrian Institute of Economic Research, hired Hayek in 1923. Then, in 1927, he appointed Hayek to be Director of the Institute. Four years later Lionel Robbins hired Hayek as Tooke Professor of Economic Science and Statistics at the London School of Economics, in order to bring the economic ideas from Continental Europe to England.

Following publication of the *Road to Serfdom* in 1944 Hayek became a world-renowned social theorist. Receiving many teaching offers, he accepted an appointment at the University of Chicago in 1950. He retired in 1962 and returned to Europe, accepting a position at the University of Freiburg. In 1974 Hayek shared the Nobel Prize for Economics with Gunnar Myrdal. The committee singled out Hayek's original way of advocating political ideas when announcing the award.

Early in his career (in the 1930s) Hayek made contributions to monetary theory and the theory of business cycles. Then he began to focus on the problems of inflation and unemployment. By the 1940s Hayek became a strong critic of socialism, of government planning, and of all government intervention in the economy. He blamed governments for creating economic problems and for making economic problems worse by meddling with the market economy.

In his first major book, Hayek (1933) examined the role that money played in economic expansions and contractions. This work attempted to develop and explain the dynamics contained in Wicksell's (1898) *Interest and Prices*. Hayek argued that monetary factors were a necessary condition for the business cycle, but that changing the money supply was not enough to cause fluctuations in output. Changes in relative prices were also necessary to explain the business cycle.

Following Böhm-Bawerk, Hayek believed that capitalist economies produce goods in ever more roundabout ways. The length of time it takes to bring goods to market constantly increased because machinery and tools had to be developed before they could be employed in the production of goods and services.

When money is created by banks, but no additional saving takes place, there is immediately a greater demand for consumer goods.

This pushes up the prices of consumer goods relative to other goods. Businesses, in an attempt to meet this demand, adopt less *roundabout* means of *production*. But soon after prices begin to rise, interest rates must rise so that banks do not incur great losses when the loans they made in the past are paid back with money that can buy much less than the money they lent. Higher interest rates, in turn, will slow down consumer spending. Industries that produce consumer goods will go idle and lay off workers. Now past excesses begin to take their toll. The failure to produce more investment goods means that firms producing investment goods cannot absorb the labor no longer needed to produce consumer goods.

This analysis of the causes of unemployment was quite different from that of Keynes. For Hayek it is not a lack of demand that creates unemployment; rather, unemployment stems from the composition of demand, or demand for the wrong types of goods (consumer goods rather than investment goods). It can only be remedied by reducing consumer demand so that extra savings become available for businesses to use for additional investment, enabling them to adopt longer production processes.

For this reason, Hayek opposed attempts to employ Keynesian expansionary policies to deal with unemployment during the Great Depression. He was against stimulating consumer demand, expanding public works projects, or propping up prices. He argued that these Keynesian policies helped convert what might have been a mild recession into a prolonged depression. In addition, by creating inflation, Keynesian policies ultimately hurt the economy.

Hayek pointed out several harmful consequences of inflation. First, for Hayek (1945) one of the most important characteristics of the market system is that it provides information. Prices tell consumers which goods require less effort and fewer resources to produce; prices also tell businesses which inputs and means of production are least costly. Inflation distorts this signaling function of prices. When all prices are continually rising, it is hard to know which goods cost less to produce and how to produce those goods in the least expensive way. As a result, inflation distorts the economy by moving resources to where they should not be employed (inefficient and unwanted activities). This reduces economic efficiency and thus the standard of living for the nation. Second, by causing greater spending in order to beat the price increase, more consumer goods get produced and less roundabout means of production get employed by businesses. This too reduces future economic growth.

While opposed to inflation, Hayek was even more opposed to using *incomes policies* as a tool to combat inflation. He saw this as a step down the road to a totalitarian state. In addition, incomes policies, like inflation, destroy the informational function of prices. Finally, Hayek saw incomes policies as ignoring the real cause of inflation – too much money. Since inflation stemmed from too much money, money creation had to be slowed down to eradicate inflation. And excessive money creation, Hayek (1976a) argued, was the result of government monopolization over the printing and circulation of money. Monopoly control over money creation by the government leads to inflation for two reasons, according to Hayek. First, the government is always tempted to print more money in order to pay its bills. Second, governments are tempted to print money and create inflation in order to repay borrowed money with money that is worth much less because it can purchase fewer goods.

To keep governments from deliberately creating inflation, Hayek (1976a) proposed allowing private businesses to issue their own currency. Thus large firms, or more likely large banks, would each print up their own money. People and firms would choose to hold those currencies they expect to be most accepted by others and least likely to decline in value. Privately issued money, Hayek felt, would keep inflation in check because it would keep the inflationary tendencies of government in check. Also, private money issuers would have to be concerned about their reputation and the value of the money they created. As a result, Hayek thought that they would *not* tend to issue too much money.

The argument that economic problems arise due to government intervention became a dominate theme in the economics of Hayek starting in the 1940s. He increasingly relied on philosophical and psychological insights when making his case against government involvement in economic affairs. He stressed that there were finite limits to the amount of knowledge that any one individual or institution can acquire, as well as limits to human reason. Men and women could understand general economic relations, but could never understand the exact relationships operating at any time. Hayek (1955, pp. 53–63) also stressed that the social sciences were fundamentally different from the natural sciences. People do not obey psychological or economic laws the way that matter obeys the laws of physics, and so all attempts to control society in the way that science controls the environment are misplaced. Both of these beliefs have implications for economics, and each supports Hayek's case against government involvement in economic affairs.

One argument for economic planning in the 1930s and 1940s was that central planners could figure out the supply and demand for all goods in the economy and manipulate prices accordingly. Going even further, some economists argued that because the economy was so complex, planners with a good mathematical model could do better than the market in setting prices (Lange and Taylor 1964). Others (see **Galbraith**) argued that, as firms became larger and more monopolistic, government planning was needed to countervail this power.

Hayek turned these arguments on their head. For Hayek, the complexity of the economy means that *no* person could understand the workings of the whole economy. As a result, supply and demand equations could not be known by planners, and planning would only lead to inefficiencies. Moreover, planners would respond slowly to changes in supply or demand. They would have to wait until reports about shortages or surpluses were confirmed. In contrast, people will react quickly, and even if they make mistakes, will learn quickly from experience (Hayek 1948, p. 45).

Similarly, Keynesian macroeconomic management (fine-tuning) was flawed since policy-makers cannot understand all the intricacies and subtleties of the market system. The knowledge requirements were just too large for any government bureaucrat, according to Hayek. Instead of improving economic performance, government policy would only stifle the economic system that is responsible for improving our living standards.

In addition, before making any decision, a socialist government or ministry of economic planning would have to gather an immense amount of information, and derive hundreds of thousands (Hayek 1935) of equations. They would then have to solve all these equations in order to find the set of market clearing prices. Moreover, by the time this set of equations was solved mathematically the economy would have changed, and the information upon which the solution was based would be obsolete. Planners would thus have to re-estimate all the equations and solve this new set of equations. Of course, by the time this was done, the economy would have changed again, and the prices set by an economic planning board would again be out of date.

Hayek also turned on its head the case that government power had to be used to counter monopoly power. He held that monopoly power is usually the result of government actions. For example, domestic producers lobby the government to keep out imports and restrict entry into an industry or profession through licensing requirements. Hayek also thought that, even if large firms become powerful, potential competition (or the threat of new rivals starting up) would force firms to operate efficiently and produce the goods demanded by their customers at the lowest possible cost.

But Hayek (1944) went even further than this. His main contention is that government policy has limited individual liberties and taken us down *The Road to Serfdom*. This applies to socialist economies as well as capitalist economies that undertake planning for the future or attempt to reduce unemployment. Similarly, it is true of government policies that attempt to redistribute income in the name of economic justice. Hayek (1976b) contends that it is illegitimate to describe the outcome of the market process as either just or unjust. Income distribution is a fact about the world, the result of impersonal market forces. The notion of justice does not apply to such situations. In addition, attempts on the part of government to redistribute income will do more harm than good. The poor are hurt because redistribution reduces economic incentives and therefore decreases the economic pie. This leaves less for everyone, wealthy and poor alike. The poor are also hurt because the wealthy perform important economic functions like taking risks, supporting the arts and education, and testing new and expensive products that, if successful, get mass produced at lower prices.

Going even further, Hayek (1944; also see Butler 1983, ch. 4) argued against government attempts to provide equal economic opportunity to all individuals in order to obtain equality of results. For Hayek the notion of equal opportunity is illusory. If the government attempted to give all children an equal starting point, this would mean redistributing the wealth of their parents so that no child starts out ahead of others. It would also mean keeping the income of all parents equal so that some children do not gain any advantages. Again, in seeking to provide equal opportunity, governments by necessity must become more totalitarian.

Hayek did support equity in another sense, however. He thought that all men and all women should be treated as equals before the law. Equality of the law, or equal rules that apply to all citizens, would preserve liberty against the coercive power of government (Hayek 1976b).

Hayek's main contribution as an economist has been his arguments about the benefits of free markets and the information provided by prices. These arguments lead to the conclusion that attempts to alter or control markets should be opposed because they inevitably limit individual freedom, reduce economic efficiency, and lower living standards. Markets, for Hayek, were self-regulating devices that promote prosperity. Government policy and other attempts to hinder the workings of markets make us worse off economically and reduce individual liberty.

Works by Hayek

Prices and Production (1931) 2nd edn, London, Macmillan, 1934
Monetary Theory and the Trade Cycle (1933), Fairfield, New Jersey, Augustus M. Kelly, 1975
"The Nature and History of the Problem," in *Collectivist Economic Planning*, ed. F. A. Hayek, London, Routledge, 1935, pp. 1–40
The Pure Theory of Capital, London, Routledge & Kegan Paul, 1941
The Road to Serfdom (1944), Chicago, University of Chicago Press, 1956
"The Use of Knowledge in Society," *American Economic Review*, 35, 4 (September 1945), pp. 519–30
Individualism and Economic Order, Chicago, University of Chicago Press, 1948
The Counter-Revolution of Science: Studies on the Abuse of Reason (1955), Chicago, Liberty Press, 1979
The Constitution of Liberty, Chicago, University of Chicago Press, 1960
The Denationalization of Money, London, Institute of Economic Affairs, 1976a
Law, Legislation and Liberty, Vol. 2, Chicago, University of Chicago Press, 1976b
New Studies in Philosophy, Politics, Economics and the History of Ideas, London, Routledge & Kegan Paul, 1978
The Fatal Conceit: The Errors of Socialism, Chicago, University of Chicago Press, 1988
The Collected Works of F. A. Hayek, 10 vols., Chicago, University of Chicago Press, 1989–94

Works about Hayek

Barry, Norman E., *Hayek's Social and Economic Philosophy*, London, Macmillan, 1979
Barry, Norman E., "Restating the Liberal Order: Hayek's Philosophical Economics," in *Twelve Contemporary Economists*, ed. J. R. Shakleton and G. Locksley, New York, Wiley, 1981, pp. 87–107
Butler, Eamon, *Hayek: His Contribution to the Political and Economic Thought of Our Time*, New York, Universe Books, 1983
Caldwell, Bruce, *Hayek's Challenge*, Chicago, University of Chicago Press, 2004
Ebenstein, Alan, *Friedrich Hayek: A Biography*, New York, Palgrave, 2001
Kasper, Sherryl, *The Revival of Laissez-faire in American Macroeconomics*, Cheltenham, UK, Edward Elgar, 2002
Machlup, Fritz, "Hayek's Contribution to Economics," in *Essays on Hayek*, ed. Fritz Machlup, Hillsdale, Michigan, Hillsdale College Press, 1976, pp. 13–59

Other references

Lange, Oskar and Taylor, Fred, *On the Economic Theory of Socialism*, New York, McGraw Hill, 1964

Wicksell, Knut, *Interest and Prices* (1898), London, Macmillan, 1936

SIMON KUZNETS (1901–85)

Simon Kuznets is best known for helping to transform economics into an empirical science. He did this by developing the system of national income accounts that all countries employ to measure economic activity. He also did this by measuring income distribution and examining how the distribution of income in the US changed during the twentieth century. But the work of Kuznets went beyond measuring economic phenomena. He also sought to determine the causes of economic growth and changing income inequality, studied the cycles of growth that economies go through, and attempted to understand the consequences of economic growth on income distribution.

Kuznets was born in Pinsk (then part of the Soviet Union, now part of Belarus) in 1901. His father was a skilled furrier, who moved the family to Kharkov, a city noted for its intellectual life, at the beginning of World War I. After graduating from the local public school, Kuznets enrolled at the University of Kharkov. There he began to study economics and was exposed to Joseph Schumpeter's theory of innovation and the business cycle. When the Russian Revolution closed the university and led to civil war in Russia, the Kuznets family fled Russia, going first to Turkey and eventually to the United States (Kapuria-Foreman and Penman 1995).

Kuznets taught himself English over one summer and then enrolled at Columbia University. At Columbia, Kuznets studied under Wesley Clair Mitchell, who trained Kuznets in empirical economic methods and sparked his interest in business cycles. He received a BA from Columbia in 1923 and a PhD in 1926. His dissertation (on fluctuations in wholesale and retail trade) involved questions of both economic measurement and cyclical variations in economic activity (Kuznets 1926).

After receiving his doctorate, Kuznets worked at the National Bureau of Economic Research (NBER) for around three years. Then in 1931 he accepted a position at the University of Pennsylvania. Kuznets went to Johns Hopkins University in 1954, and then to Harvard in 1960, where he remained until his retirement in 1971. All the while, Kuznets maintained his connections with the NBER.

Over the course of his academic career Kuznets received many professional accolades. In 1949 he was made President of the American Statistical Association; in 1953 he became President of the American Economic Association; and in 1971 he was awarded the Nobel Prize for Economic Science.

While the Nobel Prize committee singled out his work in the area of economic growth and changing social structure, the most important contribution of Kuznets was probably his work developing a system of national income accounting.

Macroeconomics studies the overall performance of national economies. To test hypotheses about macroeconomic relationships, or to find the causes of good macroeconomic performance, it is necessary to have some measure of overall economic activity. In the seventeenth century, William Petty made some rudimentary attempts at calculating economic activity in England, and national income estimates for Britain were made several times subsequent to the pioneering work of Petty. However, no one attempted to make such measurements on an annual basis, and few estimates were done carefully or systematically. Still, in the 1920s, Britain was far ahead of the US in compiling national income data. Kuznets was primarily responsible for changing this. He moved the US from the position of laggard to being a world leader in national income statistics.

At the NBER Kuznets was responsible for developing the first estimates of US national income for the years from 1929 to 1932. He then went on to develop estimates of national income for all the years between 1919 and 1938, and to provide estimates of US economic activity going back as far as 1869 (Kuznets 1941, 1946a, 1946b, 1952a).

Kuznets (1933) carefully described the methodology that he used in compiling measures of economic activity, as well as some of the problems he encountered in making such estimates. As such, he set the standards for measuring economic activity and developed the procedures that are still employed today.

For example, Kuznets was aware that estimates of national income excluded goods and services that were not marketed and sold. When households cook their own meals, mow their own lawns, and clean their own houses, they are producing goods and services; but these goods and services are not counted in government figures of economic activity. Likewise, illegal activities like prostitution and the drug trade are difficult, if not impossible, to measure and so cannot be included in estimates of overall economic activity.

Kuznets was also careful to distinguish final goods from intermediate goods, and was able to use this distinction to avoid the problem of double counting. An automobile, a final good sold to consumers, is assembled from intermediate goods such as tires, glass, engines, and brakes. To count the value of tires sold to the automobile manufacturer and also the value of the whole car would be to count twice the tires that are produced. In order to get a more accurate measure of economic activity it is necessary to subtract the value of all parts from the final price of the car sold to the consumer. Taking this difference, or computing the value added by the car manufacturer, provides the foundation for measuring national income. National income is simply the sum of the value added by every firm in the economy over a specific time period. It can be derived from the periodic reports business firms must make to the government about their revenues from sales, their expenditures on parts, and their quarterly profits.

Kuznets understood that national income measures had severe limitations as indicators of national well-being or national welfare. Just because national income increased, it did not mean that some country was necessarily better off. Income could have become distributed more unequally; so despite higher incomes overall, a large majority of households might be worse off. Kuznets also noted that the growth process itself might lead to undesirable outcomes like urbanization, traffic congestion, and pollution. Finally, national income accounts do not take into account how much output goes to the government and gets paid for by compulsory taxation.

This work on measuring national income led naturally to a study of business cycles, or the periodic expansion and contraction of economic activity. Prior to Kuznets, Nikolai Kondratieff (1984), a Russian economist, noted the existence of long-run economic cycles lasting between 45 and 60 years. Examining several hundred years of price data for the US, France, and Germany (plus data on the production of iron, coal, and other products, throughout the world), Kondratieff noticed that there were regular 20–30 year periods during which prices rose and then 20–30 year periods during which prices declined. These long-run economic changes have since been called "*Kondratieff waves*." Shorter cycles, of around ten years, have been associated with changes in business investment (see **Schumpeter**).

In his study of economic fluctuations, Kuznets (1930) found intermediate cycles of growth and decline lasting around 20 years. These cycles have come to be called "*Kuznets cycles*" (Abramovitz 1961) in honor of their discoverer. Kuznets thought that demographic changes could explain these 20-year cycles. Increasing population can result from waves of immigration or from growing birth rates due to favorable economic circumstances. Whatever the cause, population growth leads to a greater demand for consumer goods, especially for more and larger housing. Additional demand encour-ages additional business investment. This, plus the ability to take advantage of *economies of scale*, contributes to more rapid productivity growth. As a result, living standards rise as the population grows. But soon the new citizens will become part of a larger labor force, and this will lead to a downward pressure on wages. As wages fall, so too does spending and investment, and the downward phase of the economic cycle begins.

Kuznets (1965) expanded his work on economic cycles to study the structural economic changes that result from economic growth and decline. Here he studied how the business cycle affects savings and consumption rates, productivity, income distribution and other factors (like the international flow of capital, goods, and people).

Kuznets (1953, 1955) also examined the impact of economic growth on income distribution, and pioneered the measurement of income distribution. Using both income tax data and US Census Bureau survey data, he examined the fraction of total income received by each of ten income groups (the top 10 percent of income earners, the next 10 percent, the third 10 percent, etc.) for virtually every year between 1913 and 1948. He (1953) found that in the interwar years the top 1 percent of the US population received 15 percent of all national income and the top 5 percent of the US population received between 25 percent and 30 percent of all income. He also found a decline in income inequality in the US during and after World War II, with the top 1 percent of the popu-lation getting only 8.5 percent of all income and the top 5 percent receiving 18 percent of all income. The business cycle, Kuznets argued, could explain these changes. Low rates of unemployment during and after World War II increased the fraction of total income going to low-income groups. At the same time, lower interest rates and higher income taxes reduced the fraction of income going to the most affluent. Looking at data over longer-term horizons and for many different nations, Kuznets (1955) found that income equality followed a U-shaped pattern – it declined during the early stages of economic development making the poor relatively worse off, but it rose at later stages of development thus benefiting those with lower incomes.

Another important empirical finding by Kuznets involved savings rates in the US, or its converse, the ratio of consumption to national income. Kuznets (1946b, 1952b) found that saving rates in the US were remarkably constant, and did not change as the US economy grew. This contradicted the prediction of the simple Keynesian consumption function, C=a+bY, where C is consumption and Y is current income. If this hypothesis were true, then spending rates should fall as incomes increase. Falling spending rates mean rising savings rates. Essentially, the simple Keynesian view was that people would save more as their incomes increased. Kuznets's discovery that savings rates were constant led to numerous attempts at revising and extending the macroeconomic theory of consumption. As a result, Milton Friedman developed the *permanent income hypothesis* and Franco Modigliani developed the *life-cycle hypothesis* as a means of explaining constant savings rates.

Finally, Kuznets devoted substantial attention during his lifetime to the factors affecting productivity growth. This was a natural extension of his focus on economic growth, since growth is due to the combined effects of greater productivity and a larger population. Of the two factors, productivity growth is certainly the more important, for as Adam Smith pointed out it is productivity growth that leads to improvement in living standards. Studying productivity growth allowed Kuznets to incorporate his diverse interests in population changes, in making precise empirical estimates, and in improving living standards.

Kuznets placed heavy emphasis on technological change and innovation as the means to improve productivity growth. He estimated (Kuznets 1946) that, over a 50-year period, three-fifths of the gain in US productivity was due to technological advances and two-fifths was due to redistributing labor from less productive sectors (agriculture) to more productive sectors (manufacturing). Since technology was the more important factor historically, and since redistributing labor becomes less important over time as fewer Americans work in agriculture, he thought that the effort to improve productivity must focus on technological breakthroughs and advances.

At the end of the twentieth century, most work in economics was highly abstract and theoretical. Economists even looked down upon empirical studies seeking to measure economic variables and examine how these variables change over time. Kuznets stands firmly within the empirical tradition in economics that began with Petty's political arithmetic. The work of Kuznets has allowed a substantial body of knowledge to be developed about economic growth and development. It has also yielded an enormous amount of data that lets economists test their theories. And it has allowed governments to compile and report macroeconomic data on a regular basis. If economics is to be regarded as a study of the behavior of real-world economies, Kuznets must be regarded as one of its half dozen or so most important figures.

Works by Kuznets

Cyclical Fluctuations: Retail and Wholesale Trade, United States, 1919–1925, New York, Adelphi, 1926

Secular Movements in Production and Prices, Boston, Houghton Mifflin, 1930

"National Income," *Encyclopedia* of *the Social Sciences,* Vol. 11, New York, Macmillan, 1933, pp. 205–24

National Income and Its Composition, 1919–1938, 2 vols., New York, National Bureau of Economic Research, 1941

National Income: A Summary of Findings, New York, National Bureau of Economic Research, 1946a

National Product since 1869, New York, National Bureau of Economic Research, 1946b

Income and Wealth of the U.S.: Trends and Structure, Cambridge, Bowes & Bowes, 1952a, with Raymond Goldsmith

"Proportion of Capital Formation to National Product," *American Economic Review,* 42, 2 (May 1952b), pp. 507–26

Shares of Upper Income Groups in Income and Savings, New York: National Bureau of Economic Research, 1953

"Economic Growth and Income Inequality," *American Economic Review,* 45, 1 (March 1955), pp. 1–28

Economic Growth and Structure: Selected Essays, New York, Norton, 1965

Economic Growth of Nations, Cambridge, Massachusetts, Harvard University Press, 1971

Population, Capital, and Growth, New York, Norton, 1973

Growth, Population, and Income Distribution: Selected Essays, New York, Norton, 1979

Works about Kuznets

Abramovitz, Moses, "The Nature and Significance of the Kuznets Cycle," *Economic Development and Cultural Change,* 9 (April 1961), pp. 349–67

Fogel, Robert, *Simon Kuznets,* Cambridge, Massachusetts, National Bureau of Economic Research, 2000 (abstract available online at http://www.nber.org/papers/w7787)

Hinck, Harriet, "Simon Kuznets 1971," in *Nobel Laureates in Economic Science: A Biographical Dictionary,* ed. Bernard S. Katz, New York, Garland, 1989, pp. 143–59

Kapuria-Foreman, Vibha and Penman, Mark, "An Economic Historian's Economics: Remembering Simon Kuznets," *Economic Journal,* 105 (November 1995), pp. 1524–47

Lundberg, Erik, "Simon Kuznets' Contribution to Economics," *Swedish Journal of Economics*, 73 (December 1971), pp. 444–61

Ben-Porath, Yoram, "Simon Kuznets in Person and Writing," *Economic Development and Cultural Change*, 36, 3 (April 1988), pp. 435–47

Other references

Kondratieff, Nikolai, *The Long Wave Cycle* (1925), New York, Richardson and Synder, 1984

JOHN VON NEUMANN (1903–57)

John von Neumann (pronounced NOY-mon) was trained as a mathematician, and is regarded as one of the most brilliant mathematical geniuses of the twentieth century. Nevertheless, he made several contributions to economics. As might be expected, these contributions involved applying mathematics to economic analysis. But unlike other major figures who brought mathematical techniques to economics, von Neumann did not employ the calculus to explain economic relationships. Rather, he brought to economics the insights from games of strategy. By so doing, he shed new light on the human interactions that form the basis of economic life.

Von Neumann was born in Budapest, Hungary, in 1903. His father was a successful and wealthy Jewish banker. Early in life von Neumann's mathematical talents became obvious. By the age of six he could divide two eight-digit numbers in his head; by eight he mastered calculus (Halmos 1973, p. 383). At school he was excused from regular math classes to receive private tutoring from college mathematics professors. By the end of his senior year of high school he was regarded as a professional mathematician and had published his first mathematical paper.

Although registered as a student at the University of Budapest, von Neumann did not attend classes. Instead, he studied at the University of Berlin and returned to Budapest only to take exams. After two years he transferred to the Swiss Federal Institute of Technology, where he encountered the outstanding mathematicians of his time. He received a diploma in chemical engineering from the Swiss Federal Institute in 1923 and a doctorate in mathematics from the University of Budapest in 1926.

From 1926 to 1930 von Neumann taught mathematics at the University of Berlin and then at the University of Hamburg, while also publishing articles on set theory, algebra, and quantum physics.

Fearing the consequences of remaining in Germany, he accepted a teaching position at Princeton University in 1930. In 1933, he was hired by the Institute for Advanced Studies at Princeton, a post that he held for the rest of his life.

When World War II began, von Neumann was called to serve on important war committees and advisory groups. He helped develop the world's first computer for the US military and, at the behest of J. Robert Oppenheimer, he participated in the Manhattan Project, which led to the development of the first nuclear weapons. After the war, von Neumann worked for the RAND Corporation, a think-tank set up to study strategies for a possible nuclear war. Strongly anti-Communist because of his experiences in Hungary in 1919, van Neumann vigorously defended US nuclear testing and supported development of the hydrogen bomb. In 1954 he was appointed to the Atomic Energy Commission (AEC) by President Eisenhower. Soon after his arrival in Washington, von Neumann was diagnosed with cancer and his health rapidly deteriorated. Because he attended AEC meetings in a wheelchair, and because of his strong pro-nuclear position, Poundstone (1992, p. 5) contends that von Neumann was likely the model for Dr. Strangelove in the 1963 Stanley Kubrick film with that title.

Fellow Hungarian Nicholas Kaldor met von Neumann while they were both on vacation in Budapest in the late 1920s. Von Neumann expressed interest in mathematical economics, and Kaldor suggested he read Walras (Macrae 1992, p. 250). According to Walras, *general equilibrium* can be shown to exist if the set of mathematical equations representing supply and demand is equal to the number of unknowns (the price of each good and the quantities of each good bought and sold). In this case, the system of equations could be solved for the price and the quantity of each good (see **Walras**). Von Neumann pointed out that this procedure of counting equations and unknowns fails to rule out negative prices, which makes no sense and can never exist in the real economic world. Consequently, counting equations and unknowns fails to demonstrate that all markets can achieve equilibrium at the same time; a more sophisticated mathematical technique was needed to deal with this problem. It was von Neumann (1945–6) who first applied this technique (typology and its main result, the fixed point theorem) to economics, by showing that economies could grow and develop without running into the problem of negative prices. The fixed point theorem later became the basis for Arrow's proof of the existence of general equilibrium (without negative prices).

Von Neumann had another problem with Walrasian general equilibrium theory, one that led to the development of game theory as an alternative tool for economic analysis. Von Neumann noted that most economic analysis is not concerned with interdependencies among markets. At one level, this approach is perfectly satisfactory. Many economic decisions and many economic outcomes are independent of what others do. For example, when I go to the supermarket and purchase a box of cornflakes cereal, this does not affect the cereal purchases of others. However, in many instances the reaction of others will play an important role in economic decisions. Large firms are likely to set prices based not just on costs of production and demand for the goods they produce, but also on the likely impact of these decisions on their competitors. For example, an airline may increase its prices in the expectation that other air carriers will follow the price increase, thereby giving all firms in the industry higher profits. Or, a firm may cut prices, believing that its competitors will have to cut their prices also, and that these competitors will not be able to survive when selling goods at such low prices.

When Oskar Morgenstern arrived in Princeton in 1939, he and von Neumann quickly became close friends. Morgenstern read von Neumann's (1928) paper on strategy for parlor games and recognized that the framework von Neumann developed could be applied to many economic situations. The two then became collaborators on the theory of games and the use of game theory for economic analysis.

Game theory is about conflict situations in which individuals compete against one another but do not know what their opponent or competitor will do; yet all individuals know that the outcome of their choice depends upon what each party decides. Essentially, game theory analyzes the interaction between two or more people and the strategic decisions they must make.

Together, Von Neumann and Morgenstern (1944) began by describing the characteristics of a game. Each game could be described by three features: (1) a number of players; (2) a set of decisions that each player had to make; and (3) a payoff matrix or table showing the outcome for every combination of decisions made by each player. The key new element was the fact that outcomes were affected by what other people chose.

Once a game is defined in these terms, each player can calculate their gains or losses from each decision they might make or each strategy they might employ in playing the game. Von Neumann and Morgenstern assumed that each player would try to achieve the best possible result, meaning that each player would employ a strategy that would likely lead to the largest gain for them.

Figure 9 illustrates the payoff matrix for a simple game with two players, each of whom has two possible moves. This gives us four possible outcomes, each with a different payoff for the two players. For each outcome, the first payoff goes to Player 1 and the second payoff goes to Player 2. Thus, if Player 1 selects *a* and Player 2 selects *b*, then Player 1 gains 1 and Player 2 loses 1. We can think of the payoffs as monetary gains and losses (say $1000), but strictly speaking the numbers in the boxes should represent the utility received by each player.

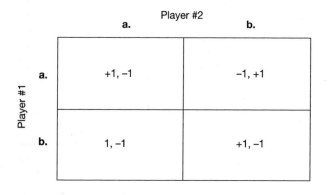

Figure 9 A game theory payoff matrix

Von Neumann (1928) demonstrated that there is always a rational course of action for two players in a game when the gains and losses for both players are always equal to zero (called a "zero-sum game," for obvious reasons), or when one person's loss was another person's gain. John Nash (1950), the subject of the movie and the book *A Beautiful Mind* (Nasser 2001), extended the work of von Neumann to show that there was a rational course of action in all games, regardless of whether they were zero-sum and no matter how many people were playing the game.

The rational course of action may be to use a pure strategy (always making the same choice) or a mixed strategy, which involves selecting each option or choice with some probability. With a pure strategy, a player would choose the same alternative all the time because that is the very best the player could do. With a mixed strategy, the best a player could do would be to select each alternative with some fixed probability.

Figure 9 describes a game where a mixed strategy is required. It is best known as the game of matching pennies. Player 1 wins the game, and wins a penny, whenever both players show heads or both players show tails; otherwise Player 2 wins. If Player 1 tends to choose strategy *a*, then Player 2 would soon recognize this and could gain by choosing strategy *b*. On the other hand, if Player 1 tends to choose strategy *b*, Player 2 gains by employing strategy *a* more frequently. The only way for Player 1 to break even over the long run is to randomly select strategy *a* half the time and strategy *b* half the time. What is true for Player 1 is likewise true for Player 2.

Various extensions and applications of this simple framework are possible. For games of more than two people, von Neumann and Morgenstern (1944) studied the conditions under which players would form coalitions in order to gain at the expense of other players who are not in the coalition. In the real world, this is analogous to studying the conditions under which it would make sense for two firms to merge, thus forming a very large firm and reducing the number of competitors in the industry. It is also analogous to studying the conditions under which it makes sense for business firms to collude and raise prices, for workers to get together and form a union, or for groups of individuals to form a special interest group and lobby the government for legislation that would confer economic benefits on the members of the group.

Perhaps the most famous and most studied extension of game theory is the *prisoner's dilemma*, which shows how two individuals pursuing their own best strategy can wind up in a less than optimal situation. The prisoner's dilemma game was invented in 1950 by two RAND scientists, Merrill Flood and Melvin Drescher, but its basic idea comes from the *Theory of Games and Economic Behavior* (Poundstone 1992, p. 125).

A typical prisoner's dilemma appears in Figure 10 (page 192). The following story usually goes along with the payoff matrix. Two suspected criminals have been captured and are put into separate rooms. If neither confess to their crime (i.e., if both choose *a*), they both get off scot-free. If both confess (i.e., if both choose *b*), they each get three years in prison. But if one prisoner confesses and the other prisoner does not, the confessor gets rewarded (with a new identity and new life) while the other prisoner serves five years in jail.

Player 1 is better off confessing (choosing *b*) regardless of what Player 2 does. If Player 2 refuses to confess (choosing *a*), Player 1 does better by confessing than by not confessing (gaining 3 rather than gaining nothing). Likewise, if Player 2 confesses (choosing *b*), Player 1 does better by confessing, because *b* gives him a loss of 3 rather than a loss of 5. The same thing is true for Player 2. No matter what Player 1 does, Player 2 is better off confessing. The paradox here is that the outcome of the game (both players confessing and spending three years in jail) is worse than the outcome that results from the "irrational strategy" of not confessing.

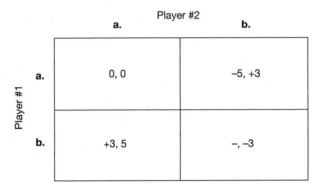

Figure 10 The Prisoner's Dilemma

Prisoner's dilemma situations are common in everyday life and in economic life. They are the heart of the *free rider problem*. Like the prisoner who confesses, the free rider does not pay to support community services that everyone takes to be desirable. The outcome of free riding is a lack of important community services.

The prisoner's dilemma has been used to study a wide range of topics. It has been used to explain the arms race (Schelling 1966; Russell 1959). Under this analysis both the US and the Soviet Union had to build nuclear missiles (strategy *b*) because, had they not done this, they would have been at the mercy of their adversary. The prisoner's dilemma has also been used to explain the advantages of oligopolists colluding to raise prices rather than competing and earning little or no profit. It has been employed in international trade theory to explain why two nations might adopt protectionist policies (strategy *b*), even though both countries would gain from free trade (see **Ricardo**). Finally, 2005 Nobel Laureate Thomas Schelling (1978) has used the prisoner's dilemma to explain why racial segregation exists in neighborhoods and why hockey players do not want to wear helmets even though all players gain from the safety provided by helmets.

Economists and other social scientists have used the prisoner's dilemma and similar games to study actual human behavior (see **Kahneman**). One important study is the prisoner's dilemma tournament that was conducted in 1980 by Robert Axelrod (1984). The tournament was a series of prisoner's dilemma games played over and over again. Axelrod invited numerous people to submit computer programs that described how they would play in the first round of the series of games, and then how they would play in all following rounds based upon the previous responses of their opponent. For example, if one's opponent selected confess in the previous two rounds of the game, one may decide to confess oneself in the next round; otherwise one would not confess. Or one could always confess; or one could confess with any random probability. Axelrod found that the simple strategy of tit-for-tat, which starts by not confessing and then does what one's opponent did in the previous round, was able to beat all the other strategies. This means that in competing against all other programs, tit-for-tat got the highest number of points at the end of the 200 games that formed the series. Axelrod concluded from his studies that human behavior is adaptive and strategic, rather than rational in the economic sense (which would require always confessing).

One potential drawback of game theory is that it does not always provide determinant solutions. Thus, it does not allow economists to make concrete predictions. For example, the prisoner's dilemma does not let us predict exactly what each player will choose to do. It can only help us analyze the decision facing each player. However, the real world itself may not always have definite or determinate results. Rather, actual results may depend on a number of different factors. Game theory is a useful tool in analyzing these situations, capturing the different factors that go into making decisions and helping people to see their best strategy in a particular situation. As Leonard (1995, p. 756) has observed, game theory was "part of a general shift in science which involved ... the abandonment of determinism, continuity, calculus, and the metaphor of the 'machine', to allow for indeterminism, probability, and discontinuous changes of state." In large part von Neumann was responsible for this shift of focus and orientation on the part of economists.

Although he was a professional mathematician, von Neumann is an important economic figure because his path-breaking work is responsible for two trends in contemporary economics. First, his discovery of game theory allowed economists to analyze strategic decision-making. Second, game theory allowed economists and other social scientists to perform experiments that would allow them to better understand human behavior.

Works by von Neumann

"Zur Theorie der Gesellschaftsspiele" ("Theory of Parlor Games"), *Mathematische Annalen*, 100 (1928), pp. 295–320. Translated and reprinted in *Contributions to the Theory of Games*, ed. Tucker and Luce, Vol. 4, Princeton, New Jersey, Princeton University Press, 1950, pp. 1–27

"A Model of General Equilibrium" (1937), *Review of Economic Studies*, 13 (1945–6), pp. 1–9

Theory of Games and Economic Behavior, Princeton, Princeton University Press, 1944, with Oskar Morgenstern

Works about von Neumann

Halmos, Paul, "The Legend of John von Neumann," *American Mathematical Monthly*, 80, 4 (April 1973), pp. 382–94

Leonard, Robert J., "From Parlor Games to Social Science: von Neumann, Morgenstern, and the Creation of Game Theory 1928–44," *Journal of Economic Literature*, 33, 2 June 1995, pp. 130–61

Macrae, Norman, *John von Neumann*, New York, Pantheon Books, 1992

Morgenstern, Oskar, "The Collaboration between Oskar Morgenstern and John von Neumann on the Theory of Games," *Journal of Economic Literature*, 14, 3 (September 1976), pp. 805–16

Poundstone, William, *Prisoner's Dilemma*, New York, Doubleday, 1992

Other references

Axelrod, Robert, *The Evolution of Cooperation*, New York, Basic Books, 1984

Nash, John, "Equilibrium Points in n-Person Games," *Proceedings of the National Academy of Sciences*, 36 (1950), pp. 48–9

Nasser, Sylvia, *A Beautiful Mind: The Life of Mathematical Genius and Nobel Laureate John Nash*, New York, Simon & Schuster, 2001

Russell, Bertrand, *Common Sense and Nuclear Warfare*, New York, Simon & Schuster, 1959

Schelling, Thomas, *Arms and Influence*, New Haven, Connecticut, Yale University Press, 1966

Schelling, Thomas, *Micromotives and Macrobehavior*, New York, Norton, 1978

JOAN ROBINSON (1903–83)

Joan Robinson made major contributions in two areas of economics. Early in her career, she focused the attention of economists on market forms in between perfect competition and monopoly. Later she was instrumental in defending and expanding the theories of Keynes, and became one of the founders of Post-Keynesian economics.

Robinson was born Joan Maurice in Surrey, England, in 1903. Her family was upper middle class, and put a high premium on education and independent thinking. Her father was a military general, an author, and later in life, head of one of the colleges making up the University of London. Her mother was the daughter of a Cambridge University professor. Robinson attended St Paul's, a leading school in London for girls, where she studied history, then Girton College at Cambridge University, where she studied economics. She became interested in economics in order to learn why poverty and unemployment existed in the world, and because she thought economics could help solve these problems (Shaw 1989, p. 145).

With the exception of a few years spent in India with her husband (the economist Austin Robinson), Robinson spent the half century following her 1925 graduation teaching and lecturing at Cambridge. However, because she was a woman, she did not become a full-time member of Cambridge University until 1948.

In the 1930s, Robinson was an active participant in the "Cambridge Circus," a small group of economists helping Keynes to develop his *General Theory*. She then helped defend Keynes from his many critics, and worked on expanding and devloping his ideas along several lines. In 1974 Robinson was made President of the American Economic Association, becoming its first female President and one of its few non-American Presidents. She is the first woman to have made the list of finalists for the Nobel Prize in Economics.

As an undergraduate, Robinson studied Marshall's *Principles of Economics*, the standard textbook at the time. What she found especially unsatisfactory was the conclusion of this work – that producers and consumers jointly maximized their well-being. This conclusion seemed incompatible with the actual British economy of the 1920s, which was plagued with high unemployment and industries operating at low capacity. Robinson was also dissatisfied with the fact that Marshall and other economists focused on just two extreme types of industries – perfect competition and monopoly. The real world, she thought, was somewhere in between these two extremes. *The Economics of Imperfect Competition* (Robinson 1933) analyzed these real-world industries that fall part way between a highly competitive industry with many small firms and an industry made up of only one firm.

To explain decision-making by the firm, Robinson used the concept of *marginal revenue* (see **Cournot**), the additional revenue a firm gets when it produces and sells one more thing. For competitive firms, marginal revenue would always equal price, since firms can always sell more goods without having to run a sale or lower the price they charge. But under imperfect competition firms faced downward-sloping marginal revenue curves. To sell more, goods had to be put on sale. But when firms run sales, consumers pay less than they would have otherwise paid, and the firm loses this revenue. Taking into account both the lower price and the greater sales, firms might cut prices in an attempt to sell more goods, but this does not mean that they will actually get any more revenue (i.e., their marginal revenue from selling more could be zero or negative). Conversely, firms might receive more revenue if they increased their prices and sold fewer goods.

By showing how raising prices and producing less could yield more revenue for the large firm, Robinson was able to explain why imperfect competition was characterized by insufficient production and underutilized resources. Imperfect competition could thus explain (while the theory of perfect competition could not) the high rates of unemployment prevailing in Britain during the 1920s and during the Great Depression of the 1930s.

Economics of Imperfect Competition (Robinson 1933, ch. 25) also showed that, under imperfect competition, workers received wages less than the value of what they produced. Consequently, the *marginal productivity theory of distribution* fails to hold when imperfect competition exists. With imperfect competition, labor is exploited by powerful businesses. To help drive home this point, Robinson developed the notion of *monopsony*, a case in which there is only a single employer in a particular geographic region or one employer for workers with certain skills. With only one potential employer, and with many individuals looking for work, people are at a competitive disadvantage. They are forced to accept the wage offered by the single employer. Robinson recognized that the world did not consist of monopsonistic labor markets, any more than it was comprised of monopolistic product markets. However, the notion of monopsony helped focus attention on wage determination as a bargaining process and the *exploitation* of workers due to their lack of bargaining power against a few large firms.

Another important contribution in *Economics of Imperfect Competition* was its analysis of *price discrimination*. Economists knew that large, monopolistic firms charged different prices to different people, but

Robinson (1933, ch. 15) was the first to explain its operating principles and its consequences. Robinson (1933, p. 179) first pointed out that price discrimination was possible only with monopoly or imperfect competition. Through price discrimination, monopolistic firms would be able to increase their revenues and their profits.

To engage in price discrimination, firms needed to segment the market for their product into two parts – those consumers willing and able to pay high prices and those consumers who were price-sensitive. Then the firm needed some way to charge higher prices to the first group. One way of doing this would be to charge different prices at different times of the day. Thus, telephone companies offer lower rates in the evenings and on weekends. Business customers, generally insensitive to price, pay the higher daytime rates; and price-conscious consumers generally pay the reduced off-peak phone rates. Discount coupons also help to segment the market and allow for price discrimination. Those who are concerned about spending too much money will clip coupons and buy goods at a lower price; those who are not will pay full price. Likewise, the practice of pricing through haggling, as often takes place at automobile dealerships, will lead to price discrimination. Here the hagglers, those unwilling to pay higher prices, will buy a car for less money than those who do not want to negotiate over price for hours and hours.

An economic world characterized by imperfect competition also led to a new theory of price determination, one hinted at by Robinson and developed later by Post-Keynesian economists (see Eichner 1976). In competitive markets, firms were all price takers; they had to set their prices equal to what the market would bear and what all the other firms in the industry were doing. With imperfect competition, however, prices were set by producers, who added a mark-up to their prime costs (primarily wages). The less competitive the industry, the greater the mark-up; and the more that firms needed funds for expansion, the greater they would mark up their costs.

Despite its many advances, Robinson grew dissatisfied with the *Economics of Imperfect Competition* almost as soon as she finishedwriting it. Her dissatisfaction came from the numerous problems she saw with microeconomic analysis. On a theoretical level, Robinson became aware of logical problems with supply and demand analysis. On a practical level, the Great Depression and the work of Keynes made her lose interest in the pricing and output decisions of firms.

One problem with supply and demand analysis, according to Robinson (1980, vol. 5, pp. 48–58) was that it ignored time and expectations; instead, a timeless notion called "equilibrium" took center stage. Robinson thought that the stability inherent in equilibrium analysis was inappropriate for a discipline like economics, which deals with growing and changing economies. Contrary to standard economic theory, consumers and businesses do not respond to current prices in ways that move the economy towards an equilibrium price. Rather, consumers and businesses respond to prices today based upon what they think prices will be in the future. Moreover, changing prices can change expectations. Lower prices can lead to expectations of even lower future prices, making consumers less willing to buy some good despite a sharp drop in its price. Under such conditions, no equilibrium or market-clearing price is possible; and supply and demand analysis fails to illuminate what is going on in the real world. To understand real economies requires a new theoretical orientation – one that focuses on how prices fluctuate over time rather than on how prices move toward some fixed equilibrium point.

A second problem with supply and demand analysis for Robinson concerned the nature of capital. Robinson began the so-called *Cambridge Controversy* with her critique of the marginalist theory of distribution. According to this theory (see **Clark**), the rate of profit was determined by the marginal productivity of capital. The question Robinson (1953–4) raised was how to measure capital in order to find its marginal product. This relatively simple and innocuous question sparked a heated debate between Cambridge, England, and Cambridge, Massachusetts, over the possibility of measuring capital when you do not know the rate of profit (see Harcourt 1972).

Robinson pointed out that the marginal productivity theory of distribution requires that we know the demand for capital in order to measure marginal productivity. Constructing such a demand curve requires relating the profit rate and the quantity of capital. The problem is that capital is not something homogeneous (like workers) that can easily be counted and added up. Capital consists of large plants and small plants, automated assembly lines, hammers and screwdrivers, computers and computer software. These goods have nothing in common that we can use to find "a quantity" of capital; so some other approach must be used.

The traditional means of counting capital is to measure its value, or future profitability. This works fine as a practical or accounting matter, but is unsatisfactory as part of a theory that explains what determines the rate of profit. As Robinson pointed out, if economic theory is supposed to *explain* the profit rate, it cannot assume it knows the profitability of capital in order to measure the quantity of capital. This procedure is circular; therefore, she argued, the marginal productivity theory of distribution must be abandoned.

Robinson's critique of microeconomic theory also supported the macroeconomic approach of Keynes. If we reject marginal productivity as a theory of distribution, labor supply and labor demand do not determine wages and employment. We therefore have no reason to believe that unemployment will disappear simply by waiting for wages to fall. Similarly, if the notion of equilibrium is useless for studying real economies, there is no reason to assume that the labor market will clear at full employment equilibrium.

Robinson was also instrumental in extending the economics of Keynes so that it could address the problems of a global economy. Traditionally, economists held that changes in exchange rates or money flows (see **Hume**) would correct any trade imbalances. Countries with trade surpluses would experience either an influx of money or an appreciating currency. This would make their goods more expensive to citizens of other countries and reduce their exports. Countries running trade deficits would experience the reverse set of changes – their goods would be less expensive abroad and they would export more goods. Price changes thus bring trade into balance according to standard economic theory.

Contrary to this conventional view, Robinson (1980, vol. 1, pp. 182–205; vol. 4, pp. 212–40) argued that there is a Keynesian adjustment mechanism. Trade problems are resolved through income changes rather than through relative price changes. Countries running a trade deficit fail to sell enough goods throughout the world. Consequently, production declines and unemployment rises. As a result, people in this country buy fewer goods and services from abroad and their trade deficit moves to a position of balance. But this affects surplus countries, which now experience reduced demand for the goods they produce. Their trade surplus gets reduced, but their unemployment rate also goes up.

Robinson further extended the work of Keynes by examining international trade in dynamic terms, or examining how trade balances change over time. Rather than viewing international trade as the study of how and why different countries tend to produce different goods (see **Ricardo**), Robinson (1980, vol. 4, pp. 14–24; vol. 5, pp. 130–45) saw foreign trade as part of a national growth strategy. Trade surpluses, especially when achieved by specializing in manufacturing industries, would raise the domestic rate of profit and lead to greater investment and technological improvements. This, in turn, would create more domestic employment and greater income. Trade surpluses could thus lead to long-term improvements in productivity and living standards. By attempting to generate trade surpluses, trade policy became part of the arsenal of tools that governments might use to spark economic growth (see **Kaldor**).

The economics of Joan Robinson was always focused on the real world. But it was also critical of accepted economic theories that were not realistic or plausible. Her analysis of imperfect competition looked at how large firms actually make decisions about price, production, and employment. Her contributions to Post-Keynesian macroeconomics and the theory of international trade were also important in helping economists understand how real economies worked.

Economics has always been a male-dominated profession. Somewhat surprisingly, it seems that the mathematical nature of the discipline is not responsible for this. Economics has smaller fractions of female undergraduate majors and smaller fractions of female PhDs than in either mathematics or the natural sciences (Kahn 1995). Within this male bastion, Joan Robinson stands out as the most distinguished female economist.

Works by Robinson

Economics of Imperfect Competition, London, Macmillan, 1933

Introduction to the Theory of Employment, London, Macmillan, 1937a

Essays in Theory of Employment, London, Macmillan, 1937b

An Essay on Marxian Economics, London, Macmillan, 1942

"The Production Function and the Theory of Capital," *Review of Economic Studies*, 21, 2 (1953–4). Reprinted in Robinson (1980), Vol. 2, pp. 114–31

The Accumulation of Capital, London, Macmillan, 1956

Economic Heresies: Some Old-Fashioned Questions in Economic Theory, New York, Basic Books, 1971

An Introduction to Modern Economics, New York, McGraw Hill, 1973, with John Eatwell

Collected Economic Papers, 5 vols, Cambridge, Massachusetts, MIT Press, 1980

Works about Robinson

Gram, Harvey, and Walsh, Vivian, "Joan Robinson's Economics in Retrospect," *Journal of Economic Literature*, 21, 2 (June 1983), pp. 518–50

Marcuzzo, Maria Cristina, "Joan Robinson and the Three Cambridge Revolutions," *Review of Political Economy*, 15, 4 (October 2003), pp. 545–60

Rima, Ingrid (ed.), *The Joan Robinson Legacy*, Armonk, New York, M. E. Sharpe, 1991

Shaw, G. K., "Joan Robinson 1903–83," *Pioneers of Modern Economics in Britain*, Vol. 2, ed. David Greenaway and John R. Presley, New York, St. Martin's Press, 1989, pp. 144–69

Skouras, Thanos, "The Economics of Joan Robinson," in *Twelve Contemporary Economists*, ed. J. R. Shackleton and G. Locksley, New York, Wiley, 1981, pp. 199–218

Turner, Marjorie, *Joan Robinson and the Americans*, Armonk, NY, M. E. Sharpe, 1989

Other references

Eichner, Alfred S., *The Megacorp and Oligopoly: Micro Foundations of Macro Dynamics*, New York, Cambridge University Press, 1976

Harcourt, Geoff, *Some Cambridge Controversies in the Theory of Capital*, Cambridge, Cambridge University Press, 1972

Kahn, Shulamit, "Women in the Economics Profession," *Journal of Economic Perspectives*, 9, 4 (Fall 1995), pp. 193–205

JAN TINBERGEN (1903–94)

Jan Tinbergen was a pioneer in econometrics and economic modeling. He constructed the first statistical economic models, and then used these models to study business cycles and the effect of economic policy on national economies. But Tinbergen was not just a number-cruncher. Rather, as Baum (1989, p. 305) points out, all his statistical work was driven by a "deep-seated concern for human welfare and a conviction that scientific, mathematical analysis can be combined with a broader humanistic approach."

Tinbergen was born in 1903 in The Hague, which borders on the North Sea in the Netherlands. His father was a language teacher who stressed the need to express complicated ideas in simple terms. Despite the influence of his father, Tinbergen gravitated towards science and mathematics in high school rather than to language courses.

After graduating from high school, Tinbergen enrolled at the University of Leiden to study physics. During this time (the mid-1920s), Einstein gave annual lectures at Leiden and stayed with Paul Ehrenfest, the professor under whom Tinbergen was studying. Tinbergen got to meet Einstein on several occasions. None the less, Tinbergen lost interest in physics and shifted his course of study – first to mathematics and statistics, and then to economics. One reason for the latter change was that the economic conditions in Leiden during the 1920s were among the worst in Holland. Unemployment and poverty were high and there was virtually no public assistance.

Tinbergen felt a responsibility to help improve the lives of the Dutch people, and economics was the logical means towards this end. Tinbergen also developed personal concerns for peace, justice, and the welfare of humanity. He became an active member of the Dutch Social Democratic Labor Party and a conscientious objector. Rather than serve in the army, he agreed to perform alternative service to his country in the Rotterdam prison administration.

After completing a dissertation on minimization problems in economics and physics in 1929, Tinbergen joined the Dutch Central Bureau of Statistics. He spent most of the next sixteen years there studying business cycles, except for a short stint working for the League of Nations. From 1945 to 1955, Tinbergen served as director of the Central Planning Bureau of the Dutch government. During this time he devoted his energies to economic planning. After a one-year teaching position at Harvard, he became a professor at the Netherlands School of Economics (now Erasmus University). In 1969, Tinbergen shared the first Nobel Prize for Economics with Ragnar Frisch. The prize was awarded for their contributions to the development of econometrics.

Tinbergen made several important contributions to economics. Most of these were statistical in nature. He is responsible for developing the first economic model of an entire economy, and then he used this model to study and explain economic fluctuations in Holland. He was also instrumental in creating and developing econometrics. *Econometrics* is a set of mathematical techniques that economists use to estimate the quantitative relationship between two or more variables. For example, by studying historical relationships between interest rates and savings, economists can estimate how much more people are likely to save when interest rates rise. Putting interest rates (the independent variable) on the x-axis and savings rates (the dependent variable) on the y-axis, we can construct a two-dimensional graph of the relationship between these variables (see Figure 11).

Each point on the graph represents the savings rate (the amount of savings relative to household disposable income) and the interest rate in one particular year. Regression analysis is a statistical technique that enables economists to find the best line depicting the relationship between interest rates and savings rates, where "best" means the line that minimizes the difference between individual data points and the line, so that the set of points lie as close to the line as possible. It enables economists to find this line in the form of a mathematical equation such as $y=a+bx$, where a is the y-intercept and b is the slope of the line, or the *regression coefficient*. The regression coefficient b measures *how much* y changes for each unit change in x, or how much more households save out of their income when interest rates rise by one percentage point. Other explanatory or independent variables can be easily added to the model (but cannot easily be shown on a two-dimensional graph).

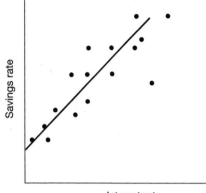

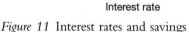

Figure 11 Interest rates and savings

Macroeconomic models are just large sets of regression equations. Each equation relates one part of the economy to other parts of the economy. The equation derived above relates consumer behavior regarding saving money to the rate of interest in the economy. A good regression equation is one where a set of independent variables can explain a large percentage of the variation in the dependent variable. This would occur, for example, if all the data points for savings rates and interest rates were very close to the estimated regression equation. In this case, knowing the interest rate would enable us to be pretty confident in predicting the national savings rate. On the other hand, if the data points were rather far away from the estimated regression equation, the interest rate would not be a good predictor of consumer savings behavior.

In 1936 Tinbergen developed a macroeconometric model of the Dutch economy containing twenty-four equations (see Tinbergen 1959, pp. 37–84). These equations described the key macroeconomic relationships of the Dutch economy – what determined consumer spending, business investment, exports, and so on. In many cases, lags were introduced so that consumption (and other macroeconomic variables) did not change immediately whenever income rose; rather, consumption (and other variables) changed slowly as income changed, and would adjust to higher income levels only after several years. Mathematically, this was shown by having consumption depend on a weighted average of present and past income (rather than just on present income).

Shortly after building his macroeconomic model of the Dutch economy, Tinbergen (1939) developed a model of the US economy for the 1919–32 period. This model contained forty-eight equations. During World War II, Tinbergen (1951) built a similar model for the UK.

This statistical work led to a heated debate between Tinbergen and Keynes about the nature and usefulness of econometrics. Critically reviewing a book by Tinbergen (1939), Keynes (1939) claimed that econometrics merely gave quantitative precision to what is already known to be true qualitatively about economic relationships. Tinbergen (1940) replied that regression coefficients can help test theories and that they might also suggest new economic theories. To prove his point, Tinbergen began using his macroeconomic models to study economic fluctuations and to develop theories about the business cycle.

In the 1930s, macroeconomists studied the different phases of the business cycle and provided different explanations for each of the different phases. Moreover, they mainly paid attention to how economies move towards equilibrium (static analysis), but they gave little attention to how economies grow and oscillate over time. Tinbergen made an important contribution when he provided a single, unified explanation of the business cycle. He also showed how and why economies change over time. His inspiration for this came from the cobweb theorem, which Tinbergen discovered in 1930.

Traditional economic theory assumes that prices and markets move in a straightforward manner towards an equilibrium or point of rest (see **Marshall**). Thus, if price is too high, there will be excess goods in the market. This will push down prices and reduce the supply of goods brought to the market. Conversely, if price is too low, a shortage will lead to higher prices and a greater supply of goods brought to the market. The problem, however, was that in many agricultural markets it was not uncommon to see prices and quantities move in opposite directions – prices would fall and more goods would be produced for sale. Or, like a cobweb, we would continually move around from high prices and shortages to low prices and surpluses, and then again to high prices and shortages.

Tinbergen provided an explanation for this phenomenon. His explanation was that output in agricultural markets responded to prices with a lag. Farmers needed time to react to changes in the market and some types of production, for example raising pigs, required considerable time. If too many pigs were brought to market, this would reduce the price of pigs. Because of the lower price, farmers would raise fewer pigs for sale in the following year. At the same time, the low price would lead to a large demand for pigs as consumers became used to consuming pork, bacon, and other pig products. This combination of low supply and high demand would create a shortage of pigs and push up prices. In response, farmers would produce too many pigs the following year, while consumers reduce their demand for pig products due to the high prices, thereby leading to another surplus.

This insight about markets provided the foundation for Tinbergen's (1937) analysis of the business cycle. He developed twenty-two statistical equations, each of which showed how supply and demand respond over time to shortages and to excess supply. Each equation also modeled the change taking place in different economic sectors. From these equations Tinbergen was able to show how economies oscillated over time, just like the production of pigs.

After developing his macroeconometric model, Tinbergen diverted his attention to policy issues. He showed how policy-makers could use macroeconomic models to measure the effects of any proposed policy. Then he showed how his statistical model could help politicians make policy decisions when facing contradictory or conflicting economic goals. Prior to the work of Tinbergen, different economic policies were studied in isolation from each other and no method existed for dealing with multiple policy targets. Tinbergen (1952, chs 4, 5) saw that multiple targets required multiple policies. Thus, if one wanted to lower unemployment and strengthen the national currency, two different policies were needed to achieve these two aims. In general, if policy-makers had a certain number of quantitative targets, they must have at their disposal at least an equal number of policy instruments.

Tinbergen also explained how economic analysis could be used to help national governments develop plans to improve economic outcomes. First, policy-makers needed to determine the collective preferences of the nation's citizens regarding economic targets. Then they needed to manipulate policy instruments in order to best satisfy the collective preferences of its citizens. The preferences led to policy targets that could either be fixed or flexible. The means to this end could be either far reaching *reforms* in the way economies operate (for example the introduction of social security legislation, guaranteed employment, or incomes policies), *qualitative changes* affecting the structure of the economy (such as new forms of taxation or changes in the laws governing monopoly and competition), or *quantitative changes*, which involve manipulating policy instruments such as the money supply, exchange rate or amount of government spending (Tinbergen 1952; van der Linden 1988).

In the 1970s, Tinbergen shifted his attention from economic planning to income distribution. Several factors are probably responsible for this change. First, interest in economic planning was waning throughout the world (see **Leontief**). Second, income disparities were large and growing in most countries, as well as between countries. This conflicted with Tinbergen's desire to increase social justice and economic welfare.

Like his other work, Tinbergen approached income distribution from a dynamic perspective. Rather than seeking the causes of the present distribution of income, Tinbergen (1975) sought to find the root causes of *changes* in the distribution of income over time. He located these in the factors affecting both the supply of labor and the demand for labor. The two most important factors affecting labor supply and labor demand, according to Tinbergen, were education and technological development. His analysis also relied upon the *dual labor market hypothesis* (see Piore and Doeringer 1971), which sees two different labor markets operating in developed countries rather than one large labor market. According to the dual labor market theory, one labor market exists for highly skilled workers while a separate market exists for those lacking skills and adequate education. Workers cannot easily cross from one market to the other, and employers usually demand workers from only one of the two labor pools.

From this perspective, expanded education tends to reduce income inequality because it tends to equalize the abilities of individuals in a country. In addition, education will equalize the wages received by these two groups of workers. A greater supply of educated workers will reduce their (higher) wages. At the same time, more education reduces the supply of less-educated workers. This means that the remaining low-skilled workers receive higher wages.

On the other hand, technological advances tend to increase income inequality. Technology requires skilled and educated manpower, thus increasing the demand for skilled workers and hence their earnings. Technology also displaces those who do not meet the higher qualifications. This reduces the demand for unskilled workers and their earnings.

Tinbergen (1975, p. 2) saw changing income inequality as the outcome of a race between education and technological development. If education improves more rapidly than technology, income inequality declines; if technology has the upper hand, income inequality becomes greater. This analysis provides the foundation for most studies of changing income distribution today. Economists see technical change as the main cause of rising inequality in the developed world (Bound and Johnson 1992), and they see more education and better education as the way to address this problem (Reich 1991).

Three policy implications follow from this analysis. First, government support for education needs to be increased so that education expands faster than technological development. Second, policies should direct technological innovation so that it requires more low-skilled labor. Increasing the demand for low-skilled labor would push up the wages of those at the bottom of the distribution and would mitigate the tendency for technology to increase income inequality. Finally, Tinbergen suggested using tax policy as a means of reducing inequality. He thus advocated higher taxes on wealth, capital gains, and inheritances.

Today, macroeconometric models built up of hundreds of equations exist for virtually every developed country. These models are used to study economic activity and to predict the future course of the national economy. They are also used (both by governments and by central banks) to help formulate economic policies. The existence of these macroeconometric models is due to the pioneering work of Tinbergen. This work makes Tinbergen one of the half-dozen most important economists of the twentieth century.

Works by Tinbergen

"Annual Survey of Significant Developments in General Economic Theory," *Econometrica*, 2, 1 (January 1934), pp. 26–8

An Econometric Approach to Business Cycle Problems, Paris, Hermann, 1937

Statistical Testing of Business Cycle Theories, 2 vols, Geneva, League of Nations, 1939

"On a Method of Statistical Business Cycle Research: A Reply," *Economic Journal*, 50 (1940), pp. 141–54

Business Cycles in the United Kingdom, 1870–1914, Amsterdam, North-Holland, 1951

On The Theory of Economic Policy, Amsterdam, North-Holland, 1952

Centralization and Decentralization in Economic Policy, Amsterdam, North-Holland, 1954

Economic Policy: Principles and Design, Amsterdam, North-Holland, 1956
Selected Papers, Amsterdam, North-Holland, 1959
Shaping the World Economy: Suggestions for an International Economic Policy, New York, Twentieth Century Fund, 1962
Lessons from the Past, Amsterdam, North-Holland, 1963
Income Distribution: Analysis and Policies, Amsterdam, North-Holland, 1975

Works about Tinbergen

Baum, Sandra R., "Jan Tinbergen 1969," in *Nobel Laureates in Economic Science*, ed. Bernard S. Katz, New York and London, Garland Publishing, 1989, pp. 304–17

Bos, Henk C., "Jan Tinbergen: A Profile," *Journal of Policy Modeling*, 6, 2 (1984), pp. 151–8

Hansen, Bent, "Jan Tinbergen: An Appraisal of His Contributions to Economics," *Swedish Journal of Economics*, 71, 4 (1969), pp. 25–36

Keynes, John Maynard, "Professor Tinbergen's Method," *Economic Journal*, 49 (September 1939). Reprinted in *The Collected Writings of John Maynard Keynes*, XIV, London, Macmillan, 1973, pp. 306–20

Kol, J. and de Wolff, P., "Tinbergen's Work: Change and Continuity," *De Economist*, 141, 1 (1993), pp. 1–28

Van der Linden, J. T. J. M., "Economic Thought in the Netherlands: The Contribution of Professor Jan Tinbergen," *Review of Social Economy*, 46, 3 (December 1988), pp. 270–82

Other references

Bound, John and Johnson, George, "Changes in the Structure of Wages in the 1980's: An Evaluation of Alternative Explanations," *American Economic Review*, 82, 3 (June 1992), pp. 371–92

Piore, Michael and Doeringer, Peter, *Internal Labor Markets and Manpower Analysis*, Lexington, Massachusetts, D. C. Heath, 1971

Reich, Robert, *The Work of Nations*, New York, Alfred Knopf, 1991

JOHN HICKS (1904–89)

John Hicks is best known for developing several pictorial diagrams used to demonstrate economic principles and techniques of analysis. These now form the basis of contemporary economics, especially as it is taught to undergraduate students.

Hicks was born in Warwick, England, in 1904 into a middle class family. His father was a journalist and an editor. He received a good high school education at private British schools, and then earned a scholarship to Balliol College, Oxford. Hicks began studying mathematics at Oxford, but soon changed fields and concentrated on economics. He received his degree in philosophy, politics, and economics in 1926.

After graduating, Hicks taught at the London School of Economics, at Cambridge University, and briefly in South Africa. He was not enamored with Cambridge, disliking both the physical climate and the intellectual climate (a great tendency to quarrel), but he found the London School of Economics a congenial place to work. Hugh Dalton of the LSE got Hicks to read Pareto's (1906) *Manual*, an event of great importance in his life. When he got to the mathematical appendices, Hicks realized Pareto did not finish what he set out to do – make economic analysis clearer and more precise by translating it into mathematics. At that moment Hicks decided to devote his career to completing what Pareto started (Klamer 1989, p. 169).

In 1938 Hicks was appointed to the Jevons Professorship at Manchester University. Eight years later he returned to Oxford, where he taught until his retirement in 1965. Hicks was knighted in 1964, thus becoming Sir John Hicks. In 1972 he shared the Nobel Prize for Economics with Kenneth Arrow.

Hicks has made important contributions to both macroeconomics and microeconomics – a rare feat in the twentieth century, when macroeconomics and microeconomics became separate and distinct fields, and when specialization prevailed in all academic disciplines. As a macroeconomist, Hicks (1937) is best known for formalizing the macroeconomic theories of Keynes. Later in life he (1974) considered this a misinterpretation of Keynes because it ignored the uncertainty of economic relationships that Keynes stressed in *The General Theory*. None the less, Hicks's (1937) paper, which translated Keynes into a set of two curves (see Figure 12, page 210), remains one of the most-cited economic papers of all time and the paper that forms the foundation for macroeconomic modeling.

Standard Keynesian theory never made clear the relationship between the goods market and the money market. In the goods market, businesses produce things and sell these things to consumers, to the government, to other businesses, and to foreign countries. Equilibrium in the goods markets requires that the supply of goods brought to market equals the demand for these goods. In the money market, people and businesses demand a fixed stock of money that is set by the nation's central bank. Equilibrium in the money market requires that the demand for money equals the supply of money.

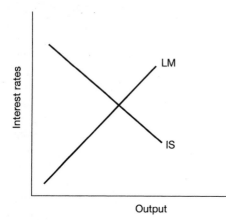

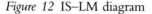

Figure 12 IS–LM diagram

These two markets, however, are interrelated rather than independent of each other. If the supply of money were increased, this would lower interest rates in the money market. But with lower interest rates, investment would rise and the total demand for goods and services would increase in the goods market. Of course, with more goods and services being produced, people would need more money so that they could buy more things. But a greater demand for money would push up interest rates, reduce investment and output, and thereby lower the demand for money.

Interactions between the goods market and the money market could conceivably go back and forth forever, yielding no final and stable outcome. The *IS–LM model* demonstrated that the goods market and the money market would achieve equilibrium simultaneously. This diagram now serves as the basis for most undergraduate education in macroeconomics, and has made IS–LM and Keynesianism synonymous in the minds of most economics students.

The IS curve in Figure 12 represents equilibrium positions in the goods market of the economy. It assumes that the rate of interest will come from the money market, and it considers the different levels of output produced in the economy for each possible interest rate that we get in the money market. IS stands for the fact that, in the goods market, investment (I) must equal savings (S). The downward–sloping IS curve shows that, as interest rates fall, economic output must expand to keep the goods market in equilibrium. This is because lower interest rates will increase business investment, but they will also reduce savings. To get savings up, and ensure that savings and investment are equal, the economy must produce more goods, more jobs, and greater incomes.

The LM curve shows possible equilibrium positions in the money market. It assumes that the level of output comes from the goods market, and it considers the different interest rates we get in the money market for each possible level of output in the goods market. LM stands for the fact that money demand (L) must equal money supply (M) in the money market. LM slopes upward showing that, as output rises, interest rates must increase to keep the money market in equilibrium. This is because with greater output people will want to hold more money to buy more goods. Given a fixed supply of money, in order to keep money demand and money supply equal, interest rates must rise so that people will want to hold less money (which pays no interest) and to hold more bonds and other assets (due to the fact that they now pay higher rates of interest).

Simultaneous equilibrium is achieved at the point of intersection between the IS and LM curves. Since the goods market moves towards points on the IS curve and the money market moves to points on the LM curve, the whole economy must move towards the single point at which the two curves meet.

Hicks then went on to show how the differences between Keynesian and non-Keynesian macroeconomists arise from different assumptions about the two curves. If the LM curve was flat rather than steeply sloped, *fiscal policy* (which works in the goods market or shifts the IS curve) would be needed to expand employment, and we are in the world described by Keynesian economists. On the other hand, if the IS curve were flat, *monetary policy* (which operates in the money market or shifts the LM curve) would be needed to expand output and employment, and we are in the world described by non-Keynesian economists.

A second macroeconomic contribution due to Hicks involves interest rates. Economists frequently talk about "*the* rate of interest" as if there were only one rate of interest existing in the economy. But, as everyone knows, there are many different rates of interest at any given time. Rates on credit cards are higher than rates for home mortgages, and rates are higher for fixed-rate mortgages than for variable-rate mortgages. Interest rate theory attempts to explain the relationship among all these different rates.

Hicks devised two ways to make sense of the vast array of interest rates. One focuses on the risk of lending money, and the other on the length of time for which money is lent. It is easiest to see these forces at work in the case of bonds. A bond is just a promise to pay back a certain amount of money (the face value of the bond) at some point in the future. When governments and large corporations borrow money they typically print up and sell bonds. Of course, they want to receive the largest amount of money for the bond because that gives them more money now, and because they are paying a lower rate of interest on the money they borrow since the difference between the selling price of the bond and the face value of the bond is effectively the interest rate that is being paid on the bond. It is this that establishes the inverse relationship between bond prices and interest rates. When bond prices are high, interest payments and interest rates are low; and when bond prices are low, firms and governments are paying a great deal of extra money on what they borrow, and so borrowing costs or interest rates rise (see **Keynes** for more details).

The greater the risk to the lender, the higher the rate of interest needs to be. More interest is required to compensate the lender for the greater probability that the loan will not be repaid. Bond-rating agencies, such as Standard & Poor's, grade corporate bonds and give them ratings like AAA, AA, A, BBB, BB, B, etc., based on their default probability. That is why junk bonds (corporate bonds with a rating of less than BB by Standard & Poor's) pay much higher interest rates than AAA corporate bonds with a default probability of close to zero, and why firms and governments are so concerned about their bond ratings.

The *yield curve* is a graphic device for looking at the rate of interest on bonds that mature (or get repaid) at different future dates. A yield curve might show that a three-month loan to the US government pays 3.5 percent, a two-year loan pays 5.5 percent, a 10-year loan pays 7 percent, and a 30-year loan pays 8 percent (see Figure 13).

One question that arises concerning the yield curve is whether there is any linkage among interest rates for assets with different maturities – say 6-month and 1-year government bonds. Hicks (1939, chs 11–13) answered this question with a resounding "yes," and developed the expectations hypothesis to explain the relationship among assets with different maturity lengths.

Hicks reasoned that if a 6-month bond paid 5 percent now and a 1-year bond paid 5.5 percent now, then investors must expect that six months in the future the rate on a 6-month bond will be 6 percent. Investors earn 5.5 percent either way. They can make 5.5 percent over the whole year by purchasing a 1-year bond now; alternatively, they can make 5 percent for the first six months of the year, and 6 percent for the second six months of the year. This averages out to the same 5.5 percent that could be earned from a 1-year bond. In general, the expectations hypothesis holds that returns on assets of longer maturities will equal the average of the current return on shorter-term assets and the expected return on shorter-term assets in the future.

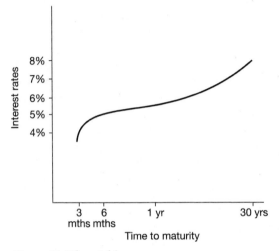

Figure 13 The yield curve

Hicks then went on to explain why the expectations hypothesis was true. His explanation essentially relies on the process of *arbitrage* (see **Cournot**). If a 1-year bond paid 5.5 percent when a 6-month bond paid 5 percent and was expected to pay 5.5 percent at 6 months in the future, very few people would want to own 6-month bonds. Over a 1-year time period, two 6-month bonds are expected to earn only 5.25 percent. People would prefer to have 1-year bonds paying 5.5 percent; so they will sell their 6-month bonds and buy 1-year bonds. This drives down the price of the 6-month bond and drives up the price of the 1-year bond. Since bond prices are inversely related to interest rates, the interest rate on the 6-month bond will rise and the interest rate on the 1-year bond will fall. This process will continue until the equilibrium condition identified by the expectations hypothesis is finally achieved – the rate on a 1-year bond will be equal to the average of the rate on a 6-month bond right now and the rate expected on a 6-month bond a half year from now.

While Hicks made many contributions as a macroeconomist, it is as a microeconomist that he first achieved fame. Although Edgeworth drew the first indifference curve diagrams, it was Hicks (1934) who incorporated indifference curve analysis into standard microeconomic theory. He showed how indifference curves could be used to construct a downward-sloping demand curve for any good. He then used indifference curves to separate the *income effect* of a price change from the *substitution effect* of a price change.

The key to developing this analysis is the introduction of a new notion – the budget line. This line represents how much of each good a consumer could purchase given their current income and the current prices of goods. For example, with $10 cash, and with pretzels and beer each costing $1, a consumer can buy any combination of pretzels and beer that adds up to 10. This is shown by the negatively sloped line in Figure 14. At one extreme, the consumer can buy 10 bags of pretzels and no beer. At the other extreme the consumer can buy 10 beers and no pretzels. In between these extremes many combinations are possible. All of these possibilities are shown by the budget line.

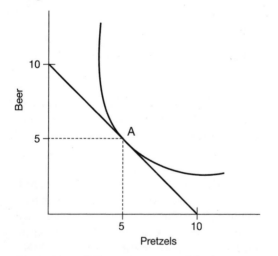

Figure 14 Indifference curve and budget constraint

Hicks next added indifference curves (see **Edgeworth**) to this diagram in order to explain consumer behavior. Consumers would choose the combination of pretzels and beer that yielded the highest utility. This indifference curve would be just tangent to the consumer budget line (see Figure 15).

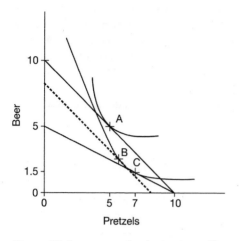

Figure 15 Income and substitution effects

Hicks then looked at the effects of a change in price. Suppose that the price of a beer were to increase to $2. With the price of beer relatively higher, people will want to purchase more pretzels and less beer. This is the *substitution effect*, whereby an increase in the price of a good reduces demand for that good and increases demand for most other goods (all goods that are not complementary goods). Yet, there is also an income effect. When beer costs more, consumer income can buy less of everything. Spending on both beer and pretzels will fall, due to the income effect. Together, the two effects together change spending from 5 beers and 5 pretzels to 1.5 beers and 7 pretzels. These effects are shown by the rotation of the budget line. Due to this rotation, point C is now where our consumer gets the greatest utility.

Hicks then figured out an ingenuous way to separate the income and substitution effects. The slope of the budget line represents the relative prices of the two goods. If there were a substitution effect, but no income effect, we should be on our original indifference curve, but choosing different combinations of pretzels and beer based on the new $2 price of beer or the new budget line. Hicks suggested that we show the income effect by taking the old budget line and moving it up the graph until it is just tangent to the original indifference curve. This is shown as the dashed line on Figure 15. At point B the relative prices of beer and pretzels are the same. It thus shows the change in consumer spending habits that must be due to the income effect alone.

Because the income effect and the substitution effect each reduce the consumption of beer, it follows that, when the price of beer rises, people buy less beer. The demand curve for beer must therefore slope downward – as the price of beer rises, the quantity consumed falls, and conversely, as the price of beer falls, the quantity consumed will increase.

Finally, Hicks (1932) is responsible for introducing the notion of the *elasticity of substitution*, a natural extension of Marshall's notion of *elasticity*. Marshall applied the notion of elasticity to consumer demand and producer supply, and studied how much more consumers would buy and how much more producers would sell given some change in price. Hicks took this elasticity notion and applied it to the decisions businesses had to make about production.

From a firm's point of view, goods can be produced in several different ways, each using different combinations of labor and capital. A more labor-intensive production process would employ less capital and more labor, and a more capital-intensive production process would use less labor and more capital. In general, firms face a trade-off in production – each additional worker employed requires less machinery, and each additional machine used in production requires fewer workers. The *elasticity of substitution* measures how much machinery could be dispensed with if one more worker were used in producing goods, or alternatively how many workers could be dispensed with by purchasing and using one more machine.

Hicks pointed out that workers should not necessarily oppose labor-saving technical change since it could lead to higher wages. This would arise if the elasticity of substitution between labor and capital is large, and it is easy to substitute capital for labor. With more capital, workers will be more productive and thus will be paid more.

Hicks has justly been called (Hamouda 1993) "the economist's economist." Writing exclusively for his professional colleagues, he developed numerous tools and diagrams that have enabled economists to depict the principles of economic analysis more clearly and concisely. Hicks showed how to combine an analysis of the money market with an analysis of the goods market, how to understand the relationships between interest rates of different maturities, and how to combine utility theory and the theory of demand. For his many advances and for the many areas in which he made important contributions, Hicks must be regarded as one of the half-dozen most important twentieth century economists.

Works by Hicks

The Theory of Wages, London, Macmillan, 1932

"A Reconsideration of the Theory of Value," Economica, 1 (February and May 1934), pp. 52–76, 196–219, with R.D.G. Allen

"A Suggestion for Simplifying the Theory of Money," Economica, 2 (February 1935), pp. 1–19. Reprinted in Hicks (1967)

"Mr. Keynes and the 'Classics': A Suggested Interpretation," Econometrica, 5 (April 1937), pp. 147–59. Reprinted in Hicks (1967)

Value and Capital: An Inquiry into Some Fundamental Principles of Economic Theory, Oxford, Clarendon Press, 1939

Capital and Growth, Oxford, Clarendon Press, 1965

Critical Essays in Monetary Theory, Oxford, Oxford University Press, 1967

The Crisis in Keynesian Economics, New York, Basic Books, 1974

Collected Essays on Economic Theory, 3 vols, Oxford, Basil Blackwell, 1981–3

Works about Hicks

Baumol, William, "John R. Hicks' Contribution to Economics," Swedish Journal of Economics, 74 (1972), pp. 503–72

Hagemann, Harald and Hamouda, Omar F., The Legacy of Hicks: His Contributions to Economic Analysis, London and New York, Routledge, 1994

Hamouda, Omar F., John R. Hicks: The Economist's Economist, Oxford, Blackwell, 1993

Klamer, Arjo, "An Accountant among Economists: Conversations with Sir John R. Hicks," Journal of Economic Perspectives, 3, 4 (Fall 1989), pp. 167–80

Morgan, Brian, "Sir John Hicks' Contribution to Economic Theory," in Twelve Contemporary Economists, ed. J. R. Shackleton and G. Locksley, London, Macmillan, 1981, pp. 108–40

Other references

Pareto, Vilfredo, Manual of Political Economy (1906), New York, A. M. Kelly, 1971

WASSILY LEONTIEF (1906–99)

Wassily Leontief (pronounced LAY-yon-TEE-F) is best known for developing *input–output analysis*. This technique, which describes the interrelationships among the different sectors or industries of an economy, has a number of important applications and provides broad insights into how economies work. Input–output analysis has been used to understand how production bottlenecks might arise when economies expand, and how the inflationary process is distributed and diffused throughout the economy (Leontief 1946). The technique was also used by socialist economies and by developing economies after World War II for constructing five-year economic plans.

Leontief was born into an educated and wealthy family in St. Petersburg, Russia, in 1906. His father taught labor economics at the University of St. Petersburg, and his mother was an art historian. Something of a child prodigy, Leontief entered the university when he was only fifteen years old. There he studied philosophy, sociology, and then economics. Leontief frequently got into trouble for criticizing the new Communist government, and was jailed several times while attending the university.

In 1925, at the age of eighteen, Leontief received an MA in Social Science with the title "Learned Economist." The Leontief family then left Russia because of their differences with the Communist government and settled in Germany. Leontief enrolled at the University of Berlin to continue his studies in economics, and in 1928 received his PhD. A chance encounter in a Berlin cafe with Chinese visitors led to a job as consultant and advisor to the Minister of Railways in China. In this capacity Leontief spent a year traveling through China collecting data to help plan the Chinese railway network. This work provided him with insights about economic interrelationships, and the opportunity to map out these relationships using real-world data.

In 1931, Leontief came to the United States. He worked first as a research associate at the National Bureau of Economic Research in New York, then for many years at Harvard University. It was at Harvard in the 1930s that Leontief began developing his input–output model for the US economy. In the decades after, he further refined and expanded this model, and found many ways to use the model for studying economic problems. Leontief left Harvard in 1975 to assume a position at the Institute of Economic Research at New York University.

Over the years, Leontief received many accolades and awards. In 1970, he served as President of the American Economic Association. In 1973 he was awarded the Nobel Prize for Economics. In selecting Leontief for this prize, the Nobel Committee cited his work in input–output analysis. This undoubtedly constitutes Leontief's major contribution to economics.

Although the vision of the economy as a set of interrelated sectors (with one sector buying goods from other sectors, and with money flowing from sector to sector and back again) was originally set forth by Cantillon and Quesnay, it was Leontief who put these relation-ships into mathematical terms and who gathered the data necessary to construct real-world input–output tables. Leontief also drew out the policy implications of the mathematical representation of the econ-omy that he developed. This tool allows an analyst to work out how the changes in any one sector or industry of the economy will affect every other sector or industry. Moreover, input–output analysis allows for comprehensive government planning, something Leontief regarded as the next stage of capitalist development.

The major insight behind input–output analysis is that, if an economy is to produce more of one good (say, automobiles), it will need to be sure to have all of the inputs or parts that are needed to build another car. Thus more tires, more hubcaps, more axles, more glass windows, more engines, etc., will all be required. In turn, pro-ducing each part will require other parts. Tires will require more rubber, more machinery, etc. Making things even more complicated, to produce more engines or hubcaps or axles the economy will need to produce more cars, since vehicles are needed to transport parts and raw materials. To produce these additional cars, of course, will require more of all the inputs necessary for car production.

Labor inputs are easily handled in this framework. The workers who assemble automobiles are viewed as an input that requires other inputs. If they are to produce cars, workers will need food, clothing, shelter, and yes, cars to get them to and from work. What is true of these assembly workers is true of all other workers in the economy.

Through extensive study of production and the technological needs of numerous US industries, Leontief (1941) was able to repre-sent the technical production relationships for major industries in mathematical form. This accounting-like framework specified all other goods in the economy that were needed to produce any parti-cular good. This gave Leontief a large set of mathematical equations, one for each good produced in the economy. With the aid of a computer, Leontief was able to solve this set of equations. His solu-tion told him how much more of all other goods had to be produced in order to get one more car. If these other goods were not produced as needed, production bottlenecks would arise; there would be shortages of engines, or tires, or window glass, and the extra car could not be made. On the other hand, if all the inputs were pro-duced in the required amounts, there would be just enough parts and materials available to give us one more car.

Input–output models are not merely technological relationships. They also allow policy-makers to determine the consequences of changing economic policy. For example, reduced government spending on defense inevitably hurts the armament industry, their suppliers, and all their suppliers' suppliers. In contrast, greater spending on infrastructure (such as roads, bridges, and railways) aids the construction industry, their suppliers, and their suppliers' suppliers. Putting these two sets of changes together would allow the government to calculate the total impact of military reconversion on different geographic regions in the country and on different industries or sectors of the economy (Leontief 1961, 1965; 1986, chs 9, 10).

Leontief (1986, chs 5, 6) demonstrated how input–output techniques could be used to test economic theories when he studied US trade relations with other nations. Surprisingly, he found that American exports used less capital and more labor in their production than American imports. This contradicted traditional trade theory, which held that a capital-rich country (like the US) should export capital-intensive goods and import labor-intensive goods. The result has come to be known as *the Leontief Paradox*. Leontief's finding led to numerous efforts to revise trade theory in order to account for these real-world findings.

Another real-world application of input–output analysis stems from the work Leontief (1977; 1986, chs 11, 12) did for the United Nations beginning in 1973. This work has attempted to develop a world input–output model that incorporates the environment as an "economic sector." One can think of economic sectors producing not only their normal output, such as cars, but also a number of pollutants. Likewise, one can think of a pollution-abatement sector, whose inputs are the pollutants produced by other sectors. This sector destroys these pollutants and returns the environment to its original state or quality. Leontief has used this model to study the environmental impact of expanding production as well as how to get more economic growth with limited additional environmental pollution.

From the 1940s to the 1960s there was a great deal of interest in input–output analysis worldwide. The development of the computer meant that increasingly complex and realistic input–output models could be developed for every country. During World War II, governments used input–output analysis to determine which sectors of the economy were likely to experience shortages, and to develop policies that would expand production by these sectors. Furthermore, after World War II, nations became interested in taking charge of their own economic future rather than leaving it to the whimsical forces of the market. Planning agencies and bureaucracies arose in both developed countries and developing countries, and input–output models provided a simple and useful tool to assist in this endeavor.

However, during the 1970s interest in input–output analysis began to wane. First, the mood at the time shifted away from planning and back towards allowing the market to determine the pace and direction of development. Second, some limitations of input–output analysis became apparent. Because it is both difficult and expensive to estimate all the actual input–output relationships for a large and complex economy, national governments infrequently revise the national input–output model. Consequently, policy analysis using input–output tools would rely on figures that were considerably out of date (Marshall 1989, p. 162).

Third, and most important, in the real world, growth and development has been associated with changes in technology and the means of production. Technological improvement has meant that production can take place with fewer inputs (especially labor requirements). That means input–output relationships are always changing. Input–output analysis, however, takes these relationships as fixed.

Besides input–output analysis, Leontief has also been concerned with the methodology of economic science and the everyday practices of contemporary economists. Here Leontief has shifted from being a model builder, interested in establishing empirical relationships, to being a sharp critic of professional practices. His first critique of the methodology of economics (Leontief 1937) attacked Keynes and his followers for constructing abstract, theoretical models whose conclusion was already built into the premises of the model. Leontief felt that, without good empirical estimates of the way an economy actually worked, such model building could shed no light on the problems facing real economies. The nature of this criticism is essentially that economics has ceased to be an empirical science and instead has become too theoretical.

In his Presidential address to the American Economic Association, Leontief (1971) continued his criticism of how his colleagues actually did economics. This time his complaint was about the mathematical formalism dominating the economics profession. He argued that economists have become intrigued with developing formal models and then logically deducing the characteristics or properties of that model without bothering to ask whether or not the assumptions of these models were realistic. The conclusions of these mathematical derivations were irrelevant, Leontief asserted, because they began with assumptions that are not true (see **Friedman** and **Samuelson**).

Leontief also criticized his fellow economists for performing sophisticated statistical analysis on data of questionable meaning and validity. More positively, he recommended that economists devote more time and attention to gathering data, and spend less time developing sophisticated testing techniques. Finally, Leontief argued that economic relationships, unlike relationships in the physical sciences, change over time because the individual behaviors on which these relationships depend also change. Econometric testing, which assumes that economic relationships always stay the same, is therefore misplaced, and helps disguise the weaknesses in the data sets and the fact that economic relationships do change over time. This argument anticipates the *Lucas Critique* of macroeconomic model building (see **Lucas**).

Leontief also has called for economists to be more interdisciplinary, by studying and working with sociologists, engineers, and management scientists. These areas give more value to empirical and practical work, and their practitioners are knowledgeable and skilled in data gathering and analysis. Studying more empirical disciplines can teach economists a great deal about the use and importance of data collection and theory testing.

While similar criticisms have been made by others about the everyday practices of economists (see **Bergmann**, Mayer 1993), none of these critics has the prestige of Leontief or the broad experience that comes from years of doing empirical economics. Unfortunately, these criticisms have fallen on deaf ears within the economics profession. Even worse, much of the profession remains unaware of this line of criticism coming from such a prestigious figure.

The one unifying theme in all of Leontief's work is that economics should be an empirical and practical science, devoted to gathering data and solving problems through the application of analytical tools to real-world data. Input–output analysis is about seeing how the economy really works, and using that knowledge to improve economic performance. Leontief's methodological complaint is that economists are not doing this anymore.

Works by Leontief

"Implicit Theorizing: A Methodological Criticism of the Neo-Cambridge School," *Quarterly Journal of Economics*, 51, 1 (1937), pp. 337–51
The Structure of the American Economy, 1919–1929: An Empirical Application of Equilibrium Analysis, Cambridge, Massachusetts, Harvard University Press, 1941

"Wages, Profits, and Prices," *Quarterly Journal of Economics*, 61, 1 (1946), pp. 26–39

Studies in the Structure of the American Economy, New York, Oxford University Press, 1953

"The Economic Effects of Disarmament," *Scientific American*, 204, 4 (1961), pp. 47–55, with M. Hoffenberg

"The Economic Impact–Industrial and Regional – of an Arms Cut," *Review of Economics and Statistics*, 47, 3 (1965), pp. 217–41, with others

"Theoretical Assumptions and Nonobservable Facts," *American Economic Review*, 61 (March 1971), pp. 1–7

The Future of the World Economy, New York, Oxford University Press, 1977

"Foreword" in *Why Economics is Not Yet a Science*, ed. Alfred Eichner, Armonk, New York, M. E. Sharpe, 1983, pp. vi–xi

Input–Output Economics, 2nd edn, New York, Oxford University Press, 1986

Works about Leontief

Cave, Martin, "Wassily Leontief: Input–Output and Economic Planning," in *Twelve Contemporary Economists*, ed. J. R. Shakleton and G. Locksley, New York, Wiley 1981, pp. 160–82

Dorfman, Robert, "Wassily Leontief's Contributions to Economics," *Swedish Journal of Economics*, 79 (1977), pp. 430–49

Marshall, James N., "Wassily Leontief 1973," in *Nobel Laureates in Economic Sciences: A Biographical Dictionary*, ed. Bernard S. Katz, New York and London, Garland Publishing, 1989, pp. 160–73

Pietzbacher, Erik and Lahr, Michael (eds), *Wassily Leontief and Input–Output Economics*, New York, Cambridge University Press, 2001

Other references

Mayer, Thomas, *Truth versus Precision in Economics*, Hampshire, UK, Edward Elgar, 1993

NICHOLAS KALDOR (1908–86)

Nicholas Kaldor spent most of his career devising policies to improve economic performance. He argued for taxing spending rather than income, and taxes that would favor and spur production in the manufacturing sector of developed economies. Kaldor also opposed tight money policy as a means of controlling inflation; instead, he advocated policies to control the wage–price spiral that caused inflationary pressures.

Kaldor was born in Budapest, Hungary, in 1908. His father was a criminal lawyer and legal consultant; his mother came from a wealthy family of businessmen and bankers. Kaldor thus grew up in fairly affluent surroundings and received an excellent education. He attended a model high school in Budapest that was famous for using the Socratic method of teaching.

Although his father wanted him to study law, Kaldor became interested in economics. In part, this stemmed from his interest in politics; but he was also fascinated by the German hyperinflation of 1923, which he had witnessed first-hand while on vacation in the Bavarian Alps.

In 1925 Kaldor enrolled at the University of Berlin. Two years later he went to the London School of Economics (LSE), where he studied under Friedrich Hayek. Graduating in 1930, Kaldor accepted a teaching job at the LSE, but left in 1947 to become Director of the Research and Planning Division for the European Economic Commission. Kaldor returned to academia in 1949, accepting a position at King's College, Cambridge, home to the followers of Keynes. Throughout the 1950s and 1960s, Kaldor served as an advisor to both British and foreign governments. He was a special advisor to the Chancellor of the Exchequer from 1964 to 1968 and again from 1974 to 1976.

When he began teaching at Cambridge, Kaldor shifted from his early focus on economic theory to a focus on economic policy. He also rejected his earlier views that economies work best when left alone by the government, and adopted a more activist policy orientation. In particular, he developed several tax policies to improve overall economic performance. Also, in the 1970s and early 1980s Kaldor advocated active government intervention to control price inflation.

In 1951 Kaldor was appointed to a Royal Commission on the Taxation of Profits and Income. This committee was charged with examining the British tax system and making recommendations for improving it. Kaldor found himself in the opposition during the Commission hearings. He was also opposed to the main Commission recommendations and wrote a lengthy minority report. This was then expanded into a book (Kaldor 1955) that advanced a radical plan to tax spending rather than income. Throughout the 1950s, Kaldor (1960–80, vols 1 (Part 3), 7, 8) pushed expenditure taxation on both developed and developing countries (advising the governments of India, Sri Lanka, Guyana, Turkey, Iran, Venezuela, and Ghana).

Kaldor (1955) was opposed to income tax for several reasons. First, income does not adequately measure the ability of an individual to pay taxes. To cite just one glaring problem, capital gains are taxed only when assets get sold; unrealized gains remain untaxed with an income tax. As a result, income from property escapes taxation and the income tax treats wealthy individuals too leniently. Moreover, the very wealthy have inherited most of their wealth and do not earn much additional income. Taxing income allows these individuals virtually to escape taxation.

Second, Kaldor noted serious economic defects with the income tax. Because interest and profits are subject to taxation, the income tax discourages the savings and investment that are required to receive such income. In addition, because returns to successful risk-taking get taxed at very high rates, income taxation discourages this important engine for economic growth.

To remedy these problems, Kaldor proposed converting the income tax into an expenditure tax. One should think of the expenditure or consumption tax as an income tax that allows all new savings to be deducted from taxable income. New savings can easily be measured as additions to stock portfolios and bank balances. If a household dissaves, or uses its wealth to finance current spending, that household would be taxed on its negative savings for the year (which get used for consumption). A "new savings" tax deduction allows annual savings to escape taxation, and so only spending gets taxed. Of course, a tax deduction for savings will cause tax collections to fall unless higher tax rates are imposed. Also, to keep income tax a *progressive tax* when large deductions are given to wealthy families for saving, very high tax rates will have to be imposed for high levels of consumption. Kaldor himself (1955, p. 241) suggested that the highest tax rate on expenditures would have to be set above 100 percent, and possibly as high as 300 percent.

The major benefit of moving from income to expenditure taxation is that savings would be encouraged. People would save more because spending would be highly penalized by high taxes while saving escapes taxation. More savings, in turn, would lead to technological improvements, productivity growth, greater incomes, and even more savings and investment.

Although Kaldor served as an economic advisor to two British Labour governments, and as an advisor to several developing countries, few nations followed his tax policy prescription. The only two countries that Kaldor convinced to follow his advice experienced popular uprisings against the expenditure tax. As a result, both countries (India and Sri Lanka) abandoned the expenditure tax soon after it was implemented (see Pressman 1995).

Following these failures, Kaldor took a new approach to tax policy. He suggested that taxation should be structured to help particular industries or economic sectors.

Kaldor wanted to develop Britain's more productive economic sectors, an idea that harks back to Quesnay's distinction between productive and unproductive economic sectors. Kaldor (1981) placed great emphasis on *increasing returns* to scale as a factor contributing to economic growth. Increasing returns means that, as firms produce more of some good, each worker becomes more productive. This improved productivity then spurs both domestic expansion and greater competitiveness in a global economy (Kaldor 1981).

Kaldor (1967) was convinced that increasing returns ruled in the manufacturing sector. His belief stemmed from three empirical regularities that he found when looking at the growth experiences of various developed countries (see Thirlwall 1983). First, Kaldor found a high correlation between economic growth and the growth of manufacturing output for twelve industrial countries during the 1950s and 1960s. He argued that aggregate growth rates were dependent upon manufacturing growth rates (rather than vice versa), and that this could be explained by increasing returns to scale in industrial activities.

Second, Kaldor found a high correlation between productivity growth in the manufacturing sector and the growth of manufacturing output. Here, he argued that productivity growth in manufacturing was dependent on the growth of manufacturing output. When people want more manufactured goods, the firms producing those goods will expand production. Due to *economies of scale*, productivity growth accelerates and costs fall because of the greater demand for manufactured goods.

Third, Kaldor found that the growth of a country's manufacturing output was correlated with the growth of productivity in other economic sectors. He argued that, as the manufacturing sector grows, it is able to absorb surplus agricultural labor. Consequently, productivity and living standards rise in the agricultural sector. In addition, "industrialization tends to accelerate the rate of change of technology, not just in one sector, but in the economy as a whole" (Kaldor 1967, p. 23). Hence, productivity rises in all economic sectors, and living standards improve throughout the nation.

From these facts Kaldor concluded that economic growth depends first and foremost on the growth of an industrial sector. A healthy and thriving manufacturing sector means rapid economic growth and rising standards of living. The policy conclusion that Kaldor drew from this analysis is that governments must support domestic manufacturing industries. Governments can do this through the direct purchase of manufactured goods, or by supporting manufacturing industries with tax breaks, regulatory relief, and other incentives or assistance.

A particular policy proposal that followed from this analysis was the selective employment tax. Kaldor (1960–80, vol. 7, pp. 200–29; 1966, ch. 7) proposed that firms in the service sector should be taxed based upon the number of workers they employed. This would encourage employment in manufacturing industries experiencing increasing returns to scale and discourage employment outside manufacturing.

During the 1970s, as inflation became the main economic problem in the world economy, Kaldor changed the focus of his attention and policy efforts. But first he had to contend with the rising tide of monetarism.

Modern monetarism (see **Friedman**) holds that changes in the supply of money are the cause of higher prices. The way to control inflation was to make sure the money supply grows at a constant and slow rate, 3–5 percent per year, which monetarists took to be the rate at which economic output grows from year to year.

Kaldor (1982) raised several objections against monetarism. First he noted that, according to the *equation of exchange*, MV=PQ (see **Fisher**), more money leads to greater inflation only if the velocity of money (V) is stable. Kaldor denied that the velocity of money was constant, and produced substantial empirical evidence to show how the velocity of money changed over time and how it differed from country to country.

Second, Kaldor held that the direction of causation was actually the reverse of that claimed by the monetarists. For Kaldor, a rise in economic activity or a rise in prices causes a rise in the money supply. In modern economies, money is created when banks make loans. When economic activity expands, firms and individuals want to borrow money. It is this borrowing that causes the money supply to rise. In contrast, when economic activity slows down, there is less demand for borrowed funds. As banks stop making new loans, the money supply stops growing.

Finally, Kaldor felt that slow money growth would create too much unemployment. He objected to the constant harping about inflation by monetarists. He noted that, even for the monetarists themselves, there are relatively few costs to inflation, since inflation was by definition a *general* rise in the price level. When all prices and all incomes go up by roughly the same proportion, there are only trivial costs to the economy, essentially the time and expense of having to increase prices (these costs are sometimes called "menu change costs"). Creating unemployment, on the other hand, creates severe hardship for those thrown out of work. Advocating joblessness in order to avoid the trivial costs of inflation, as monetarists did, was clearly a bad policy prescription.

Rejecting tight monetary policy to control inflation, Kaldor (1982, pp. 61–5) argued for an *incomes policy* to replace the current wage bargaining system. According to Kaldor, inflation was not caused by too much money, but rather by costs and prices pushing each other up in an endless spiral. Workers would demand pay increases to keep their wages up in the face of higher prices. But higher wages mean higher costs for businesses, which get passed on to consumers in the form of higher prices, starting another cycle.

Kaldor suggested that government get into the wage bargaining process in order to stop this inflationary spiral. It could do this either by freezing all wages and prices, or it could get labor and business to sit down together and cooperate on keeping inflation under control. Labor, for example, would agree to keep its wage increases in line with productivity improvements (and thus not contribute to rising costs); business, in turn, would agree not to raise prices.

Kaldor developed a name and reputation for himself by developing policy proposals to improve the market system by using economic incentives. If saving was good for the economy and spending was bad for the economy, then spending should be penalized through higher taxes. Likewise, if manufacturing production was good and a large service sector led to slower growth, the government should tax the latter sector and provide tax breaks for the former sector. This focus on developing economic policies to improve economic outcomes makes Kaldor (along with Joan Robinson) one of the founders of the Post Keynesian School of Economics.

Works by Kaldor

An Expenditure Tax, London, Allen & Unwin, 1955

Causes of the Slow Rate of Economic Growth of the United Kingdom, Cambridge, Cambridge University Press, 1966. Reprinted in Kaldor, 1960–80, vol. 5, pp. 100–38

Strategic Factors in Economic Development, Ithaca, New York State School of Industrial and Labor Relations, 1967

"The Irrelevance of Equilibrium Economics," *Economic Journal*, 82 (December 1972), pp. 1237–55

"The Role of Increasing Returns, Technical Progress and Cumulative Causation in the Theory of International Trade and Economic Growth," *Economic Applique*, 34, 4 (1981), pp. 593–617

The Scourge of Monetarism, Oxford, Oxford University Press, 1982
Economics without Equilibrium, Armonk, NewYork, M. E. Sharpe, 1985
"The Economics of the Selective Employment Tax," in *Collected Economic Essays*, vol. 7, pp. 200–29
Collected Economic Essays, 9 vols, New York, Holmes & Meier, 1960–89

Works about Kaldor

Blaug, Mark, "Nicholas Kaldor 1908–86," in *Pioneers of Modern Economics in Britain*, vol. 2, ed. David Greenway and John R. Presley, New York, St. Martin's Press, 1989, pp. 68–95

Pressman, Steven, "The Feasibility of an Expenditure Tax," *International Journal of Social Economics*, 22, 8 (1995), pp. 3–15

Targetti, Fernando, *Nicholas Kaldor: The Economics and Politics of Capitalism as a Dynamic System*, New York, Oxford University Press, 1992

Thirlwall, Anthony, "A Plain Man's Guide to Kaldor's Growth Laws," *Journal of Post Keynesian Economics*, 5, 3 (Spring 1983), pp. 345–58

Thirlwall, Anthony, *Nicholas Kaldor*, New York, New York University Press, 1987

Turner, Marjorie S., *Nicholas Kaldor and the Real World*, Armonk, New York, M. E. Sharpe, 1993

JOHN KENNETH GALBRAITH (1908 –)

The economics of John Kenneth Galbraith has had both a negative side and a positive side. On the negative side Galbraith has been a gadfly, highly critical of traditional economic theory. He has criticized economic theory for assuming perfect competition and ignoring the economic power accumulated by large corporations. He has criticized politicians for caving in to the power of large corporations rather than acting in the public interest. And he has criticized his fellow economists as *idiot savants*, who can do sophisticated mathematical analysis but fail to understand the real economic world. On the positive side, Galbraith has emphasized the importance of bringing power and power relationships into economic analysis if we are going to understand how economies actually work.

Galbraith was born in Iona Station, a small town on the northern shore of Lake Erie, in 1908; and he grew up in Southern Ontario, part of Scottish Canada. Galbraith (1981) regrets that his schooling was frequently interrupted by farm work, and that his academic record was undistinguished.

In 1926, Galbraith enrolled at Ontario Agricultural College (now the University of Guelph) to study agricultural economics. He then did graduate work in agricultural economics at Berkeley. His PhD thesis on the expenditures of Californian counties "was without distinction. . . . The purpose was to get the degree" (Galbraith 1981, p. 22).

After receiving his degree Galbraith accepted a teaching job at Harvard University. He spent most of his academic life at Harvard, although taking much time off to write and pursue his political interests. In 1941 he became deputy administrator of the Office of Price Administration, which gave him control over the prices of most US goods until 1943. During the 1950s and 1960s Galbraith was especially active in politics. He was an adviser and speechwriter in the Presidential campaigns of Adlai Stevenson and John Kennedy. In 1961 Galbraith was made Ambassador to India, a position he held until 1963 (see Galbraith 1969). During 1968 he worked on the Presidential campaign of Senator Eugene McCarthy, and during 1972 he worked on the Presidential campaign of Senator George Mc-Govern.

The economic work of Galbraith has been concerned primarily with the question of economic power. Galbraith has written about the tendency for firms to acquire economic power, the consequences of this, and the need for government intervention to counter the power of business interests and assert the public interest.

Galbraith (1967) argues that the industrial sector of the US economy is not at all as it is portrayed in economics textbooks. The US economy does not have competitive markets with a large number of firms subject to the will of the people. Rather, it has non-competitive markets and large firms that control the market. Large, monopolistic firms do not attempt to maximize the profits of shareholders; rather, they attempt to make the market more reliable and predictable.

Large firms plan because they must plan. The market and the forces of competition contain too much uncertainty for the firm. Investment in new technology is very costly; hence the firm cannot take the chance that, after undertaking expensive investment, there will be no demand for the goods they produce. To thrive, firms must eliminate market forces wherever they arise; they must attempt to control the market rather than be controlled by it.

The large corporation frees itself from the market in several ways. Through vertical integration it takes over suppliers and outlet sources. By developing many diverse products, the firm can absorb the consequences of a drastic change in consumer tastes or the aversion of consumers to a particular product. By spending money on advertising the firm controls consumer tastes. Finally, long-term contracts between producers and suppliers attempt to eliminate the uncertainty of short-term market fluctuations.

Traditional economic theory assumes that the firm is run by the owner. Galbraith thinks this view is severely antiquated. The firms that produce most of the goods and services we buy are run by professional managers. Those managers are the decision-makers for the firm; Galbraith calls them "the technostructure." It is here that corporate power lies. Professional managers have usurped power from the entrepreneurial owner because the important decisions of the large modern firm require the technical and scientific knowledge of many individuals. One person cannot be familiar with all the aspects of engineering, procurement, quality control, labor relations, and marketing necessary for doing business. As group decision-making and technical expertise become more important, power passes from the individual owner to the group that runs the firm.

But unlike owners, who have a vested interest in maximizing profits, professional managers gain little from profit maximization. Rather, members of the technostructure desire survival, growth, and technical virtuosity. Survival means a minimum amount of earnings so that the independence of the decision-makers can be maintained. Growth prevents firing members of the technostructure as a cost-saving measure. Growth also serves the psychological needs of the technostructure – prestige comes from working for a large, well-known firm. Finally, technical virtuosity means more jobs and promotions for members of the technostructure.

Galbraith (1958) has also examined the power held by large corporations over consumers. He has attacked the doctrine of *consumer sovereignty*, which holds that consumers know what they want and that businesses produce goods to meet consumer needs. This, Galbraith argues, runs counter to common sense and counter to what we know occurs all the time in the real world. Demand does not originate with the consumer; it is contrived for the consumer by the firm through advertising. Large firms have thus developed power over consumer spending.

If consumers decide on their own that they want certain goods, this would indicate some primacy for the goods that businesses produce. But since demand is contrived, there is no primacy for goods produced by the business sector of the economy. Public goods may be equally important. Moreover, many of the goods produced by businesses are quite frivolous and not of paramount importance. Even the economic principle of *diminishing marginal utility* recognizes that, as we consume more and more of the goods produced by the private sector, we receive less and less satisfaction from each additional good.

Years of favoring private production and neglecting the provision of public goods have created a situation of private affluence and public squalor. A much-quoted passage describes this contrast:

> The family which takes its mauve and cerise, air-conditioned, power-steered and power-braked automobile out for a tour passes through cities that are badly paved, made hideous by litter, blighted buildings, billboards, and posts for wires that should long since have been put underground. ... They picnic on exquisitely packaged food from a portable icebox by a polluted stream and go on to spend the night at a park which is a menace to public health and morals. Just before dozing off on an air mattress, beneath a nylon tent, amid the stench of decaying refuse, they may reflect vaguely on the curious unevenness of their blessings (Galbraith 1958, pp. 98f.).

To redress this imbalance the state must provide more public goods. Of necessity, this will mean higher taxes. Funds must be diverted from private hands, where they will purchase less-needed commodities, to the public treasury, where they will satisfy public needs.

Galbraith's Presidential address to the American Economic Association (in Sharpe 1973) criticized economists for ignoring power relationships. Economic thinking removes power from the realm of discourse by denying its existence and by assuming that the market will mitigate the power of the firm. Yet the most serious problems of modern society – war, inequality, and environmental decay – stem from power struggles between corporations wanting growth and profits, and public concerns about economic security, the environment, and the arms race. By ignoring these power struggles, Galbraith claims, economics has become increasingly irrelevant.

When important economic and social issues are viewed as conflicts between two competing powers, the state comes to acquire an additional function. The state must side with the public purpose in order to counter the power of the large corporation. This theme is developed further in *Economics and the Public Purpose* (Galbraith 1973), which argues that the US economy has become bifurcated. Large firms, part of what Galbraith calls the "planning system," have acquired enormous economic power. They have the power to control prices, and they have the resources to mold public opinion.

Advertising by the large firm equates happiness with goods produced by the private sector of the economy. Advertising can also urge the public that environmental damage is imaginary, benign, or being eliminated. Finally, large firms can influence the political process to their advantage.

In contrast, small firms are subject to the dictates of the market. They have little economic power and little ability to sway public opinion or the political process. They are thus at a competitive disadvantage relative to the planning system. The result is unequal economic development – the planning system produces too many goods and the market system produces an inadequate supply of goods.

Power between the planning and the market systems must be made more equal, according to Galbraith. Income must be redistributed from the planning system to the market system. Price controls, minimum wage legislation, guaranteed minimum incomes, protective tariffs, and support for small businesses are among the policies required.

Galbraith (1952b) has supported controls on wages and prices in order to control inflation for most of his career. Controls are required because inflation is caused primarily by the pressures of higher incomes on prices and of higher prices on incomes. The only practical solution is for the government to prevent the market power of labor unions and the market power of large businesses from generating inflation.

Most economists hold that the most efficient way to allocate goods and services is to let the free market set prices and wages. On this view, government-administered pricing and government interference in the labor market misallocate resources. Most economists also contend that controls create a needless bureaucracy to monitor compliance, and that they would require rationing of goods (see **Hayek**). In contrast, *A Theory of Price Control* argues that oligopolistic firms do not take prices that are set in the market. Firms in the oligopolistic sector of the economy are price makers rather than price takers, and "it is relatively easy to fix prices that are already fixed" (Galbraith 1952b, p. 17).

In imperfect markets there is a strong element of convention, with prices habitually set by a mark-up on costs of production. Moreover, the mark-up itself is conventional. Government controls on prices attempt to change conventions, thereby leading to a more desirable outcome – less inflation. Monitoring price controls is made easier, according to Galbraith, by the fact that prices need to be controlled only in the oligopolistic sector of the economy, since market power exists only in this sector. Consequently, only a thousand or so firms need to be monitored. And enforcement is assisted by the fact that large oligopolistic firms are all in the public eye because they are so large.

Several themes stand out in the work of Galbraith. First, large firms have substantial economic power, which they use to dominate modern economies. Second, this power encourages technological development and contributes importantly to economic well-being; hence, it is better to counter the power of the large firm than to eliminate that power by breaking up large firms. Governments must therefore help to develop countervailing power in the private sector of the economy through supporting labor unions and smaller competitive businesses. Finally, the government must itself counter the power of the large corporation by providing an adequate supply of public goods, protecting the environment, resisting the arms race, assuring employment and decent incomes to all workers, and controlling prices.

Galbraith is certainly not an economist's economist. In fact, many economists probably would claim that Galbraith is not really an economist at all. None the less, his work is important for its focus on economic power and on the role of government policy as a means to control the power of large corporations.

Works by Galbraith

American Capitalism, Boston, Houghton Mifflin, 1952a
A Theory of Price Control, Cambridge, Massachusetts, Harvard University Press, 1952b
The Great Crash 1929, Boston, Houghton Mifflin, 1954
The Affluent Society, Boston, Houghton Mifflin, 1958
The New Industrial State, New York, New American Library, 1967
Ambassador's Journal, New York, New American Library, 1969
Economics and the Public Purpose, New York, New American Library, 1973
A Life in Our Times, Boston, Houghton Mifflin, 1981
The Anatomy of Power, Boston, Houghton Mifflin, 1983
A Short History of Financial Euphoria, New York, Penguin Books, 1990

Works about Galbraith

Dunn, Stephen and Pressman, Steven, "The Economic Contributions of John Kenneth Galbraith," *Review of Political Economy*, 17 (April 2005), pp. 161–209
Parker, Richard, *John Kenneth Galbraith: His Life, His Politics, His Economics*, New York, Farrar, Straus & Giroux, 2005
Reisman, David, *Galbraith and Market Capitalism*, New York, New York University Press, 1980

Sharpe, M. E., *John Kenneth Galbraith and the Lower Economics*, White Plains, New York, International Arts and Sciences Press, 1973

Stanfield, James R., *John Kenneth Galbraith*, New York, St. Martin's Press, 1996

MILTON FRIEDMAN (1912–)

The two main themes in the work of Friedman are that money matters and that freedom matters. Money matters because only changes in the money supply can affect economic activity. Money also matters because inflation results from too much money in the economy. Freedom matters because economies run better when governments do not attempt to control prices, exchange rates or entry into professions. And freedom is also important as an end in itself.

Friedman was born in Brooklyn, New York, in 1912 to poor immigrants from the Austro-Hungarian Empire. Shortly after he was born, his parents moved to Rahway, New Jersey, which is where Friedman grew up. At Rahway High School, Friedman developed a love for mathematics and planned to be an insurance actuary. But while attending Rutgers College (then a small private school, now a large State University in New Jersey), he developed an interest in economics, and decided to major in both economics and mathematics.

After receiving his bachelor's degree in 1933, Friedman went to the University of Chicago to pursue graduate work in economics. However, a generous fellowship led him to transfer to Columbia University the following year. When Friedman completed all his course work at Columbia, he returned to the University of Chicago, where he worked as a research assistant to Henry Schultz. He then went to work in Washington, first providing consumption statistics as part of Roosevelt's New Deal administration and then working for the National Bureau of Economic Research. At the National Bureau, Friedman teamed up with Simon Kuznets to study the market for independent professionals such as lawyers, doctors, and accountants. This study eventually became his PhD dissertation from Columbia, and then a book (Friedman 1946). One finding of this work – that physicians earn high salaries because the medical profession was able to impose high entry barriers and reduce the supply of doctors – was regarded as highly controversial and delayed publication of Friedman's book for many years.

After teaching briefly at the University of Wisconsin and the University of Minnesota, Friedman returned to the University of Chicago in 1946, where, with George Stigler, he developed the

Chicago School of Economics (Reder 1980). Regular *Newsweek* columns from 1966 to 1984 (some of which are collected in Friedman 1975), a best-selling economics book (Friedman 1962a), and a ten-part TV series (Friedman 1980), helped make "Milton Friedman" a household name.

In 1967 Friedman became President of the American Economic Association, and in 1976 he received the Nobel Prize for Economics. The award committee singled out three aspects of Friedman's work for special mention – his study of the consumption function, his arguments about the problems with employing stabilization policy, and his contributions to monetary theory and history. Friedman retired from Chicago in 1977 to become a senior scholar at the Hoover Institute in California.

Among economists, Friedman is best known for his crusade against the Keynesian revolution. This involved arguing against the use of stabilization policies to control either inflation or unemployment. For a number of reasons, Friedman held that *fiscal policy* would not work and active *monetary policy* would worsen the business cycle and lead to greater inflation. Friedman's work on the consumption function, the role of money in the economy, and the natural rate of unemployment, all had the effect of countering the interventionist vision of Keynes and his followers. It also supported his own vision of an economy that functions best without outside interference by economic policy-makers.

The simple theory of consumption, outlined by Keynes, held that consumer spending was mainly influenced by *current* income. Friedman's alternative, known as the *permanent income hypothesis*, held that consumers geared spending to their expectations about income over a longer time period. Friedman (1957) provided substantial empirical support for this hypothesis. The hypothesis itself also allowed Friedman to solve a number of puzzles that stemmed from the simple Keynesian consumption function. One implication of the simple Keynesian theory was that the fraction of income consumed should fall, and the fraction saved should rise, as incomes increased. Studies of income, consumption, and savings for the US (first done by Kuznets) found this not to be true. The fraction of income saved has stayed relatively the same in the US over many decades; if anything it has declined a bit, despite large increases in income.

Recognizing that spending depends on expected future income helps explain this fact. Whenever my income rises, I am likely to expect more pay increases in the future. As a result, I need to save less money now for future consumption.

The permanent income hypothesis also explains why some groups, such as small business owners, sometimes save large fractions of their income and at other times reduce their savings balances. This would not occur if saving depends on current income, but is quite plausible if actual spending depends on average income over a number of years.

Furthermore, the permanent income hypothesis has important policy implications that contradict the policy prescriptions of Keynes. Keynes advocated fiscal policy to generate additional spending and employment during a recession. But if attempts by the government to generate additional incomes lead to little additional spending (because people view their additional income as temporary rather than permanent), fiscal policy will have little economic impact.

In contrast to the emphasis on fiscal policy by Keynesian economists, Friedman (1962, 1963) argued that money and monetary policy play the major role in determining economic activity. His theoretical argument for the importance of money stems from the *quantity theory of money* (MV=PQ), which holds that the amount of money in the economy (M) times the number of times each dollar is used in a year to buy goods (V) must equal economic output sold during the year (PQ). Given this relationship, changes in M or changes in V must be related to changes in economic activity.

In contrast to classical monetary theorists, who took the velocity of money (V) as institutionally determined (see **Fisher**), Friedman acknowledged that velocity could depend on economic factors such as interest rates and expected inflation. In addition, Friedman recognized that people might want to hold money for reasons other than buying goods, namely for security or because they thought that stock prices and other asset prices were likely to fall. However, empirical studies by Friedman (1963) found that these economic factors had only a small impact on velocity and that their impact tended to decline over time. Since the velocity of money was relatively stable, it was the quantity of money that primarily affected the level of economic activity.

Going even further, Friedman held that, while money might be able to affect economic activity in the short run, in the long run money must be neutral and can have no economic impact. More money would affect the level of output with a lag of around 6–9 months. But another 6–9 months after that, the impact of money would be only on prices. Thus, 12–18 months after any increase in the money supply, prices would start to rise and inflation would become a problem. While economists have traditionally distinguished cost-push from demand-pull inflation, Friedman has argued that all inflation stems from too much demand for goods, and that there is too much demand when too much money is created.

Since inflation for Friedman is solely a monetary phenomenon, the only solution to the inflation problem must be to restrain the growth of the money supply. Towards this end, Friedman has proposed that the US central bank be required to increase the supply of money by around 3–5 percent every year, the normal growth rate of the US economy. This would provide the money needed to purchase additional goods, but not so much money that it would cause inflation.

Friedman (1963, 1992) showed that monetary authorities have produced depressions, inflation, and other undesirable economic results through their misguided attempts to manage the money supply. He blames the Great Depression on the Federal Reserve, showing how they first tightened the money supply because of their fears about stock market speculation, then did nothing from 1930 to 1931 when depositors came running to banks to withdraw their money, and finally raised interest rates when Britain left the gold standard in September 1931. All these actions led to a sharp drop in the US money supply, reduced spending, and created a depression. Because the central bank cannot be trusted to put the right policy into effect, Friedman argues, central banks should be forced to follow a monetary rule rather than being allowed to continually mismanage the money supply.

Monetary policy frequently goes wrong, Friedman says, because of the long and variable lags between current economic problems and when any change in the money supply will affect the economy. Friedman (1953, pp. 144–8) identifies three such lags. It will take time for the central bank to recognize that an economic problem exists. It will take time to actually change the money supply. And it will take time for any change in the money supply to impact the economy. As a result of these lags, monetary policy is not likely to be of the right magnitude. Nor is it likely to be the right sort of policy, for by the time any policy starts to affect the economy, the problem it was designed to address is no longer likely to exist.

Friedman (1962b) also claims that monetary authorities are unduly influenced by fiscal authorities and the national treasury. Central bank heads are appointed by the head of the government and approved by legislative bodies. Whenever government officials want to expand the money supply and inflate the economy, the central bank invariably caves in to political pressure. Again, the solution is to tie the hands of central bankers and force them to increase the money supply by 3–5 percent every year.

The *natural rate of unemployment* was an idea that Friedman (1968) introduced in his Presidential address to the American Economic Association. He held that there was an equilibrium rate of unemployment in the economy. Everyone will not always have a job. There will always be some people in between jobs, and new entrants to the labor force will not immediately find work. The equilibrium or natural rate of unemployment, Friedman suggested, depended upon various structural characteristics of the labor force and the labor market that left some people without jobs. For example, the availability of unemployment benefits and other social programs allows people to spend a longer period of time looking for work. Likewise, having a working spouse allows for longer job searches. Any attempt to reduce unemployment below the natural or equilibrium rate would soon generate rising inflation, according to Friedman. But with higher prices for goods, people will be able to buy less. As spending falls, so too will production and employment. This eventually will lead to an economic contraction and a return to the natural rate.

The natural rate hypothesis also challenged one very important idea from Keynesian economics – the existence of a trade-off between inflation and unemployment or the *Phillips Curve* (see **Samuelson**). Friedman held that there was no such trade-off in the long run. Attempts to lower unemployment would generate higher inflation, yet unemployment would always return to the natural rate. In the long run, therefore, the Phillips Curve was really a vertical line at the natural rate of unemployment. Policy-makers could do little or nothing to permanently lower unemployment; but, in a vain desire to reduce unemployment, they would only increase inflation.

Taking this argument one step further, Friedman (1977) contended that higher inflation would cause greater volatility in the inflation rate and thus lead to greater economic uncertainty. This, he contended, might lead to an even higher natural rate of unemployment. Thus, not only was there no trade-off between inflation and unemployment, but the two might move together in the same direction. Keynesian attempts to lower the rate of unemployment not only would fail in their objective, and not only would contribute to inflation, but they might also have the perverse effect of increasing unemployment. Friedman thus ultimately blames the stagflation of the 1970s on the bad ideas about economic policy that came out of Keynesian economics.

In the international realm, as well as in the domestic realm, Friedman set his sights upon Keynesian orthodoxy. Keynes, as we have seen, favored fixed exchange rates rather than flexible exchange rates, and was responsible for helping set up a system of fixed exchange rates after World War II. In contrast, Friedman (1953, pp. 157–203; 1967) argued that flexible exchange rates were preferable to fixed rates on several grounds.

First, with fixed exchange rates, central banks have to use monetary policy to keep the exchange rate fixed. For example, in the early 2000s, the central bank of China kept printing yuan (and demanding dollars) in order to keep the yuan valued at 8.28 yuan per one US dollar. But this meant the Chinese central bank could not alter the national money supply (and interest rates) to affect the domestic Chinese economy. In contrast, floating rates allow monetary authorities to concentrate on domestic monetary policy without worrying about the value of the national currency.

Second, Friedman argues that flexible exchange rates help promote trade among nations. With fixed rates, trade restrictions become a common response to trade problems; with flexible exchange rates, the rate adjusts automatically in response to a trade deficit. The national currency of a nation with a large trade deficit will fall, thereby making its exports cheaper and imports more expensive.

Finally, flexible exchange rates keep inflation from being exported from one country to another. Under a system of fixed exchange rates, countries experiencing inflation will buy more foreign-made goods because they are cheaper. This will increase the spending for goods in other nations and will lead to greater inflation in other nations. With flexible exchange rates, this would not happen. Countries experiencing inflation would see the value of their currency fall, and so foreign nations would not be subject to higher-priced imports.

In addition to these many contributions to macroeconomics, Friedman has made several other important contributions to economics. He was involved in one of the two main methodological or philosophical disputes in the history of economics (for details on the other methodological dispute see **Menger**). One frequent criticism made about economists is that they always make unrealistic assumptions whenever they study the economy. A favorite joke about economists concerns several professionals stranded on a deserted island with many cans of food, but no way to open them up. After all the other castaways fail to use their professional know-how to open the food cans, the economist comes to the rescue: "Let's *assume* we have a can opener," he proudly suggests.

In a controversial essay, Friedman (1953, pp. 3–43) defends this methodology and argues that the realism of assumptions does not matter in scientific analysis. According to Friedman, all theory involves abstraction, and so all the assumptions of a theory have to be, in one sense, unrealistic. The only important thing is whether the implications of the theory are true; that is, whether the theory works and makes good predictions. If the theory is supported by the data, it does not matter whether the assumptions of the theory are completely accurate. On the other hand, if data does not support the theory, the theory has to be discarded even if it employs realistic assumptions. Although many economists have raised objections against this position, Boland (1979) has persuasively made the case that Friedman was right in arguing that theories are meant to be tools and that economic assumptions can be unrealistic as long as they work well and help to predict economic performance.

As noted earlier, Friedman's work has not only been directed at fellow economists. He has also written extensively for a larger audience. This work has argued for individual freedom and against all forms of government intervention in the economy. Friedman (1962a, 1979) argues that capitalism is the best economic system because it promotes political freedom, and because the market can help offset political power.

Friedman's more popular writings have also had a clear policy slant. He has opposed all government controls on economic activity because they are obtrusive to individual decision-making. Friedman (1975) has argued against wage and price controls, against rent controls (Friedman 1946), against tariffs and other restrictions to international trade (Friedman 1979), and against minimum wage laws. He also opposed a number of popular government programs such as social security (because it breaks down family bonds and is actually a transfer from the less well-off to the wealthy who tend to live longer and therefore collect benefits for longer), and government support for higher education (because the money primarily benefits those who are well off). On the other hand, Friedman has supported the all-volunteer army (Friedman 1975, ch. 8) and has advocated that all parents be given vouchers and allowed to select the school where they will send their children (Friedman 1979, ch. 4).

Milton Friedman is the rare economist who has managed to span two very different worlds. On the one hand, he is regarded as a giant within the economics profession, and is one of the two or three most referenced and revered economic figures of the twentieth century. This work has stressed the importance of money and the importance of markets to improve economic well-being. At the same time, Friedman has written voluminously for the general public. This work has stressed the importance of individual decision-making and freedom, and made Friedman one of the two or three best known and most recognized economists of the late twentieth century.

Works by Friedman

Roofs or Ceilings? The Current Housing Problem, with George Stigler, Irvington-on-Hudson, New York, Foundation for Economic Education, 1946

Income from Independent Professional Practice, with Simon Kuznets, New York, National Bureau of Economic Research, 1946

Essays in Positive Economics, Chicago, University of Chicago Press, 1953

Studies in the Quantity Theory of Money, Chicago, University of Chicago Press, 1956

A Theory of the Consumption Function, Princeton, New Jersey, Princeton University Press, 1957

Capitalism and Freedom, Chicago, University of Chicago Press, 1962a

"Should There Be an Independent Monetary Authority?," in *In Search of A Monetary Constitution*, ed. Leland B. Yeager, Cambridge, Massachusetts, Harvard University Press, 1962b

A Monetary History of the United States, with Anna J. Schwartz, Princeton, New Jersey, Princeton University Press, 1963

The Balance of Payments: Free Versus Flexible Exchange Rates, with Robert V. Roosa, Washington, D.C., American Enterprise Institute, 1967

"The Role of Monetary Policy," *American Economic Review*, 58 (1968), pp. 4–17

There's No Such Thing as a Free Lunch, Lasalle, Illinois, Open Court, 1975. Reprinted and updated as *Bright Promises, Dismal Performance: An Economist's Protest*, San Diego and New York, Harcourt Brace Jovanovich, 1983

"Nobel Lecture: Inflation and Unemployment," *Journal of Political Economy*, 85 (1977), pp. 451–72

Free to Choose, with Rose Friedman, New York, Avon, 1980

Tyranny of the Status Quo, with Rose Friedman, New York, San Diego and London, Harcourt Brace Jovanovich, 1984

Money Mischief: Episodes in Monetary History, New York, San Diego and London, Harcourt Brace Jovanovich, 1992

Works about Friedman

Burton, John, "Positively Milton Friedman," in *Twelve Contemporary Economists*, ed. J. R. Shackleton and G. Locksley, London, Macmillan, 1981, pp. 53–69

Butler, Eamonn, *Milton Friedman: A Guide to His Economic Thought*, New York, Universe Books, 1985

Hirsch, Abraham and de Marchi, Neil, *Milton Friedman: Economics in Theory and Practice*, Ann Arbor, Michigan, University of Michigan Press, 1990

Kasper, Sherryl, *The Revival of Laissez-Faire in American Macroeconomic Theory*, Cheltenham, UK, Edward Elgar, 2002

Walters, Alan, "Milton Friedman," *The New Palgrave: A Dictionary of Economics*, ed. J. Eatwell, M. Migate and P. Newman, New York, Stockton Press, 1987, pp. 422–7

Other references

Boland, Lawrence A., "A Critique of Friedman's Critics," *Journal of Economic Literature*, 17 (June 1979), pp. 503–22

Reder, Melvin W., "Chicago Economics: Performance and Change," *Journal of Economics Literature*, 20, 1 (March 1982), pp. 1–38

PAUL SAMUELSON (1915–)

Paul Samuelson is a paradoxical figure. More than anyone else he bears responsibility for the mathematical bent of economics in the late twentieth century. Yet Samuelson made a name for himself, and a great deal of money, by writing an immensely successful introductory economics textbook (Samuelson 1947a). Yet again, Samuelson has written on virtually every area within economics. For someone so mathematical, such breadth is both remarkable and unique.

Samuelson was born in 1915 in Gary, Indiana; but his parents soon moved to Chicago, so Samuelson was educated in the Chicago public school system. He then enrolled at the University of Chicago. Intending to major in mathematics, Samuelson took a course in economics and immediately recognized how mathematics could revolutionize economics.

As a result of winning a Social Science Research Council Fellowship, Samuelson had his graduate education paid for; yet there was a price to be paid. According to the fellowship rules, he could not continue at the University of Chicago. Samuelson chose to attend Harvard, which awarded him a PhD in 1941. His doctoral dissertation (Samuelson 1947b) is regarded by most economists as providing the mathematical foundations for contemporary economics.

Samuelson liked Harvard, and he wanted the school to offer him a full-time teaching position. But Harvard decided not to keep him on. Determined to stay in Cambridge, Samuelson accepted a position at the Massachusetts Institute of Technology (MIT). He remained at MIT for his entire professional career, becoming a full professor at the age of 32. In 1947 Samuelson received the first John Bates Clark Medal from the American Economic Association, awarded annually to the most promising economist under the age of 40. During 1951 he served as President of the Econometric Society, and during 1961 he served as President of the American Economic Association. In 1970 Samuelson was awarded the Nobel Prize for Economics.

In all his professional work, Samuelson sought to provide mathematical underpinning for economic ideas, believing that economic theory without formalization was unsystematic and unclear. Unlike Marshall, who felt that converting prose into mathematical equations was a waste of time, Samuelson (1947b, p. 6) held the reverse to be true – converting mathematical equations into prose was wasteful. Mathematical formalism for Samuelson clarified the nature of models and arguments, and established the validity of economic theories. Through the influence of Samuelson (1947b, 1987), economic instruction at the graduate level has increasingly come to employ the tools and techniques of linear algebra plus differential and integral calculus, and communication among economists has become increasingly mathematical.

Yet Samuelson has not supported rigor for the sake of rigor, or formalism for the sake of formalism. Rather, he has looked at mathematics as a tool. Mathematics illuminates arguments and proves economic theorems that can be empirically tested.

Concern with the relevance and testability of economic theories underlay the methodological dispute between Samuelson and Milton Friedman in the post-war years. Friedman (1953) had argued that the truth of economic assumptions was unimportant; the only thing that mattered was whether the predictions made by these assumptions were correct. Samuelson (1963) responded that the factual inaccuracy of assumptions could never be a virtue in science. He also showed that the distinction between assumptions and predictions is never very clear; what counts as an assumption and what counts as the consequence of some assumption is quite arbitrary. The unrealistic assumptions praised by Friedman could therefore be thought of as unrealistic or false predictions derived from a different set of assumptions. Finally, Samuelson pointed out that, according to the principles of logic, true premises can only produce true conclusions, but false premises could produce both, and what one wants in economics is true conclusions.

Although this methodological dispute might seem abstract, important real-world issues were at stake. For years Friedman had been using the model of a perfectly competitive economy to argue that the absence of any government intervention yields the best economic outcomes. In contrast, Samuelson was a proponent of Keynesian economics and had been advocating greater government intervention to improve economic outcomes. The Friedman–Samuelson debate therefore was not just about how to do economics, but also about the justification for using government policy to improve economic performance. In defending the assumption of perfect competition, Friedman was opposing government intervention; by arguing that economic assumptions must be realistic, Samuelson opened the door for Keynesian macroeconomic policies.

The five-volume *Collected Scientific Papers* of Samuelson (1966–77) contains 388 essays written over a 50-year period, and covers virtually every topic within economics. These papers contain many substantive advances in economics. From this prolific output, three areas stand out as being those where Samuelson has made his mark the most: consumer choice, international trade, and macroeconomics.

Following his methodological principles, Samuelson attempted to make the assumptions of microeconomics empirical and testable. In particular, he sought to move the theory of consumer demand away from the arena of psychological introspection and away from the untestable assumption that consumers maximized utility.

The traditional theory of consumer behavior held that consumers, by definition, bought the goods they wanted most; hence whatever consumers bought maximized their utility. Consumer behavior is explained in terms of preferences, which are in turn defined only by behavior. This appears to be a case of circular reasoning, whose conclusion is that people behave as they behave. It is also a theorem with no empirical implications, since it contains no hypothesis and is consistent with all conceivable behavior, while refutable by none (Samuelson 1947b, pp. 91–2).

To escape from this circle, Samuelson (1938) argued that observed consumer spending could be used to reveal consumer preferences regarding the utility they received from different goods. This data could then be used to test various assumptions about consumer behavior. For example, economic theory holds that consumer preferences will be consistent and transitive. Consider a consumer faced with three goods costing the same amount of money. If the consumer buys good A rather than good B, and good B rather than good C, then that consumer should also purchase A rather than C. This is something that could be tested experimentally, and that has been tested many times. Most of these tests have found consumer preferences to be consistent and transitive, and have thus confirmed the assumptions economists make about consumer preferences (see Caldwell 1982, pp. 150–8). However, in some cases, consumer preferences have been found to be inconsistent and to vary based upon a number of different factors including the number of choices presented to consumers and how choices are framed (see **Kahneman**).

A second area where Samuelson has made important contributions is international trade theory. This work examines the economic consequences of free trade and protectionism. Samuelson (1948, 1949) showed that, even if it is hard for people to migrate, and even if it is hard for capital to move around the world in search of the highest rate of return, free trade will make the rewards going to factors of production in different countries more equal. Consider potato chips made almost entirely by hand. If wages in the US are higher than wages in France, French workers will be able to make potato chips at lower cost than American workers. When there is free trade between the US and France, French potato chips will be exported and sold in the US. This increased demand will increase the price received by French potato chip makers and, according to the *marginal productivity theory of distribution* (see **Clark**), this should raise the wages of French workers making potato chips. In contrast, American potato chip makers, facing greater competition from abroad, will be forced to lower their prices and reduce workers' wages. The wages of French and American workers thus tend to become more equal due to free trade.

This result, which has come to be known as the *"factor price equalization theorem,"* has quite important policy implications for an increasingly global economy. One consequence of the theorem is that free trade arrangements between the US and Mexico should tend to equalize the wages received by Mexican workers and by unskilled American workers. NAFTA should therefore tend to raise the wages of Mexican workers and lower the wages of American workers who must compete with Mexican workers.

The *Samuelson–Stolper theorem* took this one step further and examined the impact of imposing a tariff on some imported good. Samuelson and Stolper (Samuelson 1941) showed that tariffs increase the incomes of those inputs used to a large extent in domestic industries that compete with the foreign good on which the tariff was placed. However, the tariff will reduce the incomes of everyone else. For example, a tariff on foreign automobiles will raise the price of foreign cars. This, in turn, will raise the price of domestically produced cars, since higher prices for imports spur greater demand for domestic cars. The greatest American beneficiaries of this tariff will be those factors of production or inputs used most in automobile manufacturing. If automobile production is capital intensive (i.e. if it uses relatively large amounts of machinery), business owners will gain; but everyone else will lose because of the higher car prices they will have to pay. On the other hand, if automobile production uses a good deal of skilled labor, then skilled workers will benefit from the tariff at the expense of everyone else.

Samuelson was also instrumental in bringing Keynesian economics to America. This was done, in part, through his popular introductory economics textbook (Samuelson 1947a), which introduced to American economists and students Keynesian notions like the *consumption function*, the *multiplier*, and *fiscal policy*. Samuelson also wrote many articles for newspapers and magazines that explained Keynes to the non-economist. And he served as an economic advisor to Presidents Kennedy and Johnson, explaining to them the importance of expansionary macroeconomic policies to lower unemployment.

Within macroeconomic circles at the time there was much debate about the relative effectiveness of fiscal and monetary policies. Monetarists, led by Milton Friedman, argued that only monetary policy could affect economic performance. They looked upon fiscal policy as a circuitous route to have banks create more money. On the other side of the debate, Keynesians like John Kenneth Galbraith described monetary policy as a string; no matter how hard we pull on this string, they argued, we could not create more jobs. Samuelson adopted a middle position, insisting that both fiscal and monetary policies would be effective in expanding the US economy and arguing that both policies had to be used for stabilization purposes. He also adopted a middle position regarding the form that expansionary fiscal policy should take. While Galbraith pressured President Kennedy to increase government spending, and while conservative Keynesians urged tax cuts, Samuelson argued for both an expansion of government programs and a sizeable tax cut.

Samuelson also made his own contributions to the development of Keynesian economics. Keynes showed that additional spending has a multiplied impact on the overall economy. If Americans purchase more French wine, then French vintners will make more money. The *consumption function* tells us that these vintners will spend most of their additional income, and the additional spending on French-made goods will generate more income and more jobs in France. Large developed countries typically have a spending *multiplier* somewhere around 2, meaning that each additional dollar (or euro) that Americans spend on French wine will increase total output in France by two dollars (or two euros).

Keynes also held that investment was driven by the expectations of businessmen. But he did not analyze any interactions between the multiplier and business investment. Samuelson developed the notion of *the accelerator* to show that, as the economy expanded, business decision-makers would become more optimistic and would accelerate, or increase, their investment spending. This increase in investment would then have a multiplier impact and possibly another accelerator impact.

Samuelson (1939a, 1939b) formalized the accelerator notion and derived mathematically the combined economic impact of the multiplier and accelerator processes – with the multiplier expanding output, and with expanding output leading to improved expectations, more investment, and a new multiplier process. He also demonstrated the formal conditions under which the multiplier-accelerator process would lead to economic instability (either too much growth or to a sharp decline in economic activity as less spending reduced the desire of business firms to invest). Finally, he drew out the policy implications of the accelerator – because it made the economy more unstable, government intervention to stabilize the economy was even more important.

In another contribution to Keynesian macroeconomics, Samuelson (1960) and his MIT colleague Robert Solow developed the famous *Phillips Curve* relationship. A. W. Phillips (1958), in an extensive study of wage increases and unemployment in Great Britain, found that small increases in wages were associated with high rates of unemployment and vice versa. Samuelson and Solow reasoned that, since wages were a major component of costs (60–70 percent for most developed countries), and since higher costs usually become higher prices, the rate of inflation should also be inversely related to the unemployment rate. The higher the rate of inflation, the lower the rate of unemployment; and the lower the inflation rate, the higher the rate of unemployment. Looking at US data from 1933 to 1958, Samuelson and Solow indeed found such a trade-off, and in honor of Phillips they named it "the Phillips Curve."

Samuelson regarded the Phillips Curve as a tool that could identify the policy options available to government officials. If there was concern about unemployment, macroeconomic policy could expand the economy; but this would also move the economy along its Phillips Curve and lead to a higher rate of inflation. On the other hand, if policy-makers were concerned with inflation, they could slow down the economy, but at the cost of higher unemployment. Good policy-making thus became a job of selecting the best point on the Phillips Curve, or making the best of the given inflation–unemployment trade-off.

As Lindbeck (1970, p. 353) has noted, Samuelson "set the style" for professional economic discourse in the last half of the twentieth century. But Samuelson also made many substantive, technical contributions as well, and he made them in virtually every area of economics. His most important contributions have been in the areas of macroeconomics and international trade. They have involved explaining how domestic economies worked, how they are impacted by engaging in trade with other nations, and how economic policies could be used to improve economic performance. For very many reasons, Samuelson became one of the two or three best-known and most respected economists during the last half of the twentieth century.

Works by Samuelson

"A Note on the Pure Theory of Consumer's Behaviour," *Economica*, 5 (February 1938), pp. 61–71

"Interactions between the Multiplier Analysis and the Principle of Acceleration," *Review of Economics and Statistics*, 21 (May 1939a), pp. 75–8

"A Synthesis of the Principle of Acceleration and the Multiplier," *Journal of Political Economy*, 47 (December 1939b), pp. 786–97

"Protection and Real Wages," *Review of Economic Studies*, 9 (November 1941), pp. 58–73, with Wolfgang Stolper

Economics, 1st edn (1947a); 18th edn, New York, McGraw Hill, 2004, with William D. Nordhaus

Foundations of Economic Analysis, Cambridge, Massachusetts, Harvard University Press, 1947b

"International Trade and Equalisation of Factor Prices," *Economic Journal*, 58 (June 1948), pp. 163–84

Linear Programming and Economic Analysis, (1958), New York, Dover Publications, 1987, with Robert Dorfman and Robert Solow

"Analytical Aspects of Anti-Inflation Policy," *American Economic Review*, 50 (May 1960), pp. 177–94, with Robert Solow

"Problems of Methodology – Discussion," *American Economic Review*, 53 (May 1963), pp. 231–6

The Collected Scientific Papers of Paul A. Samuelson, 5 vols, Cambridge, Massachusetts, MIT Press, 1966–77

Works about Samuelson

Breit, William and Ransom, Roger L., "Paul A. Samuelson – Economic *Wunderkind* as Policy Maker," in W. Breit and R. L. Ransom, *The Academic Scribblers*, New York, Holt, Rinehart and Winston, 1971, pp. 111–38

Brown, E. Cory and Solow, Robert M. (eds), *Paul Samuelson and Modern Economic Theory*, New York, McGraw Hill, 1983

Feiwel, George (ed.), *Samuelson and Neoclassical Economics*, Boston, Kluwer, 1982

Kendry, Andrian, "Paul Samuelson and the Scientific Awakening of Economics," in *Twelve Contemporary Economists*, ed. J. R. Shackleton and Gareth Locksley, New York, Wiley, 1981, pp. 219–39

Lindbeck, Assar, "Paul Anthony Samuelson's Contribution to Economics," *Swedish Journal of Economics*, 72, 4 (December 1970), pp. 342–54

Other references

Caldwell, Bruce, *Beyond Positivism: Economic Methodology in the Twentieth Century*, London, Allen & Unwin, 1982
Friedman, Milton, "The Methodology of Positive Economics," in *Essays in Positive Economics*, Chicago, University of Chicago Press, 1953, pp. 3–43
Phillips, A. W., "The Relation between Unemployment and the Rate of Change in Money Wage Rates in the United Kingdom, 1861–1957," *Economica*, 25 (1958), pp. 283–300

FRANCO MODIGLIANI (1918–2003)

Franco Modigliani (pronounced mo-dil-lee-ani) is best known for two innovations in macroeconomics. To explain total consumer spending, he developed the life-cycle theory of household savings and consumption. To explain business behavior, Modigliani helped formulate the famous Modigliani–Miller theorems. These theorems explain why corporate decisions about obtaining funds for investment, and about repaying investors, should not affect the market value of a firm.

Modigliani was born in Rome, Italy, in 1918 to Jewish parents. His father was a doctor and Modigliani, wanting to follow in his father's footsteps, enrolled at the University of Rome to study medicine. Realizing that he could not stand the sight of blood, he decided to switch from the study of medicine to the study of law (Modigliani 2001, p. 9).

Finding the law curriculum relatively easy, Modigliani earned extra money translating economic articles from German into Italian. A national essay competition on price control sparked his interest because he had previously translated several articles on this subject. Modigliani entered the contest. Not only did the essay win first prize; the judges were so impressed with his essay that they told him he would make an excellent economist.

After receiving his law degree in 1939 Modigliani decided to leave Italy, primarily because of the conflict between his beliefs and those of the Fascist government of Mussolini. After a short stay in France, he arrived in the United States and enrolled in the social science PhD program at the New School for Social Research. The New School was a refuge for intellectuals fleeing the tyranny of Europe in the 1930s and early 1940s, and became known as a sort of "university in exile" (Rutkoff 1986). While at the New School, Modigliani came under the influence of Jacob Marschak, who taught him macro-economic theory as well as the importance of formulating testable economic hypotheses. Modigliani received his PhD in 1944 and then taught economics for several years at the New School.

In 1949 Modigliani accepted a job at the University of Illinois, and in 1952 he went to the Carnegie Institute of Technology. After several visiting professorships in the late 1950s, Modigliani finally settled down at MIT, where he taught from 1962 until his retirement. In 1976 Modigliani was elected President of the American Economic Association, and in 1985 he was awarded the Nobel Prize for Economics. The Nobel committee cited the *life-cycle hypothesis* and the Modigliani–Miller theorems as his most significant contributions.

Modigliani formulated the life-cycle hypothesis with Richard Brumberg while returning to Illinois following a conference on savings at the University of Minnesota. Brumberg, a graduate student of Modigliani's, died tragically of a brain tumor shortly after their famous paper (Modigliani 1954a) was published; thus Modigliani (1963, 1966) was forced to develop and test the hypothesis on his own.

The key assumption of the life-cycle theory is that rational individuals will try to keep their level of consumption fairly constant from year to year. Personal income, of course, will vary due to changing circumstances. In good economic times people will make more money; in bad economic times and during retirement people will earn much less. Even though income changes from year to year, people want to keep their lifestyle from changing every year. This requires that people gear their consumption to their expected lifetime income (or the expected average income over their life). They will thus save larger fractions of their income when they make relatively more money and will save little in years when their income is relatively low. On this view, the main purpose of savings is to accumulate money to spend later in life (during retirement).

Supporting the work of Keynes, the life-cycle hypothesis can explain why improved expectations about future income will increase consumption while poor expectations, or worries about the possibility of layoffs, will reduce consumer spending. In the former case, people spend more money now, believing they will be able to pay back in the future (when their income is greater) any borrowing they need to do now. Also, in good times, people will spend more (believing that they do not need to save for the proverbial rainy day) because the future looks so good. In contrast, when people expect economic prob-lems in the future, they spend less and save more now so that they have money in reserve in case they are laid off from their jobs.

One important implication of the life-cycle hypothesis is that economic growth is the main determinant of the national savings rate. When the economy is growing rapidly, people do not feel the need to save for the future, since incomes will be greater in the future. Savings rates thus plummet. In contrast, when incomes and economic output grow slowly, people save more money out of their income and savings rates are higher.

A second implication of the life-cycle theory is that wealth needs to be considered when attempting to explain and predict consumer spending. For any person, the value of their wealth is the future returns expected from that wealth. If I have $1 million in stocks, and stocks earn 5 percent on average each year, I can expect $50,000 every year from my money. Thus, wealth can be used to measure one part of expected future earnings, and it will affect both household spending and savings behavior. Large changes in aggregate wealth (for example, a sharp increase in stock prices or real estate values) will mean that people have more wealth and need to save less money for retirement.

A third implication of the life-cycle hypothesis is that demographics will play an important role in explaining national savings behavior. A country with a large proportion of older, retired individuals will not be saving as much as a country with a large proportion of working-age people. And as the population of a nation ages – as is taking place now in many developed nations – national savings rates should decline.

The life-cycle hypothesis can also explain why temporary policy changes will have little impact on either spending or overall economic activity. A temporary change in taxation may have a large impact on current income, but it will have little impact on lifetime income. Therefore, temporary changes in taxation should affect consumer spending very little. The 1968 tax surcharge in the US provides considerable support for this view (Springer 1975). Contrary to the expectations of many economists at the time, this tax increase did not reduce spending by much and did not help reduce inflation. The life-cycle view, however, predicts that this tax surcharge should have virtually no impact on spending, precisely because it was temporary and therefore had little effect on lifetime incomes.

The life-cycle hypothesis remains a useful theoretical tool in macro-economic analysis because it allows economists to take factors such as wealth, demographics, and expectations about future income into consideration when attempting to explain and predict the consumption decisions made by households. It is for this reason that, when economists try to understand aggregate consumption and savings behavior, they start from the life-cycle theory.

The second major innovation due to Modigliani helped to establish modern finance theory. Finance studies the decisions made by business firms about borrowing money to undertake investment as well as decisions about repaying investors. In general, the chief financial officer of a corporation must decide whether to finance investment by borrowing (debt financing) or by printing up stock certificates and allowing investors to own part of the company (equity financing). Financial officers must also decide whether to pay all earnings to shareholders in the form of dividends, or to retain some earnings for emergencies and future expansion.

Modigliani and Miller (Modigliani 1958) showed that (ignoring taxes and financial market imperfections) the cost of capital for a firm does not depend on its capital structure or how the firm obtains money. In the 1950s, most economists thought that there was an optimal percentage of debt financing that firms should incur. Small amounts of debt provided insufficient leveraging, and large amounts of debt led to difficulties repaying that debt. High debt levels increased the risk of default, leading lenders to demand a greater return to compensate them for greater risk; but with higher interest rates, firms were less able to repay their debt.

Modigliani and Miller showed that it made no difference whether a firm used debt financing or equity financing, and that there was no optimal percentage of debt financing for a firm. All investors, they noted, carry a large portfolio of assets with various degrees of risk. As a result, investors should not be concerned if part of their portfolio becomes riskier because one firm relies heavily on debt financing. Even if investors do become concerned about the added risk of lending to one firm with a high debt ratio, they can always compensate for this by adding low-risk investments like bank deposits or government bonds to their total investment portfolio.

In a later paper, Modigliani and Miller (Modigliani 1961) argued that corporate dividend policy should not affect the value of corporate stock. As a result, the value of a corporation should be independent of its choice between retained earnings and paying dividends to shareholders. Two firms, identical in all respects except for the percentage of profits they pay out as dividends, should have the same market value. This, too, contradicted the beliefs of most economists in the 1950s, who saw corporate dividend policy as a sign of future expected profits, and thus as related to stock prices of the firm. Modigliani and Miller argued that (in the absence of differential tax treatment) it should not matter whether profits are paid out in the form of dividends, or are re-invested in the firm and paid to investors in the form of capital gains and future dividend payments.

Modigliani's work in corporate finance has one important implication. Instead of focusing on the financial structure of their firm, and instead of trying to maximize expected profits, management should focus on maximizing market value for existing stockholders. For Modigliani profit maximization is a flawed principle because it takes no account of the risks undertaken by the firm in pursuit of profits.

Modigliani has made several contributions to economics that go beyond these two key advances in consumption theory and corporate finance. In the 1960s, Modigliani and other economists began constructing large econometric models of the US economy. These models were mathematical equations expressing the relationships among the many parts of the whole economy (see **Tinbergen**). They allowed economists and policy-makers to determine the precise effects of any policy change or shock to the economy, and they supported the use of Keynesian economic policies to fine-tune the national economy. Macroeconomic models let economists figure out the amount that taxes must be cut in order to put the unemployed to work, or the decline in interest rates required to spur needed investment and employment during a recession.

Modigliani defended these models against some very sharp criticism that has been raised against them. In particular, Modigliani (1954b) responded to those objecting to macroeconomic modelingLucas Critique. His response was that forecasters needed to take into account the effect of any forecast on economic behavior. When this is done, and included in macroeconomic models, good forecasting is possible. One important implication of this work is that, if economic forecasts are poor, it is the forecaster who should be blamed rather than the behavior of people.

Probably no economist is more responsible for extending Keynesian macroeconomics than Modigliani. He developed the contemporary theories of consumption and business investment, and he developed the macroeconometric models that assisted in implementing Keynesian economic policy. Virtually every aspect of contemporary macroeconomic analysis has been improved by his insights and his work.

Works by Modigliani

"Liquidity Preference and the Theory of Interest and Money," *Econometrica*, 12, 1 (January 1944), pp. 45–88

"Utility Analysis and the Consumption Function: An Interpretation of Cross-Section Data," in *Post-Keynesian Economics*, ed. Kenneth Kurihara, New Brunswick, New Jersey, Rutgers University Press, 1954a, pp. 388–436, with Richard Brumberg

"The Predictability of Economic Events," *Journal of Political Economy*, 62 (December 1954b), pp. 465–78, with Emile Grunberg

"The Cost of Capital, Corporation Finance and the Theory of Investment," *American Economic Review*, 48, 3 (June 1958), pp. 261–97, with Merton Miller

"Dividend Policy, Growth, and the Valuation of Shares," *Journal of Business*, 34, 4 (October 1961), pp. 411–33, with Merton Miller

"Corporate Income Taxes and the Cost of Capital: A Correction," *American Economic Review*, 53, 3 (June 1963), pp. 433–43, with Merton Miller

"The 'Life Cycle' Hypothesis of Saving: Aggregate Implications and Tests," *American Economic Review*, 53, 1 (March 1963), pp. 55–84, with Albert Ando

"The Life Cycle Hypothesis of Saving, the Demand for Wealth and the Supply of Capital," *Social Research*, 3 (Summer 1966), pp. 160–217.

"The Monetarist Controversy, or, Should We Forsake Stabilization Policies," *American Economic Review*, 67, 1 (March 1977), pp. 1–19

The Debate over Stabilization Policy, Cambridge, Cambridge University Press, 1986

Adventures of an Economist, New York and London, Texere, 2001

Works about Modigliani

Bhattacharya, Sudipto, "Corporate Finance and the Legacy of Miller and Modigliani," *Journal of Economic Perspectives*, 2, 4 (Fall 1988), pp. 135–47

Samuelson, Paul A., "The 1985 Nobel Prize in Economics," in *Macroeconomics and Finance: Essays in Honor of Franco Modigliani*, ed. Rudiger Dornbusch, Stanley Fischer, and John Bosons, Cambridge, Massachusetts and London, MIT Press, 1987, pp. 29–35

Seyedian, Mojtaba, "Franco Modigliani 1985," in *Nobel Laureates in Economic Sciences: A Biographical Dictionary*, ed. Bernard S. Katz, New York, Garland Publishing, 1989, pp. 203–17

Other references

Rutkoff, Peter M., *New School: A History of the New School for Social Research*, New York, Free Press, 1986

Springer, W. L., "Did the 1968 Surcharge Really Work?," *American Economic Review*, 65, 4 (September 1975), pp. 644–54

JAMES M. BUCHANAN (1919–)

James Buchanan is an important figure in economics because of his role in developing the field of *public choice*, which examines the links between economics and politics. Buchanan has employed economic analysis to study politicians and political decision-making. At the same time he has stressed that understanding the political process is important for the study of economics.

Buchanan was born into a poor rural family in the village of Gum, Tennessee, in 1919. His grandfather was elected Governor of Tennessee in 1891 on the populist Farmers Alliance ticket. Buchanan (1992) credits his mother, a voracious reader, with developing his academic abilities through home instruction and by helping him with his homework assignments.

Buchanan planned to attend Vanderbilt University and become a lawyer, but the Great Depression destroyed these dreams. Middle Tennessee State Teacher's College, in nearby Murfreesboro, was the only school he could afford. Buchanan majored in mathematics, English literature, and social science, and then went on to earn a Master's degree in Economics at the University of Tennessee in Knoxville. Following a brief stint in the navy, Buchanan used the G.I. Bill to enroll at the University of Chicago and pursue a PhD in Economics. Had it not been for his experiences at officer training school in New York, Buchanan would have probably attended Columbia rather than Chicago. His feeling that "the Eastern Establishment" discriminated against outsiders (especially poor Southerners) led him to spurn Columbia in favor of Chicago (Buchanan 1992, p. 4).

In 1948 Buchanan received his PhD and began a teaching job at the University of Tennessee. Since then he has held positions at a number of US and European institutions, including UCLA, the University of California at Santa Barbara, the London School of Economics, and Cambridge University. But Buchanan has spent most of his adult life teaching at three schools in Virginia. From 1958 to 1969 he taught at the University of Virginia and established the

Thomas Jefferson Center for Political Economy there. From 1969 to 1983, he taught at Virginia Polytechnic Institute and founded the Center for the Study of Public Choice. Then Buchanan moved his center to George Mason University, where it has remained ever since. In 1986, he was awarded the Nobel Prize for Economics, primarily for changing the way that economists study government and politicians. Due to the work of Buchanan, economists now look at the world of politicians and policy-making more skeptically and with greater cynicism.

Many of his life experiences contributed to Buchanan's anti-state economics and his libertarian sentiments. Growing up in the rural South made him feel like "a member of a defeated people" (1999, p. 15). Then there were his officer training school experiences in New York (1992, p. 49). There was also the general libertarian atmosphere at the University of Chicago. Last, but certainly not least, Buchanan (1992, p. 113) felt that in the US Presidential election of 1960 a rich man had purchased the presidency for his son.

Buchanan's major contribution to economics is his role in developing the area of public choice, a study of exchange in the political realm. Public choice emerged out of the field of *public finance*, which studies the relationship between governments and individuals. Just as economists assume that economic man is rational and seeks to maximize utility, the public choice school holds that politicians and government bureaucrats should be viewed in the same light. Political exchange, like economic exchange, will be made with the expectation of gain.

It is perhaps easiest to understand the significance of his economic contributions by starting where Buchanan began, with Keynes. Keynes, as we have seen, argued that market economies frequently experience problems, and that economic policy tools should be used to remedy these problems. Buchanan did not dispute the fact that market economies can malfunction; in fact his personal experiences during the Great Depression support this analysis. What Buchanan disputed was the policy solution advanced by Keynes. He denied that government officials can improve upon market outcomes. His case consists of two parts, one of them philosophical and the other economic.

Philosophically, Buchanan begins from a position of *radical subjectivism* – a belief that only individuals can know what is good for them and what benefits them. This perspective denies that any outside party or body could determine objectively what is good for people. In particular, governments and government bureaucrats cannot distinguish what is good for society from what is bad for society; nor can they promote the public good through economic policy-making.

Radical subjectivism entails rejecting modern welfare economics (see **Pigou**), which seeks to improve national economic welfare by contributing to a more efficient allocation of resources. More importantly, radical subjectivism entails rejecting Keynesian economics. Buchanan (1977, 1978) has been highly critical of Keynesian economics, claiming that bureaucrats are unable to make choices that maximize anything for society since the whole notion of maximizing benefits for society makes no sense. On the contrary, by attempting to promote the public good, governments restrict individual freedom and choice, and thus reduce the welfare of their citizens.

But there is also an important economic case against government intervention. By explaining how economic forces affect government employees, Buchanan has shown how the desire to make things better will likely fail and lead to even worse problems. This is the essence of the public choice argument against Keynes and against economic policy-making.

Buchanan (1977) contends that Keynesian macroeconomic policy depends on the assumption that policy-makers will act in the public interest rather than in their own interest. But since all policy-makers are human, Buchanan claims, they will behave like other human beings; they will attempt to maximize their own utility rather than behaving altruistically and enacting legislation and policies that are best for the whole nation. Thus, politicians will act in ways that further their election (and continued employment) rather than in ways that promote the welfare of their constituents.

In addition, Buchanan notes that politicians are unlikely to be drawn from those who prefer a minimal role for government, for such people are unlikely to be attracted to government service. Rather, politicians will be interested in social engineering or in improving social well-being. This will require large budgets. Also, politicians will need to be re-elected periodically. Control of large budgets enables politicians to pass out the largesse that improves their chances of re-election. Likewise, unelected public employees will recommend and propose large budgets, since this will create jobs for them, and also give them more people to supervise and bring them greater incomes. The system is thus biased towards large budgets and large government, according to Buchanan. Finally, because of its large size and scope, government will face difficult and complex decisions. Expert economists will need to be hired, who will point out instances of market failure as the cause of particular problems and recommend an even greater role for government.

Going even further, Buchanan (1980) identifies another sort of wastefulness that stems from big government and government policy-making. When government forms a large part of the national economy, any decisions made by government will have a large impact on business firms. Firms will, of necessity, be extremely concerned with government policy and will try to influence policy-makers. In their attempt to influence government decisions, businesses will devote enormous resources to lobbying government officials. This takes away from the resources that they could put into the production of goods.

Rather than being a mechanism to improve economic performance, Buchanan (1978) sees Keynesian economics as "a disease that over the long run can prove fatal for the survival of democracy." It leads to permanent government deficits and a public debt that is rationalized with the motto "we owe it to ourselves, so it is okay." Keynesian economics, according to Buchanan (1977, p. 4), is also a disease because it has ended the moral restraint on politicians to behave in ways that are fiscally responsible; in particular, Keynesian economics has led politicians away from balanced budgets.

Buchanan (1958, 1977, 1986) has argued vigorously against government deficits and public debt. He contends that public deficits have many negative effects. They reduce the capital of the nation. When the government sells bonds to finance its debt, it competes with private sellers of debt and pushes up the cost of borrowing (interest rates). As a result, private investment declines. In the long run, problems are even greater. A rising debt, with rising interest burdens, increases the likelihood of a government default. In addition, Buchanan (1986) has argued that future generations suffer from the deficit because they must pay higher taxes, whose burden is not offset by interest payments to bond holders.

As we have seen, Buchanan does not deny that economic outcomes can be less than ideal. In contrast to Keynes, however, he contends that sub-optimal outcomes always arise because individuals cannot benefit from trade. Government policies that further constrain individual action cannot therefore be part of the solution. Rather, the solution must involve creating opportunities for mutually beneficial trade. This involves changing the rules of the economic game by finding institutional, organizational, or constitutional changes that will allow such trade to flourish. Buchanan sees the political economist as someone who identifies rule changes and makes everyone aware of the benefits that would follow from them.

Thus, his solution to the problems of excessive government is a "constitution revolution" (Buchanan 1969), which reassesses and changes the rules of government. Without constitutional limits, democratic governments expand too much and become too intrusive. Constitutional constraints must be placed on governments to keep them from trampling on individual rights, while at the same time channeling individual self-interest towards the common good. Frameworks, institutions, or rules must be developed that limit the ability of politicians to act in ways that advance their own interests but not the public interest.

One institutional change that Buchanan has long advocated is a constitutional amendment for a balanced budget. He believes that only through a change in the constitutional framework can fiscal responsibility and economic health be restored. "Just as an alcoholic might embrace Alcoholics Anonymous, so might a nation drunk on deficits and gorged with government embrace a balanced budget" (Buchanan 1977, p. 159).

Constitutional rules are also important because they keep a bare majority of the nation from imposing costs on everyone else. For example, a simple majority, by imposing higher taxes on others, could benefit itself at the expense of a large minority. The way to prevent such a tyranny of the majority is to change the rules, or the national constitution, and require that all tax increases be approved by large majorities (say, two-thirds of elected representatives).

While other economists tend not to rate Buchanan highly (he does not have an Ivy League education and does not do highly mathematical economics), Buchanan has had a policy impact that goes far beyond that of any other late twentieth century economist, with the possible exception of Milton Friedman.

Rising dissatisfaction with government, public support for tax reductions and reductions in government spending, and balanced budget amendments can all be seen as instances of the influence that Buchanan has had in the policy arena. None the less, his greatest contribution is undoubtedly the public choice perspective, which has forced economists to take a more complex and realistic view of political agents and policy-makers.

Works by Buchanan

Public Principles of Public Debt, Homewood, Illinois, Richard D. Irwin, 1958
The Calculus of Consent: Logical Foundation of Constitutional Democracy, Ann Arbor, Michigan, University of Michigan Press, 1962, with Gordon Tullock

"Pragmatic Reform and Constitutional Revolution," *Ethics*, 17 (1969), p. 95–104, with A. de Pierro

The Limits of Liberty: Between Anarchy and the Leviathan, Chicago, University of Chicago Press, 1975

Democracy in Deficit: The Political Legacy of Lord Keynes, New York, Academic Press, 1977, with R. E. Wagner

The Consequences of Mr. Keynes, Institute of Economic Affairs, 1978, with J. Burton and R. E. Wagner

Towards a Theory of the Rent-Seeking Society, ed., with Robert Tollison and Gordon Tullock, College Station, Texas, Texas A&M University Press, 1980,

"Budgetary Bias in Post-Keynesian Politics: The Erosion and Potential Replacement of Fiscal Norms," in *Deficits*, ed. James M. Buchanan, Charles Rowley and Robert Tollison, Oxford and New York, Basil Blackwell, 1986, pp. 180–95.

Better than Plowing and Other Personal Essays, Chicago, University of Chicago Press, 1992

Public Finance and Public Choice: Two Contrasting Visions of the State, Cambridge, Massachusetts, MIT Press, 1999, with Richard Musgrave

Works about Buchanan

Atkinson, Anthony, "James M. Buchanan's Contributions to Economics," *Scandinavian Journal of Economics*, 89, 1 (1987), pp. 5–15

Kasper, Sherryl, *The Revival of Laissez-Faire in American Macroeconomic Theory*, Cheltenham, Edward Elgar, 2002

Locksley, Gareth, "Individuals, Contracts and Constitutions: The Political Economy of James M. Buchanan," in *Twelve Contemporary Economists*, ed. J. R. Shakleton and G. Locksley, New York, Wiley, 1981, pp. 33–52

Reisman, David, *The Political Economy of James Buchanan*, London, Macmillan, 1990

Romer, Thomas, "On James Buchanan's Contributions to Public Economics," *Journal of Economic Perspectives*, 2, 4 (Fall 1988), pp. 165–79

DOUGLASS CECIL NORTH (1920–)

Douglass North has made contributions to three areas of economics. He has brought statistical methods to the study of economic history. He has examined and explained the role of institutions in regulating human behavior. And he has attempted to understand the historical forces that make economies rich or poor. These three lines of research are not quite as diverse as they might first appear. North has explained economic growth in terms of adopting the right institutions. He has also used statistical techniques to test his institutional theories about the causes of economic growth.

North was born in Cambridge, Massachusetts, in 1920. His father, a manager for the Metropolitan Life Insurance Company, was transferred frequently while North was growing up. As a result, North went to school in Connecticut, Ottawa, Lausanne, New York City, and on Long Island. He attended college at the University of California in Berkeley because his father had been transferred to San Francisco and North did not want to be far from his family.

At Berkeley, North triple majored in political science, economics, and philosophy. He seriously considered going to law school after graduation, but the start of World War II put this plan on hold. North (1995, p. 253) claims that, because of "the strong feeling that I did not want to kill anybody, I joined the Merchant Marine." Three years at sea gave North the opportunity to do a great deal of reading and reflecting, and he decided to become an economist rather than a lawyer.

Returning to Berkeley after the war, North received his PhD in 1952, writing a dissertation on the history of life insurance in the United States. From the 1950s until 1983 North taught at the University of Washington. He then became Professor of Economics and History at Washington University in St. Louis. In 1993, North and Robert Fogel were made joint recipients of the Nobel Prize for Economic Science.

In announcing this award the Nobel Prize committee cited the pioneering work of North and Fogel in the development of cliometrics, which involves the application of mathematical and statistical methods to the study of economic history. Until the late twentieth century, economic history was primarily a descriptive area within economics, one shunning statistical analysis. Consequently, North and Fogel encountered great resistance when, during the 1960s, they brought mathematical methods to this field. But they continued to push their project and eventually succeeded in revolutionizing the study of economy history. North and Fogel required that all work in economic history yield testable or refutable predictions, and that these predictions actually be tested against an alternative, null hypothesis that some factor was not important. This was to be done by gathering relevant historical data and then analyzing this data with the same statistical tools used by all other economists.

Some of the earliest cliometric work by North and Fogel studied the causes of economic growth. North (1961) examined the extent to which trade in the US among the South, the North and the West was responsible for US economic growth. He argued that advances in transportation (canals linking the West and the North; ocean transport linking the North and the South; and steamboats linking the

South and the West) created three different, yet interrelated, economic regions of the US. Each area had a different specialization – the South produced cotton, the North became the financial and manufacturing center, and the West specialized in animal skin and food products. Furthermore, each area depended upon goods from the other two areas.

North then performed a sort of controlled experiment. He tested the hypothesis that regional specialization led to faster economic growth against the alternative hypothesis that regional division was not responsible for growth. He found that the three different regions did tend to expand and contract together. Moreover, he found that this was primarily due to the fact that growth in one region led to demand for goods in the other regions. North took this evidence as supporting his hypothesis that regional specialization and trade led to faster growth in the US.

North (1977, p. 192) later came to recognize that, while cliometrics can test proposed explanations for historical change, it cannot provide any *new* explanations for economic growth. Another approach was therefore necessary, and so he began to study institutions and social rules. North (1990) defined institutions as constraints devised by people and imposed on their political, economic, and social behavior; they include habits and customs as well as formal constraints such as laws. He then tried to explain the impact of these institutions on individual behavior and economic performance, as well as the reasons that certain institutions come into existence at certain times in history. This line of inquiry makes North one of the founding fathers of the *new institutionalist economics*.

Most economists take economic institutions and rules as given; for example, they assume markets exist, but say nothing about how markets develop and evolve. Institutions, however, affect both economic performance and the market because institutions are all about human beings – how they interact with one another and how they structure their world. These institutions affect the costs of producing goods, the ability to sell goods, and thus economic growth rates.

For North, institutions matter in three critical ways. First, they establish property rights and economic incentives. Without some agreement about who owns things, people will not produce and will not attempt to better themselves economically. With property rights come incentives to acquire new technology and to employ more efficient production methods. For example, without patent laws there would be little incentive for an individual or a firm to spend money on research and development. Those who had not invested so heavily in research and development would be able to copy and cheaply reproduce any discovery. These copycats would gain from the new discovery without paying the research and development costs needed to make the discovery. As a result, it would not pay for firms to engage in research activities and have competitors merely copy the results; each firm would wait and let others spend the money to make the new discoveries. But under such economic rules, everyone loses, since virtually no one engages in research and development spending and there will be few new discoveries.

Second, institutions matter for North because they must enforce the rules of the economic game. Here the state becomes an important economic actor, an actor that faces key trade-offs.

On the one hand, the state must not let people cheat and get away with cheating. At the simplest possible level, the state must protect citizens and businesses from robbery and from extortion, for no one would work and produce if their gains were likely to be stolen by someone else. At a more complex level, the state must make sure that rules are not broken that will harm economic performance. The state must ensure that people do not cheat on their taxes, that firms (as well as their CEOs) do not conspire to raise prices and reduce quality, and that firms do not engage in deceptive or dangerous practices. Successful cheating by some will encourage cheating by others, and thus reduce the economic incentives to work hard, which is a necessary ingredient for a successful, thriving economy. If cheating, especially when it takes place in the public eye, were not punished in a clear and obvious way, people would believe that such actions are tolerated and they would try to make money this way rather than by producing efficiently and innovating.

On the other hand, monitoring and enforcement costs rise as the state tries to prevent more and more cheating. This will require higher taxes and lead to greater dissatisfaction with government meddling in private affairs. Consider the costs of ensuring that everyone complies with income tax laws. If no one is audited, many people will cheat; but if everyone is audited, the cost to the government becomes extremely high and the public becomes extremely dissatisfied with the tax laws. The state must walk a fine line between allowing some cheating on taxes and eliminating almost all cheating through greater monitoring and higher taxes, which itself creates economic disincentives and slower economic growth. This decision should create an institutional framework or set of rules in which businesses and people are mostly honest about paying the taxes they owe the government. In more general terms, governments must establish an environment in which most everyone plays by the economic rules, but in which the rules are not oppressive to economic actors.

Third, institutions matter according to North because they are closely related to ideology, or the psychological and social make-up of an economic community. Institutions help determine how people view fairness and correct behavior. These factors, in turn, affect how people will react to different situations. In contrast to traditional economic theory, which sees individuals as always acting rationally based upon their own self-interest, North (1994, p. 3) sees individuals as uncertain about what to do and unclear about what is in their own self-interest. Consequently, they fall back on myths, ideologies, popular beliefs, and habits. For example, if workers believe they are treated well, they will work hard and be productive; if citizens believe in political democracy, they will vote; and if people believe that the government guarantees the quality of goods, they will purchase more goods. Contrary to Gary Becker, who believes that penalties and rewards imposed on individuals are more important than institutional ideology, North holds that if people believe the economic system is fair, there is less chance they will steal; and if people have faith in their government they will be less likely to cheat on their taxes and more likely to vote. In fact, for North, excessive penalties may increase undesirable behavior if people come to believe that the system is not fair and that penalties are far out of proportion to the seriousness of crimes.

As such, institutions are important because they can keep economies from reaching their growth potential. This will occur when institutions provide incentives to engage in unproductive activities. If people view institutional rewards as arbitrary and unfair, and therefore fail to work hard, this will slow down economic growth. If firms lobby government officials for special benefits, rather than create goods and services, economic growth will suffer.

Conversely, the right set of institutions will lead to greater economic growth and benefit everyone. North (1981, ch. 5) argues that ideology or belief systems may reduce undesirable behavior (like stealing) by imposing extra-legal penalties on thieves. As a result, individuals will be less likely to engage in behaviors that undermine the foundations of the economic system.

One question frequently asked of North is why "inefficient" rules or institutions would continue to exist. North (1981) has answered that political markets are inefficient. Special interest groups have an incentive to organize and get the government to pass favorable legislation; but since the loss to everyone else from these benefits is small, they have little incentive to organize and oppose special interest groups. Voters have little incentive to be informed since there is really no chance that one single vote will determine the outcome of any selection. In addition, issues tend to be complex, which leads voters to ignore the issues. As a result, ideology takes over – people vote for simple but wrong-headed ideas, for candidates with charisma but no substance, and for the status quo. This analysis also helps explain why voters are so dissatisfied with the candidates they must continually vote for as well as the level of political campaigning.

The new institutionalism of North straddles both traditional economics and traditional institutional economics (see **Veblen**). Yet, it occupies an uneasy place relative to both. The behavioral assumptions that North employs are quite different from the assumptions made by most economists. For North, individuals are socialized to behave according to rules, and these institutional constraints are an important influence on behavior. This view has made traditional economists uneasy with his work. On the other hand, the work of North is highly quantitative and formal. This had made traditional institutionalists skeptical of his work.

Although he has caused unease in many corners, North has been creative and a pioneer. He is one of the few economists in the last 50 years who have dared to ask big questions, such as what causes economies to grow and decline? And he has attempted to provide a big answer to this question, one that recognizes the uneasy relationship between social institutions and individual self-interest.

Works by North

The Economic Growth of the United States, 1790–1860, New York, Prentice Hall, 1961

Institutional Change and American Economic Growth, Cambridge, Cambridge University Press, 1971, with Lance E. Davis

The Rise of the Western World: A New Economic History, Cambridge, Cambridge University Press, 1973, with Robert Paul Thomas

"The New Economic History after Twenty Years," American Behavioral Scientist, 21 (December 1977), pp. 187–200

Structure and Change in Economic History, New York, W. W. Norton, 1981

Institutions, Institutional Change and Economic Performance, Cambridge, Cambridge University Press, 1990

"Shared Mental Models: Ideologies and Institutions," Kyklos, 47, 1 (1994), pp. 3–31, with Arthur T. Denzau

"Douglass C. North," in Lives of the Laureates: Thirteen Nobel Economists, 3rd edn, ed. William Breit and Roger W. Spencer, Cambridge, Massachusetts, MIT Press, 1995, pp. 251–67

Understanding the Process of Economic Change, Princeton, Princeton University Press, 2005

Works about North

Goldin, Claudia, "Cliometrics and the Nobel," *Journal of Economic Perspectives*, 9, 2 (Spring 1995), pp. 191–208

Libecap, Gary D., "Douglass C. North," in *New Horizons in Economic Thought: Appraisals of Leading Economists*, ed. Warren J. Samuels, Hampshire, Edward Elgar, 1992, pp. 227–48

Myhrman, Johan and Weingast, Barry R., "Douglass C. North's Contributions to Economics and Economic History," *Scandinavian Journal of Economics*, 96, 2 (1994), pp. 185–93

Sutch, Richard, "Douglass North and the New Economic History," in *Explorations in the New Economic History*, ed. Roger L. Ransom, Richard Sutch, and Gary M. Walton, New York, Academic Press, 1982, pp. 13–38

KENNETH J. ARROW (1921–)

Kenneth Arrow is best known as a theoretical economist with extremely broad and diverse interests. His many important contributions have gone beyond economics proper, to include mathematical programming, social and political philosophy, and health care. Yet Arrow is best known for two very technical contributions – his impossibility theorem, which established social choice as a field within economics, and his proof of the existence of general equilibrium.

Arrow was born in New York City in 1921 to a middle class family of Romanian Jewish origins. A voracious reader as a child, Arrow preferred to stay home with his books rather than play outside with friends. This presented a problem for his mother when he misbehaved.

> At first, she would send him to his room, but soon realized that nothing suited Kenneth better. He would trudge away with a volume of the encyclopedia under his arm and enjoy himself immensely. She then reversed the procedure: Kenneth's punishment was to be sent out to play (Feiwel 1987, pp. 3–4).

Through exposure to the works of Bertrand Russell, Arrow developed interests in mathematics and mathematical logic in high school. He attended the City College of New York, mainly because it was free: his father, whose business was highly successful in the 1920s, lost everything during the Depression of the 1930s. At City College Arrow studied mathematics, logic, and statistics. He graduated in 1940 with the Gold Pell Medal, awarded to the student with the highest grades in the graduating class.

Arrow intended to be a high school teacher, but with no employment prospects he enrolled at Columbia University to study mathematical statistics with Harold Hotelling. Hotelling's course in mathematical economics provided Arrow with his first exposure to economics. In 1941, Arrow received an MA in mathematics and then went off to serve in World War II. After the war, he returned to Columbia to continue his studies in mathematics and statistics. Flaunting a fellowship, Hotelling enticed Arrow to enroll in the PhD program in economics. Arrow then became interested in the logic of social decisions. His dissertation, *Social Choice and Individual Values* (Arrow 1951), was completed in 1951.

Upon completing his PhD, Arrow accepted a position at Stanford University. Four years later he became a full professor there. In 1968 he accepted a position at Harvard, but returned to Stanford in 1979. Arrow was awarded the Nobel Prize for Economic Science in 1972.

Arrow's major contribution to economics is the proof of the impossibility theorem in his doctoral dissertation. This contribution concerns the way that groups of individuals, such as family members or the owners of a firm, make decisions or choose among alternatives. When analyzing individual choice, economists assume that each individual is rational and can rank order the different alternatives available to them (see **Edgeworth**). Specifically, rational choice requires that individual preferences among alternatives are consistent and transitive. To be consistent, an individual choosing good A over good B cannot also choose good B over good A. For transitivity, an individual who prefers good A to good B, and also prefers good B to good C, must also prefer A to C.

Arrow proved that social choice, or social decision-making, is not rational. In particular, he demonstrated that the decisions made by groups of people will not necessarily follow the transitivity principle. Consider, for example, the choices that have to be made by a family To keep things simple we assume three choices (A, B, and C). To keep things concrete we can think of the choices as three movies that a family considers renting – *Aladdin*, *Barney*, and *Cinderella*. Three children have to choose among these alternatives; they cannot see all three movies. Each child wants to maximize his or her utility. If all the children agree on which movie they want to see, there is no problem. However, many times this does not happen, and the children have different preferences among the three movies.

In particular, suppose that child 1 prefers *Aladdin* to *Barney* and *Barney* to *Cinderella*; that child 2 prefers *Barney* to *Cinderella* and *Cinderella* to *Aladdin*; and that child 3 prefers *Cinderella* to *Aladdin* and *Aladdin* to *Barney*. Each child has consistent and transitive preferences, as defined above. But problems arise when the children get together and must decide which movie to watch. Taken together, the three children prefer *Aladdin* to *Barney* since child 1 and child 3 both prefer *Aladdin* to *Barney*. They also prefer *Barney* to *Cinderella*, since child 1 and child 2 prefer *Barney* to *Cinderella*. The transitivity principle requires that *Aladdin* is preferred to *Cinderella*. However, child 2 and child 3 prefer *Cinderella* to *Aladdin*, thus violating the transitivity principle. The implication Arrow drew from this analysis was that social choice could not be rational because it violates the transitivity principle. Put another way, it is impossible (hence, the "impossibility theorem") to derive a social or group choice from individual preferences. Put yet another way, "there cannot be a completely consistent meaning to collective rationality. We have at some point a relation of pure power" (Arrow 1974, p. 25). What all of this means is that, while economics can explain individual choices, it cannot explain group decision-making.

Robert Paul Wolff (1970) has drawn out the implications of the impossibility theorem for political philosophy. In the example given above, if A, B, and C refer to different bills before the legislative branch, or different candidates for elected office (rather than different movies), it turns out that the order in which A, B, and C are presented will determine the final outcome. If the first choice is A versus B, A will win since legislator 1 and legislator 3 will vote for A over B. Then when A goes up against C, C will win since legislator 1 and legislator 2 prefer C to A. But suppose we made the first choice A versus C. Now C wins since legislator 2 and legislator 3 will vote for C over A. But B will win against C, because of votes from legislator 1 and legislator 2. Finally, let B versus C be the first choice. Legislators 1 and 2 both prefer B to C, so they each vote for B. But when B comes up for a vote against A, A will win based upon votes from legislator 1 and 3. Thus, the order in which bills (or candidates) get presented to voters ultimately determines the winner. Winners are thus determined arbitrarily in the political arena. Wolff argues that, by removing the philosophical backing for democratic decision-making, Arrow has inadvertently provided a philosophical justification for political anarchism.

A second major contribution by Arrow was to prove mathematically that a *general equilibrium* existed. As far back as Walras and Pareto, and possibly as far back as Quesnay, economists recognized the possibility of describing equilibrium for an entire economic system. Within this system, each market would clear at the equilibrium price for that market. What was missing from this vision was a proof that there could actually be one set of equilibrium prices to clear all markets simultaneously. It is this proof that Arrow (1954; and 1971) set forth in mathematical terms. This proof required four assumptions: (1) Households supply labor services and consume goods; (2) Households know what they want, know the utility they will get from different choices, and make rational choices about consumption and work; (3) Firms transform inputs into outputs using the best technology available; and (4) Households receive profits from production.

Proving the existence of general equilibrium also required two behavioral assumptions and two conditions. The behavioral assumptions are that firms maximize profits and that individuals maximize utility. The two conditions Arrow stipulated were that there could be no negative prices, and that any good for which an excess supply existed had a price of zero (see **von NEUMANN**). From all this, Arrow was able to prove mathematically the existence of a competitive equilibrium; that is, he showed that there was a set of prices for all goods and services such that the supply and demand for all goods and services were equal to one another. The entire economic system could thus be shown to exist in a state of equilibrium.

While this proof will likely appear to be abstract and pointless to the non-economist, it was important because it helped to convince economists of the viability of general equilibrium analysis. General equilibrium was not just some theoretical idea, but a real possibility, and economies could be thought of as moving to this general equilibrium. Economists thus moved further away from the *partial equilibrium* method of Marshall, and began to study the impact of all economic changes on all markets in the economy. This proof was also important because it confirmed for many economists the insight of Adam Smith, that the free market could allocate resources efficiently throughout the entire economy, and that the free market would lead to a highly desirable outcome. If markets were allowed to operate without hindrance, all markets would clear and consumers would maximize utility (given the resources they began with).

One important assumption made in the proof of general equilibrium was contained in (2) above. For households to maximize their utility, they have to know whether to buy various goods today or to wait and buy these goods in the future. This decision requires the existence of forward markets. Forward markets occur where we pay today in order to obtain delivery of some goods in the future, or the promise of repayment in the future. The simplest future market that most people are familiar with is the certificate of deposit offered by banks. Banks take your money today and promise to deliver more money to you in the future (your original money plus interest). For many goods, however, no future markets exist. Future markets exist for foreign currency, but only for a few months into the future. This allows importers to buy the foreign currency they will need to pay for foreign goods when they order these goods, and means that importers will not encounter a large depreciation of their home currency and much higher prices when the goods they ordered are delivered. These future markets in foreign currency thus facilitate foreign trade. For most goods, however, there are no future markets at all. Certainly, it would be hard to find someone willing to sell me food or oil ten years from now at some agreed upon price. The lack of future markets disturbed Arrow and much of his subsequent work (1971) has attempted to show that general equilibrium results still held in a world without complete future markets.

The lack of complete markets has also been a theme of Arrow's work in the economics of health care. Arrow began with the observation that health economics had to be studied from the standpoint of a less than perfect outcome in the health sector of an economy (Arrow 1983–5, vol. 6, chs 3, 7, 15). A first problem is that individuals do not have knowledge about the quality of care they will receive from doctors, especially when specialists are involved. It is important to find good doctors, since an incompetent doctor can cost you your life. But finding good doctors is time-consuming and difficult for consumers. In such cases, Arrow sees entry barriers as the only means to reduce uncertainty. Licensing requirements guarantee that doctors have some medical training and possess competence in medical matters. In contrast to Milton Friedman, who sees licensing requirements as government-mandated monopoly power (which reduces supply and increases prices) and who believes that market forces would drive out incompetent doctors, Arrow views an unregulated medical market as a game of Russian roulette that fails to benefit society.

A second problem in the health care market is what economists refer to as "*moral hazard*," a term coined by Arrow (1970). The idea behind this notion is that insurance changes individual behavior. For example, because our money in the bank is insured, we do not worry about what our bank is doing with our money. This makes it more likely that banks will gamble with our money by making risky loans. Many people have identified this as a major cause of the US savings and loan crisis of the 1980s (Barth 1991). To take another example, fire insurance makes people less careful around the home because they have insurance to pay the costs of any fire. This attitude, though, will lead to more fires. Similarly, people with health insurance are more likely to behave in ways that increase their risks of getting certain diseases or disabilities because their medical expenses will be paid for by someone else. As a result of moral hazard, the demand for health services will rise and health care spending will soar. Arrow (1970) showed that one solution to the moral hazard problem is co-insurance, where individuals pay a large proportion of their health bill. When people are forced to pay more for their health problems, they will behave in less risky ways, have fewer health problems, and so health care spending in the nation is reduced.

A final problem in the health care market *is adverse selection.* Naturally, individuals will know more about their own health than any insurer. Insurers can obtain additional information about a person's health, but only at great cost. Moreover, people who are great health risks, and who will cost the insurance company more money, have strong economic incentives to hide their health problems from their insurance company (because this would entail greater insurance premiums). This uncertainty about the health risks of different individuals creates a prob-lem for insurers. If insurance companies set their rates based upon average risks, high-risk groups will purchase a lot of insurance and low-risk groups will buy little or no insurance. The insurance company will therefore lose money and have to raise rates. But this will drive out even more low-risk groups. Premiums will continue to rise, while more and more people will opt out of insurance coverage. Arrow showed that these problems disappear with a single-payer system. If everyone is covered by health insurance, no one can attempt to provide plans that appeal only to low-risk groups and insurance companies do not have to worry abut low-risk individuals dropping out of the system and significantly raising the average costs of insuring people.

Rather than writing for the general public, and rather than providing economic advice to politicians, Arrow has written primarily for his fellow economists. He has studied the logic of group decision-making, the logic of general equilibrium analysis, and the logic of a health care market that is plagued by uncertainty. The breadth of Arrow's interests, and the penetrating insights that result whenever he studies a specific problem, make him one of the half-dozen most important economists of the late twentieth century.

Works by Arrow

Social Choice and Individual Values, New York, Wiley, 1951
"Existence of Equilibrium for a Competitive Economy," *Econometrica*, 23 (July 1954), pp. 265–90, with G. Debreu
Uncertainty and the Welfare Economics of Medical Care," *American Economic Review*, 53 (1963), pp. 941–64.
Essays in the Theory of Risk-Bearing, Amsterdam and London, North-Holland, 1970
General Competitive Analysis, San Francisco, Holden-Day, 1971, with Frank H. Hahn
The Limits of Organization, New York, Norton, 1974
Collected Papers, 6 vols, Cambridge, Harvard University Press, 1983–5

Works about Arrow

Feiwel, George R. (ed.), *Arrow and the Foundations of the Theory of Economic Policy*, London, Macmillan, 1987
Hammer, Peter J. *et al. Uncertain Times: Kenneth Arrow and the Changing Economics of Health Care*, Durham, North Carolina, Duke University Press, 2004
Heller, Walter P, Starr, Ross M. and Starrett, David A. (eds), *Social Choice and Public Decision Making: Essays in Honor of Kenneth J. Arrow*, 3 vols, Cambridge, Cambridge University Press, 1986
von Weizsacker, Carl Christian, "Kenneth Arrow's Contribution to Economics," *Swedish Journal of Economics*, 74 (1972), pp. 488–502

Other references

Barth, James, *The Great Savings and Loan Debacle*, Washington, D.C., AEI Press, 1991
Wolff, Robert Paul, *In Defense of Anarchism*, New York, Harper & Row, 1970

BARBARA R. BERGMANN (1927–)

Barbara Bergmann spent her career studying how labor markets work. These studies examined the causes of unemployment and poverty as well as the potential cures for these problems. They also examined why women receive such low wages. Bergmann identified discrimination in the labor market, mainly due to excluding women from certain jobs, as a major cause of low wages for women and of child poverty. To remedy these problems, she has advocated a strong affirmative action program.

Bergmann was born in New York City in 1927 and grew up in the Bronx. Her father left the family while Bergmann was still a child, instilling in her a strong belief that women "should have their own money." But when she received her BA in mathematics and economics from Cornell in 1948, she could not find a job and so could not be financially independent. Bergmann has said that she felt the problem was the job ads, which seemed to want only men for professional positions (Saunders and King 2000, p. 307). At the suggestion of her mother, she enrolled at Teacher's College, Columbia University. One year later she accepted a job offer from the Bureau of Labor Statistics. Encouraged by the economists at the Bureau to pursue graduate study, Bergmann went to Harvard, and received her PhD in economics in 1959.

In the early 1960s, Bergmann spent two years as a Senior Staff Economist on the Council of Economic Advisors, and three years at the Brookings Institution, a prestigious Washington think tank. From 1965 to 1988 she taught at the University of Maryland, before being hired by the American University in Washington, D.C., where she taught until her retirement. In the early 1970s she helped found the Eastern Economic Association (EEA), and in 1974 she became its first President.

Bergmann has made two main contributions to economics. First, she has argued that discrimination is a pervasive characteristic of labor markets. Second, she has argued against the traditional economic methodology of drawing conclusions from a set of unrealistic assumptions. Instead she has argued that economists need to go out into the real world and find out how economies actually work.

It is well known that female workers earn on average much less than male workers. Ever since income data was first collected in the late nineteenth century, the numbers revealed that full-time female employees in the US earn around 60 percent as much as full-time male employees (Smith and Ward 1984; Goldin 1990). While these facts are not in dispute, it is a matter of great contention why women earn so much less than men. *Feminist economics* (see Ferber and Nelson 1993) sees this pay differential as evidence of women's second class economic status. It also seeks to understand the causes of women's inferior economic status. Bergmann has been a pioneer of feminist economics; and she has identified exclusion, or *occupational segregation*, a major cause of women's low wages. Furthermore, she has blamed the methodology of her fellow labor economists for failing to see this fact.

Occupational segregation involves keeping some jobs open primarily to women while excluding women from another set of jobs. Usually women get excluded from high-paying jobs and are concentrated in relatively low-paying jobs. For example, most doctors are men, while women are more likely to be nurses; men are more likely to be bank managers, while women are more likely to be bank tellers. Bergmann has pointed out that occupational segregation also frequently occurs *within* occupations. Consider food service jobs. "Men who wait tables generally work in expensive restaurants where the tips are high and no women are hired. Women tend to work in the cheaper restaurants, with no male colleagues" (Bergmann 1996a, p. 42).

Although the phenomenon of occupational crowding or segregation was originally noticed by Edgeworth (1922), it was Bergmann (1971, 1974) who first explained why such discrimination was so prevalent. According to standard economic theory, discrimination should be eliminated by the market because it is not profitable for firms to discriminate (see **Becker**); non-discriminating firms will pay lower wages on average, earn higher profits, and eventually drive discriminating firms out of business.

Bergmann has pointed to substantial evidence that the real world is not like the world of standard economic theory. Court cases against large firms like Hertz, Pizza Hut, and Chase Manhattan all demonstrate the existence of discrimination against women. However, these firms have not been hurt through lower profits and they have not been driven out of business by their less bigoted competitors (Bergmann 1986, p. 139). In addition, traditional economic theory focuses primarily on wage discrimination, or why two people with identical skills and abilities might be paid different wages. It says little about discrimination that systematically excludes women from occupations paying relatively high wages.

Bergmann has also explained why firms discriminate against women and minorities, and why they tend to hire white men at higher wages. This explanation has focused on other employees rather than employers. If white male workers feel uncomfortable having women or minorities as their peers or colleagues, they may not train them and may not assist them with difficult, work-related problems. Or, morale problems (as a result of having to work with women) may lower the productivity of white males. To avoid these possible "costs," employers may decide not to hire either women or minorities.

Going even further, Bergmann (1971) has explained how advantaged groups gain at the expense of disadvantaged groups due to occupational segregation. If women can only be secretaries (and a few other things), but cannot hold managerial positions, there will be more job applicants for secretarial positions than the number of available jobs. This pushes down wages for secretaries. Moreover, even when women are offered non-secretarial jobs, they will receive meager pay offers since employers know that their main option is likely to be a low-wage secretarial job. In contrast, wages will be higher in managerial jobs because, by excluding women from these positions, there will be fewer job applicants and so greater incentives will be necessary to attract workers.

To remedy the problem of occupational sex segregation, Bergmann (1996a) has advanced a strong program of affirmative action. She notes that affirmative action is not meant to remedy past wrongs; it is meant to deal with current practices. Discrimination continues to exist in the workplace today. Women are paid less than men, even after controlling for such factors as education and experience levels. Occupational sex segregation also shows that women are currently discriminated against in the labor market. A final piece of evidence that discrimination exists today comes from controlled experiments in which closely matched pairs of individuals applied for actual jobs. These studies have found that both women and minorities were less likely than white males to progress in the hiring process (EEA Symposium 1995; Turner *et al.* 1991).

Bergmann (1996a) has argued that the benefits of affirmative action exceed the costs of imposing this policy on business firms. One important benefit is that affirmative action leads to more qualified people being hired. This increases economic efficiency. Another benefit from affirmative action is greater workplace diversity. Moreover, Bergmann claims that there are many ways to measure quality or merit; judgments about quality are inherently subjective and are affected by factors such as the gender, race, and age of the candidate. In many instances, there is not one unambiguously best candidate for a job. In these cases, affirmative action says that firms should hire women and minorities.

Bergmann has stressed that numerical goals for affirmative action are important because, in the absence of such goals, firms will promise to do better but will not hire more women or minorities. Only affirmative action will help end discrimination. The alternative, legal action to prevent discrimination, is both lengthy and costly. In addition, individuals discriminated against in the hiring process are not in a position to know this or prove this. For example, job applicants can hardly be expected to know that all female candidates, no matter what their qualifications, were denied an interview for a particular position.

Bergmann (2003) has also stressed the need for better and more affordable child care. Without this, she argues, women will be burdened with most child care duties. This will limit their ability to take jobs that require more time and effort, and deprive everyone of the productivity to be gained from these women. This will also increase the chances that women and children end up in poverty (Bergmann 1996b). Bergmann does not believe that the market has provided, or that it could provide, adequate child care. So she looks to government regulation and government subsidies to make sure that decent and affordable child care is available.

Reinforcing her work in feminist economics, Bergmann has advocated the use of alternative research methodologies in economics. Her Presidential address to the Eastern Economic Association (Bergmann 1974) criticized economists who sit in their ivory towers and maintain limited contact with the real world. These economists study the economy either through introspection or through performing statistical tests of economic theories using data compiled by the government. These methods, Bergmann claims, are inadequate because they are too divorced from the real world and therefore cannot help understand how the real world works.

The work of Robert Lucas provides one good illustration of this problem. Lucas has held that unemployment is the result of a choice that people make about leisure and labor; we choose leisure over work whenever current wages are too low. Bergmann (1989) contends that Lucas made a number of highly unrealistic assumptions about the rationality of laid-off workers and the way that labor markets work in order to reach this conclusion. Moreover, he failed to test any of these assumptions. As a result, he came up with the absurd (albeit logical) conclusion that unemployed individuals are just enjoying time off from working.

In place of deducing the consequences that follow from unrealistic or false assumptions, Bergmann (1973, 1990; and, with Bennett, 1986) has advocated that economists go out into the world and collect information. One way to do this is actually to survey people. Another approach would be to perform controlled experiments, like those showing that qualified women and minorities do not progress as well as white males in the hiring process. Finally, economists can perform computer simulations of labor markets. The basic idea behind this approach is to use the computer to model individual, firm, and government behavior in response to various changes. But to do this, we need to find out how workers actually respond to wage cuts and how firms actually respond when workers demand higher wages. Only then is it possible to determine the impact of wage changes on employment.

For example, interviewing workers who have just been laid off would help economists understand how these individuals think about their options. It would help economists understand why laid-off workers do not immediately apply for cashier openings at the local fast food restaurant. Surveys would also help understand why managers of fast food establishments are unable to find employees at the given wage despite the existence of people looking for work, and why these managers do not increase wages to attract more applicants. Interviews might also allow economists to discern how the manager of a fast food restaurant would view the employment application of someone who has recently lost a high-paying job. Only after conducting these interviews, and simulating the behavior of individuals in response to changing circumstances, would economists understand whether people are out of work because there are not enough jobs, or because workers prefer leisure to labor, or for other, more complex, reasons. This more adequate and more scientific approach would also enable economists to explain how labor markets actually work and to understand the causes of unemployment. Work along these lines is just beginning (see Bewley 2000), but this work still does not have the same professional prestige as abstract economic theory.

Bergmann has yet to receive the highest accolades and awards possible for an economist. She has not been made President of the American Economic Association and she has yet to make the list of Nobel Prize finalists. Part of this neglect certainly stems from the fact that she is a woman (see **Robinson**). Another likely factor is a feminist orientation that makes male economists rather uncomfortable. None the less, Bergmann has helped set the agenda for feminist economics, and her work has forced traditional labor economists to sit up and take notice.

Works by Bergmann

"The Effect of White Incomes on Discrimination in Employment," *Journal of Political Economy*, 79 (March/April 1971), pp. 294–313

"Combining Microsimulation and Regression," *Econometrica*, 41, 5 (September 1973), pp. 955–63

"Occupational Segregation, Wages and Profits When Employees Discriminate by Race or Sex," *Eastern Economic Journal*, 1 (April–July 1974), pp. 103–10

The Economic Emergence of Women, New York, Basic Books, 1986

A Microsimulated Transactions Model of the United States Economy, with Robert L. Bennett, Baltimore, Maryland, Johns Hopkins University Press, 1986

"Women's Roles in the Economy: Teaching the Issues," *Journal of Economic Education*, 18, 4 (Fall 1987), pp. 393–407

"Why Do Most Economists Know So Little About the Economy?," in *Unconventional Wisdom: Essays in Honor of John Kenneth Galbraith*, eds Samuel Bowles, Richard Edwards and William G. Shepherd, Boston, Houghton Mifflin, 1989, pp. 29–37

"Micro-to-Macro Simulation: A Primer with a Labor Market Example," *Journal of Economic Perspectives*, 4, 1 (Winter 1990), pp. 99–116

"Curing Child Poverty in the United States," *American Economic Review*, 84, 2 (May 1994), pp. 76–80

A Defense of Affirmative Action, New York, Basic Books, 1996a

Saving Our Children from Poverty: What the United States Can Learn from France, New York, Russell Sage, 1996b

America's Child Care Problem: The Way Out, with Suzanne Helburn, London, Palgrave Macmillan, 2003

Works about Bergmann

Paulin, Elizabeth "The Seditious Dissent of Barbara Bergmann," in *Economics and Its Discontents*, ed. Richard P. F. Holt and Steven Pressman, Northampton, Massachusetts and Cheltenham, UK, Edward Elgar, 1998, pp. 1–19

Polkington, Betty and Thomson, Dorothy Lampen, *Adam Smith's Daughters: Eight Prominent Women Economists from the Eighteenth Century to the Present*, Cheltenham, UK, Edward Elgar 1998, pp. 104–17.

Saunders, Lisa and King, Mary "An Interview with Barbara Bergmann," *Review of Political Economy*, 12 (July 2000), pp. 305–16

Other references

Bewley, Truman, *Why Wages Don't Fall During a Recession*, Cambridge, Massachusetts, Harvard University Press, 2000

(EEA Symposium) "Symposium: Race, Gender and Discrimination," *Eastern Economic Journal*, 21, 3 (Summer 1995), pp. 339–98

Edgeworth, Francis Y., "Equal Pay to Men and Women," *Economic Journal*, (December 1922), pp. 431–57

Ferber, Marianne A. and Nelson, Julie A. (eds), *Beyond Economic Man: Feminist Theory and Economics*, Chicago and London, University of Chicago Press, 1993

Goldin, Claudia, *Understanding the Gender Gap: An Economic History of American Women*, New York, Oxford University Press, 1990

Smith, James E. and Ward, Michael P., *Women's Wages and Work in the Twentieth Century*, Santa Monica, California, Rand Corporation, 1984

Turner, Margery Austin, Fix, Michael, and Struyk, Raymond J., *Opportunities Denied, Opportunities Diminished: Racial Discrimination in Hiring*, Washington, D.C., Urban Institute Press, 1991

GARY BECKER (1930–)

Gary Becker is among the most original economists of the late twentieth century. His unique approach involves taking the economic assumption of rationality and applying it to a large number of social problems not normally studied by economists. This approach has led to many new areas of specialization within economics – the economics of crime and punishment, the economics of addiction, the economics of the family, human capital theory, and the economics of discrimination.

Becker was born in Pottsville, a small coal mining town in eastern Pennsylvania, in 1930 and grew up in Brooklyn, New York. His father was a small-business owner. Neither of his parents had more than an eighth-grade education. His father left school early to make money, and his mother did not continue her education because "girls were not expected to get much education" (Becker 1992b).

After graduating from high school he went to Princeton University, where he received a BA in economics. Becker majored in economics because he was attracted to the mathematical rigor of the subject. However, he was dissatisfied with his economic education at Princeton because "it didn't deal with important social problems" (Becker 1996b). Nevertheless, he decided to pursue graduate work in economics at the University of Chicago. There, Milton Friedman renewed Becker's excitement about economics and how economic analysis could help understand real-world problems. Becker received an MA in 1953 and a PhD from the University of Chicago in 1955. His doctoral dissertation (Becker 1957) on the economics of discrimination was supervised by Friedman and was cited by the Nobel Prize Committee as an especially important contribution to economics.

Becker taught at the University of Chicago from 1954 to 1957, and then accepted a teaching position at Columbia University. Largely in response to the 1968 student riots, Becker left Columbia and returned to the University of Chicago in 1970. In 1983 the Sociology Department offered him a joint appointment, which he accepted. Since 1985 Becker has written a regular economics column in *Business Week*, explaining economic analysis and ideas to the general public. In 1992 he was awarded the Nobel Prize for Economic Science.

Becker has made two key contributions to economics. First, he has taken the assumptions economists make about human rationality and applied them to all forms of behavior, including matters that do not involve market transactions between individuals. Starting with the assumptions that human beings act rationally and attempt to maximize utility, Becker has analyzed decisions regarding fertility, marriage, and divorce (Becker 1973, 1974, 1977), crime and punishment (Becker 1968), and addiction (Becker 1988, 1991, 1992b). Second, Becker has been instrumental in explaining the way that labor markets work. He has helped develop the notion of human capital (Becker 1964) and he has helped economists to better understand discrimination in labor markets (Becker 1957).

Becker analyzes marriage decisions and family relationships in a manner analogous to the traditional theory of the business firm. Individuals spend time searching for the spouse who will provide them with the maximum amount of utility, just as firms search for the best possible employee. Longer searches lead to better information about whether any possible spouse would be the most desirable one. Consequently, this theory predicts that those marrying young would be more likely to get divorced, a prediction that receives considerable support from data on marital stability. Also, just like a firm attempting to maximize profits, a family can maximize utility through specialization; thus the husband typically specializes in market production and the wife typically specializes in household production. One consequence of such specialization is that women receive lower market wages. According to Becker, this is not due to discrimination, but rather is the result of decisions made within the household about which jobs will be performed by different family members.

Family decisions about having children can also be analyzed using the logic of economic analysis. In contrast to Malthus, who held that people could not control their reproductive urges, Becker looks at the decision to have children as analogous to consumer decisions about purchasing goods like cars and vacations. Raising children involves many costs. Parents must pay for food, shelter, clothing, toys, and education. Most important of all, parents must spend time raising the child, which reduces the time available to earn income and consume goods. Unless parents are compensated for these losses, through greater pleasure from their children, they will not have children. This compensation can come from the joy of raising children, a desire for offspring, or the desire to have someone care for you in your old age.

But whatever the cause of this additional utility, according to Becker, children compete with cars and vacations (which also give pleasure) for each unit of family income.

Given this perspective, it is possible to formulate many testable hypotheses about birth rates. Greater costs of child rearing should reduce fertility; greater family incomes should allow the family to purchase more of everything, including children. Higher incomes for women will increase the costs of rearing children, because the time spent at home with children results in a greater income loss, and will therefore reduce fertility. Finally, government income guarantees to the elderly should reduce fertility rates, since one benefit of children is that they will be around to support you in your old age.

The economics of crime and punishment is another area where Becker has taken the rationality assumption, applied it to a new and different arena, and pushed out the boundaries of economics. One popular view in the 1950s and 1960s was that criminal behavior resulted from mental illness or social oppression. In contrast, Becker assumed that potential criminals behave rationally, and are affected by the expected rewards and costs of criminal activity. Putting more money into law enforcement should raise the probability of being caught, increase the costs of criminal activity, and reduce crime. Likewise, if penalties are increased, the expected cost of criminal actions would rise, and crime rates would fall. Similarly, if more jobs were available, and if the financial rewards from these jobs were to increase, employment begins to look relatively better when compared to criminal activity. As the relative gains from criminal activity fall, crime should be less prevalent. Further offshoots of this approach have looked at how firm compliance with government regulations and individual compliance with tax laws depends upon the penalties and the likelihood of detection. Empirical studies carried out by both economists and criminologists (see Heineke 1978) provide a good deal of support for the theories of Becker on the determinants of criminal activities.

Further drawing out the consequences of the rationality assumption, Becker has argued that drug and alcohol addiction can be viewed as rational behavior. Becker starts by noting that habits can be either good or bad. They are good if they increase future well-being. Habits such as regular exercise, eating well, and wearing seat belts all fall into this category. On the other hand, habits that reduce future well-being, such as smoking cigarettes and experimenting with drugs, are harmful. But, Becker argues, people who develop bad habits are not necessarily irrational; they merely prefer current pleasures to future well-being. An addiction, according to

Becker, is just a strong habit and the result of rationally balancing expected present and future pleasures. This analysis leads to the conclusion that drug use should be made legal in order to allow each individual to maximize his or her own well-being. However, Becker does introduce some qualifications to this conclusion. He notes that some habits, like drug use, can reduce our concern for future consequences and thus lead to powerful addictions. Furthermore, legalizing drugs may lead to a sharp increase in drug addiction since the negative consequences of drug taking are less severe because with legalization the price of drugs will fall. Moreover, peer pressure may rise with legalization, leading to further drug use and greater likelihood of addiction.

Becker has also made significant contributions in the area of labor economics. Becker (1962) was one of the pioneers who developed the notion of human capital and then used this notion to help economists understand how labor markets worked. Analogous to physical capital, like machinery and plants, people can invest in themselves through education, through training, and through developing new skills. In fact, the concept of human capital is even broader than this; it encompasses the purchase of health care, time spent searching for better jobs, and migrating to other areas in search of better employment. Like new plants and machinery, these human investments will yield a flow of future income.

But also like physical capital investment, human capital investment comes with some costs. Perhaps the most important of these will be the lost earnings due to the time spent acquiring human capital. In addition, the difficulty of acquiring new skills and knowledge imposes a cost on the individual. People will invest in themselves, according to Becker, as long as the future gains exceed the present costs. Most empirical studies of human capital theory have focused on comparing the costs and the returns to schooling, especially a college education. Empirical tests of human capital theory have found that human capital investment does increase with greater returns and does fall with greater costs (Mincer 1974).

Several important and controversial points about economic inequality and discrimination follow from the theory of human capital. First, Becker (1971) has pointed out that inequality between two groups (such as men and women, or blacks and whites) does not show that the group receiving lower earnings is discriminated against. Differences in earnings will depend on differences in factors such as education, skills, and experience (or the human capital accumulated by members of each group). Only after we factor out the effect of these differences in human capital on earnings are we left with earning differences reflecting discrimination.

Second, Becker (1998) contends that the desire to discriminate is a kind of taste or preference held by employers, just like the desire to have Grape Nuts cereal for breakfast every morning is a taste or preference. Moreover, Becker (1993) contends that discrimination depends more on the tastes and attitudes of consumers and employees than on the attitudes and beliefs of employers. Consumers may not want to deal with minority salesmen; and current employees may not want to work with women or blacks. In such cases, firms will tend not to hire qualified women and qualified blacks, since such hiring will reduce sales or worker productivity and thus be costly to the firm.

Third, Becker notes that discrimination costs employers money. If an employer could hire a woman or a black, but wants to discriminate against members of this group, the employer will have to pay a price for indulging this taste. The price paid is the wage difference between the white male hired and the woman or minority not hired. This means that in competitive markets discrimination will be less likely to occur since firms that do discriminate will face higher costs and firms that do not discriminate will face lower costs. Non-discriminating firms will tend to force discriminating firms out of existence. These hypotheses regarding discrimination have been the subject of much criticism and debate (see **Bergmann**).

Becker has expanded the range of economic analysis by looking at all individual choice as a form of rational decision-making. He has thus pioneered the study of discrimination, crime, education, and marriage by economists. Every time that he has ventured outside the traditional boundaries of economics he turns up unique and interesting results with clear and testable predictions. More important, his approach has opened up new avenues of research and new ways of viewing non-market human activities. For these reasons Becker remains the most creative economist of the late twentieth and early twenty-first centuries, as well as one of the most influential. One measure of his influence is the large number of citations to his work. Medoff (1989) ranked Becker first among economists under the age of 65 based upon the total number of citations in the *Social Science Citation Index*.

Works by Becker

"Investment in Human Capital: A Theoretical Analysis," *Journal of Political Economy*, 70, 5 (October 1962), pp. 9–49
Human Capital, New York, Columbia University Press, 1964

"Crime and Punishment: An Economic Approach," *Journal of Political Economy*, 76, 2 (March/April 1968), pp. 167–217

The Economics of Discrimination (1957), Chicago, University of Chicago Press, 2nd edn, 1971

"A Theory of Marriage: Part I," *Journal of Political Economy*, 81, 4 (July/August 1973), pp. 813–46

"A Theory of Marriage: Part II," *Journal of Political Economy*, 82, 2 (March/April 1974), Part 2, S11–S26

The Economic Approach to Human Behavior, Chicago, University of Chicago Press, 1976

"An Economic Analysis of Marital Instability," *Journal of Political Economy*, 85, 6 (December 1977), pp. 1,153–89, with E. M. Landes and R. T. Michael

A Treatise on the Family, Cambridge, Massachusetts, Harvard University Press, 1981

"Human Capital, Effort, and the Sexual Division of Labor," *Journal of Labor Economics*, 3, 1 (January 1985), pp. 533–58

"A Theory of Rational Addiction," *Journal of Political Economy*, 96, 4 (August 1988), pp. 675–700, with Kevin M. Murphy

"Rational Addiction and the Effect of Price on Consumption," *American Economic Review*, 81, 2 (May 1991), pp. 237–41, with Michael Grossman and Kevin M. Murphy

"Autobiography" 1992a (available online at www.nobelprize.org/economics/laureates/1992/becker-autobio.html)

"Habits, Addictions, and Traditions," *Kyklos*, 45, 3 (1992b), pp. 327–45

"Nobel Lecture: The Economic Way of Looking at Behavior," *Journal of Political Economy*, 101, 3 (June 1993), pp. 385–409

Accounting for Tastes, Cambridge, Massachusetts, Harvard University Press, 1998

Works about Becker

Fuchs, Victor R., "Gary S. Becker: Ideas about Facts," *Journal of Economic Perspectives*, 8, 2 (Spring 1994), pp. 183–92

Posner, Richard A., "Gary Becker's Contributions to Law and Economics," *Journal of Legal Studies*, 23 (June 1993), pp. 211–15

Rosen, Sherwin, "Risks and Rewards: Gary Becker's Contributions to Law and Economics," *Scandinavian Journal of Economics*, 95, 1 (1993), pp. 25–36

Shackleton, J. R., "Gary S. Becker: the Economist as Empire-builder," in *Twelve Contemporary Economists*, ed. J. R. Shackleton and G. Locksley, New York, Wiley, 1981 pp. 12–32

Other references

Heineke, J. M. (ed.), *Economic Models of Criminal Behavior*, Amsterdam, North-Holland, 1978

Medoff, Marshall H., "The Rankings of Economists," *Journal of Economic Education*, 20, 4 (Fall 1989), pp. 405–15

Mincer, Jacob, *Schooling, Experience, and Earnings*, New York, Columbia University Press, 1974

AMARTYA SEN (1933–)

Over the last thirty years or so Amartya Sen has been a leading figure in the areas of *welfare economics* and economic development. His work has broadened the view of economists about how to improve human well-being, so that it encompasses not just increasing consumption but also developing human potential. He has also shown how poverty and underdevelopment adversely affect women, and he has argued that economists who study economic development need to focus more on developing opportunities for people (especially women) and less on trying to increase national income.

Sen was born in the village of Santinikeran, in Bengal (then part of India) in 1933. His father was a professor of chemistry at Dhaka University, which is now in Bangladesh. As a child, Sen lived through the Great Bengal Famine of 1943. He claims (Klamer 1989, p. 136) that this event had a prolonged and lasting effect on him, and that it sparked his interest in economic development.

While an undergraduate at Presidency College in Calcutta, Sen studied ethics and political philosophy in addition to economics. He received a BA degree in Economics from Presidency College in 1953, and then BA, MA, and PhD degrees in Economics from Trinity College, Cambridge. At Cambridge, he studied economics with both Piero Sraffa and Joan Robinson. Robinson supervised his doctoral dissertation (Sen 1960), and attempted to move his research away from "ethical rubbish" and towards abstract theory (Klamer 1989, p. 139).

After graduating from Cambridge in 1959, Sen taught at Jadaupur University, at Cambridge University, and then at Delhi University. He returned to England yet again in 1971, accepting a teaching position at the London School of Economics. In 1977 Sen moved to Nuffield College, Oxford. Three years later he became Drummond Professor of Political Economy at All Souls College, Oxford, a position previously held by Edgeworth and by Hicks. In 1987 Sen moved to the US, becoming Professor of Economics and Philosophy at Harvard University. Sen returned once more to England in 1998, this time as head of Trinity College, Cambridge, although he has maintained his position at Harvard. In 1994 Sen served as President of the American Economic Association; in 1998 he received the Nobel Prize for Economic Science. The Nobel Committee singled out Sen's work on social choice and individual decision-making; surprisingly, it ignored his most unique contribution and what most inspires his economic work – how to make life better for people in less developed countries.

The main theme in the work of Sen is the importance of developing human potential. For Sen, economics should be about developing the capabilities inherent in people, and increasing the options open to them, rather than about trying to produce more goods or figuring out how to maximize utility. Consequently, he has been highly critical of traditional welfare economics, which holds that free exchange will always maximize the well-being of rational individuals (see **Edgeworth**). Sen has also rejected the traditional economic assumption of human rationality, and he has rejected *Pareto Optimality* (see **Pareto**) as a criterion for economic well-being.

The heart of the rationality assumption is the belief that individuals are rational utility maximizers. Most economists believe that individuals behave in a highly rational and logical fashion. They see people attempting to figure out the consequences of different possible actions and the utility they can expect to receive as a result of each action. They believe that people will act to get themselves the greatest (expected) utility, and that allowing people to act in this manner leads to a Pareto Optimal situation. Sen (1976–7) has criticized this view on a number of grounds.

He contends that utility maximization provides a bad description of how people actually behave. To take just one example, individuals should expect to receive no gain from voting in political elections. The chance that my vote will decide the outcome of any election is minuscule. In fact, the likelihood of my getting struck by lightning while waiting in line to vote is greater than the probability that my vote will decide an election. None the less, I regularly vote; and so do large numbers of other people.

Furthermore, Sen notes that if people did actually behave according to the rationality assumption they would become "rational fools," acting rationally but foolishly. "'Where is the railway station?' he asks me. 'There', I say pointing at the post office, 'and would you please post this letter for me on the way?' 'Yes' he says, determined to open the envelope and check whether it contains something valuable" (Sen 1976–7, p. 332). Left out of this interaction is a concern for other people, for the sort of person one wants to be, or for the sort of society one wants to be part of. Similarly, the Prisoner's Dilemma (see **von Neumann**) shows how individual rationality can lead to collective irrationality (Sen 1974).

Sen (1985b, 1987) has also pointed out several problems with using Pareto Optimality as a welfare criterion. Relying on his experiences living through a time of famine, he notes that outcomes can be Pareto Optimal and yet disastrous. For example, a case in which a few people are very rich and everyone else is starving would be Pareto Optimal, since the situation cannot be improved without taking income from the very wealthy and reducing their utility. However, the fact that many people are starving is obviously a highly undesirable outcome, and one that can be improved through redistribution.

Finally, Sen (1970, 2002) rejects the utilitarian underpinning of traditional welfare economics because it conflicts with liberalism, or the belief that people should be able to do whatever they want so long as it does not keep others from doing what they want. If many people want pornography to be banned, utility maximization would require that pornography should be banned. Similarly, if a great many people prefer that everyone read pornographic novels, utility maximization demands that pornography be forced on people. Yet concern for liberty would allow each individual to make that decision.

Since the utilitarian analysis of individual welfare is inadequate, another perspective is needed. Sen's (1985a) alternative, the capability approach, sees individual welfare depending on the things people can do and the things that they can do well. Human well-being is maximized when people are able to read, eat, and vote. Literacy is important not because of the utility it yields, but because of the sort of person that one becomes when one can read. Food is important not because people love food, but because food is necessary for life and health. And people vote, not to increase their utility, but because they value a certain political system (democracy) and certain types of political activity (McPherson 1992).

The number of options that people have, and their freedom to choose among options, is another important part of human well-being. This means that when a consumer buys some good but has no other options, consumer well-being would be enhanced by giving the consumer greater choice, even if the consumer does not get any more goods. In contrast, on the utilitarian approach, welfare comes from consuming goods, and so greater choice but the same outcome would not make life better for people.

Going even further, Sen notes that traditional economics has got the relationship between preferences and actions backwards – preferences do *not* determine human actions. People do *not* value illiteracy and then decide not to learn how to read. Rather, people who cannot read adapt their preferences and devalue literacy. On the standard utilitarian doctrine, because individual preferences are valued more than anything else, welfare is maximized when illiterate people are not encouraged to read. But for Sen, greater literacy would improve human welfare because it increases the opportunities available to people and enhances their capabilities.

Sen has applied his capabilities approach first and foremost to the area of economic development. This work begins by distinguishing economic growth from economic development. Growth means producing more things regardless of what happens to the people producing and consuming these goods; development involves "expanding the capabilities of people" (Sen 1984, p. 497). Economic growth raises per capita incomes and output. Economic development involves improving the life expectancy, literacy, health, and education levels of people. It means making people part of their community and allowing them to appear in public without shame because they are regarded as worthwhile individuals.

Growth and development often go together. But as the experience of countries such as Sri Lanka and Costa Rica illustrates, the right sort of public policies can expand capabilities and opportunities despite low rates of economic growth. When developing countries must decide to focus on either promoting economic growth or the development of capabilities, Sen contends that they should focus on the real goal, which is the development of human potential. Moreover, the success of a developing economy (as well as developed countries) should be judged on its growing literacy rates and life expectancy rather than on its growth in production or income levels.

To aid in this endeavor, the United Nations created a Human Development Index with the assistance of Sen. The index is a weighted average of mean income (adjusted for distribution and purchasing power), life expectancy, literacy rate, and educational attainment. It seeks to measure success and failure in development based on the key capabilities attained in the community. The index is expressed in relative terms, having a value between 0 and 1, and so it provides a measure of both how individual countries are doing over time and how one country is doing relative to another country at any fixed point in time. A Human Development Index for every country in the world has been published in the UN *Human Development Report* every year since 1995.

Sen has also established that gender issues are an integral part of the development process. He has questioned the assumption that low levels of economic development affect men and women equally, and that development policy should focus on men and women more or less equally.

Sen (1990b) has shown how a parental preference for sons leads to discrimination against women in developing countries. All families must constantly make decisions about how to use the limited income at their disposal. One important decision concerns how to allocate income among all family members. For more affluent families such decisions are usually not critical, but for poor families they can become life-and-death decisions. Family members who do not receive sufficient food will die; likewise family members who fail to receive adequate medical care when they are sick may die.

Sen (1993) has shown that women and men do not have the same access to health care and nutritious food. Women are less likely to be taken to the hospital than men, and women have to be sicker before they get taken to the hospital. Women are also less likely to be given adequate supplies of food (Sen 1984, ch. 15).

Sen (1990b, 1993) has documented in stark and concrete terms the consequences of this unequal treatment. In the developed world there are around 105 women for every 100 men. In the developing world, however, there are only 94 women for every 100 men. If men and women were treated equally in developing countries, these countries should also have a ratio of between 100 and 105 women for every 100 men. Put another way, if women were treated by their families in the same way that men were treated there would be another 100 million women alive today in developing countries.

For ethical reasons, as well as for efficiency reasons, Sen suggests that development efforts should focus on women. In India, for example, direct feeding programs have been more successful at improving the nutrition of girls than general food disbursements consumed by families at home. Programs that encourage women to work outside the house give women greater status within the family, and will enable them to claim more economic resources within the family. Moreover, Sen argues that, if the economic contribution of women were greater and received greater recognition, female children would likely receive more attention and more family resources (Sen 1996).

Finally, Sen's work on famines and hunger has helped economists understand the causes of these important real-world problems. It has also changed the way that many international agencies approach famine prevention and relief. *Poverty and Famines* (Sen 1981) points out that famines do not occur in democracies. Sen (1996) points out that India has had no famines since 1943, but China had a disastrous famine (with 15–30 million people dying of starvation) from 1958 to 1961, despite the fact that China has generally done a better job than India in eliminating hunger. Mass starvation has less to do with the higher output resulting from democratic forms of government, and more to do with the fact that democratic governments must respond to political pressure from the electorate. Prior to the work of Sen, development economists assumed that famines were the result of insufficient food production. Sen pointed out that distribution issues were separate from, and more important than, the question of food supply. Famines could result from poor or unequal distribution mechanisms; famines could also result from great food demand in some sectors or regions of a country and insufficient food supplies elsewhere.

The work of Sen has attempted to broaden the horizon of economic analysis. He has pressed economists to take a different view of human economic agents. He has made a strong case that people have some intrinsic worth, and are not just rational utility maximizers. And he has pointed out that the goal of a well-performing economic system is not just more goods and services, but improving the lives of people by making sure that they have access to food, education, and health care. The unifying theme in the work of Sen has been a focus on creating human potential or capabilities, and showing how this leads to greater well-being in society and within the household. He has seen the development of human abilities, and greater freedom to develop our human potential, as the real end of economic growth and development.

Works by Sen

Choice of Techniques: An Aspect of The Theory of Planned Economic Development, Oxford, Basil Blackwell, 1960

"The Impossibility of a Paretian Liberal," *Journal of Political Economy*, 78, 1 (January–February 1970), pp. 152–7

On Economic Inequality, Oxford, Clarendon Press, 1973

"Choice, Orderings and Morality," in *Practical Reason*, ed. Stephan Körner, New Haven, Yale University Press, 1974, pp. 54–67

"Rational Fools: A Critique of the Behavioral Foundations of Economic Theory," *Philosophy and Public Affairs*, 6 (1976–7), pp. 317–44

Poverty and Famines: An Essay on Entitlement and Deprivation, Oxford, Clarendon Press, 1981

Resources, Values and Development, Oxford, Basil Blackwell, 1984

Commodities and Capabilities, Amsterdam, North Holland, 1985a

"The Moral Standing of the Market," in *Ethics and Economics*, eds Ellen Frankel, Fred D. Miller, Jr., and Jeffrey Paul, Oxford, Basil Blackwell, 1985b, pp. 1–19

On Ethics and Economics, Oxford, Basil Blackwell, 1987

Hunger and Public Action, with Jean Dréze, Oxford, Clarendon Press, 1989

"Gender and Cooperative Conflicts," in *Persistent Inequalities*, ed. Irene Tinker, London, Oxford University Press, 1990a, pp. 123–49

"More than 100 Million Women Are Missing," *New York Review of Books*, 37 (December 20, 1990b), pp. 61–6

The Political Economy of Hunger: Famine Prevention, Oxford, Clarendon Press, 1991

Inequality Reexamined, Cambridge, Massachusetts, Harvard University Press, 1992

"The Economics of Life and Death," *Scientific American*, 268, 5 (May 1993), pp. 40–7

The Political Economy of Hunger: Selected Essays, Oxford, Clarendon Press, 1995, with Jean Dréze and Arthur Hussain

India: Economic Development and Social Opportunity, Oxford, Oxford University Press, 1996, with Jean Dréze

Development as Freedom, New York, Random House, 1999

Rationality and Freedom, Cambridge, Massachusetts and London, Harvard University Press, 2002

Works about Sen

Arrow, Kenneth, "Amartya K. Sen's Contributions to the Study of Social Welfare," *Scandinavian Journal of Economics*, 101, 2 (June 1999), 163–72

Klamer, Arjo, "A Conversation with Amartya Sen," *Journal of Economic Perspectives*, 3, 1 (Winter 1989), pp.135–50

McPherson, Michael, "Amartya Sen," in *New Horizons in Economic Thought: Appraisals of Leading Economists*, ed. Warren J. Samuels, Hampshire, UK, Edward Elgar, 1992, pp. 294–309

Pressman, Steven, and Summerfield, Gale, "The Economic Contributions of Amartya Sen," *Review of Political Economy*, 12, 1 (January 2000), pp. 89–113

DANIEL KAHNEMAN (1934–)

Why a psychologist in a book on major economists? The answer to this question is that Daniel Kahneman has been a leader in two areas of economics – *experimental economics* and *behavioral economics* – that seek to understand how people actually behave in economic situations.

As noted earlier (see **Menger** and **Leontief**), economics has frequently been criticized as being too deductive. One key criticism has been that economists employ unrealistic assumptions about human behavior. For example, economists believe that people are generally rational and seek only to maximize their own gains (see **Locke**). In addition, economists have encountered great difficulty setting up controlled experiments to test their theories.

The work of Kahneman has addressed these concerns. It employs actual experiments to understand human decision-making and the economic implications of real human behavior. Kahneman has objected to the rationality assumption because it is not a good description of how people actually behave. His research experiments support this by showing that people use shortcuts when making decisions instead of seeking to maximize utility. They may do what their friends do, or what they think other people are doing. People also have a sense of what is fair, and they think about this when they make decisions. But using shortcuts, and thinking about fairness, means that people sometimes make decisions that are not rational and that fail to serve their own self-interest.

Kahneman was born in Tel Aviv, Israel, in 1934. His parents were Lithuanian Jews who emigrated in the early 1920s to Paris, where his father was head of research for a large chemical factory. After the Germans swept into France in 1940, they sent Kahneman's father to Drancy, a way station for the extermination camps. Like something out of the movie *Schindler's List*, he was released due to the intervention of his firm. The family then moved to Vichy and stayed on the French Riviera until the Germans arrived there. This time they escaped to the center of France. Just before the end of the war his father died, and Kahneman, along with his mother and sister, emigrated to Palestine.

As an adolescent, Kahneman developed interests in philosophical questions such as the existence of God and the difference between right and wrong. But over time he became less interested in these philosophical issues and more interested in why people believe in God, and in their beliefs about what is right and wrong.

In 1954 Kahneman received his undergraduate degree from the Hebrew University in Jerusalem, majoring in psychology and mathematics, and then was drafted into the Israeli army. After a year as a platoon leader he was transferred to the psychology branch of the army and assigned to assess candidates for officer training. Here he encountered his first behavioral anomaly. Aviators in training were not responding to positive reinforcement after a very good performance, as psychological theory predicted they would. Instead, reinforcement seemed to have no effect on subsequent performance. Kahneman later recognized this as an example of a statistical error called "regression to the mean."

When he left the army in 1956, Kahneman decided to pursue a PhD in psychology. He received a grant to study abroad, and in 1958 began studying at the University of California at Berkeley. His program there was quite eclectic. Besides psychology courses, Kahneman took courses on Wittgenstein and the philosophy of science as part of his degree program. Graduating in 1961, Kahneman returned to the Hebrew University to teach.

During the 1968–69 academic year, Kahneman taught a graduate seminar on the application of psychology to real-world problems. He asked Amos Tversky, a younger colleague at the Hebrew University, to speak to his class about human judgment and decision-making, the two topics on which Tversky was doing research. Thus began a long and fruitful collaboration. Most of Kahneman's important ideas were developed with Tversky, and many of his key papers were written with Tversky. They worked together, studying, documenting, and explaining the many biases that people have when they make decisions.

In 1978, Kahneman left Israel and took a position at the University of British Columbia. Eight years later he moved back to Berkeley. In 1993 he accepted a position at Princeton University in order to be closer to his friends and relatives in Israel. In 2002 Kahneman won a Nobel Prize (with Vernon Smith, who was doing similar work) for his pioneering work in behavioral and experimental economics. Had Tversky not died of cancer in 1996 it is likely that he would have shared in the Nobel Prize.[1]

The work of Kahneman (and Tversky) has focused on errors in judgment, particularly around decision-making. Kahneman (2002) sees human judgments as having two different components. First, humans are able to directly perceive things; we take in information from the environment around us. However, our perceptual systems are not perfect. Optical illusions are one well-known class of perceptual error.

Second, we have a deliberative or evaluative system, which knows that our perceptions can be mistaken and may try to correct them. Unfortunately, we cannot and do not always do this. Kahneman has identified several types of decision-making mistakes. These occur when our perceptual system generates errors and our deliberative system fails to correct them. Moreover, Kahneman (1973) has shown that these errors are not mitigated through either education or experience. People do not seem to learn from their past mistakes; instead, they tend to make these same errors over and over again.

One type of error stems from faulty memory. In large measure, our decisions today depend on what we remember about our past experiences. If our memories about what happened in the past are defective, it hinders our ability to make good choices now.

In one experiment Kahneman (1993) tested how people remember unpleasant experiences such as undergoing a colonoscopy. When an unpleasant experience was immediately followed by a less unpleasant experience, Kahneman found that it is remembered as less unpleasant. In addition, even though adding a less unpleasant experience at the end *increases* the total unpleasantness, and increases the time that one is experiencing something unpleasant, people still prefer this to a single very unpleasant experience.

Similarly, Kahneman found that a pleasant experience followed by an experience that is not so good is remembered less fondly. For this reason lottery winners are less happy after they win than they expected they would be when buying a ticket. Kahneman concludes from this work that, because we have defective memories, people frequently make wrong choices about what will give them pleasure.

A second class of error judgments concerns probability. Probability assessment is important because when we make decisions we do not know the outcome of our choice with certainty. However, if we can make good guesses about the probability or chance of each possible outcome, we can choose what is most likely to make us happy.

Kahneman found that people are not good at making probability judgments. One example of this problem is raised by the following description that Kahneman (1982) gave to numerous subjects: "Linda is 31 years old, single, outspoken, and very bright. She majored in philosophy. As a student she was deeply concerned with issues of discrimination and social justice, and also participated in anti-nuclear demonstrations." He then asked how likely it is that "Linda is a bank teller" and how likely it is that "Linda is a bank teller and is active in the feminist movement." According to mathematical laws of probability, the latter *must* be less likely than the former, since it requires that Linda be *both* a bank teller and a feminist. Yet, nearly 9 out of 10 people said the latter description was more likely to be true.

Kahneman believes that this error arises because the description of Linda made her seem like a feminist and that people tend to give more vivid evidence disproportionate weight. For this reason, the second statement appeared right or was more representative. In the real world, this type of error occurs when we give great weight to a friend's story about their car problems rather than relying on assessments from places like *Consumer Reports* that independently test and evaluate products.

The famous *Sports Illustrated* cover jinx is another real-world example of faulty probability judgments at work. Athletes whose picture appears on the cover of the American magazine *Sports Illustrated* generally perform worse after their picture has appeared, and many athletes and sports fans think that getting their picture on the cover of the magazine is bad luck. However, faulty thinking about probability is at work here. A picture appears on the cover of the magazine because of an extraordinary performance, one that is not likely to continue. In the future, the athlete should have a more average performance. Hence the origin of the *Sports Illustrated* jinx. Statisticians call this "the regression to the mean." It is a normal part of life. At times we do much better than average, but the next time we are likely to perform near our average. This is the phenomenon Kahneman noted when working for the Israeli military, and it explains why positive reinforcement did not seem to work there – aviators who did well in one instance and were reinforced, then reverted to a more average performance.

Another type of judgment error has come to be called "the endowment effect" and "the status quo bias." Kahneman (1984) saw that people value a thing more when they own it or possess it. The owner of a bottle of rare wine may refuse to sell it for $200 but would not pay $100 to replace if it was stolen. This raises the problem of how that individual values the bottle of wine. According to standard economic theory, if the person will not sell the bottle for $200, it must have a value of more than $200. On the other hand, because he would not pay $100 for replacing it, its value must be less than $100.

Another example of the endowment effect concerns how people behave when planning to attend a concert or sporting event. Many people report that they would likely buy a ticket if they lost cash equal to the cost of a ticket, but they would not buy a second ticket if they lost a ticket that they had previously bought. The amount lost, and the decision, is the same in both cases – do you want to spend a certain sum of money to see a concert? Yet the specifics of the situation lead to different actual behavior.

One real-world consequence of the endowment effect is that consumers will be reluctant to return goods that they purchase and that fail to live up to their expectations. Similarly, people will be reluctant to sell stocks and other assets that do not perform well. Such behaviors raise important questions about whether markets are able efficiently to allocate resources and produce the goods that people really want.

A final category of judgment errors concerns framing. Kahneman (1992) demonstrated this phenomenon experimentally as follows. Subjects were asked to decide between two public health programs to deal with a life-threatening epidemic on a tiny island village. They were told that one program would save 200 lives, while the other program had a chance of saving all 600 villagers and a chance of saving none. Given these choices, most people preferred the program that would definitely save 200 lives. Subjects were then given an identical version of the two programs, but with a slight wording change – one program was described as leading to 400 deaths, rather than saving 200 lives, while the other program was described as having a chance of saving no one and a chance of saving everyone. In this later formulation, most people preferred the gamble rather than 400 sure deaths. In addition, subjects given the two sets of choices on separate occasions tended to give inconsistent responses, favoring saving 200 lives in the first formulation and the gamble in the second formulation.

Framing effects appear to play an important role in the real world. They can explain why consumers are less averse to a cash discount than to a surcharge for using one's credit card, even though the two are identical. Framing effects may explain why pollution taxes are more acceptable than letting firms bid on pollution permits. In the former case, it appears that firms are being penalized for polluting the environment. In the latter case, it looks like they are being allowed to pollute, and are paying for the right to pollute. Yet, both cases are really identical – firms pay to pollute.

Framing effects also provide some insight into the debate over Social Security privatization in the US. The US system, as of 2005, faces a shortfall of around 2 percent of taxable wages. President Bush's call for privatization replaces a sure loss for current workers with a gamble that high stock market returns will prevent these losses. The political gamble here is that most Americans are ready to accept the economic gamble rather than a sure loss.

A final question that has concerned Kahneman involves fairness. He has been interested in whether people will punish those who treat them unfairly, even at some individual cost. This issue arose initially in repeated prisoner's dilemma games (see **von Neumann**). Kahneman (1986a) invented two games to study this phenomenon further – the ultimatum game and the dictator game – and had subjects play these games to determine how our sense of fairness affects our behavior.

In the ultimatum game, two people are given a fixed sum of money to divide. The first subject can propose any division of the money that they like; the second subject can only accept or reject that division. If the division is accepted, each person receives the amount of money proposed by the first subject; if the division is rejected, each person receives nothing.

The dictator game is similar to the ultimatum game, but with one key difference. Here there is really no second subject, for the second subject has no power at all. Whatever the first subject, or dictator, decides determines how the money gets divided up.

Kahneman (1986b) ran a number of experiments where individuals played these games for real stakes. He found that people do not behave as predicted by the rationality assumption employed by economists. In the ultimatum game people chose to make substantial offers to the second subject, when they could have offered close to zero, reasoning that the second subject would not reject even a very small amount of money. Furthermore, most people rejected unfair offers. Similarly, in dictator games, Kahneman found that the dictator did not take all the money, even though they had the (dictatorial) power to do so.

This work has several economic implications. Notions of fairness help explain sticky wages, or why wages usually don't fall in times of high unemployment. Cutting wages of current workers because someone else is willing to work for less would be considered unfair, and may lead to less work effort by employees. Likewise, product markets may not clear because firms might be reluctant to charge high market-clearing prices, fearing consumers may judge them to be unfair and by so doing reduce their future demand for the good.

All of this work challenges subjective utility theory, which holds that rational individuals will choose alternatives that maximize their expected gain or utility, and that preferences are stable, context free, and consistent. It also provides a psychological underpinning for Keynesian and Post Keynesian economics because it relies on a correct description of how people actually behave (see Akerlof and Yellen 1987). And, perhaps most important of all, it opens the door for economic policy to improve economic well-being. As Kahneman (1994, pp. 758–60) put it, "it is plausible that the state knows more about an individual's future tastes than the individual knows presently."

For many reasons it is hard to evaluate the importance of Kahneman's work for economics. He is a trained cognitive psychologist rather than an economist; and recognition of his work has come only recently to economics. Thus, the future impact of his research program and his approach to economics remains uncertain.

One of the most astute and thoughtful observers of trends within the economics profession, David Colander (Colander, Holt and Rosser 2004), sees both psychological and experimental economics at the forefront of the profession and expects to see much more work in these and related areas in the future. If this prediction comes true, Kahneman will turn out to be one of the most important economic figures of the late twentieth and early twenty-first centuries.

Note

1 Tversky received a citation from the Nobel Prize committee, but could not share in the award because only living individuals are eligible to receive a Nobel Prize.

Works by Kahneman

"Belief in the Law of Small Numbers," *Psychological Bulletin*, 76 (1971), pp. 105–10, with Amos Tversky

"On the Psychology of Prediction," *Psychological Review*, 80 (1973), pp. 237–51, with Amos Tversky

"Judgments of and by Representativeness," in *Judgment Under Uncertainty: Heuristics and Biases*, ed. Daniel Kahneman, Paul Slovic, and Amos Tversky, New York, Cambridge University Press, 1982, pp. 84–98, with Amos Tversky

"Choices, Values and Frames," *American Psychologist*, 39 (1984), pp. 341–50, with Amos Tversky

"Fairness as a Constraint on Profit Seeking: Entitlements in the Market," *American Economic Review*, 76 (September 1986a), pp. 728–41, with J. Knetch and Richard Thaler

"Fairness and the Assumptions of Economics," *Journal of Business*, 59 (October 1986b), pp. S285–S300, with J. Knetch and Richard Thaler

"When More Pain is Preferred to Less," Charles Schreiber, and Donald Redelmeier, *Psychological Science*, 4 (November 1993), pp. 401–5, with Barbara Fredrickson

"New Challenges to the Rationality Assumption," *Journal of Institutional and Theoretical Economics*, 150 (March 1994), pp. 18–36

"Representativeness Revisited: Attribute Substitution in Intuitive Judgement," in *Heuristics and Biases: The Psychology of Intuitive Judgment*, ed. T. Gilovich, D. Griffin, and Daniel Kahneman, New York, Cambridge University Press, 2002, with S. Frederick

Works about Kahneman

Altman, Morris, "The Nobel Prize in Behavioral and Experimental Economics: A Contextual and Critical Appraisal of the Contributions of Daniel Kahneman and Vernon Smith," *Review of Political Economy*, 16 (January 2004), pp. 3–41

Maital, Shlomo, "Daniel Kahneman: On Redefining Rationality," *Journal of Socio-Economics*, 33 (March 2004) pp. 1–14

Rabin, Matthew, "Daniel Kahneman and Amos Tversky," *American Economists of the Late Twentieth Century*, ed. Warren Samuels, Cheltenham, UK, Edward Elgar, 1998, pp. 111–37

Rabin, Matthew, "The Nobel Memorial Prize for Daniel Kahneman," *Scandinavian Journal of Economics*, 105 (June 2003), pp. 157–80

Other references

Akerlof, George, and Yellen, Janet, "Rational Models of Irrational Behavior," *American Economic Review,* 77 (June 1987), pp. 137–42

Colander, David, Holt, Richard P. F., and Rosser, J. Barkley, Jr., "The Changing Face of Mainstream Economics," *Review of Political Economy*, 16 (October 2004), pp. 485–99

ROBERT E. LUCAS, JR. (1937–)

Robert Lucas is known for developing the new classical or rational expectations approach to macroeconomics. This approach seeks to provide microfoundations to macroeconomics. It assumes that macroeconomic actors, like microeconomic actors, are rational and self-interested human beings who use all available information when making decisions and who attempt to anticipate the future consequences of their actions. When macroeconomic actors are seen in this light, the conclusions of Keynesian economics can be rejected – unemployment will remedy itself and stabilization policy is neither necessary nor desirable.

Lucas was born into a middle class family in Yakima, Washington, in 1937. Shortly thereafter the family restaurant (the Lucas Ice Creamery) went bankrupt, a victim of the Great Depression. As a result of the personal hardships they had to endure during the Depression, Lucas's parents, both descendants of a long line of Republicans, rejected their Republican leanings and became ardent supporters of the New Deal.

Lucas attended public schools in Seattle, and excelled in science and mathematics. His parents expected him to attend the University of Washington in Seattle and become an engineer. But Lucas was anxious to leave home, and a scholarship let him attend the University of Chicago, where he majored in history. After receiving his BA degree in 1959, he received a Woodrow Wilson doctoral fellowship and began graduate study in history at Berkeley. Recognizing that economic factors were the key forces moving history, Lucas shifted his focus to economic history and decided to return to the University of Chicago in order to pursue a PhD in economics. At Chicago he studied with Milton Friedman, whose libertarian-conservative bent forced Lucas to rethink the New Deal politics he had grown up with. His PhD dissertation, awarded in 1964, was an econometric study of the ease with which businesses can substitute capital and labor in production (see **Hicks**).

From 1963 to 1974 Lucas taught at Carnegie-Mellon University, where he came into contact with John Muth, who first developed the notion of rational expectations. He then accepted a teaching position at the University of Chicago. In 1980 Lucas became the John Dewey Distinguished Service Professor at the university. In 1995, he received the Nobel Prize for Economic Science, primarily for his contribution to rational expectations macroeconomics.

Beginning with Keynes, macroeconomists recognized that expectations affect the overall performance of the economy; but they had only a rudimentary understanding of how expectations were formed. Some macroeconomists took expectations as static or fixed. Others saw expectations as formed by past experience. On this view, if inflation had gone up 2 percent in the past, people would come to expect 2 percent inflation to continue indefinitely. Only after a few years of 4 percent inflation would people change their views and expect future inflation to be 4 percent.

Lucas insisted that people were smarter than this and more sensible when it came to forming expectations. With *rational expectations* people look forward as well as backward. Expected inflation depends not just on past price changes, but on how current conditions or current economic policies might change things. Just because inflation has been 2 percent for many years does not mean people believe that inflation will continue to be 2 percent. Falling unemployment rates or rapid money growth, for example, might lead people to expect that prices will start to increase more rapidly in the future.

Although Muth (1961) first set forth the notion of rational expectations, Lucas has been its strongest proponent and has made this approach part of contemporary macroeconomics. It was Lucas who pointed out that rational expectations were just a logical extension of the normal economic assumptions about people. On this view, individuals are seen as rational agents who seek out all information and who learn from past mistakes. It was also Lucas who insisted that rational expectations be incorporated into all macroeconomic analysis, thereby giving macroeconomics solid microfoundations. And it was Lucas who drew out the consequences of this assumption for macroeconomic theory and policy.

The main consequences of rational expectations are that there is no short-run trade-off between inflation and unemployment, and that economic policy tools are ineffective and cannot improve economic outcomes. These two consequences have led people to call this approach "the *new classical school*" of macroeconomics because of its pre-Keynesian or non-Keynesian conclusions. Lucas himself (1981, p. 215; Klamer 1984, p. 56) regarded his work as a mathematical representation of the ideas of Hayek on *laissez-faire*, and also saw them as supporting the policy conclusions of Friedman and Buchanan rather than Keynes (Lucas 1981, pp. 17, 234–52).

One good way to understand new classical macroeconomic analysis is through the conflict between the macroeconomics of Keynes and traditional labor economics. Keynesian macroeconomics attempted to explain why economies might experience prolonged bouts of high unemployment. Labor economics, in contrast, sees unemployment as the consequence of too high wages creating a surplus of workers. On this view, if workers would accept pay cuts, they would be able to find jobs; if workers do not accept pay cuts, they could be viewed as preferring more leisure to working for lower wages. Macroeconomists from the 1940s through the 1960s generally sided with Keynes and viewed unemployment as primarily involuntary. Lucas changed all that.

New classical economics harks back to the classical approach to macroeconomics. It assumes that markets, including labor markets, always reach a point at which supply equals demand. Unemployment will therefore be the exception rather than the norm, and will tend to disappear as labor markets adjust. It is a temporary, disequilibrium phenomenon that will remedy itself. The reason for this is that Lucas assumes economic actors will be rational and will behave in ways that maximize their well-being.

Lucas (1969b) sees the labor supply decision as a choice that each worker makes between labor and leisure. Workers have some sense of the real wage they would receive from working. They then decide whether to work or not by comparing this real wage against the benefits from leisure time. If expected real wages are higher than normal, workers will have an incentive to work more. In contrast, if expected real wages are lower than usual, workers will take more leisure and wait until real wages rise before working. Within this framework, unemployment is explained as a voluntary choice made by workers who are waiting for real wages to rise to the normal level.

A similar decision must be made by business firms (Lucas 1972, 1973). When prices rise for the goods it produces, a firm must decide whether that price rise is due to a greater demand for what it produces (thus necessitating additional production) or to a general rise in all prices, which would not call for greater production. Like the worker, business owners face labor–leisure trade-offs; like the worker, the business firm will want to produce more only when it really gets more for what it produces.

Because people do not have all relevant information at their disposal, they will sometimes make errors in their labor and production decisions. For example, workers may assume that a given pay increase represents an increase in real wages, or businesses may think that a price rise for what they produce is an increase in the relative price for their product rather than part of an overall price increase. According to Lucas, unemployment results when individual workers and businesses make mistakes of this sort. When workers mistake their real wage, they withhold their labor by quitting their job or turning down job offers with too low wage offers. Businesses can also make mistakes about demand, and so they will sometimes produce too little and hire too few workers. But because people are rational beings, and are forward-looking in how they form expectations, any mistakes will be corrected shortly and unemployment will disappear shortly.

This analysis of the causes of unemployment dovetails with a second contribution due to Lucas, one that has come to be known as "the *Lucas Critique.*" One normal exercise in economic analysis is to employ a macroeconomic model to study how changing *fiscal policy* and/or *monetary policy* impacts the whole economy. In the 1960s it was assumed that these models could help policy-makers guide the economy towards full employment with low inflation. In the 1970s, *stagflation* seemed to show that fiscal and monetary policies were relatively ineffective in solving macroeconomic problems. Economists needed some explanation for this policy failure. Lucas provided that explanation.

Lucas (1976, 1978) criticized the use of large-scale macroeconomic models to evaluate the consequences of different economic policies (see **Tinbergen**). His criticism was that these models all assumed that macroeconomic relationships would remain unchanged in the face of any change in policy. But this will not be true, Lucas (1978, p. 52) contends, because "a change in policy *necessarily* alters some of the structural parameters ... in a highly complex fashion." Without knowing which economic relationships remain the same, which change, and how they change, an econometric model is of *no* value in assessing alternative policies. Going even further, Lucas (1978, p. 56) claims that the poor track record of economic forecasting models (for example, their failure to explain the stagflation of the 1970s) shows that macroeconomic relationships frequently change.

In practice, the Lucas Critique means that economic behavior will change in response to a policy change. Rational individuals who attempt to maximize their own well-being should change their behavior in the face of changing economic policy. In turn, these behavioral changes will change macroeconomic relationships. These behavioral changes will also make macroeconomic policies ineffective because they will work against any policy changes that are announced or anticipated.

One simple example of this, pointed out by Barro (1974), concerns the effects of government deficits. According to the Keynesian view, a tax cut by the government will lead to increased demand for goods and services. But tax cuts also lead to larger government deficits. According to rational expectations macroeconomics, rational citizens will realize that these deficits must be paid back in the future and that the government must raise taxes to do so. People will therefore save most of their tax cut so that they can pay their higher taxes in the future. Tax cuts no longer increase consumer spending and employment; instead, saving is stimulated and fiscal policy will not increase demand or lower unemployment.

Another important example of the Lucas Critique in action concerns the *Phillips Curve* (see **Samuelson**). Lucas (1972) pointed out that the traditional argument for the Phillips Curve assumes irrational macroeconomic actors. He then went on to explain why the Phillips Curve would likely be vertical in the long run. If policy-makers attempt to expand the economy and lower unemployment they will generate expectations of higher inflation among rational economic agents. Workers will not want to work more if they are paid less, and so employment will not increase and unemployment will not fall. The only impact of stimulative demand policy is to increase prices. In the long run, then, economic policy can only change prices or the rate of inflation; it can do nothing about unemployment. There is no inflation–unemployment trade-off; there is only, following Friedman, a *natural rate of unemployment*. This rate is determined by the decisions made by workers and firms, and cannot be modified by any economic policy.

Lucas argues that stimulative fiscal policy can only increase employment by fooling workers into believing that the higher wages offered by businesses represent an increase in their real wages. But Lucas also points out that rational workers can be fooled once or twice. After that, whenever the government tries to stimulate employment through additional government spending, workers will expect to see higher inflation and no increase in their real wages. As a result, people will not seek more work and prefer less leisure, and these policies will fail to stimulate employment. The same thing is true for money policy. Central banks cannot continually increase the money supply and fool people about what they are doing in order to expand the economy.

Since economic policy cannot stabilize the economy, Lucas (2002, 2003) has emphasized that macroeconomics needs to focus on what can be done to encourage economic growth in the long run. Moreover, he notes that business cycles are really a minor problem and cause only small income losses, but that small differences in long–run growth have the ability to raise incomes a great deal over the course of several decades. To generate more rapid growth in the long run, Lucas has emphasized the importance of rules, such as a balanced budget for fiscal policy and a fixed money growth rule for monetary policy. And in a somewhat ironic twist, because it sounds more like Keynesian and Post Keynesian macroeconomics, Lucas has emphasized the importance of greater investment as a means of spurring economic growth rather than higher savings rates.

When the Royal Swedish Academy of Sciences awarded him the Nobel Prize in 1995, it noted that no one has had a greater impact on macroeconomics since 1970 than Lucas. Lucas explained how rational economic agents form expectations and how these expectations, in turn, affect economic outcomes and performance. In so doing, he has challenged the Keynesian orthodoxy that economic policy must be used to remedy the problem of unemployment. As a result of his work, the new classical or rational expectations approach came to dominate macroeconomics in the late twentieth century.

Works by Lucas

"Price Expectations and the Phillips Curve," *American Economic Review*, 59, 3 (June 1969a), pp. 342–50. with Leonard A. Rapping

"Real Wages, Employment and Inflation," *Journal of Political Economy*, 77, 5 (September/October 1969b), pp. 721–54, with Leonard A. Rapping

"Expectations and the Neutrality of Money," *Journal of Economic Theory*, 4 (April 1972), pp. 103–24

"Some International Evidence on Output–Inflation Tradeoffs," *American Economic Review*, 63, 3 (June 1973), pp. 326–34

"An Equilibrium Model of the Business Cycle," *Journal of Political Economy*, 83, 6 (December 1975), pp. 1113–44

"Econometric Policy Evaluation: A Critique," in *The Phillips Curve and Labor Markets*, ed. K. Brunner and A. Meltzer, Amsterdam, North-Holland, 1976, pp. 19–46

"After Keynesian Macroeconomics," in *After the Phillips Curve: Persistence of High Inflation and High Unemployment*, Boston, Federal Reserve Bank of Boston, 1978, pp. 49–72, with Thomas J. Sargent

"Rules, Discretion and the Role of the Economic Advisor," in *Rational Expectations and Economic Policy*, ed. Stanley Fischer, Chicago, University of Chicago Press, 1980, pp. 199–210

Studies in Business Cycle Theory, Cambridge, Massachusetts, MIT Press, 1981

Models of Business Cycles, Oxford, Basil Blackwell, 1987

"Nobel Lecture: Money Neutrality," *Journal of Political Economy*, 104, 4 (August 1996), pp. 661–82

Lectures on Economic Growth, Cambridge, Massachusetts, Harvard University Press, 2002

"Macroeconomic Priorities," *American Economic Review*, 93, 1 (March 2003), 1–14

Works about Lucas

Chari, V. V., "Nobel Laureate Robert E. Lucas, Jr.: Architect of Modern Macroeconomics," *Journal of Economic Perspectives*, 12, 1 (Winter 1998), pp. 171–86

Fisher, Stanley, "Robert Lucas's Nobel Memorial Prize," *Scandinavian Journal of Economics*, 98, 1 (March 1996), pp. 11–31

Kasper, Sherryl, *The Revival of Laissez-faire in American Macroeconomic Theory*, Cheltenham, UK, Edward Elgar, 2002

Klamer, Arjo, *Conversations with Economists: New Classical Economics and Opponents Speak Out on the Current Controversy in Macroeconomics*, Totowa, New Jersey, Rowman & Allenheld, 1984

Other references

Barro, Robert, "Are Government Bonds Net Worth?," *Journal of Political Economy*, 82, 6 (November–December 1974), pp. 1095–117

Muth, John E., "Rational Expectations and the Theory of Price Movements," *Econometrica*, 29, 3 (July 1961), pp. 315–35

JOSEPH STIGLITZ (1943–)

Joseph Stiglitz has been a pioneer in studying the economics of information, which examines individual decisions to obtain information and how the economy is affected when people have insufficient information. One result of this work is that the lack of information generates economic problems. This result has made Stiglitz a leader of the *new Keynesian* school of economics, which seeks to explain why economies can experience high unemployment even if people are perfectly rational.

Stiglitz was born and grew up in Gary, Indiana, a mid-western industrial city. His mother came from a long line of New Deal Democrats and worshipped Franklin Delano Roosevelt. His father was a Jeffersonian Democrat, who possessed a deep sense of moral responsibility. Stiglitz (2001) claims his father always made Social Security contributions for all household help, and that he followed his father's example when he grew up. For this reason, unlike other Clinton cabinet appointees in 1993, Stiglitz was easily confirmed by the US Senate.

After graduating from high school, Stiglitz went to Amherst College. He majored in physics until the spring of his junior year, when he switched to economics because it let him apply his mathematical interests and abilities to social problems. His economics professors at Amherst told him that if he was serious about economics he would need a doctorate, and that his senior year at Amherst would not be much different from his first year in graduate school. They also helped him get into the MIT PhD program, and arranged for the necessary financial assistance.

At MIT he studied with some of the top economists of the time – Paul Samuelson, Franco Modigliani, and Robert Solow – all prominent Keynesians and all future Nobel Laureates. After graduating, Stiglitz received a Fulbright Fellowship to study at Cambridge University for a year. There he worked with a number of the Post Keynesian followers of Keynes. Joan Robinson was originally his tutor, but they did not get along well and so Stiglitz had to find a new tutor. Robinson "wasn't used to the kind of questioning stance of a brash American student" (Stiglitz 2001).

Following his year at Cambridge, Stiglitz returned to MIT to teach; and at the young age of 26 he became a full professor. The position was offered only on the condition that he sleep in an apartment rather than in his office, and that he always wear shoes around the office (Chait 1999). This reputation for eccentricity has grown, rather than diminished, over the years. Rosser (2003, p. 7) reports that Stiglitz once showed up at a Clinton cabinet meeting with his tie outside his shirt collar.

Stiglitz left MIT in 1970, and then held a series of academic positions for short periods of time. From 1970 to 1974 he taught at Yale. From 1974 to 1976 he taught at Stanford University. From 1976 to

1979 he was Drummond Professor of Political Economy at Oxford University. Beginning in 1979 Stiglitz taught at Princeton, and then returned to Stanford in 1988.

From 1993 to 1997 Stiglitz served on President Clinton's Council of Economic Advisors, and was its chair from 1995 to 1997. In this position, he continually fought with the US Treasury Department and the International Monetary Fund (IMF). The IMF was created after World War II to lend money to countries facing economic problems. These loans were supposed to let countries employ expansionary macroeconomic policies (see **Keynes**). The US has the largest number of votes on the IMF, and the US Treasury is effectively the US representative on the IMF. Stiglitz felt that the Treasury and the IMF were furthering the interests of the US financial community rather than the interests of global economic stability or the interests of countries facing economic problems.

Fed up with the political battles, Stiglitz resigned from the Council of Economic Advisors in 1997 and became Chief Economist at the World Bank. Created with the IMF after World War II, the mission of the World Bank is to reduce poverty in the poorest areas of the world.

However, the political battles continued and intensified. Stiglitz complained about the hardships imposed on poor countries by the US Treasury and the IMF, especially the high interest rates that the IMF was charging them to borrow money. This, he felt, increased loan defaults and worsened the problems facing poor nations. After the US Treasury pressured the World Bank to silence him, Stiglitz had had enough of politics. In 2000 he left the World Bank and Washington politics and returned to academia, accepting a teaching position at Columbia University.

In 2001, Stiglitz was awarded the Nobel Prize for Economics, along with George Akerlof and Michael Spence. The Prize Committee singled out his work on the economics of information. To this we can add his role as a leader of one of the main schools of contemporary macroeconomics – new Keynesian economics.

New Keynesian economics begins where Robert Lucas and the *rational expectations* school begin – with very smart and very rational individuals. But unlike rational expectations macroeconomists, new Keynesians seek to explain why markets fail to work perfectly, thereby resulting in financial crises at times and high unemployment at other times.

On the standard economic view, people are rational and have all the information needed to make optimal choices. Stiglitz disputed whether rational people would have sufficient information to make good choices. There are two main reasons for his doubt, one stemming from the demand side and one from the supply side. Demanding information is costly – time, effort, and even money are required. As 1978 Nobel Laureate Herbert Simon (1955) pointed out, it is not rational for people to get all the information needed to make the best possible choice. Instead, we consider a few reasonable options and then make a choice that seems satisfactory.

Stiglitz also recognized that information is different from tangible goods in an important way. When we buy cars and bread we can try them out to see if we like them. We can take a car for a test drive and kick its tires. We can taste a piece of bread, checking its texture and flavor before we buy an entire loaf. But we cannot do this with information. If I am given information to inspect, there would be no reason for me to buy it. When I examine a recipe for a loaf of bread, I do not need to pay to get the recipe for I have it already. Information is therefore a *public good* (see **Pigou**) once it is available, and so suppliers have an incentive to keep it hidden.

In markets where information is important, some people will lack the information they need to make rational choices. Kenneth Arrow explained how information problems plague the market for medical services and how this results in excessive spending on health care. Stiglitz has shown how inadequate information in labor and credit markets leads to macroeconomic problems.

In labor markets, employers do not know the skills of potential employees and do not know whether any job candidate will work hard or slack off if hired. Job applicants have good incentives to overstate their skills, and in interviews people always seek to give a good impression of how they will perform on the job. The only way to know if someone will work hard or not is actually to hire them and see what happens. But this advice does not help an employer who needs to make a hiring decision.

Early in his career Stiglitz (1974) suggested that firms could use education as a screening device, similar to the way that MIT used recommendations from Amherst College to accept him into their PhD program. If employers hire people with more education and who graduate from better schools, firms will likely get harder working, more productive employees. But he later recognized that this device is flawed, since firms cannot determine which well-educated applicants will work hard.

A better solution is to pay higher wages than necessary, or wages above the market-clearing wage. Economists call these "*efficiency wages.*" The term is intended to convey the idea that high wages will increase the likelihood that employees will work efficiently. Workers who are paid high wages will have more to lose if they slack off and are fired, and should have greater incentives to work hard (Stiglitz 1984). The idea of efficiency wages reverse the traditional economic view that worker wages are based on their *marginal productivity* (see **Clark**). Rather than wages being determined by worker productivity, it is worker productivity that is determined by wages.

While offering efficiency wages helps the firm get good workers, it does not help the whole economy. High wages reduce the demand for workers by firms. Since there are good reasons for firms to pay efficiency wages, wages will not tend to fall when unemployment is high. Moreover, even if wages did fall, production costs and prices would likely decline also, and so real wages would not fall to eradicate the unemployment. The Keynesian conclusion of this analysis is that we will not reach full employment by just waiting for market forces to do their job (Stiglitz 1995).

What is true of labor markets is also true of credit markets. The problem here is that some people who borrow money are unlikely to pay that money back. Moreover, lenders cannot tell whether people will try their hardest to repay a loan or will readily look to declare bankruptcy. If banks knew the actual default risk for each borrower, they could charge everyone an interest rate based on their likelihood of not repaying a loan. But informational problems prevent this.

Some useful information about borrowers is available. Home buyers making a large down-payment are more likely to repay their loan, and so they generally receive lower mortgage rates. Putting down a large sum of money plays a role similar to a good education in labor markets – it signals reliability. However, there is also a problem with this solution: not every good borrower can make a large down-payment. When borrowers cannot make a large down-payment, banks must assume the worst, and charge higher interest rates. But with higher interest rates, some people will decide not to take out the loan. As a result, borrowing and spending will be lower, and so will economic growth and employment (Stiglitz 1981).

From this analysis Stiglitz concludes that lack of adequate information in labor and credit markets means that there will be too little hiring at efficiency wages, and too little borrowing and spending at high interest rates. Without sufficient spending, the economy will end up in a recession – unless Keynesian macroeconomic policies are used.

Information problems also plague the global economy. According to Stiglitz (2000b), in the early 1980s Ronald Reagan and Margaret Thatcher appointed free market ideologues to head up the World Bank and IMF. These political appointees got rid of the exisiting first-rate economists working at these institutions, and made believing in free market economics a condition for employment. As a result, the World Bank would lend money to poor nations for roads and dams only if they made certain changes to their economy; and the IMF became concerned mainly with issues such as reducing protectionism and removing restrictions on capital flows in and out of a country.

These restrictions worsened the economic problems facing many countries. Stiglitz (2002) was especially incensed that the IMF dealt with the Asian currency crises of the late 1990s by pushing for higher interest rates. This, he argued, increased loan defaults and corporate bankruptcies, and reduced confidence in these troubled countries.

Similarly, by pushing for free markets, the World Bank and IMF made problems worse in some of the poorest areas of the world. Stiglitz (2002, p. 54) gives a good real-world example of such errors. For many years women in a poor Moroccan village received week-old chicks from the government and raised them both for food and for the market. Virtually every analyst agreed that the program helped raise the living standard of these villagers. But the World Bank and the IMF told the Moroccan government that it should not be in the business of distributing baby chicks, and it pressured them to stop this practice. As a result, the chicken raising industry disappeared in Morocco, to the detriment of the poor people living there.

The problem, according to Stiglitz, was that the IMF and World Bank thought the private sector would immediately fill the gap left by the government. In a world of perfect information, private firms would lend chicks to families that were good risks, and the process would continue as before. But in a world plagued with uncertainty and informational gaps, new firms do not start up just as the government leaves a market. The result can easily be an economic disaster.

Imperfect information also created problems for the former socialist economies of Eastern Europe as they sought to make the transition to a market economy. Stiglitz (1994) blamed the IMF for worsening the economic problems faced by the former Communist nations of Eastern Europe, especially Russia, by pushing for quick privatization of government-owned firms. Pushing for rapid privatization, Stiglitz argued, the IMF and the US Treasury virtually ensured that former

Communist bureaucrats would strip assets and send the money obtained from selling them to Swiss bank accounts. Privatization efforts worked badly because these countries had no experience with free markets, and so senior Communist bureaucrats obtained government assets cheaply and via bribes. Moreover, the IMF pushed too quickly for eliminating trade restrictions. Because many government-owned firms were too inefficient to compete in the global economy, and because new firms did not quickly arise to replace privatized firms, the people working for government firms soon found themselves unemployed.

The problem in all these cases is that markets are not perfect. They do not move immediately and painlessly to some equilibrium. In the real world, timing matters; so does the information one has. If people do not understand markets and do not have experience with markets, free markets may lead to more problems than economic benefits.

The work of Stiglitz provides a defense of Keynesian policy prescriptions against monetarism (see **Friedman**) and new classical economics (see **Lucas**). This is why Stiglitz is a leading new Keynesian economist; he provides a new justification for Keynesian policies, one based on problems with obtaining information. When information is imperfect, markets do not give us the best possible result and Keynesian economic policies are needed to improve economic outcomes.

More than anyone else, Stiglitz has been responsible for the resurgence of Keynes and Keynesian economics in the late twentieth and early twenty-first centuries. For this reason, Stiglitz has been one of the most influential economists at the turn of the new millennium.

Works by Stiglitz

"The Theory of 'Screening,' Education and the Distribution of Income," *American Economic Review*, 64 (December 1974), pp. 283–300

"Credit Rationing in Markets with Imperfect Information," *American Economic Review*, 71 (June 1981), pp. 393–410. Reprinted in *New Keynesian Economics*, Vol 2, *Coordination Failures and Real Rigidities*, ed. N. Gregory Mankiw and David Romer, Cambridge, Massachusetts, MIT Press, 1991, pp. 247–76, with Andrew Weiss

"Equilibrium Unemployment as a Worker–Discipline Device," *American Economic Review*, 74 (June 1984), pp. 433–44. Reprinted in *New Keynesian Economics*, Vol 2, *Coordination Failures and Real Rigidities*, ed. N. Gregory Mankiw and David Romer, Cambridge, Massachusetts, MIT Press, 1991, pp. 123–42, with Carl Shapiro

Whither Socialism?, Cambridge, Massachusetts, MIT Press, 1994

"Labor Market Adjustments and the Persistence of Unemployment," *American Economic Review*, 85 (May 1995), pp. 219–25, with Bruce Greenwald

"The Contributions of the Economics of Information to Twentieth Century Economics," *Quarterly Journal of Economics*, 115 (November 2000a), pp. 1441–78

"What I Learned at the World Bank," *New Republic* (April 17–24, 2000b), pp. 56–60

"Joseph E. Stiglitz Autobiography" 2001 (available online at www.nobel.se/economics/laureates/2001/stiglitz-autobio.html)

Globalization and Its Discontents, New York, Norton, 2002

The Roaring Nineties, New York, Norton, 2003

Works about Stiglitz

Bausor, Randall, "Joseph E. Stiglitz," in *American Economists of the Late Twentieth Century*, ed. Warren Samuels, Cheltenham, Edward Elgar, 1996, pp. 323–50

Chait, Jonathan, "Shoeless Joe Stiglitz," *The American Prospect*, 45 (July–August 1999)

Chang, Ha-Joon, "The Stiglitz Contribution," *Challenge*, 45 (March–April 2002), pp. 77–96

Rosser, J. Barkley, Jr., "A Nobel Prize for Asymmetric Information: The Economic Contributions of George Akerlof, Michael Spence and Joseph Stiglitz," *Review of Political Economy*, 15 (January 2003), pp. 3–21

Other references

Simon, Herbert, "A Behavioral Model of Rational Choice," *Quarterly Journal of Economics*, 69 (1955), pp. 99–118

GLOSSARY

Absolute advantage A theory holding that whichever country can produce a good more efficiently will export that good (also see *comparative advantage*).

Accelerator A theory of investment which holds that investment increases whenever the economy expands.

Adding up problem This concerns whether summing the marginal productivity of all inputs used by the firm will equal the value of output, and thus whether sales proceeds can pay factors of production.

Adverse selection A problem in the insurance industry, whereby people take out insurance who are more likely to file claims than the population in general.

Arbitrage The simultaneous purchase and sale of some asset in two different markets in order to make money from the price differential.

Asymmetric information Differences in knowledge by two parties to some trade or transaction.

Behavioral Economics An approach to economics that seeks to provide economics with more realistic psychological foundations by focusing on actual human decision-making and behavior.

Cambridge Controversy A dispute between Cambridge, England and Cambridge, Massachusetts in the mid-twentieth century concerning how to measure capital.

Cantillon Effect The differential impact of money on the economy depending upon how money enters the economy and who gets the money.

Cardinal utility The belief that consumers can distinguish how much more they prefer one bundle of goods to another bundle of goods (see *ordinal utility*).

Class struggle A conflict between capitalists and workers.

Cliometrics The new economic history, which uses advanced statistical techniques to test hypotheses about economic history.

Comparative advantage   The doctrine that it is relative efficiencies (or relative inefficiencies) that determine the goods a country will export (see *absolute advantage*).

Complementary goods   Two or more goods usually consumed together, like gasoline and automobiles.

Conspicuous consumption   Expenditure made to impress others rather than improve one's well-being.

Constant returns to scale   Occurs when an increase in inputs leads to a proportional increase in outputs.

Consumer sovereignty   The belief that each consumer is the best judge of her own well-being and should be allowed complete freedom in purchasing goods.

Consumption function   The relationship between consumer spending and income.

Contract curve   A curve within the Edgeworth Box connecting the points at which two individuals' or two countries' indifference curves are tangent.

Correlation coefficient   A measure of the relationship between two economic variables, or the extent that they move together.

Cost–benefit analysis   A tool for evaluating investment projects and government spending programs by comparing all the benefits that will result from the project and all the costs of the project.

Creative destruction   The process by which new innovation and technological breakthroughs come to destroy old products and production processes.

Cumulative causation   A positive or negative feedback mechanism involving two or more variables, so that increases in one variable lead to increases in the second variable, which increases the first variable again, etc.

Differential theory of rent   Belief that the rent on any plot of land is determined by the difference between the productivity of that plot and the productivity of the least fertile land.

Diminishing marginal utility   Belief that the satisfaction received from consuming a good will decline with each additional unit of the good that is consumed.

Diminishing returns   When additional workers (or other factors of production) produce less than the previous workers (or factor) hired.

Division of labor   Specialization in the production process whereby tasks are divided into small operations and individual workers are assigned to do just one task.

Dual labor market hypothesis The theory that there are two different labor markets in developed countries – one for skilled workers and one for unskilled workers.

Dumping The practice of charging less for some good abroad than the firm charges in its domestic market.

Econometrics The part of economics that measures economic relationships using statistical techniques.

Economies of scale Reductions in the cost of producing goods as a result of producing larger quantities of the good.

Edgeworth Box A diagram which combines the indifference curves of two individuals or two countries in order to determine the outcome of their attempts to trade with each other.

Effective demand The demand for goods and services which is backed up with the ability to purchase those goods and services.

Efficiency wages Wages set by firms above the market-clearing level in the expectation that they will lead to greater effort and efficiency by workers.

Elasticity of demand The percentage change in consumer purchases divided by the percentage change in price of a good. This shows how much sales change given a price change.

Elasticity of substitution A measure of how much businesses will change their use of inputs into the production process as a result of changes in the cost of buying that input. If the elasticity of substitution is zero, factors of production are always used in fixed proportions no matter how expensive the cost of some inputs becomes. If it is greater than zero, then higher wages will lead business to use more machinery and less labour.

Equation of exchange MV=PQ, or the money supply (M) times the number of times each dollar gets spent (V) equals the output of the economy (prices times quantities).

Ex ante–ex post Distinguishes that which is planned (*ex ante*) from what actually occurs (*ex post*).

Expenditure tax An income tax that exempts all savings from taxation.

Experimental economics This approach to economics uses controlled laboratory experiments to study actual human decision-making and behavior.

Exploitation The appropriation of surplus value by owners of capital.

Externalities The cost (or benefit) of producing a good for consumption that is not paid for (or not received) by the ultimate consumer. For example, pollution imposes a cost on all society, but this cost is not part of the price of a polluting good.

Factor price equalization theorem Free trade in goods leads to equal wages among trading partners and equal profit rates.

Feminist economics A branch of economics that employs feminist theory in order to uncover the causes and consequences of women's economic oppression.

Fiscal policy The use of government spending and government tax policy to direct the economy.

Free rider problem Because some goods or benefits (for example, the benefit of defense spending and higher wages due to unionization) are available to everyone, people will not voluntarily pay for them; therefore, unless people are forced to pay for these goods, they will not be produced.

Game Theory The study of interdependent decision-making.

General equilibrium A situation where all markets in an economy are simultaneously in equilibrium.

Gresham's Law "Bad money drives out good money." This law stems from the fact that people will hold on to money that is more valuable (has more precious metals in it) and pass on to others money that is less valuable.

Income effect The increased quantity of some good demanded by consumers as a result of higher consumer incomes.

Incomes policy Government attempts to control wage and price increases, and thus inflation, by limiting the incomes received by workers and business owners.

Increasing returns Occurs when additional workers produce more output (on average) than previously hired workers.

Indifference curve A set of points, representing different combinations of two goods that yield the same level of satisfaction to the consumer.

Infant industry argument The claim that protection from foreign competition is justified for firms that are just starting up in an industry.

Input-output analysis A mathematical representation of the economy that shows how much of various different inputs are needed to produce one more unit of every good.

IS–LM model A macroeconomic model showing how the goods market (*IS*) and the money market (*LM*) reach equilibrium together.

Kondratieff waves Long-run (45–60 years) cycles in economic activity.

Labor theory of value A theory holding that relative prices of goods depend on relative amounts of work required to produce that good.

Law of demand The view that (other things being equal) the lower the price for some good, the more of that good the consumer will buy.

Law of supply The view that, as prices rise for some good, business firms will produce and sell more of that good.

Leontief Paradox The surprising finding that the US, rich in capital, was exporting goods that used relatively large amounts of labor and relatively small amounts of capital.

Life-cycle hypothesis The belief that individuals gear their annual consumption to their expected average lifetime income rather than to their current income.

Loanable funds theory of interest The theory that interest rates are determined by the supply of savings and the demand for loans.

Lucas Critique The argument that large-scale macroeconomic models cannot help make macroeconomic policy because making any policy change will alter the macroeconomic model.

Macroeconomics A study of the performance of the entire economy.

Marginal cost The extra cost of producing one more unit of output.

Marginal productivity Additional output that results from hiring one more worker (or using one more input).

Marginal productivity theory of distribution The view that the income received by each input in the production process is equal to its marginal productivity.

Marginal propensity to consume The proportion of any additional income that is spent by customers.

Marginal revenue The additional revenue received by a firm when it produces and sells one more good.

Marginal utility The utility consumers get from the last unit of some good that they consume.

Market socialism An attempt to combine the characteristics of capitalist and socialist economies by using the market to set prices and allocate resources but having the government own most large enterprises.

Mark-up pricing The view that firms set prices by adding a (percentage) increase to their costs.

Mercantilism   An early economic doctrine stressing that nations must run trade surpluses and accumulate money if they are to grow and develop.

Methodological individualism   The belief that economic phenomena should be explained only as a result of individual choices.

Methodology   A study of the methods used in trying to understand how economies work and how economic laws operate.

Monetarism   A doctrine holding that inflation stems from too much money in the economy.

Monetary policy   The attempt by a central bank to influence economic outcomes through its ability to control interest rates and/or the domestic money supply.

Money illusion   When individuals react to changes in monetary terms (they are happy because they received a pay rise) rather than to changes in real terms (the greater pay can buy no more than the previous paycheck because prices have gone up as well).

Monopsony   A market in which there is only one buyer of some factor of production

Moral hazard   A problem arising from insurance systems: insurance causes people to behave in more risky ways, thus increasing the chance that they will need to collect from the insurance pool.

Multiplier   The relationship between a change in spending and the impact of that change on the entire economy.

Natural rate of unemployment   The lowest rate that unemployment can reach before it results in accelerating inflation.

New classical macroeconomics   A twentieth century school of macroeconomics that combines rational expectations and a belief that there exists a natural rate of unemployment for all economies.

New institutional economics   A study of how and why economic institutions (such as property right, markets, and the state) come into existence.

New Keynesian Macroeconomics   This late twentieth century school of macroeconomics seeks to explain why unemployment exists in a world of perfectly rational individuals.

Nominal interest rate   The rate of interest in today's prices or ignoring the impact of inflation (see *real interest rate*).

Occupational segregation   The practice of hiring primarily women or minorities for certain types of jobs and hiring white males for an entirely different set of jobs.

Opportunity cost   The cost of some forgone alternative.

Ordinal utility   The belief that consumers can only distinguish that they prefer one bundle of goods to another bundle of goods (see *cardinal utility*).

Pareto Optimality   When an economy's resources are distributed in such a manner that no one can be made better off without making someone else worse off.

Partial equilibrium   Economic analysis that looks at just one market in isolation from all the other markets in the economy.

Permanent income hypothesis   A theory of consumption holding that consumer spending depends on average expected income over several years rather than on current income.

Phillips Curve   A trade-off between inflation and unemployment. The curve shows that when inflation rises unemployment falls, and vice versa.

Physiocracy   The first school of economics, headed up by François Quesnay. The Physiocrats held that only agriculture was productive.

Physiocratic theory of rent   The view that rents are determined by the surplus produced on a plot of land.

Pigou Effect (real balance effect)   The argument that, during a recession, declines in prices will increase the real wealth of consumers and thereby increase spending.

Poll taxes   Taxes of some fixed amount that everyone has to pay regardless of their income or their spending habits.

Population principle   A belief (due to Malthus) that population growth would exceed the growth of the food supply.

Predatory pricing   The practice of lowering prices to unprofitable levels in order to drive your competitors our of business.

Price discrimination   The practice of charging different prices for some good to different consumers.

Prisoner's dilemma   A famous result in game theory which shows that individual rationality and self-interest may not lead to an optimal outcome.

Progressive tax   A tax that falls more heavily on wealthy households than on low- and middle-income households. The income tax is an example of a progressive tax

Proportional tax   A tax under which all households pay the same fraction of their income to the government.

Public choice   The economic study of politics.

Public finance   A study of government spending and tax policy.

Purchasing power parity A view that exchange rates will tend towards levels so that two currencies will be able to buy the same set of goods in their respective' country.

Quantity theory of money The belief that changes in the quantity of money lead directly to changes in the price level.

Radical subjectivism The belief that only individuals themselves are capable of knowing what is best for themselves.

Rational expectations The belief that businesses and individuals will learn about the effects of government policy and change their behaviour in a way that will counteract any government policies.

Real balance effect See *Pigou Effect*.

Real interest rate Nominal interest rate minus the rate of inflation. The real interest rate represents the gain in purchasing power for a lender and the loss of purchasing power for a borrower.

Regressive tax A tax whereby the poor pay larger fractions of their income for the tax than middle class and wealthy households. Sales taxes are a good example of a regressive tax.

Roundabout production Production methods using more machinery and capital, and requiring a longer period of time between when producing decisions are made and when goods are produced and ready for sale.

Samuelson–Stolper Theorem This theorem shows that tariffs on imports increase the returns to those inputs that are heavily used in producing domestic goods which compete with the taxed good.

Social Darwinism The belief that in all social and economic interactions "the fittest," or the best competitors, will run out.

Special flow mechanism A process whereby trade imbalances automatically correct themselves because they lead to changes in the domestic money supply and price level.

Stagflation The simultaneous occurrence of high unemployment (stagnation) and inflation.

Subsistence theory of wages The view that wages will tend to fall to a level that is just sufficient to let workers survive.

Substitution effect The effect on sales for some good due to a change in price. Higher prices cause people to purchase (substitute) other goods.

Surplus The difference between the output of some economy in one year and the inputs required to produce that output.

Surplus value   The value of a product over and above the wage and depreciation costs of producing that good.

Tatonnement   A process of "groping" by which equilibrium can be reached in all markets at once.

Total utility   The total amount of satisfaction that one gets from consuming a certain quantity of goods.

Usury (laws)   Laws that regulate or prohibit charging (high rates of) interest.

Utilitarianism   The philosophical doctrine that people should seek to promote the greatest possible happiness in society.

Wage fund doctrine   A theory of the demand for labor which holds that employers must have a fund of capital available to pay workers during the production of goods.

Welfare economics   The part of economics which studies how to maximize the well-being of the nation by both increasing output and changing its distribution.

Yield curve   A diagram showing how interest rates change as the time to maturity on some asset increases.